THE RUINS LESSON

The Ruins Lesson

MEANING AND MATERIAL
IN WESTERN CULTURE

Susan Stewart

The University of Chicago Press
Chicago and London

The University of Chicago Press, Chicago 60637
The University of Chicago Press, Ltd., London
© 2020 by The University of Chicago
Published 2020
Printed in the United States of America

29 28 27 26 25 24 23 22 21 20   3 4 5

ISBN-13: 978-0-226-63261-2 (cloth)
ISBN-13: 978-0-226-63275-9 (e-book)
DOI: https://doi.org/10.7208/chicago/9780226632759.001.0001

This publication is made possible in part by support from the
Barr Ferree Foundation Fund for Publications, Department of Art
and Archaeology, Princeton University.

Library of Congress Cataloging-in-Publication Data

Names: Stewart, Susan, 1952– author.
Title: The ruins lesson : meaning and material in western culture / Susan Stewart.
Description: Chicago : University of Chicago Press, 2020. |
Includes bibliographical references and index.
Identifiers: LCCN 2019030168 | ISBN 9780226632612 (cloth) | ISBN 9780226632759 (ebook)
Subjects: LCSH: Ruins in literature. | Ruins in art. | Antiquities in literature. | Antiquities in art.
Classification: LCC PN56.R87 S74 2019 | DDC 809/.9335—dc23
LC record available at https://lccn.loc.gov/2019030168

For Alice, Leon, and Percy
new, tender, quick!

Contents

Illustrations

Color Plates (following page 154)

Black-and-White Figures

Preface

Today, in what we call the developed world, we often pursue practices that undermine our values. We know that to survive as a species we must nourish the resources of the earth, yet we continue to further an economic system based upon "creative destruction." We hold to a belief in the intrinsic worth of individuals, yet we further, through animosity or indifference alike, the physical and mental degradation of those who are impoverished and powerless. We pursue new knowledge, yet we crush its consequences by demanding it yield immediate, material benefit. Not only do we practice these and other forms of unmaking and destruction, we have also turned their image into a vital theme of our art tradition. Beyond expressing the contradictions of hypocrisy and greed, or the pressures arising from a death drive, there seems to be some sense of mastery, freedom, or even pleasure involved in the pursuit of representations of ruin. From stories of the fall of Troy to contemporary "ruins porn," we so often are drawn—in schadenfreude, terror, or what we imagine is transcendence—to the sight of what is broken, damaged, and decayed.

In this study, I have tried to understand the fascination and appeal of ruins throughout the history of Western art and literature. A scholar of other traditions, an economist, psychologist, historian, or anthropologist, would have looked elsewhere and along other paths. But I have considered works of art, in our time both revered for their metaphysical power and taken up as commodities for speculation, as paradigmatic of conflicts between beliefs and practices involving materialism and value. By representing what we find most compelling, and calling themselves for judgment and care, works of art tell us a great deal about our attitudes toward materiality. And in their autotelic discourse regarding form, formlessness, and significance, they are our most sustained meditation on the limits and possibilities of meaning.

My research has led me to founding legends of tragic flaws, broken covenants, and original sin; to the Christian rejection, appropriation, and transformation of the classical past; to myths and rituals regulating human fertility, and their consequences in the exaltation and disparagement of women; to the proliferation of ruins images in Renaissance allegory and eighteenth-century melancholy; to ancient sites of disaster and to gardens featuring new ruins. In their multiplication of ruins images, artists and writers have struggled to recover morals and lessons out of the fragility and inevitable mortality of intended forms. Beginning with ancient Egyptian memorials and ending in twentieth- and twenty-first-century responses to world war, I nevertheless focus on periods of intense interest in ruins and emerging paradigms for their reception—particularly the era of Northern humanism in the Renaissance and the "ruins craze" of the eighteenth century and Romanticism. I return several times to a set of artists and writers whom I consider to be visionaries regarding ruins: Johann Wolfgang von Goethe, Giovanni Battista Piranesi, William Blake, and William Wordsworth.

The reader will discover that this book is also a meditation on the story of the Tower of Babel. Ruins arise at the boundaries of cultures and civilizations—syncretic phenomena, their very appearance depends on an act of translation between the past and the present, between those who have vanished and those who have survived. Ruins are in this sense the alter egos of what is left unfinished, and they offer a warning to the makers of monuments. In the end, I have asked what cannot be ruined, and have found there—in the eternal resources of thought and language—a means of addressing those contradictions with which I began.

Introduction

VALUING RUIN

In Western culture, for better or worse, men and women have located themselves in time and space by marking the earth. The flags they plant, the dwellings they build, the tombs they place, the permanent settlements and cities they found—all mediate the relation between ground and sky, establishing their coordinates in line with those of rising and setting stars and recurring patterns of wind and weather. They yoke materials, plans, and, later, stories of their making, to the illusion of their permanence.

How is it, then, that ruins, those damaged and disappearing vestiges of the built environment, became so significant in Western art and literature? Derived from the Latin *ruere*, "to fall or collapse," the word *ruin* is both a noun and a verb. As a noun, *ruin* refers to a fabric or being that is meant to be upright but has fallen, often headlong, to the ground. What should be vertical and enduring has become horizontal and broken. As a verb, *ruin* means to overthrow, to destroy, or, often in the case of a woman victim, to dishonor. Persons and things can be slowly ruined by suffering the depredations of use and ordinary weather, and in times of human violence and extreme weather, they can be actively ruined.

Nevertheless, at least since late antiquity, poets, thinkers, artists, and sometimes emperors have brought an array of positive attitudes toward ruins: in the first and second centuries CE, the elder Pliny and the far-ranging Lydian physician and traveler Pausanias looked on them with some measure of reverence and nostalgia. In the early Christian period, Roman ruins were used as quarries and, although they continued to fall into rubble well into the fifteenth century, we also find a growing interest in preserving their forms. At the turn of the thirteenth century, Frederick II incorporated their remains into his castles, and in the ensuing centuries, Petrarch hoped to animate them, Francesco Colonna wove them into architectural fantasies, and Raphael protected their inscriptions.[1] Later sixteenth-century painters, engravers, and poets in

Antwerp, Prague, Florence, and Rome allegorized and dreamed over them. Antiquarians and architects of the Enlightenment looked on them with both melancholy disenchantment and scientific curiosity. Romantic poets used them as scenes of writing and speculation. Ancient emperors and twentieth-century dictators alike have taken their persistence as self-justifying grounds for claims to power.

Anomalies in the landscape of the present, ruins are the architectural equivalent of the syntactical *anacoluthon*, or non sequitur. They do not follow or precede—they call for the supplement of further reading, further syntax. These often massive and almost always empty material structures are both over- and underdetermined. They stand poised between the forms they were and the formlessness to which, in the absence of restoration, they are destined. They lose their original purposes and have the singularity of artworks, yet they are severed irremediably from their contexts of production. In the present they are fused, almost always destructively, with their immediate natural environments. They call for an active, moving viewer—often a traveler with a consciousness distinct from that of a local inhabitant—who can restore their missing coordinates and names. Their most well-known student, the eighteenth-century Venetian and Roman engraver-architect Giovanni Battista Piranesi, called them, in the dedication to his 1743 *Prima parte di architetture, e prospettive*, "queste parlanti ruine": "these speaking ruins."[2] As we respond to ruins, we transform materiality into ideas, learning something about the value of human making and the place of our made world within the natural world.

Aristotle wrote in one of the remaining fragments of his *Protrepticus* of "architecture as the art [cause] of building houses, not of pulling them down,"[3] yet a ruin is meaningful because it speaks to the destruction of something intended. That destruction can be the consequence of natural forces or of the willed actions of persons. Although the outcome of a built form, a ruin is not a work of artifice; unlike the architecture it was before its current state, a ruin does not represent the fulfillment of a plan. Nor, unless we are in the hands of a temperamental god inclined to rearrange our handiwork, are decay and damage, the forces of ruination, commensurate to human acts of willed replacement and augmentation.

The Roman poet Propertius vividly noted in books 2 and 3 of his *Elegies* the inevitable balance between formation and deformation in human artifacts and human character. Attending the opening of the "golden portico" of the Temple of Apollo on the Palatine, Augustine's most magnificent structure, what the poet sees is a catalog of narrated and potential ruins. He notes the temple doors with their images of the "Gauls cast down from Parnassus's peak" and the "deaths of Niobe and her children." His depiction of the "silent" stone lyre of Apollo, who stands "with parted lips," underscores the god's frozen state and leads him to thoughts of the infidelities of his own lover Cynthia and the consequent damage to her reputation. In book 3, he continues his study of the relations between the power of women and the power of the state. Recounting the story of the treachery of Antony and Cleopatra at 3.11, he declares, "The city set high on seven hills which presides over the whole world stands not to be destroyed by human hand." At 3.13, he describes the Arcadian simplicity of earlier ages and complains, "But now shrines suffer neglect in forsaken groves: gold commands the worship of all, with piety trampled underfoot. . . . Charred portals testify to the sacrilege of Brennus, when he attacked the Pythian realm of the unshorn god: and soon Parnassus shook its laurelled peak and scattered terrible snows upon the Gallic arms." Propertius vows, "I shall speak out. . . . Proud Rome is being destroyed by its own prosperity." Whether his pronouncements are heard or not, Propertius takes on the role of the *vates* who sees through material to its inevitable decay: as Cynthia's beauty is bound to be ruined by wine and promiscuity, so are temples, even those with golden porticos, subject to the vicissitudes of weather and human neglect.[4]

Yet Propertius is offering us a poem, not a window onto reality. For most of Western history, ruins representations have provided a means to restore irreparably damaged objects to the closure offered by the intended forms of art. And such efforts, as Propertius indicates, are often framed as restorations of, and even improvements on, the moral order. As we shall see, in ancient Egypt, ruins poems often were performative, expressing a resolve to repair and renew fallen tombs and monuments; Anglo-Saxon ruins poems, in contrast, conveyed a sense of mystified awe and curiosity regarding the engineering feats of what their authors imagined were a vanished race of giants. And from the late medieval period forward, Christian visual art and poetry addressed so-called pagan ruins by transposing and rededicating them to a new religion.

The makers of these ruins representations assumed that, through the obduracy of the works' materials or curatorship, or, eventually, via their replication in multiples, such frescos, paintings, prints, and poems could be protected. Unlike buildings and other unsheltered structures in the environment, curated forms could escape the inevitable decay of their own materials and endure. No artists held to this promise of permanence, and even immortality, more tenaciously than poets, who believed that their works could outlast the marble monuments on which they sometimes were inscribed. Propertius's contemporary Horace famously claimed such powers in the thirtieth work of his third book of odes. There he says:

Today I have finished a work outlasting bronze
And the pyramids of ancient royal kings.
The North Wind raging cannot scatter it
Nor can the rain obliterate this work,
Nor can the years, nor can the ages passing.
Some part of me will live . . .

He adds the thought that so long as the silent virgins and the Pontifex climb the steps of the Capitol, he, too, will not fully die, for his poetry will keep him "ever young" thanks to "praise in times to come." The Latin word *situ*, appearing in the opening phrase regarding the ancient environs of the pyramids (*Exegi monumentum aere perennius / regalique situ pyramidum altius*) means both "site" and "decay" and indicates that as the pyramids are built in place, so will they fall to ruin in place.[5] The poet's hope is that, in contrast to ruins, poetic memorials will both commemorate those who are honored and spark further speech about them. Deeds and qualities would thus not perish utterly, for well-shaped phrases that live in the minds, hearts, and tongues of those who hear them promise to continue in perpetuity.

Horace draws an implicit contrast between the mediums of made forms and indicates that a structure's materials, whether bronze or stone or human memory, are its destiny. Nevertheless, the thematic, and in the end moral and social, implications of the experience of ruins and images of ruins have been explored far more than their formal consequences. The power of ruins and ruin images to bestow lessons has to do with the fact that they are read—both in themselves, as presences, and as representations.[6] Leon Battista Alberti in fact suggests in his *De re aedificatoria* (*On the Art of Building*, begun in the mid-fifteenth century and published in 1485) that the moldings found on ancient ornaments can be grasped by thinking of them as letters and features of nature. This is what he says:

> The platband has a lineament like the letter L. . . . The ovolo I was almost tempted to call ivy, because it extends and clings; its lineament is like the letter C surmounted by the letter L. . . . The astragal is a little ovolo. The letter C, if reversed and surmounted by the letter L . . . produces a channel. But if the letter S is surmounted by the letter L . . . it is called a gullet, because of its resemblance to a man's throat. If, however, below the letter L an inverted S is attached . . . it is called a wave.

C, L, and S could be combined to create the representations of the profiles of platbands, coronas, ovolos, astragals, channels, waves, and gullets. He continues to explain that platbands "may be carved with seashells, volutes, or even with a lettered text; in the corona there may be dentils. . . . The ovolo is carved with eggs, or sometimes adorned with leaves. . . . Beads are cut into the astragal, as though threaded along a string. The gullet and wave are not covered except with leaves. The fillet, in any position, is always left plain."[7] Here ornaments are made from letters and natural symbols—reading them means forgetting their literal legibility; when such details survive the fragmentation or decay of a building's form, they enter a limbo between text and ornament.

We seem to have a talent for imbuing ruins with meaning, yet those meanings remind us that the material is the empty ground of meaning, where meaning stops or has not yet started—and that there is little, if any, intrinsic relation between what signs are made of and what they have to say. Ruination happens at two speeds: furious and slow—that is, sudden and unbidden or inevitable and imperceptible. We do not have a sense of a moderate or proper pace for ruination precisely because it is not intended. A systematic process of ruin would resemble, more than anything, a practice of torture. When we tell stories of divine destruction, we tell ourselves the gods are either aloof or just: it is unbearable to imagine they are merely sadists. The immediate damage brought about by such divine violence is described in scriptures and epics. In turn, we know through experience or historical accounts about the consequences of catastrophic weather events and human destruction. The stories of such events are secondhand explanations, documentations of damage and residue.

The sites of Herculaneum and Pompeii are especially disquieting because they compound the effects of both sudden and slow ruin. Created by a catastrophic and unexpected form of natural violence, they remain "snapshots" of that moment of destruction even today. The centuries since their discovery have made them slow ruins to some degree as well—weeds and erosion have taken a toll even as archaeologists have maintained their sites for scientific exploration. Yet their slow ruination has been wreaked upon their already-destroyed forms; we are seeing double: the ruin of a ruin. Unlike a ruined temple, bath, forum, or other abandoned structure that has outlived its original use, the once-vibrant cities at the bases of volcanoes, like the destroyed cities of epic and scripture, suggest the wrath of gods. Once buried and now exposed, they live on as unearthed—perpetually disturbed—graves. Their sites remain places of "unnatural death"—that is, a death that has truncated the process of aging for its buildings and human residents alike.

If since the twentieth century and into the present we have a taste for "ruins porn," or take a voyeuristic pleasure in images of ruins, perhaps this is because the immediate testimony of the photograph bears witness to what cannot be known as presence—such erupting violence, on the one hand, or the precarious and unstable conditions of extant ruined forms, on the other. (Indeed, the photograph has by now often replaced presence and banished it, elevating the vicarious to a new status.) A taste for appreciating ruins at a remove has its roots in Lucretius's thoughts on the tinge of gratification whenever a viewer's horror is mixed with a sense of "self-security."[8] And this taste is developed more specifically in the notion of "the pleasure of ruins," introduced by Bernardin de Saint-Pierre in his *Études de la nature* of 1784. There, following on a discussion of our responses to rainy weather and melancholy, he turns to this peculiar emotion. He recounts his visit to Dresden in 1765, five years after the Prussian bombardment—a scene of destruction vividly commemorated as well in Bernardo Bellotto's contemporary painting of the ruins of the old Kreuzkirche (see fig. 1). Saint-Pierre describes other structures similarly

FIGURE 1. Bernardo Bellotto (Canaletto), *The Ruins of the Old Kreuzkirche*, Dresden, 1765. Oil on canvas. Kunsthaus Zürich; gift of Betty and David M. Koester, 1994.

turned inside out: palaces exposed from their roofs to their cellars, painted ceilings and small closets "lined with Chinese papers," shards of mirrors and smoked gildings—all revealed by the destruction of the bombs. He notes the Lucretian feeling of safety in the midst of peril: *"if this were thy country!"* But, fortunately, it is not.[9] He then turns to the quite different kinds of distance and alienation that follow from the slow ruin. Thinking of the Arch of Marius near Orange, which in his time was believed to commemorate a Roman victory from 101 BCE, Bernardin concludes, "if this triumphal arch was a memorial of the victories of the Romans over the Cimbri, it was likewise a monument of the triumph of Time over the Romans." He decides that our pleasure in antiquated ruins is increased when such decayed structures were originally sites of old crimes or tyrannies.[10]

Imperceptibly continuing to fall away as moss and weeds grow through crevices and cracks in mortar and stone, the slow ruin presents a gradual balance between the breakdown of the mineral surface and the accrual of organic life on it. "Nature has made the work of art into material for its own shaping, as art originally had made use of nature's substance," wrote Georg Simmel as he explained how a ruin is a form constructed by humans and destroyed by nature.[11] The duality of ruination and reformation is evocative of the relations between the anabolic, often geometrical, processes of building in crystals, plants, and molecules and the catabolic forces of friction and general wear and tear that characterize the physical universe. Indeed, in a ruin we see the remains of an allegory of human dwelling: our striving for order within the chaos of the elements. Some ruins are on their way to formlessness by becoming vegetation; others, as exemplified in the artificial ruin of the grotto, are surrendering their edges and outlines to calciferous growths of shells and pebbles. The first give way to land, the second to water. The rate at which this breakdown happens, juxtaposed to the moment of our observation, reminds us of the strength of structures and the span of our own existence. Jean-Pierre Louis Laurent Houël's aquatint, *Vue générale de la masse de debris*, from his 1776 expedition to explore the Greek ruins of Sicily, provides an indication of how a ruin breaks down into the materials of its origin. Unlike the many identified sites Houël depicts in his series, this one, without its caption mentioning the Temple of Jupiter, would be completely formless (see fig. 2).

In a Mediterranean climate, many kinds of plants spring up in the limey soil and crevices of ruins. In the winter of 1818, Percy Shelley described walking through the Colosseum as like traversing an amphitheater of rocky hills, overgrown by wild olives, myrtles, and figs. He wrote that "a copsewood

FIGURE 2. Jean-Pierre Houël, *Vue générale de la masse de debris du Temple de Jupiter Olimpien d'Agrigente*. From *Voyage pittoresque des Isles de Sicile, de Lipari et de Malte* (Paris, 1787). Private collection.

overshadows you as you wander through its labyrinths, and the wild weeds of this climate of flowers bloom under your feet."[12] Four years later, as Lord Byron described the same spot in canto 4 of *Childe Harold's Pilgrimage*, he wrote of the Colosseum as a "garland forest." At the turn of the twentieth century, Rodolfo Lanciani describes in a footnote that he has found in the nearby Forum entire ilex oaks and fig trees with four-inch-thick trunks growing through cracks in masonry.[13] In antiquity, the Forum's three sacred plants were fig, olive, and grape. But archaeologists have found many kinds of seeds and plants there at various layers, including some from North Africa. Today you can find wild chives, broom, wild rocket, dandelion, amaranth, and crabgrass growing everywhere.

Nevertheless, many named ruins continue to resist, or are curated to resist, the encroachments of rain and wind and vegetation over time. Being given a name, becoming a place, is a means of vitality and protects a form from indifference and inevitable destruction. The Pyramid of Cestius, for example, has remained largely intact in the same ways throughout the history of extant ruins images, as glimpses from Aegidius (also known as Egidio or Giles) Sadeler, Piranesi, and a recent photo—spanning more than four hundred years—reveal (see figs. 3–5).

FIGURE 3. Marco Sadeler (after Aegidius Sadeler), *Piramide di Caio Cestio* (*Veſtigij di una Piramide di marmoro, che fu un Sepolcro*). From *Vestigi delle antichita di Roma, Tivoli, Pozzuolo et altri luochi, come si ritrovavano nel secolo XV* (Prague, 1606). This photograph from the reprinted edition by G. J. de Rossi (Rome, 1660[?]). Marquand Library of Art and Archaeology, Princeton University.

FIGURE 4. Giovanni Battista Piranesi, *Piramide di C. Cestio*. From *Vedute di Roma* (ca. 1756). Metropolitan Museum of Art, New York; gift of Edward W. Root, Elihu Root Jr., and Mrs. Ulysses S. Grant III, 1937.

FIGURE 5. Pyramid of Cestius, Rome, ca. 18–12 BCE.

With their undermining of spatial integrity and breakdown of time, ruins underscore the difficult truth that perception itself is unified only by acts of mind. Sigmund Freud contended that "what is past in mental life *may* be preserved and is not *necessarily* destroyed." Yet he also argued that "only in the mind is such a preservation of all the earlier stages alongside the final form possible," and "we are not in a position to represent this phenomenon in pictorial terms." The closest we could come to such a representation of the surviving past, he concluded, using the example of "the history of the Eternal City" (i.e., Rome), is a representation of a ruin.[14]

There is a difference between continuing in pristine condition and continuing in a process of decay. The word *value* itself stems from the Proto-Indo-European root *wal*—to be strong, and from the Latin *valere*, to be strong and well. The well-known monuments of Rome and Greece are far less precariously situated today than the colonnade of Palmyra, the temples of Baalbek, and the remains of Troy and Carthage. State and religious policy, geography, proximity to centers of art and culture, and, paradoxically perhaps, syncretism or a form of constant reinterpretation all can contribute to the long-term preservation of ruins in actuality and legend. There are also great differences in the fates of ruins, depending on who receives them in later generations. Conquering armies, arrogant settlers, and the merely ignorant will plunder and damage the structures of strangers and their ruins will have no audience. Stone cottages or farmhouses abandoned to rubble by famine, clearances, and migration are ruined, yet unmarked; they have something of the pathos of shipwrecks, the most ephemeral and untraceable of ruins.

And for those of us who live in landscapes once inhabited by peoples who lived lightly on the land—whose relation to it was, and is, a matter of marks in the landscape and spoken tradition, and who have suffered dislocation—a founding violence always haunts what remains. "Antiquities acts," such as the US law of 1906 regulating objects, structures, and excavations on federal lands, are based in notions of property foreign to native cultures and cannot, and will not, address the ways that what is monumental and treasured is inextricably bound to the land itself. Tourism, let alone an enthusiasm for ruins, can be both distorting and opportunistic. The stone relics and potsherds of nomadic hunter-gatherers in fields and forests, the vestiges of prehistoric burial and effigy mounds, kivas, cliff dwellings, platforms, towers, and observatories of settled peoples have been subjected to environmental catastrophe, the depredations of internecine violence, and, above all, the destruction exercised by the state. In the case of the Anasazi ruins at Chaco Canyon, for example, the way of life and eventual disappearance of an entire people at the end of the thirteenth century finds its explanation only in aspects of the legends of later Southwest cultures and in whatever marks and forms remain in the landscape.

Anticomanie is foreign to North Americans in additional ways: our neoclassicism always has had the cast of the unveiled and newly polished. Narratives of triumphal expansion, founding gestures, and an often-misguided resolve to "rebuild" in the face of environmental destruction characterize US culture now as in the past. It is as if time on this continent is both too slow and too fast to accommodate the gradual decay that characterizes ruins reception in other parts of the world.[15]

Only those who are belated can observe a ruined form. We may witness ruination, but we come upon a ruin. A certain distance and estimation of damage are involved; the current state of things will be compared to what was prior and depends on an ability to find the ruin intelligible. The ancient Egyptians, for instance, celebrated the kingly role of the restorer, the one who maintains works that will last forever, and held that those who cause damage are cursed.[16] When the Twelfth Dynasty governor of Elephantine, Sarenput, arrived at the cult site of the Old Kingdom general Heqaib, who had been revered in his own time and whom Sarenput claimed as an ancestor, he found the place in ruins. Three hundred years had passed since Heqaib's death. Sarenput was given permission by the pharaoh to build a sanctuary on the site, and he set up a stela there, now known as "Stela Nine." One of the poems inscribed on the stela describes the work of restoration. Here is a rough translation of its message:

> I was the one who built this sacred place for noble Heqaib
> after it was found in a ruined state.
> I built this shrine so this site would again be here.
> I renewed what I found had been damaged
> and in unexpectedly poor condition
> its walls were gone, its form obscure even to an eye-witness.
> The place was destroyed by Ti-weeds.
> Every chamber was filled with debris.
> When it rained, it was flooded with water.
> Though the name was alive, the bricks were lost
> And the well had been swallowed by the earth . . .
> Then I built it anew . . .

Sarenput goes on to recount how he made a "work of eternity," creating a shrine in stone, laying new foundations, establishing a room for the priest and a drinking place. He ends by threatening anyone who would dare to damage the site in the future.[17]

The Egyptian work of eternity is countered by the certainty of material decay and the inevitability of bodily mortality. Yet Sarenput not only knows how to rebuild this shrine; he also reminds us of his direct lineage from the Old Kingdom cult figure.[18] Contrast Sarenput's situation with that of another visitor encountering a ruin—the moment is approximately 2,700 years later, and the observer has, unlike Sarenput, little knowledge of what he is seeing. Here a man stands before a vista of broken stone walls, roofs, and towers, describing his thoughts. He is moved by what he can glimpse of the magnificence of the structures, and he struggles to speak of what he can infer, even in the works' collapsed state, regarding the skill of their builders. He knows the forms were made many generations—"fifty fathers and sons"—ago. Yet he does not know how they were made. He comes from another world, where halls and houses are made of wood. What is the explanation for what he sees? He decides these fallen forms are *enta geweorc*, "the work of the Giants."

This is the situation recounted in the fifty, in places illegible, lines of poetry on two damaged leaves branded by fire that are all that remains of an Old English poem titled by later editors "The Ruin." Written most likely in the eighth century, the poem was recorded in the late tenth-century Exeter Book. Here, in Michael Alexander's translation, we are immediately confronted with the broken wall and shattered condition of a structure (Alexander uses ellipses to indicate the places where the text is illegible):

> Well-wrought this wall; Wierds broke it.
> The stronghold burst......
>
> Snapped rooftrees, towers fallen,
> the work of the Giants, the stonesmiths,
> mouldereth.
> ....Rime scoureth gatetowers
> ....rime on mortar.
>
> Shattered the showershields, roofs ruined,
> age under-ate them.

The narrator explains that "fifty fathers and sons have passed" since "the wielders and wrights" who built the place have vanished into "gravesgrasp." He imagines the damage battles have done to the walls and the tides of fate that brought life and decay in alternation:

> Bright were the buildings, halls where springs ran,
> high, horngabled, much throng-noise;
> these many mead-halls men filled
> with loud cheerfulness: Wierd changed that.
>
> Came days of pestilence, on all sides men fell dead,
> death fetched off the flower of the people;
> where they stood to fight, waste places
> and on the acropolis, ruins.

Where once men "flushed with wine-pride, flashing war-gear, / gazed on wrought gemstones, on gold, on silver, / on wealth, held and hoarded, on light-filled amber, / on this bright burg of broad dominion," only ruins remain. The fragment concludes, inconclusively, with these lines:

. . . . it is a kingly thing
. . . . city . . .[19]

"The Ruin" gives us some sense of this astonished encounter between a northern people who built ephemeral structures from wood and a southern, imperial, people who built with stone for the ages. At the moment of the poem's composition, the Roman stoneworkers the speaker admires are three hundred years in the past, the Norman stoneworkers to come are three hundred years in the future.

The inhabitants of Rome had borne a continuous relation to their past, and the Franks came to see themselves in a continuous line with the Romans. But these Anglo-Saxon settlers of Britain happened upon signs of past habitation in wonder and, often, melancholy. With the advent of Christianity, their churches, like their dwellings and halls, were constructed with wood. At the same time, their awe of stonework extended to an association between stones and magic. The "hoar stone," *se hara stan*, was a gray boundary marker or monolith that marked the known natural world from the supernatural one inhabited by monsters and dragons.[20] Eventually they turned to a syncretic use of materials. The oldest extant English church, the Church of St. Martin at Canterbury from the sixth century, incorporates brick and tile *spolia* ("spoils" consisting of repurposed building materials or ornaments) from Roman buildings into its walls. And when, in the late seventh and early eighth centuries, bishops began to commission stone churches, they brought glaziers and masons from Gaul, artisans who built "after the fashion of the Romans."[21]

Though contemporary to the collapse of the Colosseum, the Anglo-Saxons are a world away, and when we find further traces of Roman structures in their literature, they evoke the imagination, or more specific feelings of fear, awe, or pensive sadness. The oral epic that survives in written form as *Beowulf*, which could date to anywhere between the eighth and eleventh centuries, portrays in its final scenes several structures that seem to be Roman and are, too, given the epithet of *enta geweorc*. Beowulf sees by the wall where his final foe, a great fire-breathing dragon, lurks, "stone arches standing, and a stream / shooting forth from the barrow, its surge / was hot with deadly flames" (2545–47).[22] As he realizes that his wounds are poisoned and his death imminent, Beowulf "sat / on a seat by the wall. On that work of giants he gazed, / saw how stone arches and sturdy pillars / held up the inside of that ancient earth-hall" (2716–19). Throughout the epic, an otherworld of monsters—associated with fens, moors, and desolate wild spaces, with fire and flood, and the dangers of caverns and barrows—stands in contrast to the warm companionship of the mead-halls.

Indeed, the central problem of *Beowulf* is the pollution of the great halls where sociability, and poetry itself, is practiced, by these singular, murderous, elemental, creatures. Here, too, the reward for battle is spoils: those precious metals that endure in time and that remain themselves, regardless of their provenance, scale, or form. The gold and gems that the Anglo-Saxons hoard or use to ornament their helmets, shields, and swords are valued alike by their inhuman enemies. To defeat a monster in its lair beneath the water or the earth is to raid its hoard, a practice that echoes to the inhumation of ancient graves and appropriation of their materials.

"Where is that horse now? Where are those men? Where is the hoard-sharer? / Where is the house of the feast? Where is the hall's uproar?" asks the speaker of the Old English elegy "The Wanderer."[23] Dating to the late ninth or early tenth century, this poem on an *ubi sunt* theme of the kind we first encountered in Propertius's elegies unfolds in the voice of its speaker, a *wræclastas* (wanderer), who journeys homeless without a protecting lord: he finds that "in many places, over the earth / walls stand, wind-beaten, / hung with hoar-frost; ruined habitations." Like the speaker of "The Ruin," he wonders at the cause of these desolate places, naming war, attacks by wolves, and exile as reasons for their abandonment. Here, too *enta geweorc* are credited as builders, but now "a towering wall" is "wrought with worm-shapes." *Wyrd*, or fate, is the ultimate source of power in the poem, despite its Christian-inflected opening and closing lines.

In the Old English text known as *Genesis A*, a verse paraphrase of the first book of the Hebrew scriptures recorded in the Junius 11 manuscript at Oxford's Bodleian Library, the Tower of Babel story is given a particularly Roman slant. The tower there is no longer a tower of bitumen-fused bricks but one that is likened to a "stænenne weall." The city is called a "ceastre" (fortification). And in the end that "stiðlic stantorr" or (sturdy stone tower) stood "samworht" (unfinished). That a construction can look like a ruin and a ruin like a construction is a paradox the Anglo-Saxons, whose very name included a "saxum," or stone, at its root, could surely grasp.[24]

The specific details of "The Ruin"—its inventory of walls, arches, baths, and water ducts—have led many scholars to conclude that the poem is a meditation on Aquae Sulis, the contemporary English city of Bath. By the late fourth century, the Roman settlements of Britain were decaying: in Aquae Sulis, the streets were still in use and even repaired, but the temples were crumbling and dismantled. And within a few decades, as the collapse continued, all of Britain's Roman towns vanished. Marshland covered what had been urban spaces. The city of York, for example, became the home of froghoppers, water voles, weasels, and shrews—species that do not appear in the archaeological record of the Roman era.[25] The transformation was not only one of collapsed materials: it also was one of vanished customs and meanings. Fifth-century grave sites contain skeletons wearing "antique" Roman jewelry in ways a Roman resident of Britain would find more than passing strange.[26]

Despite its fragmented state, "The Ruin" brings the scene to life. Shifting between present observations and imaginative inferences about the past, the speaker seems driven by juxtapositions. His own composing brings to mind the inspiration that must have suffused the builders who lived so many generations before: "mood quickened mind, and a man of wit, / cunning in rings, bound bravely the wallbase / with iron, a wonder." He brings *waldend* (rulers) up against *wyrhtan* (workers), an acknowledgment of skill as well as—given that all are held in "gravesgrasp"—a leveling by death. His description of the bright buildings, the armor's gold flashing, the warm nights in the mead-hall, is not merely melancholy, however: the ruins are an occasion for him to repeople, in the only terms he knows—his own—the moldering and emptied spaces.

From their earliest recorded notice, ruined structures are evocative not only of ghosts but also of our relations to living persons: to our distinctions between appearance and interiority, to the visibility of our surfaces and invisibility of our organs, to losing and saving face in relation to reputation, to imagining the breakdown of social relations. Seneca wrote movingly in his Epistle 95: "Let us possess things in common; for birth is ours in common. Our relations with one another are like a stone arch, which would collapse if the stones did not mutually support each other, and which is upheld in this very way."[27]

We cannot see our own death, but we also cannot, without access to some very high technology, gaze upon our own interiors. Alberti writes in *De re aedificatoria* that "first we observed that the building is a form of body, which like any other consists of lineaments and matter, the one the product of thought, the other of Nature; the one requiring the mind and the power of reason, the other dependent on preparation and selection."[28] In Vincenzo Scamozzi's late sixteenth-century commentary on ruins and monuments *Discorsi sopra l'antichità di Roma*, we find an extended and more specific meditation on the notion that a building is an analogue for a human body: he writes that "the profile of a building is like the human anatomy." He goes on to compare bones, nerves, and veins to the parts of ancient structures, describing the wearing down of the body until it is covered by what he calls the "bark-like hard surface of the tomb."[29] Ruins, like trees, live beyond us and raise the haunting thought that what we have made may outlive us, even as a species.[30]

The ruin's extensive relation to time, stretching beyond the span of not only a human lifetime but also the extent of the rise and fall of particular cultures, gives it a certain power. One of the most enduring concepts arising from the Western fascination with ruins has been Alois Riegl's notion of "age value"— the estimation of age and its signs of presence as valuable in themselves. In ancient Greece, China, and Japan, potters and sculptors developed techniques for sealing the surfaces of artifacts with patinas. The chemicals and firing processes used could rely on corrosion and polish at once. And objects transformed by the wear of the human hand, its oils and pressures and residues, often have inspired the arts of pottery and sculpture.[31] Yet these valued attributes of wear are not the same as the particular weight given to the effects and signs of time in the West from the Renaissance forward. Anyone who visits, for example, the Shanghai Museum of Ancient Art or the Istanbul

Archaeological Museums (İstanbul Arkeoloji Müzeleri) today, with their
thoroughly restored artifacts, some of which look as if they were completed
yesterday, will be able to grasp the difference between a concept of restoration
that aims at re-creating the conditions of origin and one that is driven by noting and preserving the marks left by wear and time.

Riegl wrote in his seminal essay, "The Modern Cult of Monuments," in
1903, "We are as disturbed at the sight of decay in newly made artifacts (pre-
mature aging) as we are at the traces of fresh intervention into old artifacts
(conspicuous restorations). In the twentieth century we appreciate particularly the purely natural cycle of becoming and passing away."[32] Writing
of monuments (by which he indicates made artifacts of visual and literary
culture) as intended structures, he distinguishes between "art-value," which
stems from the work's "conceptual, formal, and coloristic qualities," on the
one hand, and its "historical value," which resides in the specificity and irre-
placeability of the work's historical context, on the other. Implicit in Riegl's
concepts is an acknowledgment that with the emergence of a sense of historical value in the Renaissance, works of art take on a duality: to the extent they
are intended, their worth, their "art-value," is determined by their makers, but
contemporary viewers shape their historical value—a value that can only be
viewed from the standpoint of the present. And, he argues, an apprehension
of historical value eventually becomes a kind of abstracted or general sense of
the passage of time; we come to appreciate the presence of the past in the material effects it leaves, in its traces on the artifact.

For Riegl, this appreciation turns artworks into "indispensable catalysts
which trigger in the beholder a sense of the life cycle, of the emergence of the
particular from the general and its gradual but inevitable dissolution back into
the general."[33] He contended that patina, erosion, discoloration, stains, and
other forms of damage manifest the "slow and inevitable disintegration of nature."[34] Signs of age produce an immediate emotional effect which, he argues,
depends on neither scholarly knowledge nor historical education for its satisfaction, since it is evoked by mere sensory perception.[35] Under an aesthetic of
age value, we are taken not with the continuous historical specificity of an object, which we may or may not know, but rather with an allusion to time itself.

Thus as ruins acquire a value endowed by continuing in time, what endures in a ruin is not necessarily integral or intelligible. According to Riegl, the
very ambiguity of the form—the flux brought on by its constantly changing
state—is what modern viewers appreciate in a ruined monument. In contrast
to historical value, which encompasses those aspects of a structure typical
of its moment of origin, age value accrues above all from endurance and the
presence by which it is manifested.

Introducing ruins as the most ready-to-hand example of age value, Riegl
returns to them with increasing attention as his argument proceeds. He traces

the "cult of ruins" to the seventeenth century. There he finds what we might call an allegorical impulse: the baroque painters who represented the magnificence of Rome and Greece in its decayed state were taking part in an "indulgence in pain," a pathos designed to remind their viewers of the transitory glories of earthly power. In contrast, the modern appreciation of age value finds in ruins evidence of the natural laws governing all artifacts as objects of human development. The aged artifact is incomplete; it dissolves form and color; it loses much, but not all, of its integrity and shape, for it must in the end be identifiable as an entity. And, in light of the continuing presence of historical value, it is an entity relating to a period style or stage.[36]

Riegl was the first to propose and develop a theory of age value, but we can find a similar notion of the aesthetic desirability of age in aspects of the earlier, largely English and French, tradition of the picturesque. The proponents of the picturesque furthered an aesthetics of texture, contrast, and unevenness that followed from exposure to weather. And they described dynamic relations between the interior and exterior aspects of structure. Such rough surfaces were always preferable to smoothly polished and closed exteriors, according to the formulations of the most prominent theorist of the picturesque, the Reverend William Gilpin. He wrote in his 1792 essay on the picturesque and the beautiful, "To make an object in a peculiar manner picturesque, there *must be* a proportion of roughness, so much, at least, as to make an opposition."[37]

The *Encyclopédie* of 1765, the year of Saint-Pierre and Bellotto's visions of a hammered Dresden, explained, amid many entries on ruins, that "ruine" indicates "décadence, chute, destruction . . . les *ruines* sont belles à peindre" (decline, fall, destruction . . . ruins are beautiful to paint).[38] Diderot's ruin discourse in *The Salon of 1767* contains the edict, "To make a palace an object of interest one must destroy it."[39] Gilpin in turn suggested that the artist wishing to show an example of Palladian architecture in his work should use "the mallet, instead of the chisel." He explained, "We must beat down one half of it, deface the other, and throw the mutilated members around in heaps. In short, from a *smooth* building, we must turn it into a *rough* ruin."[40]

A castle or monument acquires age value because it speaks to the resistance of human effort against nature—a resistance that inverts and follows on the ontology of the structure itself as wrested from nature. Yet the work's age value resides in the authenticity of its materials. The intended destruction half-jokingly described by Gilpin raises, as we shall see, the "quick fix" or inauthentic presentation offered by the artificial ruin, symbol of luxury and aristocratic play. Bernardin de Saint-Pierre, claiming that "the passive taste for ruin is universal," wrote, "Our voluptuaries embellish their gardens with artificial ruins; savages take delight in a melancholy repose by the brink of the Sea, especially during a storm, or in the vicinity of a cascade surrounded by rocks."[41] (He does not explain how he came to witness the leisure of "savages.")

Such positive attitudes toward the signs and effects of wear and age have had a powerful and long-lasting influence on the field of architectural conservation. In the 1860s and 1870s, proponents of "scientific" restoration, who followed Viollet-le-Duc's mandate that restoration required a building be "reinstated" to a condition of completeness which may never have existed at any time,[42] argued against those who followed John Ruskin and William Morris and claimed ancient buildings should be conserved and protected in their existing state. Ruskin, condemning Romantic attitudes toward ruins, wrote in 1849, "Look the necessity full in the face, and understand it on its own terms. It is a necessity for destruction. Accept it as such, pull the building down, throw its stones into neglected corners, make ballast of them, or mortar, if you will; but do it honestly and do not set up a Lie in their place."[43] In the twentieth century and into the present, restorers have turned against both simulacral practices of tearing down and ripping out parts of structures with the aim of unifying an appearance of period style and the conservation of buildings as examples of national and collective aspirations. Instead, they have aimed to preserve a record of the ongoing continuity of buildings and sites.[44]

How did Roman ruins, in the capital itself and throughout the empire, come to serve as the prototypical examples for most later ruins representations? Was it because the sheer scale and magnitude of the ruins ensured that they were left to decay while the continuous presence of visitors ensured that they were seen? Consider the contrasting fates of the remains of Athens and Rome in this regard. Pausanias says very little in his survey of Greece about the ruins of Athens beyond noting they seemed relatively intact—this against a backdrop of ruined, deserted, and shrunken villages and cities, and the roofless and statue-less temples and other devastation that he chronicles elsewhere on his journey.[45] By 395 the Christian Neoplatonist Synesius of Cyrene complained that, as he arrived in Athens, he realized how little previous visitors to the damaged city must have seen. He writes, "They do not understand Aristotle and Plato better than we, and nevertheless they go about among us as demi-gods among mules, because they have seen the Academy, the Lyceum, and the Poecile [the Stoa Poikile] where Zeno gave his lectures on philosophy. However, the Poecile no longer deserves its name, for the proconsul has taken away all the pictures, and has thus humiliated these men's pretensions to learning."[46] The Neoplatonic Academy was closed by Justinian I in 529, and Greece's temples became Christian churches. By the twelfth century, Athens was a wilderness, and from the fourteenth century on, under successive rule by Catalans, Florentines, Venetians, and Turks, the city's monuments suffered. Nevertheless, travelers' accounts describe both the ongoing deterioration and the persistent presence of the Parthenon, Propylaea, and Erechtheum.[47]

Although, as Rose Macaulay describes, there has never been a period of more than a few decades when surveys and chronicles of Athens were not

available,[48] Rome's ruins came to dominate the sensibility of ruins appreciation in the West. By the fourth century, Christian pilgrims and travelers had
established regular routes to Jerusalem and Rome. Some traveled to Jerusalem
through Salonika, and others sailed from Venice.[49] Yet reaching Rome was an
easier objective. Roman structures were pondered and allegorized by early
church fathers and by far later critics of decadence and empire alike; Roman
building schemes involved the appreciation, measurement, and spoliation of
earlier structures; legal protection for ancient buildings developed hand in
hand with the exploitation of their materials and knowledge of their forms.
Until the turn of the fifteenth century, when Manuel Chrysolaras arrived in
Florence from Constantinople, knowledge of Greek was relatively rare. Nearly
four hundred years of Ottoman rule in Greece made continuity in cultural
practices problematic. In contrast, the Renaissance in Europe beyond Greece
was passionately engaged in establishing connections to ancient literature, art,
and architecture—after the fall of Constantinople, such knowledge was en-
hanced by the emigration of Byzantine texts and scholars themselves to the
West. Later, the establishment of the Accademia di San Luca in the sixteenth
century, the French Academy in the seventeenth century, and colonies of foreign residents and practices of the grand tour by the eighteenth century guar-
anteed the Eternal City would continue as a subject of aesthetic and scholarly
contemplation.

Perhaps another answer to Rome's domination of ruins discourse lies in
the fact that Rome has been ruined and rebuilt so many times—by earthquake and flood and fire as well as human violence and neglect. Writing in the
wake of the Sack of Rome by Alaric in August 410, Augustine of Hippo im-
plores, "My soul is like a house. . . . It is in ruins, but I ask you to remake it."[50]
In his *City of God*, he notes there was nothing particularly unusual about the
cruelty of Alaric's attack—"All the devastation, the butchery, the plundering,
the conflagrations, and all the anguish which accompanied the recent disaster
at Rome were in accordance with the general practice of warfare."[51] If Rome
is eternal, it is not because of the permanence of its forms but because it has
endured so many cycles of destruction and rebuilding. For Augustine, there
is a homology between the folly of continual imperial wars and the error of
cyclical history: he spends much of book 12 of *The City of God* arguing for the
unique and irreversible event of Christ's sacrifice and resurrection in contrast
to the "wicked circles" of conflict based on material gain.

At least before the Enlightenment, the story of ruins in Western tradition
is thus largely a story of Roman ruins, and the representation of Roman ruins has proved to be a paradigm for the apprehension of ruins. Even so, ruins
lend themselves, as we will see, to syncretism of many kinds. Contemplating
them leads to a range of thoughts and emotions—from an acknowledgment
of the utter strangeness of the past to a sense of deep connections between
past and present. Henry James wrote among his meditations on Rome in his

Italian Hours, "To delight in the aspects of *sentient* ruin might appear a heart-less pastime, and the pleasure, I confess, shows the note of perversity."[52] Of the varieties of aesthetic pleasure, ruins contemplation can seem the most heavyhearted and heavy-handed.

What we can learn of ruins necessarily comes from the legible and visible record of the past, but we might remember that ruins often are both steeped in and surrounded by absence. They invite quiet contemplation as much as response, and they immerse the viewer-listener in association and reverie. Edward Gibbon recorded in one of his numerous autobiographies the moment of inspiration for his *Decline and Fall*: "It was at Rome, on the fifteenth of October, 1764, as I sat musing amidst the ruins of the Capitol, while the barefooted fryars were singing Vespers in the temple of Jupiter, that the idea of writing the decline and fall of the City first started to my mind."[53] Gibbon hears at dusk a Christian music rising from a ruined temple; there those who have taken a vow of poverty walk on and through the damaged remains of Roman imperial might. He is inspired to register the succession of triumphs and calamities that have shaped the scene in which he finds himself—that dense canvas that will become his explanation for how a civilization betrays itself.

Two hundred years later, in the wake of a second world war, Patrick Leigh Fermor sat amid the ruins of Greece with a far more fatalistic sense of their import:

> A spell of peace lives in the ruins of ancient Greek temples. As the traveller leans back among the fallen capitals and allows the hours to pass, it empties the mind of troubling thoughts and anxieties and slowly refills it, like a vessel that has been drained and scoured, with a quiet ecstasy. Nearly all that has happened fades to a limbo of shadows and insignificance and is painlessly replaced by an intimation of radiance, simplicity and calm which unties all knots and solves all riddles and seems to murmur a benevolent and unimperious suggestion that the whole of life, if it were allowed to unfold without hindrance or compulsion or search for alien solutions, might be limitlessly happy.[54]

For Gibbon, ruins call for remembering; for Leigh Fermor, they call for forgetting. Between attention and neglect, waking and dreaming, they cast their shadows on our thought and making.

I. Matter

THIS RUINED EARTH

Before there are ruins, there must be structures, and before there are structures, there must be materials. The philosopher Hans Jonas, himself a witness to much of the worst devastation of persons and the built environment of the twentieth century, wrote in 1968 that "matter, if created by God, must have a positive, actual being of its own and cannot be merely the potency for something else to be, the empty possibility of becoming. Called forth 'from nothing,' it must be something, *aliqua res actu*, as Duns Scotus says."[1] That is, something of intelligibility and meaning. To acknowledge matter, as Duns Scotus and Jonas do, not only as potential for human appropriation but also as actuality, leads toward a view of nature as in and for itself that recognizes our alienation from nature and the often harsh antinomy between human desire and nature's course.

When John Milton tells the story of the banishment of Adam and Eve from Eden at the end of book 12 of *Paradise Lost*, he sets his final scene ablaze with light: ". . . High in front advanced, / The brandished sword of God before them blazed / Fierce as a comet; . . ." (lines 632–34).[2] Led by the Archangel Michael away from the garden, down a cliff to the waiting plain, the two outcasts catch a glimpse of the fiery destruction God is wreaking behind them: "They looking back, all th'eastern side beheld / Of Paradise, so late their happy seat, / Waved over by that flaming brand; the gate / With dreadful faces thronged and fiery arms: . . ." (641–44). The God of Genesis built the cosmos in planned stages, and here he destroys it—by stages again, rather than by fiat. And yet not all human faces and arms are trapped behind the burning gates that have made an earthly heaven into a hell: Adam and Eve survive as witnesses, turning back to see what has happened as they begin their onward journey.

A narrative constrained by material fact: facing evidence, here, before us, we must go behind its appearance and uncover its cause. A narrative overwhelmed by the trauma of experience: any account of what has happened will never be commensurate to the actuality of what has happened. Milton's source, the stories of the destructions of cities and persons in the Hebrew scriptures, moves between these two narrative forms. As it does, the reader is left wondering about the intentions of a creator God who has brought about such destruction directly or who, as the source of all that happens in the world, has allowed it to unfold.

Thus beyond any questions of local cause lies the larger question of the purpose and meaning of changing states—states of being, states of nature. The story of the Fall reveals how human beings ultimately found their destiny outside of an unchanging garden—in the painful transformations of birth and labor and death, in the decision to live despite such pain, and in their capacities for willing and loving. As Milton's last lines, with their dramatic enjambment, emphasize, "The world was all before them, where to choose / Their place of rest, and Providence their guide" (646–47). "Where to choose," for now choosing is possible and their orientation is no longer toward the present, but toward the future. Human history, contrary to the cycles of natural forms, would therein find, between will and providence, a specificity and direction.

The Hebrew scriptures record, within a perfected Creation, destructive forces of weather, human violence, and divine anger against those very forms God has made. In turn, with its theology of a creator God who takes material form—not only revealed, as the Greek and Roman gods might be, but as well manifested in human clay—Christianity lent both dignity and contempt to "mere" matter.

In Hebrew and Christian traditions, and later in Islam, prohibitions of idolatry are not only rooted in a threat to monotheism but also tied to ideas about matter's limitations as a vehicle of divine representation. In Exodus, at chapter 20, verses 3–4, we find an injunction, "Thou shalt have no other gods before me. / Thou shalt not make unto thee any graven image, or any likeness of any thing that is in heaven above, or that is in the earth beneath, or that is in the water under the earth."[3] In Leviticus 26:1, the command specifically addresses the manufacture of carved and standing forms: "Ye shall make you no idols nor graven image, neither rear you up a standing image, neither shall ye set up any image of stone in your land, to bow down unto it: for I am the LORD your God." Numbers 33:52 condemns "pictures" and "molten images," and Deuteronomy 4:16 prohibits graven images and "likenesses," as Deuteronomy 27:15 repeats the ban on graven and molten images. Whether or not these injunctions inhibited the development of crafts and arts, they emphasize a strong predilection for the metaphysical and invisible over the tangible and earthly.

As the apostle Paul looked on idols and temples of pagan gods in Athens, he preached that the Christian God was too powerful to be embodied by such finite forms. Acts 17:24 describes "God that made the world and all things therein, seeing that he is Lord of heaven and earth, dwelleth not in temples made with hands." At verse 29, Paul explains, "Forasmuch then as we are the offspring of God, we ought not to think that the Godhead is like unto gold, or silver, or stone, graven by art and man's device."

The early Christian theologian Tertullian, born in Carthage circa 155 CE, wrote in his *Apology* that idols cannot embody divine entities, for they are dumb material things: "As for your images, I shall only observe that they are material, and often of the same matter with your common utensils; and 'tis ten to one but the holy image has some sister-vessel about the house, the pots and kettles being frequently of the same metal and piece with the gods. Nay, oftentimes the vessels themselves have the good luck to change their fate, and be turn'd into gods, by the help of consecration, which alters the property, and by the help of art, which alters the form, tho' not without great sacrilege and contumely to any of the gods in their very making."[4] In succeeding generations, Lactantius wrote in his *Divine Institutes* that "body is constructed of heavy and unstable material and can be touched and seen, so it breaks up and collapses, and because it is subject to sight and touch it cannot resist attack, whereas soul cannot be undone by any act of violence."[5] Lactantius mocks, just as Augustine did in *The City of God*, the paltry material finitude of idols in the light of God's infinite capaciousness.[6]

Mountain Ruin

Idols and temples are material objects fashioned by human hands, yet the Judeo-Christian suspicion of materiality has extended as well to at least one feature of nature: mountains—those massive mineral forms so resistant to human aims. "Mountain ruin" is a strange concept to us today, but in fact well into Milton's time many people, particularly in Britain and northern Europe, believed that mountains were flaws in an otherwise harmonious world.[7] As early as Camden's late sixteenth-century *Britannia*, the ontological status of mountains is doubtful—their very "thingness" comes into question as Camden writes of a Herefordshire hill that seems to have powers of agency. He describes how the hill had

> Neere unto the place where *Lugg* and *Wy* meete together, Eastward, a hill which they call *Marcley hill*, in the yeere of our redemption, 1571. (as though it had wakened upon the suddaine out of a deepe sleepe) roused it selfe up, and for the space of three daies together mooving and shewing it selfe (as mighty and huge an heape as it was) with roring noise in a fearefull sort, and overturning all things that stood in the way, advanced it selfe forward to the wonderous astonishment of the beholders: by that kinde of Earthquake which as I deeme, naturall Philosophers call Brasmatias.[8]

The literary historian Stuart Piggott has explained some of this antipathy. He suggests that "classical landscapes necessarily included classical ruins, which had to be replaced in Britain by those of the Middle Ages.... With ruins went mountains, and in the seventeenth century mountains could arouse passionate dislike, and few found them even tolerable."[9] Nevertheless, fear of or disgust with mountain landscapes proved to be inspiring for poetry. Michael Drayton published in his 1606 collection *Poemes Lyrick and pastorall. Odes. Eglogs, The man in the Moone,* an homage to the Peake district of North Central England that would later become known as his "Ode Written in the Peake." The work celebrates the "holy fire" of poetry as a power against the "cold air," "mountains bleak / Exposed to sleet and rain," and the "grim and horrid caves / Whose looks affright the day."[10] Drayton's longer writings on the district in his topographical poem of 1612, *Poly-Olbion,* record three caves among the "seven wonders of the Peake": Eldon Hole, Peak Cavern (or the Devil's Arse), and Poole's Cavern, which his contemporaries believed reached down to Hades. Thomas Hobbes would later describe "The Devil's Arse" as well:

> Behind, a ruin'd Mountain does appear
> Swelling into two Parts, which turgent are,
> As when we bend our Bodies to the Ground,
> The Buttocks amply fticking out are found.[11]

In "An Anatomie of the World. The First Anniversarie," his meditation upon the death of the young Elizabeth Drury within a larger account of the "decay of this whole World," John Donne asked of mountains in general:

> Are these but warts, and pock-holes in the face
> Of th'earth? Thinke so; but yet confesse, in this
> The worlds proportion disfigured is.[12]

Andrew Marvell recorded similar thoughts about the deformity and "ill-design" of mountains in a poem "Upon the Hill and Grove at Bill-borow."[13]

Mountains in the Hebrew scriptures and the Gospels are often places of dramatic transformation and traumatic sacrifice, close to a heavenly God and to natural forces of water, fire, earthquakes, and landslides attributed to the deity's divine moods and powers. Among them, Mount Ararat as the scene of the end of the Flood; Mount Sinai, sometimes known as Mount Horeb, where the inscribed stone tablets of the Ten Commandments were delivered, then broken, and delivered again; Mount Moriah, site of the sacrifice of Isaac and the founding of the Temple of Solomon; Mount Carmel, where Elijah contested the priests of Baal; Mount Olivet, in the Hebrew scriptures another scene of the condemnation of idolatry and in the Gospels, the location of Christ's final earthly agony. John Wilkins, a philosopher and theologian, wrote in his 1638 *The Discovery of a World in the Moone; or, A Discovrse Tending to Prove That 'Tis Probable There May Be Another Habitable World in That Planet* that mountains "were not the effect of mans sin, or produced by the Worlds curfe the Flood, but rather at the first created by the goodneffe and providence of the Almighty."[14] His reasoning was that the inaccessibility of mountains made them refuges for those under attack. The agriculturalist Gabriel Plattes wrote in the same period that mountains were held by some people to be "produced by accretion in length of time, even as Warts, Tumours, Wenns and Excrefcences are engendred in the fuperficies of men's bodies."[15] The parson-naturalist John Ray believed this surely could not be true, for if mountains were ugly blemishes, they could never have been part of an original and per-fected Creation.[16]

Opinions veered between arguments for and against the significance of mountains within a Creation that otherwise seemed to hand. In his 1681 *Telluris Theoria Sacra* (*Sacred Theory of the Earth*), Thomas Burnet contended that, before the Flood, the earth had been a perfect orb of a soft and fertile ground that yielded to the needs of men. And then, Burnet claimed, the sun's heat led this surface to crack; the cracked soil fell into the waters below, caus-ing a flood; in consequence, mountains emerged. This process of shrinking and sinking was simultaneous, in Burnet's view, to the Fall of mankind, and the earth became "a broken and confus'd heap of bodies" reflecting man's sin-ful state. Burnet produced a map of the earth's form designed to show "the image or picture of a great Ruine" with "the true aspect of a World lying in its rubbish."[17] He wrote that although mountains are "the greatest examples of confusion that we know in Nature," they must have been even worse in the past: "'Tis true, they cannot look so ill now as they did at first; a ruine that is fresh looks much worse than afterwards, when the Earth grows discolour'd and skin'd over. But I fancy if we had seen the Mountains when they were new-born and raw, when the Earth was fresh broken, and the waters of the Deluge newly retir'd, the fractions and confusions of them would have appeared very ghastly and frightful."[18] Burnet's natural history is structured around the importance of the Deluge and throughout he looks to forces of use, beauty, and order as counters to the chaos wrought by natural disasters and divine punishments.

By the eighteenth century, such accounts of the ruin of nature as a macro-cosmic version of the Fall of man receded, and as scientists, including the De-ist James Hutton, came to understand the nature of chemical weathering and the powers of running water in molding topography, they began to use ruins themselves to determine the age of the earth. Roman sites in the Thames ba-sin, even when completely exposed, kept their forms for nearly two thousand years and gave evidence that a valley many hundreds of feet deep could not have been created by the force of the river alone.[19] The boundary between ruined nature and ruined structures also becomes blurred around both mega-lithic forms—stone posts, arches, vaults, and caves giving evidence of human habitation—and artificial mountains.

The seven wonders of the ancient world—the Great Pyramid of Giza, the Colossus of Rhodes, the Lighthouse at Alexandria, the Mausoleum of Hali-carnassus, the Temple of Artemis at Ephesus, the Statue of Zeus at Olympia, and the Hanging Gardens of Babylon—all were (and in the case of the Giza pyramid, the only surviving wonder, are) human-engineered constructions. But are the massive upright stones of Stonehenge properly ruins? Where does their nature end and their artifice begin? How can we infer their ur-form? The same is true of megalithic forms. Even later works further complicate the boundaries between made and natural forms. For example, the eroded structures of the tenth-century castle of Les Baux in Provence are situated on a rocky outcropping; it is difficult at first to distinguish the castle's stone reliefs and crenellations from the jagged outlines of the surrounding stone.

Artificial mountains are constructed by intention and happenstance alike: often, like Burnet's world lying in its own "rubbish," they are formed from the detritus or rubble of other fallen structures. Regardless of their contents, their height gives them value and significance. And yet their history is not erased by the creation of their pleasing surfaces. As the scholar of artificial mountains Michael Jakob has noted, "the artificial mountain, the positive rising-up, the built and the consolidated, the titanic self-affirmation, is directly related to that which is dug out: the negative, the hollow form, the uncanny hole and the wounded earth."[20] Among the many examples he considers are *tumuli*, or artificial small hills, associated with the cult of the dead and ancestor worship in Britain, all parts of Europe, the Middle East, Asia, and prehistoric North America. And, as we saw in the devilish "wonders" of the Peake District, mountains and caves continue to evoke not only sin but also visions of hell. Dante's spiraling, descending, funnel becomes a negative, fallen, image of the mountains of Purgatory and Paradise.

European Renaissance gardens could include representations of Parnassus made from piled rocks and soil.[21] The mound of "Monte" Testaccio in Rome and the rubble mountain of Teufelsberg (literally "Devil's Mountain") in post–World War II Berlin each began as refuse—accumulated and expelled matter. As they have acquired vegetation and external form, they have become named sites and locations of meaning. Built at the dawn of the Christian era from shards of as many as 53 million smashed amphorae,[22] Monte Testaccio was, into the nineteenth century, a place for recreation. Today it is a subway stop and working-class neighborhood. Teufelsberg was shaped from the rubble of the Allied bombing and now is a much-loved park famed for its views. Paris's Parc des Buttes-Chaumont was a gypsum quarry where rubbish and animal carcasses were discarded until 1866–1867, when Baron Georges-Eugène Haussmann's followers Adolphe Alphand and Jean-Pierre Barillet-Deschamps turned it into a twenty-three-hectare park with Anglo-Chinese landscape features and a temple modeled on the first-century BCE Temple of Vesta at Tivoli (see fig. 6).[23]

What is the legacy of this eccentric, gradually vanished, theme drawing connections between mountains and expulsion, materiality and human failings? One work deeply indebted to it is Johann Wolfgang von Goethe's

FIGURE 6. Temple of the Sibyl, Parc des Buttes-Chaumont, Paris, 1869.

lifelong meditation on human ruin, sin, and redemption: his *Faust*, parts 1 and 2.[24] Throughout Goethe's masterpiece, architecture is characterized by its physical decay and relation to waste. Faust's study, site of his tragic discontent, is described from the start as synonymous with history: ". . . A vast / Old rubbish dump, an attic of the past" (1:21) and "a moth-mumbled rubbish-bin . . ." (1:23). When, after a long absence, he returns to this room in part 2, he finds that "The stained glass seems a trifle browned, / And the room has more cobwebs covering it," while his scholar's gown is full of crickets, beetles, and moths (2:64–65). Mephistopheles is a source of material as well as spiritual decay: his presence makes the staircases and walls tremble and the floors warp. In his first appearance to Faust, the devil declares:

> I am the spirit of perpetual negation;
> And rightly so, for all things that exist
> Deserve to perish, and would not be missed—
> Much better it would be if nothing were
> Brought into being. Thus, what you men call
> Destruction, sin, evil in short, is all
> My sphere, the element I most prefer. (1:42)

The perverse ministry of Mephistopheles takes place against a backdrop of spring's contrary renewals and resurrections; thus every destruction is a blow against the new and the just-born. The antique and antiquarian in turn are linked to stultification and decay. Goethe's stage directions specify that Faust's study and the laboratory where his assistant Wagner creates a homunculus should be "gothic" and narrow. As the homunculus describes the "proper habitat" of the devil, he says Mephistopheles belongs to the "dark ages": "Black mouldering stones, arches in Gothic style / And absurd curlicues—how drab, how vile!" (2:75). Barging along a passageway to Faust's study, the Baccalaureus or Graduate declaims:

> As things were, one used to rot
> Like a corpse in such a spot;
> Life was mere disintegration,
> Death by slow anticipation.
>
> Walls and halls, you've had your day!
> Now you crumble and decay.
> Here's no place to stop; we'll all
> Squash to death here when you fall. (2:68)

Such interior scenes are as well continuous with a fallen external world: the claustrophobic, crumbling interiors of Faust's study presage the close walls of Gretchen's prison cell: the familiar village scenes of houses, wells, and gardens dissolve into the vast and solemn echo chamber of the cathedral; the restorative environs of the forest are shadowed by the Forest Cavern where Faust and Mephistopheles meet, and by the looming, ever-present mountain scenery in the distance. Here Goethe draws on actual mountains and their lore. "The Brocken," also known as "Blocksberg," or Block Mountain, is the dominant peak in the German Harz Mountain range; it is where, according to legend, devils, witches, and other evil spirits congregate on Walpurgis Night

(April 30–May 1). Goethe also mentions Ilsenstein, a granite rock formation near the peak of the Brocken, and the "Raven Stone," a formation of stone augmented with mortar that was used for executions.[25] On high, crows circle, waiting for carrion.

Part 2 of *Faust* evokes such artificially created and natural spaces on a far broader scale, incorporating flights of imagination and time travel: houses are replaced by imperial halls, staterooms, and galleries. Faust travels to the upper and lower Peneus (or Pineiós) River of Thessaly, the "rocky inlets of the Aegean," and the mountainous heights, spur, gorges, forest, cliff, and wilderness of the two final acts.

In sum, Goethe relies on a claustrophobic backdrop of demonic rocks and mountains, an ever-resistant materiality, to tell his story of the breakdown of the mind and weakness of the flesh. In "High Mountains," act 4 of part 2, Faust and Mephistopheles conduct a dialogue on geology after Mephistopheles has described how the creatures of hell were propelled by a volcanic eruption to the crests of mountains, giving to the lowest things the highest place. Faust describes the emergence of a picturesque landscape typified by a modulated order:

> Mountains keep noble silence; let them be!
> Their whence and why's no puzzlement to me.
> When Nature's reign began, pure and self-grounded,
> Then this terrestrial globe it shaped and rounded.
> Glad of their peaks and chasms, it displayed
> Mountains and mountains, rocks and rocks it made;
> The soft-curved hills it shaped then, gentling down
> Into the valleys; there all's green and grown.
> Thus Nature takes her pleasure, never troubling
> With all your crazy swirl and boil and bubbling. (2:176–77)

In Faust's account of the formation of the earth, all is ordered and in its place. The jaggedness of peaks and gorges evokes pleasure, not terror, and the "shaped and rounded" proportions of Nature herself are echoed in the gentle beauty and softened lines of the hills leading to green valleys, welcoming to human effort.

But Mephistopheles, claiming his status as an eyewitness to Creation, tells a different story:

> But I was there, my dear sir, and I know!
> I saw it all: the lower regions seethed,
> They swelled and spilled, great streams of fire they breathed,
> And Moloch's hammer, forging rock to rock,

Scattered the fragments with its mighty knock.
The land's still stiff with alien lumps of stone:
How's such momentum possible? The sages
Try to explain, but still untouched for ages
Those boulders lie, the answers still unknown.
We rack our brains to death: what more
Can thinking tell us?—Only the old lore
Of simple folk has understood, they've read it
In their tradition's ripe unchanging store:
Wonders they see, and Satan gets the credit! (2:177)

Mephistopheles is pointing to the "Devil's Rock" and "Devil's Bridge"—features of landscapes the world over that survive as manifestations of a terrifying, but no longer evident, manufacture. This is the natural architecture—the landscape planning—of demonic forces; aspects of the environment that make life difficult for human motion and plans, leaving us literally "astounded."

As Teufelsberg today is a popular green and cultivated park, and the Parc des Buttes-Chaumont accommodates more than three million visitors a year, it is not difficult to see that the remedy for the intransigence of a mountain ruin is a garden. In Goethe's long lifetime, ruins became encompassed, and tamed, by the picturesque—no longer overwhelming, they are part of a view or vista. William Gilpin wrote in 1769, "The Picturesque advantages, which a caſtle, or any eminent building, receives from a *state of ruin*, are chiefly these: It gains irregularity in it's [*sic*] *general form*. We judge of beauty in caſtles, as we do in figures, in mountains, and other objects. The ſolid, ſquare, heavy form, we diſlike; and are pleaſed with the pyramidal one, which may be infinitely varied; and which ruin contributes to vary."[26] In Gilpin's aesthetics, as in Goethe's, the mountain ruin gradually tapers and recedes, and the horror and sublimity of a destructive nature are brought under the regulation of human cult and ritual.

Substance

With the human-generated rubble or trash mountain, ruined materials acquire a form that resembles nature and that eventually, like all ruins, will be overtaken by nature. But what of the ruin of materials that have been shaped by human hands for purposes beyond mere refuse, storage, and accumulation—those materials of the built environment also subject to forces of natural wear and human violence? Our Latinate word *substance* and its corollary *substantial* yoke the very essence of being with the capacity to stand firm. Emotions regarding the ruination of buildings thus observe a certain ratio: the stronger and more valuable the initial material of the ruin, the more poignant is its decay.

And the only materials and practices we can study are those that have left some trace. Hence ruins are vestiges—from *vestigium*, Latin for "footstep," "footprint," "trace," or "mark"—which are visible signs of what once existed but no longer exists, parts indicating their missing wholes. A vestige indicates both a sign left on the ground and an impression made by an image on the brain.[27] What are we seeing when we look at the elements of a ruined structure? To go to the source of a ruin is not merely to look for the cause of destruction but also to look behind the vestige to the material origin of its construction.

All material human artifacts are drawn from the earth, and all eventually will return to the earth. Between their emergence and their disappearance, structures could be said to be undergoing a process of decay or ruination by wear, erosion, arson, or putrefaction. It is not ruin, but preservation, that is the exception. Yet the rate of decay depends on the material. A granite form sheltered from the weather, such as the interior of the Giza pyramid, will last, so far as we know, for many thousands of years beyond the more than 4,500 it already has endured. Almost all precious stones are imperishable, but they can be destroyed, lost, or ground for medicine.[28] Wooden structures exposed to insects and rain will not last a generation.

Limestone was the first mineral to be quarried for a specific purpose. Out of the limestone formations on either side of the Nile, using the strong tools they had wrought from copper—and later, bronze and iron—the ancient Egyptians were able to cleave the relatively soft stone into blocks for their buildings. Each block produced at least the same amount of rubble, and the techniques the Egyptians used continued for five thousand years, well into the early twentieth century. The Minoans were quarrying as early as 1700–1450 BCE, and Greek stoneworkers introduced the pickax toward the end of the sixth century BCE; at the same time, the Greeks began to quarry an especially fine white marble from the island of Paros. As the Egyptians had exploited cracks in sandstones and limestone by hammering them with harder dolomite, the Greeks developed an abrasive cutting technique using wet sand, harder than marble, cutting through the stone with a dull blade.

It was the Greeks who made marble, and any limestone that can be polished, a material of valued status—a status it has maintained into the present. The ancient Maya culture, like the Egyptians, also used limestone, but the Maya seem to have approached it without any particular reverence. The softness of marble made it much more suited to a figurative, gestural sculpture that conveyed the values of Greek realism. The Egyptians preferred granite and basalt, much harder stones, for their sarcophagi and sculptures. Whereas Egyptian granite emphasized an eternal permanence, Greek marble gave a sense of fleeting, lived, existence in time.

During the reign of the Athenian city-state, more than 400,000 cubic meters of stone were mined from twenty-five Pentelic marble quarries in the vicinity of the city. In Sicily, the tyrants of Siracusa owned enormous quarries, known as *latomie*. They were worked by, among others, more than seven thousand Athenian prisoners of war from the failed expedition of 413 BCE who eventually died there. Yet for the most part, Greek efforts did not involve the inhuman labor practices of earlier periods, since the Greeks often worked on a smaller scale. They also learned how to finish the stones roughly on-site at the quarry.[29]

In his seminal late nineteenth-century study *The Ruins and Excavations of Ancient Rome*, the pioneering and controversial Roman archaeologist Rodolfo Lanciani, whom we met earlier measuring oaks and figs at the Forum, listed the materials used in ancient Roman constructions: *lapis ruber* (tufa), *lapis Albanus* (peperino), *lapis Gabinus* (sperone), *lapis Tiburtinus* (travertino), and *silex* (selce), as well as bricks and tiles. Concrete was composed of pozzolana and lime. Augustus's legendary boast was that he had "found a city made of brick and left one made of marble."[30] Stones from the Luna quarry, near today's Carrara, and Greek marble became the most frequently used building materials.[31] The first white marble temples were erected by Quintus Caecilius Metellus Macedonicus in 147 BCE,[32] and the high cylindrical white tomb of his descendant Caecilia Metella remains one of the most striking ruins on the Via Appia (see fig. 7).

From the end of the Roman Republic and then throughout the imperial period, as Augustus boasted, the Romans imported marble from near and far. The Pax Romana included an enormous trade in marble from around the empire. Egypt and the Aegean provided exotic stones, and a North African quarry in what is now Chemtou, Tunisia (the Roman Simitthus) supplied *marmor numidicum*, the yellow marble known as "giallo antico."[33] Although much sought after, Numidian marble often cracked.[34] Colored marble from conquered lands was especially popular for thresholds, enabling the Romans to walk over the territory of their defeated enemies each time they entered their houses. The quarry at Portus was under imperial ownership, but in the first century it was worked through a system of contractors—imperial slaves or freedmen who leased parts of quarries and "signed" their products with inscriptions.[35] Deposits of travertine along the Aniene River near the city were heavily used; the variety known as calcareous sinter formed the walls of the Colosseum, and under the emperors Domitian and Trajan, enormous building projects demanded great quantities of stone. The expense and weight of marble led to new building techniques. Solid walls of the stone were replaced by ordinary brick covered with marble facings, while poured concrete vaults, known as *opus caementicium*, enabled massive constructions, including the Pantheon. Concrete structures, too, were faced with marble slabs and by the end of the second century CE, public buildings were no longer made purely of marble. Stucco painted to look like marble followed; the technique, so characteristic of the baroque, has been carried over to the present.[36]

FIGURE 7. Tomb of Caecilia Metella, Via Appia Antica, Rome, after 62 BCE.

Inside Out

The raising of a building moves from the structural elements of the interior to the finish or "skin"; ruin turns this process inside out. Lanciani describes the patterns of building techniques hidden beneath the marble facings, both real and painted. The oldest remains, the walls of the Palatine and the Capitol, are built in the Etruscan-derived style of *opus quadratum* in which blocks of tufa were placed lengthwise in one level and crosswise in the next. A later style, *opus incertum*, involved inserting irregularly shaped and randomly placed uncut stones or tufa blocks into concrete. The Porticus Æmilia is the most well-known example of this technique. *Opus reticulatum*, also used by the Etruscans, became popular from the first century BCE forward and can be glimpsed today in Ostia Antica, Hadrian's Villa, and Pompeii. It is made of regular tufa prisms that look like a net—hence they are "reticulated" (see fig. 8). *Opus latericium*, made of courses of unfired mud bricks, was used to face structures made of concrete and eventually came to dominate imperial buildings. The blocks were placed in only one direction, and the style was often replaced by the third century CE by plaster imitations. The Baths of Diocletian and Constantine, among other buildings, were plastered in this style.

The brickwork exposed in ruins can be dated by its use of concrete: the thinner the layer of concrete between the layers, the older the building. In the early days of the Pax Romana, the bricks are so close that the concrete is barely visible. At the end of the third century, the concrete is thicker than the bricks. Lanciani expressed surprise that so much effort was expended to create brick and tufa work of such elegance and beauty, for these forms were concealed by coatings of plaster or marble slabs. The style is common for practical buildings, including Ostia Antica's warehouses, and was used as well for the substructure of Hadrian's elegant villa.[37]

Thanks to processes of ruination, then, the hidden craftwork of Roman walls has been visible for centuries by now. As Lanciani appreciated the revealed rhythms of *opus reticulatum*, we can view many other patterns uncovered, and often as well created, by ruination: the rows of small brick columns beneath the floors of the *caldaria* (rooms with hot plunge baths) and *tepidaria* (warm rooms, environments made by heated walls and floors) of

FIGURE 8. *Opus reticulatum*, Ostia Antica, ca. 100 BCE–200 CE.

FIGURE 9. Egg-and-dart ornament, Ostia Antica, ca. 100 BCE–200 CE.

FIGURE 10. Herm at the base of the ramp to the Borghese Gardens, Rome.

Roman baths, the enormous radiant ribbed brick vaulting of domes, the herringbone brick patterns of the walls of commercial buildings once covered by plaster, the vertical grooves left by the deep runnels of wooden forms used to mold concrete, the mossy outlines of buttresses once covered in marble. In some cases, such as the magnificent coffered ceiling of the Pantheon, with its panels of receding squares framing the oculus and nesting within the great round dome, the exposed view has become the canonical one.[38]

A ruin also evokes new perspective views; the recession of a colonnade is transformed when parts of the structure are broken or missing; the shadows cast by open roofs upon interiors were never meant to be viewed; an ornament representing a facet of the natural world, such as an acanthus leaf, might now be juxtaposed to an actual acanthus leaf. Our eye continually returns to places where the facade has fallen away and what should have remained hidden is exposed. Conversely, through wind and weather, a detail such as the egg-and-dart entablature of an ancient wall will become more abstract (see fig. 9), and the face of a herm will almost vanish (see fig. 10).

A ruin confuses the interior with the exterior and the transparent with the opaque as it also shows the interrelatedness of these aspects of perception. When a cover vanishes and an interior is revealed, what was opaque no longer resists our view. We come to realize that the perception of transparency and actual transparency—in a kind of allegory of their own terms—are quite separate. As the Italian psychologist Fabio Metelli has suggested, "Physical transparency is neither a necessary nor a sufficient condition for the perception of transparency."[39] He adds, "Physical transparency is present everywhere, as we always see objects through the (physically) transparent air. But under these conditions we do not perceive transparency. We perceive transparency only when the transparent object or layer is perceived, in addition to the objects seen through it."[40] Thus, like the view through a rain-dotted window, transparency is only noticed when it is marked or semiopaque. And yet we believe transparency is greater when we see "beyond" more clearly, when the transparent layer is less visible, and when what is beyond is less altered by the superimposition of the transparent object.[41]

In a ruin, a formerly closed view will be opened to weather, light, earth, and sky, and our awareness of what was once present will be more acute because of its absence. Describing the influence of ruins on his architectural projects in the late 1950s, Louis Kahn memorably wrote, "I thought of the beauty of ruins . . . the absence of frames . . . of things which nothing lives behind . . . and so I thought of wrapping ruins around buildings; you might say encasing a building in a ruin so that you look through the wall which had its apertures by accident."[42] Kahn's radical thought is to remind us that ruins always are adjacent to us: we can enter, set up camp within, or find temporary shelter under a ruin, but our habitation of a ruin is never a matter of dwelling or "fit." The original maker of what is now a ruin never had us in mind. The perforations in a ruin open onto the space of the present where we, the viewers, stand.

To wrap a ruin around a building is as well to insert a building within a ruin—for Kahn, the practical aim was the reduction of glare, yet we can see that he has found a means to cut back on the glare not only of the sun but also of the new: "things which nothing lives behind." Transparency does not evoke clarity so much as emptiness. The self-consciousness we bring to noticing "the transparent layer" in many ways fixes our view on the structure before us. When we speak of the "resistance" of history, we have in mind a similar relation, and we can see in these perceptual frames some of the reasons why ruins are so readily aestheticized.

We are called back from looking "beyond" and blocked from looking "behind"—the ruined object fixes our attention on our frames for perception themselves. In an essay contemplating the "evidence of images," Ernst Gombrich wrote, "While we scan a picture . . . , the surface is irrelevant to our processing and disappears from our awareness."[43] But when we view ruins, surface is the ground of relevance, and in printed representations of ruins the "relief" of the image is relevant as well—there is a homology between the etched or engraved line and the ruin. As we shall explore, printmaking is an art of inscribing stone and other mineral surfaces and involves the erosion and eventual destruction of the work's own material: the print is a trace of a ruined form. This process does not characterize the tactile and accumulative art of painting, which is perhaps why, although it can incorporate every kind of line, painting has been second to printmaking as the means of ruins representation.

In viewing a ruin, we also find that the minimal aspect of the part might evoke the whole. We can recall here that Leonardo da Vinci, contemplating "a new art of invention," suggested that ideas for compositions might sometimes be inspired by shapes seen in an old wall or streaked stones. In the 1540 compilation made by one of his former students under the title "A Treatise on Painting," Leonardo explained, "Among other things, I shall not scruple to deliver a new method of assisting the Invention; which tho' trifling in appearance may yet be of considerable service, in opening the mind, and putting it upon the Scent of new Thoughts; and 'tis this; if you look at some old Wall covered with dirt, or the odd appearance of some streak'd Stones, you may discover several things like Landskips, Battles, Clouds, uncommon Attitudes, humorous Faces, Draperies, &c, out of this confused Mass of Objects, the Mind will be furnish'd with abundance of Designs, and Subjects, perfectly new."[44] Here we see an affinity between ruin and abstraction that will flower into the many forms of imaginary ruins in the eighteenth century.

Outside In

As exposure is one consequence of ruins, the inverse motion—collapse—is equally paradigmatic of ruination, and the ruin of walls takes on particular significance, for a wall is the edge between inside and outside. The destruction of a wall ends in the destruction of boundary and the end of intelligible form. The walls of a city are emblematic of this kind of disaster: without its walls, the city is no longer itself; once broken, a wall no longer functions as a wall.

Pride in the strength of walls and horror at their downfall are major themes of book 7 of the *Iliad*, for example. After the fierce duel between Hector and Ajax in that book, the Trojans and Achaeans agree to a truce to bury the dead. The Trojans retreat to light their cremation pyres and go back within their city. Troy, or Ilion, is surrounded by great walls built by Poseidon and Apollo.in a period when Zeus strips them of their divinity and makes them serve Laomedon, king of Troy and father of Priam. The Achaeans burn their dead as well, and before dawn they gather to build a barrow for the dead and their own high, strong-gated wall—with the funeral barrow and their ships on one side and a deep, wide trench filled with stakes on the other side. The wall comes to the attention of the gods, who marvel at the great feat of engineering that the Achaeans have accomplished.

But Poseidon complains that the Greeks have built their wall without remembering to offer hecatombs to the gods:

> Look there—the long-haired Achaeans
> have flung that rampart up against their ships,
> around it they have dug an enormous deep trench
> and never offered the gods a hundred splendid bulls,
> but its fame will spread as far as the light of dawn!

And men will forget those ramparts I and Apollo
reared for Troy in the old days—
for the hero Laomedon—we broke our backs with labor.[45]

Zeus answers in anger that as soon as the Achaeans return home with their
ships, Poseidon is free to "then batter their wall, sweep it into the salt breakers
/ and pile over the endless beach your drifts of sand again, / level it to your
heart's content—the Argives' mighty wall."[46]

The destruction of the wall does follow, and Homer inserts the story in the
middle of his description of battle, writing at the opening of book 12 of the
wall's eventual fate:

Defying the deathless gods they built that wall
and so it stood there steadfast no long time.
While Hector still lived and Achilles raged on
and the warlord Priam's citadel went unstormed,
so long the Achaeans' rampart stood erect.
But once the best of the Trojan captains fell,
and many Achaeans died as well while some survived,
and Priam's high walls were stormed in the tenth year
and the Argives set sail for the native land they loved—
then, at last, Poseidon and Lord Apollo launched their plan
to smash the rampart, flinging into it all the rivers' fury.[47]

Homer goes on to describe how Apollo creates one mouth from all the rivers, sending them to flood the wall with their combined fury for nine days.
Zeus watches the spectacle as Poseidon pitches in, sweeping up the "strong
supports of logs and stones," returning the mighty wall to beaches and sending the rivers backward in their courses. Homer gets ahead of himself and explains "in the years to come" Poseidon and Apollo will have done this, but at
this moment in the epic's action, the war is still crashing, blazing, and shaking
all around the "strong-built work."[48]

As the founding of Troy is linked to the creation of its great walls by the
chastised gods of water and light, stories of the founding of Rome similarly
focus on the importance and endurance of its walls. Plutarch, in *Romulus* 11,
and Livy, in his *Ab urbe condita* (1.44), tell the legend of how the pomerium
(from *post murum*—beyond the wall) was first shaped by Romulus.[49] Romulus began by making a circle on the projected site of Rome, then "the founder,
having shod a plough with a brazen ploughshare, and having yoked to it a bull
and a cow, himself drove a deep furrow round the boundary lines."[50] A wall
was then built on this plowed line and came to stand for the city itself. The
land on either side of the wall was used neither for cultivation nor for building: the Etruscans reserved it instead as a site for augury, which Romulus and
Remus themselves practiced.[51]

In book 1 of Virgil's *Aeneid*, the prophecy of Jupiter, delivered to Venus to assure her of the destiny of her son Aeneas, lists among "builders of walls" not only Romulus but also Aeneas and his son Ascanius. When, at the end of Ovid's *Metamorphoses* (15.807–15), Venus worries that the death of Julius Caesar is imminent despite her efforts to protect him, Jupiter replies with a similar assurance of the permanence of the destined, and solidly built, record:

> Child, do you mean, by your sole self, to move
> Unconquerable fate? *You* are allowed
> To enter the three Sisters' dwelling. There
> A giant fabric forged of steel and bronze
> Will meet your eyes, the archives of the world,
> That fear no crash of heaven, no lightning's wrath,
> Nor any cataclysm, standing safe
> Engraved on everlasting adamant
> The fortunes of your line. I read them there
> Myself and stored them in my memory . . .[52]

Inscription in adamant, the legendary mineral associated with both diamonds and lodestones, is invincible, "untamable," as its name—*a* (not) *daman* (to tame)—records. Yet Ovid has Jupiter offer an even more durable record: the memory of prophecy in the mind of the god.

Time's Diminution

The prophecies of Jupiter assure Venus, as they assure the reader, that Aeneas will indeed found a new city, a new Troy, made by the building of laws and walls. Yet the prospect of his achievement is haunted by an encounter with a building project that is not so much a ruin as a failed memorial to one, a work that exists as a kind of model and memento mori at once: it is a diminished Troy seen in small scale as if from a great distance. In book 3 of the *Aeneid*, Andromache has fulfilled Thetis's command to found a new colony, and yet at the same time her existence represents an insistent repetition—a mourning that has dissolved into melancholia. By now presumably a considerably older woman after her exile from Troy and period as the captive concubine of Achilles's son Neoptolemus, Andromache has herself become a ruined figure of ritualized memory. She represents the continuity of nostalgia and blood relation rather than either the true founding of a new city or a force of persistent fertility.

We see her from the perspective of Aeneas. On his erring journey toward the future, Aeneas has received, from ancestral spirits who appear to him in dreams, from the harpies and other sources, prophecies regarding his eventual path. Among his blunders, he mistakenly begins to cultivate land that should be first devoted to burial, settles prematurely in the wrong place, and eats and sacrifices what rightfully belongs to others. Then he arrives at Buthrotum in Epirus.[53]

Aeneas discovers that Andromache, Helenus, and other Trojan refugees have established in this place a miniature simulacrum of Troy. It has a river that mimics the Simois and a copy of great Pergamus, as well as "a tiny river / in a dry bed, trying to be the Xanthus." Helenus delivers a prophecy of Aeneas's future travails and gives him gifts that include the arms of Neoptolemus.

With this scene Virgil draws an implicit contrast to the burial of Hector's shield with Astyanax. Astyanax receives his father's arms, which are not to be allowed to hang in the bedroom of his killer's son. Aeneas receives the arms of that killer; he thereby reclaims for the Trojans the arms whose power Helenus was forced to yield to the Greeks. Andromache also gives Aeneas gifts—robes ornamented with gold and a Phrygian scarf for Ascanius and other objects she has made at the loom, saying,

> Take them, my child; these are
> The work of my own hands, memorials
> Of Hector's wife Andromache, and her love.
> Receive these farewell gifts; they are for one
> Who brings my own son back to me; your hands,
> Your face, your eyes, remind me of him so,—
> He would be just your age.[54]

Buthrotum is a place mired in nostalgia where sheer acts of naming only emphasize the distance between the fantasy of a vanished Troy and the reality of a dry brook.

When in 1859, describing Haussmann's ongoing destruction and rebuilding of Paris, Charles Baudelaire writes, "Andromaque, je pense à vous! Ce petit fleuve, / Pauvre et triste miroir où jadis resplendit / L'immense majesté de vos douleurs de veuve" (Andromache, I think of you! That little stream / That poor sad mirror that once glittered / The enormous majesty of your widow's grief), he calls the miniature river, "Ce Simoïs menteur qui par vos pleurs grandit" (That false Simois swollen by your tears)[55]—in other words, a kind of lie. And as Andromache's model Troy is an imitation of her vanished city, determined forever by her melancholy perspective, so are Baudelaire's memories of "Le vieux Paris" (the old Paris) a fixed and fictional image—an allegory:

> ce camp de baraques,
> Ces tas de chapiteaux ébauchés et de fûts,
> Les herbes, les gros blocs verdis par l'eau des flaques
> Et, brillant aux carreaux, le bric-à-brac confus.[56]

> that camp of huts,
> Those piles of shafts and rough-hewn capitals,
> The grass, the huge blocks stained green by puddled water,
> and, shining in the windowpanes, the jumbled bric-a-brac.

Juxtaposed to these tumbled pieces, lying on the ground, is the scaffolding of the new city:

> Paris change! mais rien dans ma mélancolie
> N'a bougé! palais neufs, échafaudages, blocs,
> Vieux faubourgs, tout pour moi devient allégorie,
> Et mes chers souvenirs sont plus lourds que des rocs.[57]

> Paris changes! But nothing in my melancholy
> Has budged! new palaces, scaffolding, blocks,
> Old suburbs, everything becomes allegory for me.
> And my dear memories are heavier than rocks.

It is the leaden weight of the past, the burden of its perspective, that keeps Baudelaire's melancholy, and Andromache's, bound to the earth. The gods of the earth are always more archaic than the gods of the sky; they pull us toward the past and haunt each aspiration.

Almost a century after Virgil's poem, Lucan gives an account, in his *De Bello Civili* or *Pharsalia*, of Julius Caesar's own melancholy visit to the collapsed walls of Troy: "Emulous of ancient glory, Caesar visited the sands of Sigeum and the stream of Simois, Rhoeteum famous for the Grecian's [Ajax's] grave, and the dead who owe so much to the poet's verse. He walked round the burnt city of Troy, now only a famous name, and searched for the mighty remains of the wall that Apollo raised. Now barren woods and rotting tree-trunks grow over the palace of Assaracus, and their worn-out roots clutch the temples of the gods, and Pergama is covered over with thorn-brakes: the very ruins have been destroyed."[58]

Emphasizing how much the dead owe to the poet's record, Lucan recounts how "a legend clings to every stone" (*nullum est sine nomine saxum*). The poet knows, as Caesar does not, that the "stream trickling through the dry dust" was the Xanthus. As Caesar steps on some "rank grass," a native of the place asks him "not to walk over the body of Hector." A set of scattered stones, which seem to have no special sanctity, are in fact the overlooked altar of Zeus Herceos, worshipped as a god in Priam's household. The twenty-something Lucan, who died at twenty-six, assures Caesar that he should not be "jealous of those whom fame has consecrated," for "posterity shall read my verse and your deeds; our Pharsalia shall live on, and no age will ever doom us to oblivion." A. E. Housman charmingly described this claim as "fought by you and told by me"[59]—a comparison that underscores Lucan's suppositions of the ephemerality of heroic action and permanence of epic.

The final consequences of the destruction of Troy and the flooding and collapse of the Achaean Wall signify a break in human consciousness. "The matter of Troy" and "the matter of Rome" continued to live, as they do at Buthrotum, in their ruined—necessarily secondary and partial—states through the virtual experiences of legend and myth. But the gods receded. Humans might continue to pray and augur and practice long-standing rituals; no longer would the Greek and Roman gods intervene in human fate.

Planned Obsolescence in the Hebrew Scriptures

What can ruin a city? Weather, war, the gods' mere dalliance with the destiny of mortals.

Mesopotamian city laments—*The Lament for Sumer and Ur, The Lament for Eridu, The Lament for Uruk,* and *The Lament for Nippur*—follow a polytheistic narrative logic telling of divine abandonment, the unleashing of consequent evil forces of destruction, lamentation, then the restoration of the cities by human hands and the return of the gods.[60] But the Hebrew scriptures emphasize, with the truly wearying repetition of a pattern of destruction, witness, and renewed beginnings, a sense of broken and renewed covenants made between a single God and humankind. These are not stories of slow ruin, of long sieges and equally balanced forces in heaven and on earth: here ruin is sudden and overwhelming.

In Genesis 18:20, God warns Abraham that he intends to destroy the inhabitants of Sodom because "their sin is very grievous." Abraham pleads with God: if he can find fifty righteous men in the city, could it be saved? God consents, even as Abraham whittles the number from forty-five to thirty, from thirty to twenty, from twenty to ten. And then even ten proves optimistic. So God sends two angels in the guise of human strangers to the house of Abraham's nephew Lot in Sodom. Lot extends hospitality to the strangers, but soon a mob comes to his door, demanding that the visitors be handed over to them. Lot holds to the laws of hospitality, protecting the strangers, and offering his virgin daughters to the Sodomites instead. The Sodomites refuse this substitution. In response, revealing themselves as angels, God's emissaries pull Lot back into the house, shutting the door and striking each member of the mob blind. The angels tell Lot that God will now destroy the city; it is time for him to escape with his family. When Lot hesitates, the angels seize the family and place them beyond the bounds of Sodom, demanding that they neither stop nor look back and granting them permission to go to the nearby small city of Zoar.

Genesis 19:24–25 further records what ensues: "Then the LORD rained upon Sodom and upon Gomorrah brimstone and fire from the LORD out of heaven; And he overthrew those cities, and all the plain, and all the inhabitants of the cities, and that which grew upon the ground." Lot's wife looks back, violating the interdiction, and becomes a pillar of salt. This salt pillar, embodiment of infertility, stands in vivid contrast to God's promise to Abraham that his descendants will be as numerous as the stars. As Abraham looks on the site of what had been Sodom, he sees that "the smoke of the country went up as the smoke of a furnace" (Gen. 19:28). The daughters of Lot will go on to lie with their uncle and bear his children—these progeny become the Moabites and Ammonites.

As God destroys Sodom by fire, he destroys the coastal city of Tyre by water. In the book of Ezekiel 26:3–6 we find his warning: "Behold, I *am* against thee, O Tyrus, and will cause many nations to come up against thee, as the sea causeth his waves to come up. And they shall destroy the walls of Tyrus, and break down her towers: I will also scrape her dust from her, and make her like the top of a rock. It shall be *a place for* the spreading of nets in the midst of the sea . . . and it shall become a spoil to the nations. And her daughters which *are* in the field shall be slain by the sword." Tyre is named as well, beside Damascus, Philistia, Edom, Ammon, and Moab, in the opening to the book of Amos, where a series of oracles predicts the destruction of each of these cities. In this version, destruction is again by fire: "I will send a fire on the wall of Tyrus, which shall devour the palaces thereof." What have these cities done to deserve their destruction? Tyre and Philistia are condemned for their traffic in slaves with Edom; in turn, Edom for aggression and Moab for attacking Edom, and Aram and Ammon for their harsh occupation of Gilead. These nations bordering Israel in the tenth century BCE were likely to have had contracts or agreements with it. In the case of Edom, they also were linked through the common ancestors of Jacob (Israel) and Esau (Edom).[61]

The Hebrew scriptures present parallel instances of devastation by divine and human agents. Indeed, the Hebrew God's policy of total destruction as the punishment for the violation of a covenant echoes to the doctrine of deporting conquered peoples and obliterating their cities. Here divine and human action alike are absolute: a towering city is scraped away to the bare earth: "the top of a rock."

During their conquest of Canaan, the Israelites continue the practice of total ruin. The destruction of Ai, whose name in Hebrew means "the ruin" or "a ruined heap," is described in Joshua: "The smoke of the city ascended" (8:21), and all that remained was, at Joshua's command, "a great heap of stones" (8:29). The carcass of the king was thrown down beside the gate of the city. Joshua is given credit for reducing the Canaanite royal city to rubble, but archaeological evidence indicates that Ai had been destroyed in the mid-third millennium BCE, long before the seventh- and sixth-century BCE texts of the book of Joshua.[62] The Hebrew scriptures record how, in the same campaign against Canaan, Israelites conquered the walled city of Jericho with an assault by means of ritualized sound. They marched around the perimeter of the city for six days. Then seven priests blew seven rams' horn trumpets before the ark, and on the seventh day they marched around the city seven times with priests blowing the trumpets and the attackers shouting. In consequence, the walls of Jericho tumbled to the ground. Only Rahab the harlot and those with her were spared, for she had protected Israeli messengers early in the confrontation. Joshua 6:24 continues with an account of spoliation: "And they burnt the city with fire, and all that *was* therein: only the silver, and the gold, and the vessels of brass and of iron, they put into the treasury of the house of the LORD."

Even so, whatever historical covenants existed between the twelve tribes of Israel and their neighbors, whatever success the Israelites had in defeating their enemies, the covenants God held with Israel, like those he held with Adam and Eve, were enforced by his wrath. The book of Amos prophesies the ruin not only of bordering nations but of Israel itself. The "tabernacle of David" will be "fallen" and in "ruins," he declares, before it is restored (Amos 9:11). This part of Amos indeed may date to the period of the destruction of Jerusalem and the fall of David's dynasty in the sixth century BCE.

Solomon's construction of the First Temple in the mid-tenth century BCE had involved not merely the establishment of an architectural monument: the building was the symbol of the united tribes within the holy city of Jerusalem; a shelter for the most sacred of objects, the ark of the covenant—the footstool of Yahweh; a site of entry, dwelling, and worship to a people who were prohibited from worshiping graven images. Cherubim carved in relief, palms, flowers, and gourds worked in wood and covered in gold—these ornaments are derived from Canaanite myth. As permanent fixtures of the building's structure, they just barely evade the interdiction upon images. Nevertheless, the project has the approval of Yahweh, who proclaims in 1 Kings 6:12–13, "*Concerning* this house which thou art in building, if thou wilt walk in my statutes, and execute my judgments, and keep all my commandments to walk in them; then will I perform my word with thee, which I spake unto David thy father: And I will dwell among the children of Israel, and will not forsake my people Israel."

This declaration of the importance of abstract, immaterial, truths—the law and the word—is set against the description of Solomon's practical achievement. The passage in 1 Kings provides the measures and materials for the temple; its great, proportional size—thirty cubits high, sixty cubits long, and twenty cubits wide—and its enduring materials: cedar, which does not rot or decay; stones so perfectly cut at the quarry that they need not be fitted or adjusted on the building site; veneers made of untarnishable, light-reflecting, gold.[63]

In turn, Jeremiah 52 tells of how all of this perfected construction is broken into redundant and innumerable pieces. In the year 586 CE, Nebuzaradan, captain of the guard for the triumphant king of Babylon, Nebuchadrezzar II (aka Nebuchadnezzar), and his men burn and pillage the temple: "The Chaldeans brake, and carried all the brass of them to Babylon. The caldrons also, and the shovels, and the snuffers, and the bowls, and the spoons, and all the vessels of brass wherewith they ministered, took they away. And the basons, and the firepans, and the bowls, and the caldrons, and the candlesticks, and the spoons, and the cups; *that* which *was* of gold *in* gold, and *that* which *was* of silver *in* silver, took the captain of the guard away" (Jer. 52:17–19). The structure collapses into metal objects, once sacred, that now seem either destined for secular, everyday use or due to be harvested for their constituting metals.

Describing the destruction of Solomon's temple, the Lamentations of Jeremiah set forth, in chapter 2, a sequence of violent verbs attributing the temple's fall to divine agency: the Lord has "covered" the city "with a cloud"; "swallowed up all the habitations"; "thrown down" the "strong holds . . . to the ground"; "polluted the kingdom"; "cut off in his fierce anger all the horn of Israel"; "drawn back his right hand"; "burned against Jacob like a flaming fire"; "bent his bow like an enemy"; "stood with his right hand as an adversary, and slew all that were pleasant to the eye in the tabernacle of the daughter of Zion." Amid this sequence, verse 6 complains, "And he hath violently taken away his tabernacle, *as if it were of* a garden." *As if it were of a garden* at first may seem an aside as the speakers of Lamentations go on to describe further acts and signs of the temple's collapse. But the phrase returns us to the redundancy of covenants broken and renewed. As a garden exists in cyclical time, harvested and replanted in turn, so will the temple need to be reinstated.

The Tower of Babel I

Jeremiah predicts that as the Babylonians destroyed the temple, further destruction awaits the Babylonians themselves and they will suffer the fate of Tyre: "How is Sheshach [the cryptic name for Babylon] taken! and how is the praise of the whole earth surprised! how is Babylon become an astonishment among the nations! The sea is come up upon Babylon: she is covered with the multitude of the waves thereof. Her cities are a desolation, a dry land, and a wilderness, a land wherein no man dwelleth, neither does *any* son of man pass thereby" (Jer. 51:41–43).

Nebuchadrezzar II left inscriptions in brick of his achievements. He is often credited not only with the destruction of Jerusalem in 587 BCE but also with the restoration of Babylon after the long period of Assyrian domination that his father, Nabopolassar, had helped end by 605. He directed the building of the Ishtar Gate now housed at the Pergamon Museum in Berlin and led the reconstruction of the imperial grounds, including the celebrated Etemenanki ziggurat—a stepped pyramid topped by a temple—that he describes as "a tower" and "an eternal house." Among the many legends of Nebuchadrezzar's achievements is the story of the city's "hanging gardens"—listed at least since the Roman writer Josephus as one of the seven wonders of the ancient world. These "hanging gardens," if they did indeed exist, were plantations built of terraces, and recent evidence indicates they may have stood hundreds of miles away at Nineveh.[64] By the early sixth century BCE, Babylon held over a quarter of a million people within its three square miles—more than twenty times the population of Jerusalem.[65] Nabopolassar (625–604 BCE) left an inscription saying he made his palace "tall like unto wooded mountains," and his son and successor, in his "Large Inscribed Stone Tablet," describes how he improved on his father's work by laying a new foundation: "firmly, and raised it mountain high with bitumen and burnt brick . . . [a] royal dwelling of asphalt and burnt bricks."[66]

The inhabitants of the Mesopotamian world placed their deities in the sky, and the Babylonians were well known for their high and extensive building projects, especially their ziggurats. Their own word for such a building, *ziqqurratu*, came from their verb *zaqaru*, "to build or raise high." The ziggurat was more than a building—it was a cosmic symbol that unified the heavens, the earth, and the underground: "the temple of the foundation of heaven and earth."[67]

A clay cylinder at the Louvre registers the story of the Etemenanki ziggurat in Nebuchadrezzar's own voice. He describes how the structure was built by carrying bricks in baskets, up to a height of thirty cubits (approximately fifty feet). Large solid cedar beams were used for the structure and covered with copper until "a high and holy temple, as in ancient times," was "built for [the god] Marduk."[68] Babylon's ziggurat is linked in legend to, and perhaps the actual prototype for, the Tower of Babel from Genesis 11:1–9. The biblical story of the tower's rise and fall that we found intriguing the Anglo-Saxon imagination is an etiological legend that explains the diversity of human languages, for in Hebrew, as now in English, *babel* is a pun indicating at once the ancient city and the sound of unintelligible communication. Here is the Genesis account in its entirety:

> And the whole earth was of one language, and of one speech.
>
> And it came to pass, as they journeyed from the east, that they found a plain in the land of Shinar; and they dwelt there.
>
> And they said one to another, Go to, let us make brick, and burn them throughly. And they had brick for stone, and slime had they for mortar.
>
> And they said, Go to, let us build us a city and a tower, whose top *may reach* unto heaven; and let us make us a name, lest we be scattered abroad upon the face of the whole earth.

And the LORD came down to see the city and the tower, which the children of men builded.

And the LORD said, Behold, the people *is* one, and they have all one language; and this they begin to do: and now nothing will be restrained from them, which they have imagined to do.

Go to, let us go down, and there confound their language, that they may not understand one another's speech.

So the LORD scattered them abroad from thence upon the face of all the earth, and they left off to build the city.

Therefore is the name of it called Babel; because the LORD did there confound the language of all the earth: and from thence did the LORD scatter them abroad upon the face of all the earth.

The "land of Shinar" is a phrase that occurs eight times in the Hebrew scriptures, indicating Babylonia and Erech. Its rulers are mentioned as Amraphael (Hammurabai), Nebuchadrezzar, and, in Genesis 10, Nimrod.[69] Nimrod is described here as "a mighty one in the earth. He was a mighty hunter before the LORD: wherefore it is said, Even as Nimrod the mighty hunter before the LORD. And the beginning of his kingdom was Babel, and Erech, and Accad, and Calneh, in the land of Shinar" (Gen. 10:8–10). Although Nimrod is not mentioned directly in the story of the Tower of Babel, he enters into later retellings and iconography as a human giant directing the building of the great tower.

Several details of the story are resonant to Babylonian building types. The tower is made of bricks joined together by bitumen, which we also call asphalt or pitch. This building technique—bricks with a pitch adhesive—was used by the Sumerians, who relied on natural asphalt deposits; at the time of Queen Semiramis (800 BCE) a tunnel was built beneath the Euphrates of fired bricks and an asphalt coating designed to keep it waterproof. Herodotus, in his fifth-century BCE *historia*, or inquiry, describes in book 1, chapter 179, that the Babylonians used hot asphalt as a mortar for their walls. He writes in great detail:

I must explain also where the earth was used that was taken from the trench and how the wall was built. As they dug the trench, they made bricks of the mud that was carried out of the trench; and when they had made enough of the bricks, they baked them in ovens. Then, using hot asphalt for cement and stuffing in mats of reeds at every thirty courses of bricks, they built first the banks of the trench and then the wall itself in the same manner. On top of the wall, along the edges, they built houses of a single room facing one another. A space was left between these houses big enough for a four-horse chariot to drive through. There were a hundred gates set in the circuit of the wall, all of bronze, and of bronze likewise the posts and the lintels. There is another city, some eight days' journey from Babylon, called Is, where there is a small river, also called Is. It empties into the stream of the Euphrates. This river Is brings to the surface, with its waters, many lumps of asphalt, and it was from it that the asphalt was conveyed for the walls of Babylon.[70]

Asphalt: this hot, black, eye-smarting, slimy, sticky substance is bituminous pitch. The "slime pits of Siddim" were exudations of liquid asphalt, and the Vale of Siddim corresponds to the Dead Sea, where asphalt still is collected. The substance enters into the New Testament book of Revelation and the imagination of the early Christians, along with other imagery of lakes of fire and trials by fire.[71]

Why is a building made of bricks and bitumen a particular expression of human overachievement? Why does the deity see it as a threat? The story of the Tower of Babel can be placed with other myths of stealing power—in the form of fire or technology—from the gods. By a principle of addition and accumulation, there is no limit to the heights to which bricks can be placed so long as they are structurally stable. Using bricks, human beings can indeed move and make mountains. Yet here God does not knock down or otherwise level the tower, as we have seen him proceed to do in these many accounts of divine punishments wreaked by means of fire and water. Instead he confuses the language of these builders who have used "the songs of men" to accomplish their achievement. The true overreaching here happens on the level of communication: if humans can perfectly understand one another, using words, one at a time, like bricks, to form their speech, enjoying a transparency of intention, there is no limit to the addition and accumulation of their knowledge.

The story of Babel's tower wonderfully inverts the account of how noise brings down the walls of Jericho. At Babel the power of work song is evoked—a shared, intelligible goal; a clear path; a rhythm allowing many workers to coordinate their plans and gestures. With the confusion—both merging and separation—of languages, human techne is humiliated at its very root in the universality of a desire for transcendence. In the curse of misunderstanding, humankind finds itself rerooted, reradicalized, and scattered. And yet God did not strike the builders mute: like Adam and Eve in a world that is wholly future, they must start over, beginning again to build structures of intelligibility, to work and re-form from the ground up.

II. Marks

INSCRIPTIONS AND *SPOLIA*

The Optimism of Inscription

Forms are ruined not only by erosion and collapse; they also are ruined through defacement. They can be marked with negative significance as they are pocked or marred by weather and intended damage, but, as we found in Jupiter's speech on records carved in adamant, they also can be marked with positive significance through inscription and more ephemeral signs of allusion that in turn are subject to wear and decay. In the West, these signs of marking have a dynamic and paradoxical history. From ancient practices of inscription and their erasure, the gestures that became known as *damnatio memoriae*, to the largely positive use of *spolia* in the early Christian and succeeding periods, to, as we have considered, the early modern development of age value, wherein forms are admired precisely because they show signs of wear or damage, attitudes toward ruin come full circle and the ruined aspect of a form turns out to be not a supplementary feature of its value but instead its defining attribute.

As Herodotus sets out on his *History*, he begins with a bold statement of purpose. David Grene translates the passage as follows: "I, Herodotus of Halicarnassus, am here setting forth my history, that time may not draw the color from what man has brought into being, nor those great and wonderful deeds, manifested by both Greeks and barbarians, fail of their report, and, together with all this, the reason why they fought one another."[1] For Herodotus, witness to history and alterity—and, as we have seen, in a later era, for the poets Ovid and Lucan as well—there is no question that such knowledge should be preserved. But what means are available for preserving memories from decay? The answer is twofold: "putting on record" through written texts, carved into stones or written on the portable surfaces of hides, paper, and papyrus that record the monumental achievements of the past; or, keeping in mind that the word *monument* comes from *monere*, to warn or show forth, "setting down" signs on the landscape. Memory is served by the creation of monuments themselves—the obelisks, temples, sarcophagi, tombs, and stelae inscribing the past, often in the place where events unfolded.

Yet these concerted and optimistic gestures toward the future are haunted from the outset by the specter of their futility. As the Hellenist James Porter has suggested, in ancient Greek culture, "monuments *imply* ruins."[2] Whether the memorial structure is as large as the sixth-century BCE Temple of Apollo at Siracusa (extending to approximately 190 by 70 feet) or as small as a few scattered stones where once there had been a tumulus, the made form, Porter explains, inevitably will be subject to decay. Rome's military domination of Greece after the defeat of Macedonia in 168 BCE was countered by the Roman surrender to an idealized vision of Greek culture—a culture that long had become more artifactual than lived; young Romans frequently toured Greece and Asia Minor, and Athens and Rhodes became important centers of education.

Pausanias's guidebook noted the monuments and traditions he encountered, or witnessed as ruins, as he traveled through the Greek mainland.[3] In a lament echoing Lucan's account of how the very ruins of Troy had been ruined, he wrote of Parapotamii, in northern Greece, "I found no ruins of Parapotamii left, nor is the site of the city remembered."[4] Even so, Lucan's account of Caesar's "misreading" of the significant landscape he traverses is corrected by the poet's own words, and Pausanias's travels hold together in mind a vanished world; he made his meticulously detailed survey of Greek monuments as an aide-mémoire for his readers. The *Periegesis* commemorates and underscores the notions of the sacred and justice meaningful to Greeks at the edges of the Roman Empire.[5]

Following the prophecy of Jupiter, Ovid writes an epilogue celebrating his own achievement:

> Now stands my task accomplished, such a work
> As not the wrath of Jove, nor fire nor sword
> Nor the devouring ages can destroy.
> Let, when it will, that day, that has no claim
> But to my mortal body, end the span
> Of my uncertain years. Yet I'll be borne,
> The finer part of me, above the stars,
> Immortal, and my name shall never die.
> Wherever through the lands beneath her sway
> The might of Rome extends, my words shall be
> Upon the lips of men. If truth at all
> Is stablished by poetic prophecy,
> My fame shall live to all eternity.[6]

Here, as in Horace's thirtieth ode, the writer's dream of being remembered in oral tradition is founded in an acknowledgment of the impermanence of inscription—all matter, even adamant, can wear down or be erased, but words passed from mouth to ear over generations can ensure the survival of thousands of epic lines and the most fragile thought.

Nevertheless, Ovid was writing during a long era of enthusiasm for inscription or "lapidarias litteras," as Petronius's indignant character Hermeros calls such works when he defends his own learning at the Banquet of Trimalchio in *The Satyricon* (58.7).[7] The Latinist Greg Woolf has described "an epigraphic boom," from the end of the last century BCE to the beginning of the third century CE. By the fourth century, the practice had fallen away.[8] In both Latin and Greek epigraphy, in every province of the empire, Romans and their subjects carved into stone a range of writings: epitaphs, building dedications, local and imperial laws, the names of civic officials, tax information, honors acquired by individuals, statements establishing the fulfillment of vows made to the gods. Above all, Woolf explains, inscriptions registered the names of individuals.[9]

It was not only the contents of inscriptions that suggested permanence. The majuscules of the Roman *scriptura monumentalis* used from the late republic into the early empire, conveyed a stability and ordered repose that would last throughout the history of lapidary forms and on into print. Cicero's *De oratore* appeared in *scriptura monumentalis* in 1465, and the script became common by the 1470s.[10] The novelist and essayist Marguerite Yourcenar commemorated its qualities in the voice of the Emperor Hadrian in her fictional biography *Memoirs of Hadrian*: "There is nothing to equal the beauty of a Latin votive or burial inscription: those few words graved upon stone sum up with majestic impersonality all the world need ever know of us."[11]

For a people who were captivated by worldly power and fame, and at the same time disinclined toward eschatology, inscription on stone augmented by, as Ovid hoped, one's words "upon the lips of men" doubled the chances of renown. Roman imperial inscriptions were addressed to no particular audience;[12] they were intended for anyone who came upon them, just as more ancient Hebrew, Greek, and Latin inscriptions may have pointed strangers to information as diverse as the locations of springs or the texts of local laws and edicts. A certain cultural confidence accompanies such carving; the assertion of one's name, and, among elites, one's image, is a gesture toward the future, which, remaining by definition ineffable, nevertheless might offer delayed forms of recognition—a "promise" for the future that is hardly reciprocal.

The Latin *monumentum* indicates physical objects, including tombs, and written records alike.[13] In contrast to the cosmological and otherworldly foci of Druid stoneworks and Egyptian pyramids, Roman monuments were concerned with the situation of the individual in the present social fabric. Not all Roman monuments bore inscriptions, and those that were inscribed did not always emphasize their written mottos, but whether made of earth, stone, or clay, monuments displayed the individual's desire to endure in public memory.[14] Unlike the Greeks, the Romans carefully recorded the deaths of children and adolescents, and those who died far from home were given a local

FIGURE 11. The Roman Emperor Septimius Severus (r. 193–211 CE), his wife Julia Domna, and his children Caracalla and Geta. From Egypt, Roman period (ca. 200 CE). Tempera on wood. Antikensammlung, Staatliche Museen, Berlin.

monument and inscription.[15] The disappearance of the practice by the fourth century raises the question of whether Romans continued to find their lives worth remembering.[16]

A monument not only expresses confidence that it will be read and of interest in the future; it also expresses an anxiety that a material form, often constructed at great expense and with painstaking labor, will be needed as a reminder. The carving of words into stone reminds us as well that writing can be ruined: in its natural form, a stone is itself all the way through and, eroded, is simply a smaller, still recognizable, version of itself. It can be diminished in magnitude and position only. But writing is only writing so long as it is legible. Erosion poses the threat of disappearance.

At the height of the epigraphic "boom," the Romans were equally taken, perhaps not surprisingly, with deliberate acts of erasure. Their practice of varieties of *damnatio memoriae* involved the destruction of all images and inscriptions relating to a person—most often discredited officials, even including emperors.[17] The practice indicates the possibility of erasing its own gesture, for if the name disappears to history, so does the erasure of the name. The Senate could go so far as to declare that a person's *praenomen* (first name) couldn't be used by descendants.[18] Caracalla's murder of his brother and rival Geta in 211 (see fig. 11) included the destruction of his image and name throughout the empire. The Codex Theodosianus records the damnation of the former palace eunuch and consul Eutropius after his death in 399 and provides further details as to how the practice was carried out: "All his statues, all his images, in bronze as well as in marble, in pigments, or in whatever material is suitable for portraiture, we order to be destroyed in all cities and towns, both in private and in public places, in order that the stigma of our age, so to speak, may not pollute the sight of those who look at such images."[19] Just a few years later, the half-Vandal Stilicho, regent for the Western emperor Honorius and ironically a frequent target of Eutropius's own hostility, was accused of collaborating with the Visigoths. Therefore, he, too, was disgraced and executed, and his name was erased wherever it appeared.[20]

Spolia: The Pagan Uses of Pagan Ruins

If the signs of damage on an old wall are a spark to visual invention and imagination in Leonardo's terms, yet another aspect of ruins came to speak to the memory and knowledge of the historical relations between buildings: this was the use of *spolia*, or reappropriated materials. Artifacts made for one structure have long been reused for another or others for purposes of economy or efficiency, but the practice of *spolia* has a particular history bound to the denigration and estimation of ruined forms.[21] Inscribed surfaces proved more vulnerable than indelible as material objects, yet they nevertheless spoke a language that could be read by anyone literate in that language—names could lose their particular meaning but could be recognized as names; statements of value could persist in a world of changed values. *Spolia*, however, often begin in intelligibility—their viewers know their sources and understand them as allusions. Unmarked beyond their difference from those materials in which they are embedded, however, they can lose their significance within a generation or two very easily. As the structure is worn, and worn unevenly, what expresses historical value and what expresses novelty may become impossible to separate.

The term *spolia* originally indicated specifically "spoils of war," and some of the most paradigmatic instances of the Roman practice, such as Egyptian obelisks and the confiscated statues and bronzes of Magna Graecia, are indeed both spoils of war and reused artifacts of the made environment. Obelisks, which suffered damage in their transport over land and sea and more often than not were buried and then restored out of fragments during the Renaissance, have a particular force as *spolia* because of the ways they command the spaces around them. Clustered about by fountains, inscribed in Latin below their hieroglyphs, topped by crosses and statues of saints, even, in the case of

Bernini's work at Santa Maria sopra Minerva, perched on a sculpture of an elephant, the obelisks of Rome "mark the spot," as Anthony Vidler has written. And yet they also are signs of an extraordinary mobility, signifying their own history of displacements as much as their supposed final resting places.[22] Their original inscriptions record their relation to the Egyptian rulers who commissioned them and the gods those rulers worshipped. The work known as the "Flaminian obelisk" (see fig. 12), which stands in the center of the Piazza del Popolo, bears a hieroglyphic inscription on its east face as follows:

> Re shines forth, rejoicing over them in his House of millions of years.
>   It is his Majesty who has completed [beautified] this monument for his
>   father, so that his name might be granted to aid in the House of Re;
> Made for him [by] the Son of Re, Ramesses II,
> The beloved of Atum, Lord of Heliopolis, and given life forever

Augustus took the obelisk from Heliopolis in 10 BCE and erected it on the spina of the Circus Maximus, rededicating it to the sun and noting its status as a war spoil:

> When Imperator for the twelfth, consul for the eleventh, and tribune of the people for the fourteenth time, Imperator Augustus, son of divine Caesar, dedicated this obelisk to the sun, when Egypt had been brought under the sway of the Roman people[23]

Obelisks stitch the urban landscape to the changing sky and, rising far above street level, often achieve an odd transparency, their Egyptian meanings remaining unintelligible for almost every viewer and masked by these many later ornaments and additions. Forms without interiors, made from monoliths of flawless granite, they were subject to burial and breakage but survived their long journeys in space and time into the present largely intact.

The best-known example of war booty from the imperial era, however, is the monumental seven-branched menorah, the golden table, the great trumpets, and other captured treasures depicted on an interior relief of the Arch of Titus showing the spoils of the Temple of Jerusalem, destroyed by the Romans in 70 CE. The relief was completed twelve years later (see fig. 13). The Jerusalem spoils continue to play an iconic role in the narrative of Roman ruins. In *The Jewish War* (6.8.3), Josephus lists among the spoils "two lampstands, tables, bowls and platters—all of gold." Procopius records various vicissitudes of the spoils; he writes that during the Sack of the Goths, in 410, Alaric and his hordes carried off the treasure. In consequence, the Franks laid siege to Carcasiana (Carcasonne) "with great enthusiasm, because they had learned that the royal treasure was there, which Alaric the elder in earlier times had taken as booty when he captured Rome. Among these were also the treasures of Solomon, the king of the Hebrews, a most noteworthy sight. For the most of them

FIGURE 12. Obelisk from Heliopolis at the Piazza del Popolo, Rome, 13th century BCE, erected at Circus Maximus 10 BCE, erected at Piazza del Popolo 1589.

FIGURE 13. Scene from a relief on the interior of the Arch of Titus, Rome, after 81 CE.

were adorned with emeralds; and they had been taken from Jerusalem by the Romans in ancient times."[24] This account is noteworthy for its own radiance, the precious metal objects further "adorned" with gemstones.

In his history of the 455 sack by the Vandals under Gizeric (or Genseric), the spoils turn up again, eighty years after the sack itself. In this account they were discovered and seized by Belisarius in Carthage—where the Vandals supposedly had taken them to Genseric's African estate. Belisarius, returned to Constantinople, staged a triumph of his victory, displaying slaves and spoils: "And there was also silver weighing many thousands of talents and all the royal treasure amounting to an exceedingly great sum (for Gizeric had despoiled the Palatium in Rome . . .), and among these were the treasures of the Jews, which Titus, the son of Vespasian, together with certain others, had brought to Rome after the capture of Jerusalem." When a Jew in the crowd speaks up to say the spoils belong in "the place where Solomon, the king of the Jews formerly placed them," a nervous Justinian sends "everything to the sanctuaries of the Christians in Jerusalem."[25] Stories of the Jerusalem spoils thus persisted into the Christian era in legends that conflated the Babylonian destruction of Solomon's temple with the Roman destruction of Herod's temple and traced the fate of individual artifacts—most particularly the menorah and the ark of the covenant—as later sacred architecture continued to borrow from the biblical account of temple forms.[26]

Despite the specificity of the Jerusalem spoils and biblical accounts of these ancient temples, *spolia* can be taken from near or far and come in marked and unmarked forms. They can be both buried and displayed in plain sight. When builders use them as mere materials, without knowledge of their provenance or of the intentions and domains of their makers, they envelop the older form in a contemporary one. But when builders take up such materials as true "spoils," it is their provenance in another style, another culture, another world that is marked and noted. The new form supersedes the old form, and that very supersession is key to the appropriation's meaning.

In 83 BCE, Sulla is said to have moved the columns of the Athenian Temple of Zeus Olympeios to rebuild the Temple of Jupiter on the Capitol.[27] At the turn of the fourth century, Diocletian destroyed a large Flavian building to make room for his baths and reused many of the stone and marble elements of the earlier structure. Soon after, Maxentius built a "Temple of Romulus" in the Forum that reused a Severan bronze door and its marble frame, as well as porphyry column shafts. He added a new cornice that imitated the style of adjacent first-century blocks. If Sulla was translating temples by linking parallel uses, Diocletian and Maxentius in contrast were finding building materials to hand that added to the opulence and complexity of their new structures.[28]

Nevertheless, ancient practices of spoliation and reuse could combine both imperial triumphalism and continuous belief. When Aurelian's soldiers sacked Palmyra after the revolt of Zenobia in 272 CE, the emperor left instructions to have the Temple of Bel restored and specified that the necessary funding should come from the confiscated gold of the queen and the silver of wealthy Palmyrenes. At the same time, he took the very imagery of the temple as spoils, removing statues of Bel and Helios and building a new temple to Sol near what is now one of Rome's central bus stations, the Piazza di San Silvestro.[29] And, as with his rededication of the Flaminian obelisk to the sun, when Augustus erected an Egyptian obelisk on the Campus Martius, it was intended to be used as a sundial.[30] Such syncretic practices of sun worship did not disappear until the suppression of non-Christian cults in 391 CE.

The Christian Uses of Pagan Ruins

The architectural historian Beat Brenk has argued that Christian architectural *spolia*, from their appearance in the reign of Constantine, had a primarily ideological function—they were intended to convey messages about the new structure and religion via allusions to the old and to transfer metaphors of Roman imperial might to Christian forms.[31] The Arch of Constantine, consecrated in 315, is built almost entirely from parts of earlier buildings, including a hodgepodge of materials from the pillaged Forum of Trajan. In a fourth-century version of "photoshopping," the reliefs were reworked from triumphal monuments of Hadrian and Aurelian as well. Columns, capitals, and architraves were saved from demolished or decayed buildings because they were valuable, but their reuse also was meant to signify the dignity of archaic tradition and to lend legitimacy to contemporary forms of power.[32]

The first Christian basilica, the Lateran, was initiated two years before the dedication of the Arch of Constantine in 313. Famed for its novel overall structure, Constantine's church was nevertheless replete with *spolia*: each of its columns and capitals came from earlier structures, and all of its decorative elements were traditional or archaic. Today its organ loft includes a Numidian yellow marble shaft taken from Constantine's arch itself.[33] The basilica's twenty-two uniform shafts of *verde antico*, a green white-veined breccia, flanking colossal statues of the apostles are likely to have come from a single earlier structure.[34] Two bronze columns there were said to have been taken from the Temple of Solomon, and a legend contended that every year on the ninth of the month of Ab (during the Gregorian calendar's July and August) they exuded moisture, weeping. As twelfth-century popes exploited myths that the treasures of the second Jerusalem Temple were stored in the church, the artifactual aspect of *spolia* dominated over the structural. In the sixteenth century, these columns disappeared and Donato Bramante's demolition broke others into parts.[35]

Very often marked *spolia* function like jewels in new settings: they need not be serving an architectural purpose; they can be valuable in themselves. They are often the surviving treasures of forms that are otherwise demolished, and they thereby evoke tropes of mining precious metals or retrieving gold from dross. One of the foremost scholars of *spolia*, Dale Kinney, has noted that "glittering" and "gleaming" are aesthetic tropes in descriptions of the fourth-century basilica of Saint Peter's with its use of gold and other precious materials and many ornaments, columns, and other forms taken from ancient buildings, including the bronze roof tiles transported from the Temple of Rome in the Forum.[36] Vasari describes how the *spolia* of Saint Peter's appear against a plainer backdrop: "The Temple of the Prince of the Apostles in the Vatican was not rich except for the columns, bases, capitals, architraves, cornices, doors, and other revetments and ornaments, which had all been taken from . . . buildings erected earlier with great magnificence."[37]

The late antique and early medieval taste for *varietas* was nourished both by the insertion of *spolia* and by the mixing of architectural orders. The Lateran seems to have been the first building alternating Ionic and Corinthian capitals.[38] Inherent in these developments is an ever-increasing process of cultural and historical syncretism: the Romans, with their free adaptation of an only occasional Greek practice of superposed orders, had used the heavier orders at the bottoms of structures, employing the more slender and ornate orders

FIGURE 14. Colosseum, Rome, 70–80 CE.

the higher they went. The most important extant example of this practice is the loggia of the Colosseum, which ascends from Tuscan to Ionic to Corinthian columns topped by pilasters with Corinthian capitals. The result is a kind of primer of the architectural orders. The intelligibility of such practices depends on the ability of the viewer to read them—so long as they can be read, they are not only structural and formal elements; they also are three-dimensional allusions (see fig. 14).

Spolia, when marked, thus have a status as figures in themselves, but they appear against dual grounds: their original context and context of reuse. Although in the first century BCE Cicero prosecuted Gaius Verres, the proconsul of Sicily, for stealing temple treasures without any legitimate claim to them as military spoils, early laws regulating spoliation were more concerned with spoiled buildings (*spoliatae aedes*) than with the illicit appropriation of objects.[39] In the first century CE, Vespasian issued an edict outlawing the destruction of buildings for their marbles, and similar laws were passed in the second and third centuries. By the early sixth century, Theodoric wrote that he hoped to build new edifices without despoiling the old, but if masonry and columns were lying "useless and dishonored" in Rome, he would like to have them sent to Ravenna for new buildings. Few *spolia* have survived in the existing buildings at Ravenna, perhaps because in turn Charlemagne took *spolia* from Theodoric's palace to build his own palace chapel at Aachen.[40]

Whether booty or reappropriated forms, *spolia* must be reframed in semantic terms, and along the way, the palimpsest of earlier meanings and uses shines through.[41] As we have seen with the Jerusalem spoils, at times this is a matter of a supplemental legend. Even today we do not know the actual history of the enormous bronze pinecone now at the Cortile della Pigna at the Vatican (see fig. 15). It seems to have been in place there by the seventh century, when it would have been protected from the fate of being sent, with so many other bronzes, to Constantinople by the Emperor Constans II. When Dante saw it in Old Saint Peter's, he used it as a metaphor in canto 31 of the *Inferno* for the face of the giant Nimrod, builder of Babel's tower.[42] Hermann of Fritzlar suggested around 1350 that when the Pantheon was rededicated to Christ, the pinecone was lifted off the top of the building by the devil and transported to Saint Peter's and that since then, the "hole in the church [the oculus] has stayed open and nobody wants to close it."[43]

Meanwhile, the theological grounds for appropriation were set out by Augustine in his *De doctrina Christiana* (*On Christian Doctrine*). There, in book 2, concerned with arguing the merits of interpretation and contending that pursuing inference and difficulty is worthwhile, Augustine explains the uses of past knowledge:

> Just as the Egyptians had not only idols and grave burdens which the people of Israel detested and avoided, so also they had vases and ornaments of gold and silver and clothing which the Israelites took with them secretly when they fled, as if to put them to a better use.... In the same way all the teachings of the pagans contains not only simulated and superstitious imaginings and grave burdens of unnecessary labor, which each one of us leaving the society of pagans under the leadership of Christ ought to abominate and avoid, but also liberal disciplines more suited to the uses of truth, and some most useful precepts concerning morals. Even some truths concerning the worship of one God are discovered among them. These are, as it were, their gold and silver, which they did not institute themselves, but dug up from certain mines of divine Providence.[44]

Despite Augustine's confidence in *spolia* as theologically edifying, this process of extraction and rededication might require explicit clarification.[45] When Sixtus V, who reigned as pope from 1585 to 1590, put a cross on the top of the Vatican obelisk and a statue of Saint Peter on top of the Column of Trajan, he ritually exorcised malignant spirits from these ancient monuments. In the case of the obelisk, the pope sprinkled holy water on it in the sign of the cross, scratched into the surface of the stone with a knife, and then

FIGURE 15. Cortile della Pigna, Vatican Palace, Vatican City, ca. 100 BCE–200 CE, moved to this site at the Vatican by 1615.

crossed himself three times. Surveying the four inscriptions that he placed on the obelisk when it was moved in 1586, we find phrases designed to banish all former uses of the form. On the south side: "by a toilsome labor transferred / to the threshold of the Apostles / the Vatican obelisk, / dedicated in unholy reverence / to the gods of the heathen." On the north side: "consecrated to the Cross invisible / the Vatican obelisk, / purified of unclean superstition." On the east side: "Lo, the Cross of the Lord! / Take flight, / hostile ranks." On the west side: an invocation, "May Christ defend / his people / from all evil," and, above that, "Sixtus the Fifth, Supreme Pontiff, / consecrated this / to the Cross most holy, / torn from its / former foundation / and legally and licitly expropriated / from Caesars Augustus and Tiberius / in 1586."[46] Such an eth-nocentric notion of legality has long persisted—even into the present. Robert Wood wrote in his preface to his 1753 *Ruins of Palmyra*, "[We] carried off the marbles whenever it was possible, for the avarice or superstition of the inhab-itants made that task difficult and sometimes impracticable."[47] Lord Elgin had the notion of removing the entire caryatid porch intact from the Erechtheum because "Bonaparte has not got such a thing from all his thefts in Italy."[48]

Ruins continue to be a source of *spolia*, and their meanings continue to be on the one hand abstracted, misrepresented, and aestheticized, and on the other taken up as sources of knowledge and imaginative reconstruction. As fragments of ruin, *spolia* are decontextualized and metonymic to their sources. And yet, even as fragments, they carry certain value as the essential and the authentic: they are what they are wherever they are. Perhaps this quality stems from the original regulation of Roman *spolia* as war booty. In the nineteenth century, Sir William Smith noted a ban on ever removing, repairing, or replac-ing the armor, weapons, and elements of ships and buildings that the Romans confiscated. Such objects were meant for prominent display—often arrayed in the atrium or hung from the doorposts or arranged in the vestibulum of the victor's house and accompanied by explanatory inscriptions. A new owner of the house would have to leave them in place; if they fell to the ground or fell apart with age, they must remain undisturbed. There would thereby be no question as to their authenticity.[49]

The reuse of the materials of earlier buildings by Sulla, Diocletian, and Maxentius; the importation of Egyptian obelisks; and the restoration of more than eighty ancient temples by Augustus all give us some sense of the energy brought to ancient building projects and the dynamic relation between spoils and construction that often manifested an imperial ideology. Yet late antiq-uity brought a change to the estimation of ancient structures. To turn to the most paradigmatic of Roman forms, the last recorded ancient repairs of the Colosseum took place in the fifth century CE; in the sixth century, the amphi-theater was sealed off with wooden barricades, and soon afterward inhabitants of the area began using it to shelter their livestock. At the same time, scaven-gers started collecting building stones from the southern side of the structure, and in the eighth century, the entire southern side suffered an enormous col-lapse. The consequent mountain of rubble the collapse created was known as the *coscia Colisei*, or "haunch" of the Colosseum.[50]

The three-dimensional circular structure now had two parts: a northern, intact, facade of great majesty and proven strength, which faced the most pop-ulous part of the city and was along the processional route linking the Lateran with Saint Peter's, and a southern stone yard destined to become a quarry. The stones of the southern side of the Colosseum may have evoked no particular veneration precisely because they had become an excess: the intact northern walls were enough to signify the building once its early functions had dis-appeared.

Ruins as Image

If Egyptian and Assyrian laments, predecessors to the biblical book of Lamentations, are our earliest sustained meditation on ruins in language,[51] and Anglo-Saxon poetry gives us some glimpse of the reception of ruins from the eighth century forward, visual images of ruins are harder to find. Whether drawn from actual devastation, including the Antioch earthquake of 556 as it was remembered in manuscripts centuries later, or imaginative visions of the ruins of Sodom, such images arise in concert with the theology of the early Christian era.[52] As the *spolia* of the early Christian basilicas, most especially the Lateran and Saint Peter's, marked the subreption of pagan materials to Christian doctrine, those visual images of ruins that have survived indicate the prior forms against which the new faith took form.

Among the earliest extant visual images of ruins are the fourteenth-century frescos of Maso di Banco (working 1325–1353) depicting the life of the fourth-century pope and saint Sylvester in the church of Santa Croce in Florence (see plate 1). In these works, Maso's vision of contemporary ruins of the Roman Forum provide the background for several episodes in the saint's life. We see Sylvester baptizing Constantine and performing various miracles that show the superiority of the Christian faith to the practices of the pagans—Sylvester closes the mouth, and hence stops up the pestilential breath, of a dragon and as well revives two powerful sorcerers who themselves have succumbed to the dragon's deadly breath. Rome is represented with shattered pagan fragments in the foreground, while the new Christian city rises behind it.[53]

Maso's frescos are of interest not only because of their primacy but also because they present us with a conflation of two causes of ruin: the forces of nature that we see represented in the plants growing in the ruins' crevices, the jagged top layer of masonry, and crumbling materials breaking back down into ground; and the human edicts that commanded the ancient constructions and objects be destroyed. In this instance, the deliberative acts of Christian leaders, rather than the frenzies of barbarian hordes, bring about ruin. At a distance of a thousand years, Maso emphasizes Sylvester as the agent of pagan destruction. The twelfth-century guidebook to Rome known as the *Mirabilia Urbis Romae* (*Marvels of Rome*) gave him similar dubious credit: "The Colosseum was the Temple of the Sun. . . . After some time the Blessed Silvester ordered that temple be destroyed and likewise other palaces, so that the orators who came to Rome would not wander through profane buildings but instead pass with devotion through the churches." The writer says that Sylvester ordered a gigantic statue of Phoebus destroyed, with the head and hands of "the idol laid before his Palace of the Lateran in remembrance of the temple."[54]

The *Mirabilia* also declares that Sylvester's pestilential dragon enemy lived below the Temple of Vesta[55]—perhaps one in a line of "damsel(s) in distress" stories of such monsters. Whether it was Sylvester or the sixth-century Pope

Gregory the Great who demanded the destruction of pagan forms is a matter of legend as well as scant record. If Sylvester were the cause of such destruction, he is associated nevertheless with great building, for as part of his healing and eventual conversion of the Emperor Constantine, he commanded the emperor to carry burdens of earth that would be used for the foundation of new churches. Jacobus de Voragine's *Golden Legend* explains in its passages on Sylvester that the emperor came to Saint Peter's and confessed his sins before all people and declared the wrongs he had done to Christian men: "Afterwards he picked up a tool and turned over the first shovelful of earth at the foundation of the basilica that was to be built there, then carried out twelve baskets of earth on his shoulders and threw it outside the building site."[56] His gesture seems designed to echo the boundary making of Romulus's plow as he established the pomerium for Rome itself.

Just decades after the *Mirabilia*, Gregory in turn is given credit for the destruction of the pagan monuments and statues—a belief held well into the sixteenth century. After the death in 526 of Theodoric, the Ostrogothic king who had protected ancient ornaments and structures, statues were toppled for lime and precious metals, and any buildings that could not be adapted for Christian worship or purposes were fair game for their materials. The built environment of Rome continued to be used as a quarry in the ensuing centuries. Jacob Burckhardt writes that in 1140, Abbot Sugerius, rebuilding Saint-Denis, thought he might be able to import the granite monoliths of the Baths of Diocletian but later decided against it, and in 1257, the senator Brancaleona had 140 fortified houses of Roman nobles torn down.[57] Gregory's injuries to pagan literature, idols, and, again, the Colosseum are listed in early fourteenth-century Dominican texts as evidence of the church's triumph over the demonic forces of the pagans. By the time of Maso, the Papal Chronicle of Urban V had claimed that Gregory accomplished the destruction of paganism.[58]

To Save and Restore

Yet in the same period a vivid inversion of this attitude toward classical culture emerges with the onset of humanism. For Maso's near contemporary and fellow Florentine Petrarch, Rome and Roman history were a *spiritus mundi* from which, despite the brevity of his firsthand acquaintance with the city, he would draw upon throughout his life. In 1341 he would be crowned as the laureate at the Capitol.[59] Heavily indebted to Plutarch and Livy for the biographies of *De viris illustribus* (*On Illustrious Men*), he began with an account of Romulus as he set out to record the lives of the most significant heroic figures in Hebrew, Greek, and Latin history. At the same time, he began work on his epic Latin poem celebrating the Roman general Scipio Africanus, his *Africa*—the epic remained unfinished at the time of his death in 1374.[60] Petrarch's "lives" and his epic work animate Rome as a place of triumph and fame. In the eighth and ninth books of *Africa*, he shows the glory of Rome through the amazed eyes of the Carthaginian general Hasdrubal. In his conclusion, he retraces the route of Scipio's triumphal entry.

Rome's literary reputation and the interplay between its remaining signs of magnificence and signs of decay are bound to Petrarch's preoccupations with literary fame and his belief in the powers of writing to animate and summon the past. As his Scipio is sailing home to Rome, sleeping on deck and under the stars next to his friend the poet Ennius, the general describes a vision he has had where Homer comes to him and predicts that a young poet from Florence will immortalize his victories and be crowned with the laurel at the Capitol. Homer has committed not only Petrarch's verses to heart; he also knows the name of Petrarch's epic and can describe the *De viris illustribus*.

Petrarch's optimism of imaginative time travel is countered by realism about what has been lost. During his first visit to Rome in 1337, he wrote to his patron the Cardinal Giovanni Colonna that he was struck dumb by his admiration for the city's ancient remains. Four years later, not long after his second visit to Rome, he wrote his famous letter 2 of book 6 of his *Familiares*, recounting to his contemporary and sometime companion the Dominican friar Giovanni Colonna the many particular scenes they have animated via both their knowledge of history and their imaginations as they roamed across and along the hills of Rome. The form of his discourse is a kind of "rewind" function: there is nothing he describes that Colonna has not seen, and yet he sets out the sites, and sights, within a perpetual tension between the base and the valiant, and includes in his long litany a reference to the familiar legend of "Old Augustus" glimpsing a vision of Christ.[61]

Thus the journey of the past becomes, in retrospection, an account of what has led to the present and future. Petrarch produces an effect of anticipation and constant motion, especially through his streams of deictic phrases: most of the letter is organized through binary comparisons of "hic" and "ibi": "Here was the palace of Evander, there the shrine of Carmentis, here the cave of Cacus, there the famous she-wolf and the fig tree of Rumina with the more apt surname of Romulus, there the overpass of Remus, here the circus games and the rape of the Sabines, there the marsh of Capri and the palace where Romulus vanished, here the conversations of Numa and Egeria, there the battle line of the *trigemini*," and so on.[62] The appreciation of ruins becomes less a matter of still contemplation than a kind of pursuit until the two friends end their peregrinations high on the remains of the Baths of Diocletian: "And as in our travels through the remains of a broken city, there too, as we sat, the remnants of the ruins lay before our eyes. . . . Our conversation was concerned largely with history which we seemed to have divided among us, I being more expert, it seemed, in the ancient, by which we meant the time before the Roman rulers celebrated and venerated the name of Christ, and you in recent times, by which we meant the time from then to the present."[63]

Petrarch famously mourned the disappearance of more than a hundred of Livy's volumes. Writing the ancient author an imaginary fan letter, he explains that purely material estimations of ancient artifacts and ideas are not adequate to their powers, arguing, "I busy myself with these few remains of yours whenever I desire to forget these places or times, as well as our present customs, being filled with bitter indignation against the activities of our contemporaries, who find no value in anything but gold and silver and pleasures. If these are to be considered among good things, then not only the dumb beasts but even inert matter enjoy a fuller and more perfect good than does rational man."[64] His friend Boccaccio, too, lamented the destruction of pagan literature, and although Petrarch sees the importance of Christian truth as a counter to pagan error, he introduces the idea that early Christianity—in the vein of natural disasters and barbarian invaders—could also be a destructive power.

Their contemporary, the Ghibelline poet Fazio degli Uberti, author of an encyclopedic survey of the world, the *Dittamondo*, introduced the idea that Gregory's actions were misguided and disastrous in their consequence, for they deprived modern artists, writers, and builders of the knowledge of the ancients.[65] Composed around 1360, the *Dittamondo* is a cosmographical travel account that also uses the technique of a view from above. Often linked because of its peregrinations and terza rima form to Dante's *Commedia*, and putting forward a narration that owes quite a bit to the *Mirabilia*, the poem nevertheless is more concerned with knowledge and naming for its own sake than with any larger moral or allegorical scheme. Fazio's title could be translated as *World Words* or *Song of the World*, and the poet is led forward in his peripatetic journey from height to height by the ancient geographer Gaius Julius Solinus. In chapter 11 they meet a wearied old woman, Roma, who wears a widow's mantle: "vecchia era in vista, e triste per costume." She shows them her city, its legends, its history, and the stories of its descendants before they go on to visit other parts of Italy. His sibylline figure of Rome cannot remember without deep sadness, but the narrator claims pessimistically and rather matter-of-factly, "perché da tanto onore caduta siete in cotanta bassezza" (because you have fallen from such honor, you have ended in such depths).[66]

Chrysolaras arrived in Florence in 1397 and became a vital force in the revival of the study of ancient Greek and Greek texts in the West. He served as Greek tutor to Leonardo Bruni, Cencio de' Rustici, and perhaps Poggio Bracciolini as well. In 1411, during a period when, as a convert to Roman Catholicism, he took part in the retinue of the Pisan Antipope John XXIII as he entered Rome, Chrysolaras wrote his *Comparison of Old and New Rome* in the form of a letter to the Byzantine emperor. There Chrysolaras records that "nothing in Rome has come down to us intact: you will not find anything that is undamaged, either crumbling beneath the natural forces of time or due to the violence of human hands. Like our own city, Rome uses itself as a mine and a quarry, and (as we say to be true of everything) it both nourishes and consumes itself. . . . Nonetheless, even these ruins and heaps of stones show what great things once existed, and how enormous and beautiful were the original constructions." Chrysolaras views the ruins and fragments of Rome as forms of testimony; he cites its aqueducts, walls, porticoes, palaces, council halls, markets, baths, and theaters, its shrines, images, statues, and sacred precincts, its funerary monuments and arches, sculptures, and reliefs as "alive" through their images and inscriptions: "They speak of Rome's victories, her general well-being, dominion, dignity, and deeds in war." Yet he values ruins for both their historical testimony and their formal pleasures: "These works were beautiful not only in their original composition and organization; they seem beautiful even in their dismembered state. Just as in a body that is beautiful as a whole, so the hand or foot or head is also beautiful; or, in a body of outstanding size, each of the limbs is large."[67]

Poggio, too, noted and meditated on the ruins of Rome. He recorded that in his lifetime, portions of the intact tomb of Caecilia Metella had collapsed. He witnessed columns from a temple on the grounds of the Capitol and a vast colonnade near the Temple of Minerva (today Santa Maria sopra Minerva) used for lime. Frequenting the Temple of Venus and Roma, which he believed was dedicated to Castor and Pollux, and other sites near the Senate, he emphasized not so much the magnificence of Roman structures but the eloquence of Roman orators: Hortensius, Cicero, Crassus, and others.[68] Poggio began his original *Ruinarum urbis Romae descriptio* (*Description of Roman Ruins*) at some point before 1431, and it was incorporated into his work on the topic of the "variations in human fortune," *Historiae de varietate fortunae*, published in 1448.[69] For Poggio, ruins were not remnants of eternally perfected forms. Instead, he took the collapse and ruination of numerous ancient buildings within the relatively brief span of his individual life as a reminder that life and fortune are fleeting and that one must register the history of one's times while one can.

In the same period, Pope Eugenius IV sponsored a survey of Roman monuments by Alberti—an experience that led Alberti to write in his *De re aedificatoria* of the damage to buildings caused not by barbarians and decay but by the negligence and avarice of his contemporaries.[70] Eugenius returned to a desolate and sparse Rome in 1443, accompanied by his secretary Flavio Biondo (Flavus Blondus) of Forli. Although Eugenius would die within just a few years, Biondo continued to serve his successors to the papacy, including both Nicholas V, who had a deep interest in monuments—and whose collection of Latin and Greek manuscripts would form the core of the Vatican Library,[71] and the devoted humanist Pius II, who had a passion for antiquarianism and was preoccupied with ancient military systems.[72]

Biondo began his thorough survey of the architecture and topography of Latin antiquity, *Roma instaurata* (*Rome Restored*), under a conviction that if Roman ruins were not sustained, a knowledge of all of Roman culture could vanish. Following Petrarch, he held that the ruins inspired their viewers to thoughts of Roman achievements. He worked to reconstruct the original grandeur of an array of Roman buildings, forms, and plans, including gates, coins, obelisks, theaters, private houses, roads, temples, and the layout of districts. As he used literary sources to uncover the names of the structures, his work became the standard guide to Roman ruins for more than a century.[73] He followed this protoarchaeological work with a companion volume, *Roma triumphans* (*Rome Triumphant*). For Biondo, *instaurare* was not merely a matter of maintaining the ancient fabric in its existing state; he had in mind a process of renewing and animating the remnants of the past. His project set the ground for mapping and modeling the rebuilding of Rome that consequent Renaissance popes envisioned. At the same time, he was aware that his own texts, and the literary sources on which he relied, were valuable in themselves. The conclusion to his dedicatory preface suggests that posterity will decide whether the *instauration* in marble, brick, concrete, stone, and bronze, or the restoration in literature will endure the longest: "*calce, latericio, materia, lapide aut aere, an literis facta solidior diuturniorve maneat instauratio.*"[74]

Romans continued to pasture their cattle within the city walls well into the fifteenth century. When the popes returned to Rome from Avignon, they found the city populated by only twenty thousand souls. Within thirty years, by the time of the Jubilee of 1450, they had begun building projects and, as always, constructing in the environs of the city revealed hidden stores of antiquities. The humanist revival of classical learning set the stage for an appreciation of these discoveries made in the progress of building commissions, and Florentines continued to play a prominent role: Ghiberti was in Rome in 1425–1430 and saw a statue of a hermaphrodite uncovered; Donatello was working in Saint Peter's in 1423–1424; Gentile da Fabriano was at the Lateran in 1427; Pisanello and Masolino worked in the city between 1428 and 1432. From the mid-fifteenth century forward, antiquities were valued for their own sake as new buildings continued to be manufactured from old materials.

In the 1480s the discovery of the Domus Aurea, or "Golden House of Nero," and the fantastical wall decorations of its subterranean vaults, or *grotte*, led to a fascination with Roman decorative painting—the *grotteschi* of vines, plants, and imaginary animals. Under Alexander VI, pope from 1492 to 1503, exploration of these "grotesques" continued, and the Apollo Belvedere was discovered at the Porto d'Anzio. Under Julius II (pope from 1503 to 1513), the Laocoön, the Venus of the Vatican, and the Torso of Cleopatra were found.[75] Much destruction of ancient buildings ensued in looking for statues and emulating ancient buildings. Leonard Barkan observes that "the imperial ascendancy of the papacy, despite all its classicizing trappings, . . . tends to ride roughshod over the very field of ancient remains it is using to validate itself." He notes the destruction of the Colosseum, the Septizodium (aka Septizonium) (see fig. 16), the Forum of Nerva, and the Triumphal Arch of Marcus Aurelius, and adds the removal of marble from the Colosseum by Eugenius IV, the demolition of the Hercules temple in the Forum Boarium under Paul II, the damage to the Meta Romuli under Alexander VI, and further destructive building projects under Julius II and Leo X, both of whom were well known for their love of classical culture.[76]

The following text appears within the engraving:

COS·FORTVNATISSIMVS·NOBILISSIMVSQVE

C·TRIB·POTV

LVCI·SEPTIMII·SEVERI·CAESARIS
IN·VIA·APPIA·QVANTVM·QVIDAM·CONSEQVI·CONIECTVRA
POTVERVNT·SEPVLCRVM·SEPTIZONII·TITVLO·TEMPORVM
INIVRIA·PAENE·DISTRVCTVM·CETERIS·PARTIB·VEL
CORRVPTIS·VEL·CONLABSIS·NEGLIGENTIA·SVPERIORIS·
AEVI·MOTI·QVOD·SVPEREST·MEMORIAM·VETERVM·
PROPAGANTES·EFFINXIMVS
ROMAE·ↀↃXLVI·

ANT·LAFRERI
SEQVANI·FORMIS

FIGURE 16. *Luci Septimii Severi Caesaris in Via Appia . . . sepulchrum Septizonii titulo temporum iniuria paene distructum* (Septizodium). From *Speculum Romanae Magnificentiae* (Rome: Antoine Lafréry [Antonio Lafreri], 1551). British Museum, London.

Further, remnants of the "medieval" view of the destruction of pagan idols continued. Despite his own aesthetic and historical appreciation for ruins, Chrysolaras had described in his *Comparison* how pilgrims denigrated monuments and buildings associated with the persecutors of early Christians, including Diocletian, Maximianus, and "that accursed butcher Nero." According to Chrysolaras, "the pilgrims pass by these physical remains, even though they once belonged to emperors and to those who persecuted and enslaved the Christians. But why do I say that they pass these by? Rather, they trample them underfoot, strike them with their fists, break off pieces, spit on them . . . and, throwing them to the ground, smash them."[77] In August 1413, a Paduan monk took a hammer to a skull in the monastery of Santa Giustina that he believed to be Livy's.[78]

Ghiberti continued to hold that Sylvester was to blame. He writes in his *Commentaries*, "The Christian faith achieved victory in the time of the Emperor Constantine and Pope Sylvester. Idolatry was most stringently prosecuted so that all the statues and pictures, noble, and of antique and perfect venerability as they were, were destroyed and rent to pieces. With the statues and pictures were consumed books, commentaries, drawings, and the rules by which one could learn such noble and excellent arts. . . . Thus ended the art of sculpture and painting and all the knowledge and skill that had been achieved in it."[79] Whether they are pointing to Sylvester or Gregory, scholars and artists considered the destruction of Roman statues to be closer to a crime than a virtue. This opinion eventually found resonance in Northern Europe as well. A century after Ghiberti, Albrecht Dürer wrote that as an artist he had been "robbed" by the vehemence of iconoclasm against the pagans.[80]

Medieval iconoclastic fervor against pagan ruins long went hand in hand with the opportunistic use of *spolia*. We have seen how, from the time of Constantine forward, colonnades of basilicas were often made of *spolia*; into the eleventh century, French, German, and English builders were eager to use such elements to claim a Roman heritage. Vasari noted that such columns kept alive an intimate knowledge of ancient building types into his own time.[81] When, in 1514, Raphael Sanzio was appointed chief architect for the new Saint Peter's by Pope Leo X and given license to collect building materials in the landscape from within a ten-mile radius of Rome, the artist found himself not only in charge of buildings but also commandeering excavations.

In the same period, Pope Leo asked the artist to reconstruct imperial Rome on paper, drawing not only what was visible at the time but also delineating everything that had become "entirely ruined or barely visible."[82] Four years later, in 1518–1519, Raphael, with editorial help from Baldassare Castiglione, wrote to the pope, "Why should we blame the Goths, the Vandals, and other perfidious enemies of the Latin name, if those who ought, like fathers and guardians, to have protected these poor remains of Rome, have themselves long expended all their zeal to extinguish and destroy? How many Popes, Holy Father, occupants of Your Holiness's throne, but lacking Your Holiness's knowledge, and Your Holiness's strength and greatness of mind, how many Pontiffs, I say, have acquiesced in the ruination and defacement of the ancient temples, the statues, the arches and the other monuments, which were the glory of their founders?"[83] The architectural historian David Karmon has argued that, although this now well-known letter is usually seen as a pathbreaking intervention, Raphael's plea was designed to imply that the numerous existing papal and civic efforts at conserving ancient structures, including those stemming from Pius II's papal bull of 1462, were insufficient. The letter thus not only alerted Leo to the urgency of the need to stop the mere mining of ancient buildings for lime; it also solidified the papal authority to do so and denigrated civic conservation efforts.

Raphael also celebrated the strength and permanence of the early forms as compared with recent ones. He singles out his mentor Bramante in the letter for his "beautiful works" but implies that he is using impermanent materials. Bramante was notoriously called "Bramante Ruinante" or "Maestro Ruinante," primarily for his demolishing of the Basilica of Constantine in preparation for the site of the new Saint Peter's. He sometimes substituted plaster, or *getto*, for actual stone in his facades—a practice that led to rapid disintegration.[84] Thus ruination became a concern of new construction and not merely an attribute of ancient buildings. By 1589, the humanist and poet Pietro Angelio of Barga introduced a contrary argument—that neither the popes nor the barbarians had destroyed ancient Rome but instead the culprits were, as they had been since massive parts of the Forum collapsed in the earthquake of 847, natural disasters, fire, and the relentless ravages of time.[85]

Debates and policies regarding preservation took place in the shadow of the remains of the most imposing ancient structures, and knowledge of their forms was continuous between the pagan and Christian eras. Earlier, and farther afield, where fourth- and fifth-century bishops undertook missionary activities against the pagans, structures were confiscated and put to new uses. Marilius of Angers, who died in 453, burned down two pagan temples in the vicinity of the city and established a church at one site and a monastery at the other. When Paternus of Avranches and his fellow monk Scubilio learned of an active pagan cult in Brittany, they punished its members and turned their temple into a pen for livestock.[86] In each case building materials were saved and reused for the Christian structures. Pope Gregory issued an edict in 601 to the missionary Mellitus in Anglo-Saxon England to retain and consecrate any pagan structures still in use as churches.[87] Some structures were abandoned for long periods, some occupied soon after they were deliberately destroyed. Some clerics fabricated descriptions of antiquities.[88]

In the late fifth and into the sixth century, many Roman buildings were adapted and reused in southern Gaul: the cathedral and baptistry of Aix-en-Provence were constructed on the site of the city's forum, the church of Saint-Étienne of Strasbourg was constructed over a Roman road, the villa of Séviac was transformed into a baptistry and small chapel and Cimiez and Saint-Pierre-aux-Nonnains in Metz were built on the sites of former thermal baths. Beyond Gaul, numerous altars of pagan goddess cults and an altar to Mercury were reused in the foundations of the fourth-century cathedral of Bonn.[89] The dispersal and dislocation of ruins stretched as far as the Christian frontier.

Ruin as the Ground of Nativity

Although in fact the Temple of Peace was built after, and to celebrate, the Roman destruction of Herod's temple, seventy years after the birth of Christ, a legend persisted that the temple collapsed at the moment of the Incarnation.[90] The death of Pan that Plutarch records, the legend of Thamus's cry "The Great God Pan is dead," echoed to the ears of Milton, too, as simultaneous to the morning of the Nativity. Here the instant destruction of one world is caused by the surprising advent of another. Pagan ruins stand as mute, humiliated witnesses to Christian accomplishments as well in one of the most prevalent medieval and early Renaissance images of ruins: the Nativity scene.

In two of Botticelli's several *Adorations*, dating from 1470 to 1475—one at the Uffizi Gallery in Florence and the other the tondo at the National Gallery in London, for example, the visit of the magi or kings is shown within and against ruined ancient buildings with pilasters, arches, and Corinthian pediments; around the stones of the structures are rough timbers, making each building a conflation of a palace and stable. In the Uffizi *Adoration of the Magi* (see plate 2), the ruins form something like a throne, despite the sprouting vegetation, rough stones, and rudimentary wooden shelter. In the London tondo *Adoration of the Kings* (see fig. 17), the crowded figures, mostly seen from the back, seem to be pushing toward not only the Nativity scene but also a vanishing point in the far rough wall of the form, just behind the animals in their stall. The outlines of the stones disappear and a blank—whether wood or plaster or something else—absorbs our focus. A peacock, reminder of human vanity, watches on the right, perched high on broken stone pilasters that lean against what remains of a supporting wall for the facade.

A similar hybrid structure stands behind Piero della Francesca's Nativity of the same era (see fig. 18). Here the remains of a stone wall are crumbling at their edges, and a simple shedlike roof has been built to shelter the animals within. The roof itself is in ruin, with a prominent jagged hole and vegetation growing between the shakes. Much of Piero's originality of conception is evident in the clustering of the figures of angels, Virgin and infant, and the paired shepherds, and the comparative solitude of Joseph, who is facing away. But most remarkable is the painting's auditory dimension—the resonant sound and attentive listening it conveys. Three angels are singing, two accompanying

FIGURE 17. Sandro Botticelli, *The Adoration of the Kings*, ca. 1470–1475. Tempera on poplar. National Gallery, London.

their voices with lutes; the infant Jesus is awake, his lips parted and his hands gesturing up toward his mother; Joseph has turned his ear toward the viewer and seems to be attending to the adjacent shepherds; at the center of the image, and adjacent to the singing angels, a donkey's protruding teeth and open mouth give a sense that it is braying along; an ox's protruding and slightly bowed head below a lute suggests more animal noise. And on the roof a magpie, the chattiest of birds, is captured in a closed-beak moment of listening.

The painting suggests the noisy celebration in speech and song of the death of Pan as well as the collapse of the old order by shouting down its walls. Yet it also evokes the account of Christ's birth by Saint Bridget of Sweden in Voragine's *Golden Legend*—a book Piero often used as the text for his paintings.

FIGURE 18. Piero della Francesca, *The Nativity*, 1470–1475. Oil on poplar. National Gallery, London.

There Bridget recounts a vision she had of Mary adoring the infant Christ on the ground while she "heard the singing of the angels, which was of miraculous sweetness and great beauty."[91]

The motif of the Christ child born in the midst of ruined buildings extended to the North and to works in woodcut and etching as well as painting. In a 1504 engraving by Albrecht Dürer from his series on the life of the Virgin (see fig. 19), thatch or hay has been destroyed by weather, vegetation sprouts in broken walls made of brick, and a section is cut away to reveal the new dispensation. The holy family is placed to the side, and central to the image is a bearded, kneeling figure pouring an abundant flow of water from a solidly constructed well. The well stands in contrast to the ruined materials here, the wooden building and the decaying Roman arch at the center that frames the distant view. The ruined wood reminds us that the grain of the wood has been worked here to make the relief. That this is the scene from the life of a god who is a carpenter in a line of carpenters and divine makers is only underscored by this image.

FIGURE 19. Albrecht Dürer, *The Nativity*, 1504. Princeton University Art Museum; bequest of Julie Parsons Redmond.

Christian narratives placed against backdrops of ruins also became a specialty of the Donau or Danube school in the first third of the sixteenth century. Among the most well-known depictions of the Nativity among ruins is a 1513 Nativity of Albrecht Altdorfer (see plate 3). Altdorfer locates his nocturnal scene of the holy family in nearly wild settings of hanging vegetation where the figures are only barely sheltered by a ruined form. The structure, notably made of bricks and beams—is cut away, with strong contrasts of shadow, moonlight, starlight, and candlelight. Everything deranges the viewer's sense of space and time, exterior and interior.[92] There is no vanishing point, and the viewer must find the sacred figures to the right and receding behind the bricks that are sheltering them. Arches, square openings (perhaps once windows), doorways, crumbling buttresses, and wooden stairs lie exposed to weather. Altdorfer conveys something of the effect of physically exploring a ruin and of spoliation once its referent has been lost to time. We witness in his ruined structures the destruction of once significant forms, no longer intelligible. Below the scene, a proliferation of finely delineated weeds and flowers; above, an elegantly figured cartouche of three massed and hovering angelic putti who seem drawn with thin ribbons of light against the black sky.

As the pagan world continually explored the boundaries of the animal and human in satyr, centaur, and other hybrid beings, it rarely produced mixtures of the mortal and immortal. The exceptions were, on the one hand, Hercules, Aesculapius, Aristaeus, Triptolemus, and others who provided valued services, and, on the other, those few, including Psyche and Ganymede, rewarded via love or fortune by individual gods. Christianity begins in a stable but departs from the literal world to pursue a transcendent duality between the mortal and immortal. Yet a notion that humans negate their animal being through considered work persists with its corollary suggestion that inventions are credentials for immortality.

Nevertheless, the contrast between Christian stable and ruined Roman palace does not present a narrative of one god replacing others as neatly as it might at first seem. The Romans carried a sustained reverence for the simple huts that were the dwellings of their founders Romulus and Evander. In the Augustan era, the Greek writer Dionysius of Halicarnassus wrote that in his own time the hut of Romulus stood on the slope of the Palatine facing the Circus Maximus and that, although no ornaments or improvements would be made to it, if any part of it was damaged, by storms or time, the damage would be repaired and thus the hut was continually restored.[93] These depictions of the Nativity reinscribe the contrast between imperial grandeur and Republican virtue as they also suggest that conservation can itself evoke renewal.

III. Mater

NYMPHS, VIRGINS, AND WHORES—
ON THE RUIN OF WOMEN

On Ruined Persons

Human beings can be agents of the destruction of the built environment, but, unless they are suicidal or subjected to an impeding violence, they do not suffer passively the effects of weather and time; they protect themselves through making and building those very forms that will be damaged in times of war. Nevertheless, we do speak of "ruined" persons, and our frames for such figures are more often than not divided by gender. A ruined man is one stripped of his material resources, damaged by fate or circumstances, unable to complete an intended future, yet continuing to exist. A ruined woman may also suffer such a fate, yet the ruin of women has been tied inextricably as well to ideas of women as material and to the cache of value that a woman's body, and particularly her virginity and chastity, can hold. Wherever women are themselves considered to be material or property, where their sexual and reproductive powers are mediums of exchange, their ruin is calculated within such a system and remains tied to the value of their bodies alone.

What is the genealogy of these ideas? Even a preliminary answer depends on returning to our most fundamental assumptions regarding persons and environments. The womb of a woman is everyone's first dwelling. Like a spring or a well, the womb holds water, the amniotic fluid that nourishes us from inception to birth. And water continues, in its pure forms from external nature, to be necessary to human life. Yet water, when contaminated, can also harm us. Furthermore, as the account of Christ's encounter with the woman of Samaria at the well in the Gospel according to John (John 4:4–10) indicates, the sharing of water involves trust and charity. Here is the passage from the King James Bible:

> And he must needs go through Samaria.
>
> Then cometh he to a city of Samaria, which is called Sychar, near to the parcel of ground that Jacob gave to his son Joseph.
>
> Now Jacob's well was there. Jesus therefore, being wearied with his journey, sat thus on the well: and it was about the sixth hour.

FIGURE 20. Rembrandt van Rijn, *Christ and the Woman of Samaria among Ruins*, 1634. Metropolitan Museum of Art, New York; Harris Brisbane Dick Fund, 1917.

There cometh a woman of Samaria to draw water: Jesus saith unto her, Give me to drink.

(For his disciples were gone away unto the city to buy meat.)

Then saith the woman of Samaria unto him, How is it that thou, being a Jew, askest drink of me, which am a woman of Samaria? for the Jews have no dealings with the Samaritans.

Jesus answered and said unto her, If thou knewest the gift of God, and who it is that saith to thee, Give me to drink; thou wouldest have asked of him, and he would have given thee living water.

This episode takes place before the return of Jesus to Galilee. Although the two peoples shared many beliefs, the Jews regarded the Samaritans as foreigners and their attitude was often hostile, as the two peoples seem to have drifted apart in the postexilic period. The Gospel of John, like the Gospel of Luke, is favorable to the Samaritans, unlike the Matthew Gospel, which quotes Jesus as telling his followers not to enter any Samaritan cities.[1]

In Rembrandt's etching from 1634, *Christ and the Woman of Samaria among Ruins*, a landscape of stone ruins extends to the background, where an obelisk and a Pantheon-shaped form can be glimpsed. Shown in the midst of conversation, the woman gestures with her hands while Jesus intently listens (see fig. 20). Like Dürer's Nativity in figure 19, Rembrandt's image implicitly marks a transition from barrenness and ruin to a life-giving hospitality where water and words can be safely shared. Yet we remember that water, as rain and weather, is inimical to human buildings—it wears wood to decay and stone to mud. Between these life-giving and form-destroying possibilities lie a set of persistent myths and images around women, dwellings, and water. Purity and contamination become attached to women; anthropomorphic qualities are given to water; bodies become dwellings and dwellings become bodies. The figures of ancient Greek and Roman nymphs, who are the guardians of springs and wells; the hearth-tending vestal virgins, whose house was next to the important Juturna spring at the foot of the Palatine[2] and who protect the rituals and integrity of ancient Rome; the contrary Christian figures of the Virgin Mary and Mary Magdalene—all contribute to the continuity of associations between women's integrity and women's ruin.

The Nymph's Freedom

The Greek term *numphê* could refer either to minor female deities associated with wild places or to mortal human women who had reached sexual maturity, most often brides.[3] If human heroines are found within the polis or city walls, nymphs are creatures of external nature and most often personify and haunt springs, rivers, and lakes. The nymph's most important mythic and ritual function is to provide fresh water. In this, too, she differs from human heroines. Ancient writers, including Homer, often provide clues that a woman is a nymph by drawing attention to her parentage by a river god or by adding *naïs* (naiad) or the suffix *rhoê* to her name to indicate the flowing movement of water.[4]

Caves, grottos, and springs have maintained their association with nymphs and persist as sites of nymphaea. For example, the shrine to Persephone at the Grotto Caruso near the Calabrian town of Locri, plundered by the Carthaginians in the Punic Wars, was an active place of ritual from the classical through the Hellenistic period. A spring there supplied fountains and wells and was believed to convey pure water from the underworld. Shepherds, travelers, and women fetching water paid tribute to the nymphs as they visited the shrine.[5] Water was most often used in Greek ritual for purposes of purification, sometimes for appeasing a divinity and shedding some pollution. At Cyrene, fourth-century sacred laws inscribed in marble included a prescription for newly married women to "go down to Artemis" (i.e., a nymphaeum) for a purifying bath—an act viewed as appeasement for the loss of their virginity. Porphyry's third-century commentary on the Cave of the Nymphs in Odyssey 13 suggests that the cave is symbolic of the generative potency of the cosmos.[6] In Callimachus's fragment, Aitia 3.4, "The Fountains of Argos," the poet tells the story of four of the fifty daughters of Danaus, who found water when Poseidon had inflicted the residents with a drought. Amymone, the most famous of the four, became Poseidon's lover. In appreciation, he gave her the spring at Lerna, three miles or so from Argos. The poem explains that the girls who weave the robe for Hera's cult statue in her temple at Argos must first bathe in Amymone's spring, pouring the water over their heads.[7]

Supernaturally long-lived, yet mortal themselves, nymphs hold an ambiguous position as brides of mortals and immortals; their progeny will be divine or human, depending on their mates. They are sexually desirable and remain free of the social and familial constraints imposed on human women. They therefore are often represented as sexually promiscuous and aggressive.[8] Dancing, singing, bathing, seeking the objects of their desire and escaping the unwanted attentions of satyrs—or, in the case of Arethusa, the unwanted embrace of a river god—nymphs exercise their individual pleasure and volition; they are chaste or not, as they like. They therefore are threats to the law. Living beyond the polis, their forms of generosity and withdrawal are their own. When we encounter them in later tradition, they are recognizable as representations of realized female desire. The gentle nymphs who help raise the infant Dionysus have their extreme counterpart in the maenads and other madwomen associated with his adult cult. Beyond regulation, such nymphs threaten devastation and their desire curdles to frenzy.

Perhaps because of these dualities between appearance and withdrawal, assertion and retreat, figures of nymphs play an important role in the earliest printed representations of ruins.[9] One of the most beautiful and mysterious of early printed texts, the *Hypnerotomachia Poliphili*, or *The Strife of Love in a Dream*, tells the story of a lover's pursuit of a nymph. Produced by the Venetian printer Aldus Manutius in December 1499, the work includes 172 intricate and exquisite woodcuts most often attributed to Benedetto Bordone. They follow the progress of the protagonist Poliphilo in a dream—his name meaning "friend of Polia" and/or "friend of all things." Within his dream, Poliphilo pursues his heart's desire, the nymph Polia, and we learn as well something of her own history. In turn, within her narrative, we hear Poliphilo's fraught appeals to Venus to further his love and their eventual happy, if merely oneiric, reunion. Reconstructing the work's narrative threads from its enveloping structure requires a form of semantic archaeology, for the stories within stories are hidden in the details, as the details are hidden in the progress of the narrative. The relations between text and pictures require an analogous attention to both frame and particulars.[10]

The work has long been attributed to the Venetian Dominican grammarian Francesco Colonna, yet a number of scholars now contend that Leon Battista Alberti was its creator—still others claim that perhaps the author was a Roman governor named Francesco Colonna, or Lorenzo de' Medici, or someone else, unknown. Yet the attribution to a Francesco Colonna—whether the friar, the governor, or another descendant—is hidden in pieces in the text, for the initial letters of each chapter, placed together, form the acrostic POLIAM FRATER FRANCISCUS COLUMNA PERAMAVIT, or "Fra Francesco Colonna loved Polia exceedingly."[11]

Written in a fabulous and convoluted idiolect, the work sets forth an Italian that itself resembles a ruin in that the Latin and Greek roots of each word are made evident, the parts of words made visible at their seams. The author created innumerable neologisms by adding Latin suffixes and prefixes to Italian words and Italian suffixes and prefixes to Latin words; his images include inscriptions not only in Latin but also in Greek, Hebrew, and Arabic, with what he thought were Egyptian hieroglyphs taken up and adapted as well. He is working with piecemeal fragments, assuming his readers would understand not only Tuscan but also these many ancient tongues. Poliphilo explains his sense of the damaged Latin language in terms of invasion and ruin, making an analogy between the destruction of the built environment and the breaking down of a language as he reveals that he cannot find words to describe "a mighty and rare work of antiquity"—a marvelous portal.

> Without a doubt, I lack the knowledge that would allow me to describe it perfectly, especially since in our time the proper vernacular and native terms peculiar to the art of architecture are buried and extinct, along with the true men. O execrable and sacrilegious barbarism, how you have invaded and sacked the noblest part of the Latin treasury and sanctuary! A once honourable art is now polluted and lost, thanks to your accursed ignorance, which in league with raging, unslaked and perfidious greed has extinguished that supreme and excellent portion that made Rome the sublime Empress of the world.[12]

And yet it is impossible not to note that these visible seams are indeed seams; word by word, sentence by sentence, passage by passage, the first-person speaker traces his narrative. The progress of Poliphilo is described as a path from site to site, with an emphasis on arrivals and encounters where his, and our, attention is arrested by what we see and hear. As he explains in his dedicatory epistle, "It is the case here that although these things are difficult by their nature, they are expounded with a certain grace, like a garden sown with every kind of flower; they are told in a pleasant manner, presented with many illustrations and images for the eyes."[13] Thus, to attempt to trace the convoluted progress of the story is to return to various sites of encounter and beholding, whether dreamed or experienced, whether framed within the fantastic architectural descriptions of book 1 or the psychological discourse of book 2. The *Hypnerotomachia*, one of the most exquisite material objects of the Renaissance—composed with finely chiseled, elegant fonts, beautiful proportions, and line-drawn woodcuts of delicate clarity of detail—often takes its allegorical themes of courtly love from the relation between appearance and ruin.

As the work begins, we first glimpse Poliphilo on a "calm and silent shore" before he enters the winding paths of a dark wood.[14] He is driven forward by his thirst: a physical thirst for water, an erotic thirst for love, and a thirst for images and evidence of antiquity. We find the conflation of these desires as he arrives in a valley where he comes upon an enormous pyramid topped by an obelisk—before it lie the fragments of an ancient peristyle, parts of a temple to Venus, Amor, and Cybele. He wants to look at "every part of the beautiful complex, examining these excellent and noble statues made from virgin stone," and goes on at length to describe the "marvelous portal," circling back to its entrance to admire its ornaments. He muses, "If the fragments of holy antiquity, the ruins and debris and even the shavings, fill us with stupefied admiration and give us such delight in viewing them, what would they do if they were whole?"[15] A dragon suddenly appears, driving Poliphilo into a labyrinth. As he comes to the end of it, he steps into a luxurious garden where the nymphs of the five senses invite him to bathe with them in an octagonal bathhouse. Here Queen Eleuterylida (the Queen of Happiness and Free Will) assigns Logistica and Thelemia (Reason and Desire), to be his guides as he pursues his love for Polia. With them, he passes artificial gardens, a twisting boat canal, and a geometrical monument. At this point he finds himself surrounded by the nymphs of Love.

When Poliphilo arrives among these "amorous nymphs," Logistica warns him about the dangerous connection between the visible and decay, exclaiming, "O Poliphilo, theirs is a feigned and cosmetic beauty, deceitful, insipid and vain! For if you were to examine them from behind, you would be sickened to realize how indecent and despicable they are, how disgusting and abominably stinking, worse than a great rubbish heap. . . . O depraved, impious and accursed desire, O detestable madness, O defrauded senses, which you seduce with the selfsame bestial pleasure for the ruin of miserable mortals!" Her opposite and cohort Thelemia tells him not to listen to Logistica—Logistica is filled with contempt and turns her back, sighs, and runs away.[16]

The *Hypnerotomachia*'s nymphs are derived from Boccaccio's 1341–1342 *Commedia delle Ninfe Fiorentine (Ameto)*, yet they also return to classical myths of nymphs.[17] When we find in the *Hypnerotomachia* a procession of virgins and nymphs, with Diana attended by virgins and nymphs riding centaurs, it is like coming directly upon a scene from a frieze. Jennifer Larson asserts in her comprehensive study, *Greek Nymphs*, "The nymphs combine the forbidden allure of the virgin Artemis with the lust of the sexually aware Aphrodite; yet as local deities believed to inhabit not Olympos but the caves, trees, and springs, they are much more accessible than these goddesses. The nymph is also an idealized mythopoetic version of the village girl at the peak of her sexual desirability, so that her interactions with mortal men can hardly avoid connotations of sexual attraction." As opposed to stories where the gods are drawn to liaisons with mortals, when nymphs and human men partner, "the nymph's supernatural power balances or overwhelms the assumed superiority of the male, so that her desires are often central to the narrative."[18]

The nymph who attracts the attentions of Poliphilo carries a cornucopia-shaped burning torch. He says that "a noble and festive nymph had separated herself from [the others] and was coming toward me with her burning torch in her hand. Since I could tell plainly from her virginal walk that she was a real and genuine girl, I did not move, but awaited her with relief." She thereby also evokes the fire of the vestal virgins. He finds that at first sight he thought this was Polia, but he was not sure. The work's complex play of desire and appearance emphasizes Poliphilo's aim to manifest the invisible—the authenticity of virginity, the causes of what he sees, the sources of antiquity. As he presents his vision of Polia, he begins with a sustained description of her that reaches a hallucinatory scale of detail that nevertheless seems unable to penetrate reality:

> The sun-like nymph had dressed her virginal and divine little body with the thinnest material, of a green silk weft woven together with a warp of gold, like the lovely colouring of the feathers on a duck's neck. She wore this over a white tunic of silk crêpe next to her delicate flesh and milk-white skin, such as the inventive Pamphila, daughter of Platis on the island of Cos, could never have woven. The graceful tunic seemed to contain white and scarlet roses, while the dress above it, elegantly fashioned in tiny pleats or wrinkles, clung to the ample hips and was tightly secured around the little breasts with a golden cord, stretching out the pleats of the fine cloth over the delicately swelling bosom. The superfluous material of the long dress was pulled up above this first belt, leaving the fringed edge to fall evenly around the fleshy heels.[19]

This description goes on in the same vein, with accounts of her "small round belly," "milk-white heels," "extended arms with their long hands, ornamented with rounded and delicate fingers with longest, pink, translucent nails." The eyebrows and cheeks take up a whole paragraph several pages later. In a consequent ceremony, Poliphilo is instructed to extinguish Polia's torch in the cold water of a basin. At that moment, Polia shows her true identity as she kisses him. Poliphilo is filled with sexual desire—in plate 17 of the work, he is depicted with an erection—and the lovers await the arrival of the god of love.[20]

As they approach the city of Poly, the luxurious vegetation about them turns suddenly into a stony ground of thistles and thorns. Poliphilo sees before him the ruined walls of the city and the remains of what was once a hexagonal temple devoted to Pluto. His description carries over to ruins the same hallucinatory detail he earlier devoted to Polia's appearance:

> What remained of it was a great ruin of walls or enclosures, structures of white marble, and nearby a broken and sea-dashed mole of the nearby harbour. In the fissures thereof I saw growing the salt-loving littoral cock's-crest, in some places ox-eye, much saltwort and the fragrant sea-wormwood, and on the sand banks iringo, purslane, sea-colewort and other well-known simples, characias and myrtites. From the port many odd-numbered stairs led to the footing of the temple gateway. Due to devouring time, the decay of age and negligence, this building had collapsed onto the damp earth, leaving here and there a shaft without a capital, or a headless trunk of some immense column of Persian stone with its red granulations, sometimes alternating with Mygdonian marble. Some were broken at the *joints*: one could see neither hypothesis, nor hypotrachelia, nor astragal. I also saw some of such *marvellous* artistry as even the temple of Gades could not boast; but everything was exposed to the sky and gnawed by decay and old age.[21]

Yet this passage also significantly inverts his discovery of his lover. As he once longed to uncover the living body of the nymph beneath the shimmer of her drapery, here his imagination uncovers, beneath the fragments of the damaged temple, an exposed skeleton—a headless trunk, a pile of broken joints, a residue of gnawed bones. Even his architectural terms refer to parts of a body: *hypotrachelia*, signifying the spaces between capitals and shafts from the Greek terms for "under the neck"; and *astragal*, the word for a molding profile with a round surface poised between two flat planes, which comes from the Greek and Latin words for "vertebrae."

Polia urges Poliphilo to look at the monument, imagining how it was once "a noble and wondrous temple." She explains, "In it . . . there are many grave-pits in which were buried the mouldering corpses of those who yielded to a dark and miserable death through base, unfortunate, and unhappy love." She describes the place as the former site of rituals to the god of the underworld

FIGURE 21. Attributed to Benedetto Bordone, *The Ruined and Deserted Temple*. Woodcut. From Francesco Colonna, *Hypnerotomachia Poliphili* (Venice: Aldus Manutius, 1499). Department of Rare Books and Special Collections, Princeton University Library.

designed to warn against those who "knowingly . . . cause their lovers' death." Polia's cautionary role continues as the lovers eventually are awaiting Cupid's boat that will take them to the isle of Cytherea. Urged on by desire, comparing himself to a "snarling dog that has reache[d] his prey," Poliphilo is "mad with greed to satisfy [himself] utterly with [his] own desired game." But Polia sees his "dishonorable condition" and suggests that, since he is "extremely fond of looking at the works of antiquity," he might pass the time admiring "these deserted temples which have collapsed through the ravages of time, or have been consumed by fire, or shattered by old age. Take your pleasure in looking at these, and examine the noble fragments that remain, which are worthy of admiration" (see fig. 21).[22]

In these "vast, lofty heaps and ruins, mostly covered with ground-ivy and ground-creepers and tangled with thorns," Poliphilo gradually discerns inscriptions made by forlorn lovers.[23] Some were betrayed, "imitat[ing] Dido," others loved "beautiful youths" or "wandering guests" or were otherwise maddened by love.[24] The lesson of temperance and consideration for the beloved emerges only for the reader of Latin and Greek. But the inscriptions tell coherent, aphoristic, and moral narratives—they are themselves fountains or sources of knowledge in the midst of the swirling, continually collapsing and fragmenting narrative of the *Hypnerotomachia* as a whole. Once the lovers reach Cythera, they will see the triumphs of Amor, and the fountains of Venus and Adonis, and Polia will tell her story, within which she reports the speech of Poliphilo. Poliphilo will die, experience a vision, and be addressed by Cupid as he witnesses a number of mysteries. He finds himself revived in Polia's arms. A priestess of Venus then lectures the lovers; Polia completes a speech to the nymphs; the nymphs thank her and leave, Polia and Poliphilo are united, and Polia dissolves. Poliphilo awakens to the song of a nightingale.

Even if we cannot identify its author, and even if it presents us with a constantly evaporating narrative structure, the *Hypnerotomachia* remains not only one of the first Western representations of an interest in ruins but also a concerted exercise in their interpretation. Our encounter with these overdetermined and broken forms, embedded in a dream within a dream, is shaped, before the systematic methods of archaeological science, by imaginative projections, by our own desires and our need to sublimate and objectify them. The architectural theorist Alberto Pérez-Gomez has suggested that the *Hypnerotomachia*'s "didactic dream" reminds us that desire is the origin of meaning, and that the harmony—the underlying geometry, order, and stability of architecture—"is always mater-ial, from the Latin notion of the Mother of All."[25] His point is well taken when we consider that the architectural frame is not merely a backdrop but as well corresponds to developments in the narrative: the atmosphere of a dream is underscored by the use of bird's-eye perspective; passages of failed love are surrounded by decaying structures—passages of happiness marked by new buildings made of precious materials.

The climax of the *Hypnerotomachia*, the ceremonial scene where Poliphilo and Polia are united, takes place at the Fountain of Venus. With obvious sexual symbolism, Poliphilo breaks the fountain's entrance curtain, which bears the inscription ΥΜΗΝ (Hymen). Fountain imagery signifies not only an association with nymphs but also notions of abundance.[26] In the economy of such images, the fountain is the opposite of the altar—sign of depletion and sacrifice. Yet here the destruction of the hymen surely is the loss of something: that virginity which, once gone, cannot be restored. Chastity, whether marital or extramarital, can be encouraged and adopted, but virginity appears in a restricted economy: whenever virginity is valued absolutely (and not as a good to be exchanged and expended in the future), we find "the corpse of the beautiful woman"—frozen forever in her perfection; a "sleeping beauty" never to be disturbed. Indeed, in Gregory of Nyssa's paradigmatic "On Virginity" of 368, the very first sentence emphasizes virginity's relation to beauty, claiming that anyone who can "discern the beautiful in purity" will prize virginity.[27]

In April 1485, just a few years before the publication of the *Hypnerotomachia*, a report circulated that the corpse of a young Roman woman of the classical period—wonderfully beautiful and in perfect preservation—had been discovered at the convent of Santa Maria Nuova on the Via Appia, not far beyond the tomb of Caecilia Metella. The Lombard masons who found it said it bore the inscription "Julia, daughter of Claudius." By order of Pope Innocent VIII, she was secretly buried in the night outside the Pincian Gate.[28] On the one hand, this anecdote exemplifies the notion that "the best virgin is a dead virgin"—that virginity, necessarily resulting in infertility and valued as a negation of bodily desire, carries with it an unworldly denial of the senses that approximates a death wish.[29] But on the other hand, it underscores the ways that the body of a virgin is inviolate, not only in relation to sexual penetration but also to the depredations of mortal decay. If an ancient corpse was held to be more beautiful than anything from the present, this young woman's remains, like those of miraculously preserved, "uncorrupted," virgin saints, represents the opposite of a ruin—a form paradoxically free from both life and harm.

Throughout the sixteenth century, nymphs continue to haunt the imagination of humanists in both the north and south along this valence of activity and passivity. At midcentury, Rosso Fiorentino, Léon Davent, Léonard Thiry, and other members of the first school of Fontainebleau pursued a fascination with landscape motifs alluding to existing and imaginary ruins and ancient statuary, although their knowledge of actual ruins was largely secondary.[30] Thiry's figures rowing boats through inundated ruined worlds; Davent's landscapes crammed with skewed obelisks, gigantic columns, glimpses of Bramante's Tempietto, and other structures; medallions showing the virginal Artemis and nymphs in hunting and fishing scenes with amorphous ruins looming in the background: all seem taken from dreams and have more to do with the world of the *Hypnerotomachia Poliphili* than with the consequences of archaeology.[31] In figure 22, for example, Ceres flies to Olympus to implore Jupiter to return Proserpina; in figure 23, a detail from the depiction of the Nymphaeum of Hecate from the same series, a nymph soars over the broken ramparts and pyramid of what looks like a ruined city on a hill.

In Paracelsus's "Book on Nymphs, Sylphs, Pygmies, Salamanders, and Other Spirits,"[32] printed posthumously in 1566, nymphs are described within a schema of elemental spirits that yokes each spirit to an element. Here, too, nymphs, or *undine*, are associated with water (and sylphs to air; pygmies or gnomes to the earth; and salamanders to fire). Paracelsus holds that even if they resemble humans, nymphs are in fact born elsewhere than from Adam. Under special terms of creation, they are subtle hybrids, difficult to categorize:

FIGURE 22. Possibly Léon Davent (after Léonard Thiry), *Ad gemitus Cereris flectuntur numina olimpi* (*Ceres on a Chariot Flying to Olympus and Imploring Jupiter*). From *La Favola di Proserpina* (1547–1550). British Museum, London.

FIGURE 23. Possibly Léon Davent (after Léonard Thiry), *At Nympharum Hecates Scapulis timor addidit alas* (*But Fear Lends Wings to the Shoulders of the Nymphs of Hecate*; detail). From *La Favola di Proserpina* (1547–1550). Istituto centrale per la grafica, Rome.

unlike humans, they do not have souls; unlike animals, they have logic and reason; unlike pure spirits, they have bodies. Yet nymphs have the special characteristic—distinct from other non-Adamic creatures—of being able to receive a soul if they have sex with a man and generate a child. The child, in consequence, receives a soul as well. Desiring souls, nymphs are driven to unite with human men and shaped entirely by their desire.[33]

Often a sleeping, if not dead, nymph evokes a fantasy of awakened desire wherein the nymph has surrendered her own powers and is caught at a moment of vulnerability. The Luxembourg humanist and antiquarian Johann Goritz chose the nickname "Corycius" for himself as an homage to the legendary nymph Corycia. He went on to build a *vigna* with a fountain of a sleeping nymph to complete the connection. An ancient legend held that a young girl, a *virgo*, had guided a legion of Roman soldiers to a spring with particularly clear and clean water. The water was channeled to an aqueduct that became known as the "Aqua Virgo" and supplied the Romans with potable water until the Gothic invasion. The channel was restored in the eighth century and again in the fifteenth century and continues to serve the Piazza del Popolo fountains and the fountain of Trevi. The garden of the del Bufalo, destroyed in the nineteenth century, contained a nymph fountain and frescos that told the story of another spring: the birth of the Hippocrene spring on Parnassus. The water is said to have arisen on the spot where Pegasus's hoof struck the earth. Nearby, Raphael's friend and collaborator, the humanist Angelo Colocci, built a Latin Academy and sculpture garden that also included a fountain of a sleeping nymph meant as an allusion to the Aqua Virgo.[34]

Nymphs also are evoked in Renaissance spaces as inhabitants of grottos. The great salon on the ground floor of the Palazzo Corsini in Florence, completed at the end of the seventeenth century, is shaped around the theme of nymphs in a grotto, suggesting they haunt the gardens of the palace. The Villa Balbi-Durazzo allo Zerbino in Genoa, overlooking the sea, includes an enormous grotto lined with seashells, mother of pearl, and colored pebbles and a "Sala delle Rovine" with the "madness of Enone," the wood nymph who married Paris, and was betrayed by him, depicted in the distance through a damaged arch. Alexander Pope's grotto at Twickenham honored Egeria, the Roman water nymph who was the legendary lover and helper of Numa Pompilius, the equally legendary king and lawgiver of Rome, successor to Romulus. Pope, who could not travel himself, was able to incorporate a souvenir stone from the Roman grotto of Egeria at Porto Capena into his fabrication. The nymph was also celebrated as late as 1812–1818 by Lord Byron in *Childe Harold's Pilgrimage*. In canto 4:

> Egeria! Sweet creation of some heart
> Which found no mortal resting-place so fair
> As thine ideal breast; whate'er thou art
> Or wert,—a young Aurora of the air,

The nympholepsy of some fond despair;
Or, it might be, a beauty of the earth,
Who found a more than common votary there
Too much adoring; whatsoe'er thy birth,
Thou wert a beautiful thought, and softly bodied forth.

This specter moves the poet to compose, in Spenserian stanzas, some of his most effervescent nature imagery:

The mosses of thy fountain still are sprinkled
With thine Elysian water-drops; the face
Of thy cave-guarded spring, with years unwrinkled,
Reflects the meek-eyed genius of the place,
Whose green, wild margin now no more erase
Art's works: nor must the delicate waters sleep,
Prison'd in marble, bubbling from the base
Of the cleft statue, with a gentle leap
The rill runs o'er, and round, fern, flowers, and ivy creep . . .

The consequent unusual cross-stanza enjambment to "Fantastically tangled" and further description is one of Byron's most clever effects, evoking the spill of water—"a gentle leap."[35]

A Virgin Queen

Robert Dallington's 1592 English translation of the *Hypnerotomachia* adapted not only its language but also its context by inserting observations regarding Elizabeth's Protestant court and the queen herself throughout. The work is dedicated to the "virtues" of Sir Philip Sidney, who had died in 1586, and is addressed to Robert Devereux, the Earl of Essex, a distant cousin of the queen and sometime favorite who would join the Privy Council in the year after Dallington's work was published. Creating a portrait of Elizabeth, Dallington adapts Colonna's descriptions of the beneficent Queen Euterilyda (his translation of Eleuterylida), ruler of a postlapsarian paradise, and Queen Telosia, an inscrutable embodiment of self-interest.[36] As a virgin queen, ruling under the sign of the moon, Elizabeth was aligned much more to the Roman Catholic position, articulated in the Council of Trent, that perpetual virginity was superior to marriage, than to the Protestant position, promoted by the Church of England of which she served as the head, that set marriage above virginity.

This near paradox, which held some personal danger for the queen, serves as the foundation for the complex and shifting figures of women as both sources of power and objects of violence in Edmund Spenser's *The Faerie Queene*. In his "Letter of the Authors," Spenser explains that "in that Faery Queene" he conceives "the most excellent and glorious person of our soueraine the Queene, and her kingdome in Faery land. And yet in some places els, I do otherwise shadow her."[37] In his proem to book 3, he suggests that Cynthia/Elizabeth will find her own portrait "in mirrours more than one."[38] Thus Elizabeth is invited to see something of herself in the figures of Gloriana, the Faerie Queene; in Belphoebe, a virgin of virgin birth and Diana's foster daughter, and in Belphoebe's twin sister, Amoret; in Mercilla, the hesitant judge; and in the warriors Britomart, Elizabeth's ancestor, and Radigund, queen of the Amazons. Spenser's allegory yokes fairy lore to stories of the virgin queen with his depictions of Amphisa and Chrysogone.[39] And in the figure of the evil Duessa, he evokes Protestant representations of the Roman Catholic Church as the "whore of Babylon"—a metaphor taken from the book of Revelation and designed to describe either pagan Rome or fallen Jerusalem, with the cities envisioned as false and corrupt "queens," betrayers of covenants and faiths. Elizabeth's successor, King James I of England (also King James VI of Scotland—son of Mary, Queen of Scots), saw in the trial and execution of Duessa a cruel and threatening recapitulation of his mother's end.[40] Yet Spenser's depiction was hardly original—nor did he have to rely on Revelation alone when the Presbyterian reformer John Knox was writing of Mary Stuart in 1566, "Let men patiently abide and turn unto their God, and then shall he either destroy that whore in her whoredom, or else he shall put it in the hearts of a multitude to take the same vengeance upon her that has been taken of Jezebel and Athaliah."[41]

The Faerie Queene is a compendium of stock female figures, valued and detested alike. It draws from British folklore and ballads telling of fairy women, who seek and evade mortal lovers, and fairy queens who rule over enchanted courts. But it also evokes, as fairy lore itself does, classical myths of nymphs and virgins. With his formal emphasis on mutability and shadows, Spenser underscores the necessary withdrawal and fleetingness of such powerful and elusive figures. Sir Walter Ralegh's first "commendatory verse" for the epic, "A Vision Upon This Conceipt of the Faery Queene," makes an explicit connection to the vestal virgins and Petrarch's own fleeting Laura:

> Me thought I saw the graue, where *Laura* lay
> Within that Temple, where the vestall flame
> Was wont to burne, and passing by that way,
> To see that buried dust of liuing fame,
> Whose tombe faire loue, and fairer virtue kept,
> All suddeinly I saw the Faery Queene . . .

The remainder of the verse describes a weeping "Petrarke" and trembling Homer, master poets superseded by the accomplishment of *The Faerie Queene*.[42] From the proem of book 1, with its apostrophe to Calliope, here "holy Virgin chiefe" of the nine Muses, to the opening glimpse of the Red Crosse Knight accompanying Una, who rides a white ass and is "much whiter" herself, "as pure and innocent" as the "milke white lambe" that accompanies her, the imagery of virginity suffuses the text.[43] The innocent reader herself has yet to experience the disguises, falsehoods, aggression, and wickedness against which Spenser, echoing Paul in Ephesians, warned Ralegh to arm himself.

Spenser's wells, fountains, temples, and altars form a literal architectonics for his epic, and, as does the *Hypnerotomachia*, speak to a love of antiquity—even to the point of uncovering, in book 5, a Temple of Isis at the origin of Elizabeth's heritage in a reference to the Temple of Isis that once stood in Roman London.[44] Spenser and his associates had long explained the collapse of the Roman Empire by its moral failings and, in a milieu of apocalyptic thought, found in that history a lesson for contemporary life. Ancient associations between fountains and nymphs are retained, negatively, for example, in the Bower of Bliss. Spenser expresses a Protestant wariness as he describes the displays of the fountain nymphs and the idolatrous procession before the Knight of Temperance, Guyon. The knight, repeating the gestures of iconoclastic zealots of the 1530s and 1540s, destroys the entire bower.[45] Here ruination is not the slow decay of time mirroring the slow growth of a garden. Instead, Guyon attacks incontinence with gestures hardly continent:

> But all those pleasant bowres and Pallace braue,
> *Guyon* broke down, with rigour pittilesse;
> Ne ought their goodly workmanship might saue
> Them from the tempest of his wrathfulnesse,
> But that their blisse he turn'd to balefulnesse:
> Their groues he feld, their gardins did deface,
> Their arbers spoyle, their Cabinets suppresse,
> Their banket houses burne, their buildings race,
> And of the fairest late, now made the fowlest place.[46]

As with Milton's irrevocably ruined Paradise, the Bower of Bliss is utterly destroyed and lives on only in the words of the poem itself. Spenser himself lived in a series of dissolved and confiscated Irish monasteries and, after 1586, in Kilcolman Castle, which was sacked by rebels in 1598. In book 1, canto 8, stanza 23, he compares the fall of giants to the collapse of a castle:

> Or as a Castle reared high and round,
> By subtile engins and malitious slight
> Is vndermined from the lowest ground,
> And her foundation forst, and feebled quight,
> At last downe falls, and with her heaped hight,
> Her hastie ruine does more heauie make.[47]

This imagery is repeated in book 5, as Artegall rips out the very foundation of Lady Munera's castle as one might pull out a weed:

> And lastly all that Castle quite he raced,
> Euen from the sole of his foundation,
> And all the hewen stones thereof defaced,
> That there mote be no hope of reparation,
> Nor memory thereof to any nation.[48]

The threat of immanent and fulfilled violence runs through *The Faerie Queene*, undermining time with the ready enactment of wishes. Spenser's iconoclastic imagination, its suddenness and irreversibility, adds to the inorganic, near-mineral quality of his epic as a whole.

Spenser's earliest poems, anonymous contributions to Jan van der Noot's *A theatre wherein be represented as wel the miseries & calamities that follow the voluptuous worldlings*, or *A Theatre for Worldlings*, included translations of ruins poetry by Petrarch and Joachim Du Bellay. Van der Noot's *Theatre* was designed as a complaint illustrating the fleetingness of the sensory world: "the vanitie and inconstancie of worldly and transitory thyngs." It begins with a laudatory epistle to Queen Elizabeth, which narrates his suffering as a refugee to England and claims that "it may truly be fayd, that the kingdome of *Saturne*, and the Golden worlde is come againe, and the Virgin *Astrea* is defcended from heauen to builde hir a feate in this your mofte happie countrey of *Englãd*" and reminds the queen of the "dyuers vertuous women"—Debora, Judith, and Hester (Esther)—who delivered the elect of God from the hands of their enemies and persecutors. "The Epistle" is followed by three sets of "emblems": poems and images concerned with ruin and the prophecies of the book of Revelation. Van der Noot sets forth an Augustinian panorama of the decline and fall of the city of man and the triumph of the city of God. He predicts that the Roman Catholic Church will follow the fate of the Roman Empire, and a New Jerusalem will arise as Elizabeth produces the new golden age.[49]

The sonnets and woodcuts of the volumes portray a Rome haunted by nymphs, ghosts, and recognizable temples and obelisks that have collapsed from earthquakes, tempests, and fires. The poems are written in the first person as testimonies to destruction, including the despairing speech of a wailing nymph, a representation of Rome, who sits with arms folded, head thrown back, and mouth open, by a riverbank meant to represent the Tiber. The volume as a whole forms a kind of anti–travel narrative, recounting the disappearance of sites and figures.

In 1591, a year after his publication of the first three books of *The Faerie Queene*, and five years before the remaining three appeared, Spenser published his own *Complaints*—a set of nine poems concerned with "the ruins of time" and including retranslations and tributes to Joachim Du Bellay's 1554 *Antiquités de Rome* (*Antiquities of Rome*). Spenser himself never visited Rome, but Du Bellay was stationed in Rome from 1553 to 1557 in the service of his relative Jean Du Bellay, French ambassador to the papal court.[50] Du Bellay's sonnets emphasize the transience of beauty, and Sonnet 7 is indebted heavily to Castiglione's sonnet "Superbi colli et voi sacre ruine," or "Lofty hills and you, sacred ruin," a poem that had appeared in the context of the plea he and Raphael made to Pope Leo X to protect the monuments of Rome. And the *Antiquités* as well imply the positive effects and consolations of ruins.

Sacrés coteaux, et vous saintes ruines,
Qui le seul nom de Rome retenez,
Vieux monuments, qui encor soutenez
L'honneur poudreux de tant d'âmes divines:

Arcs triomphaux, pointes du ciel voisines,
Qui de vous voir le ciel même étonnez,
Las, peu à peu cendre vous devenez,
Fable du peuple et publiques rapines!

Et bien qu'au temps pour un temps fassent guerre
Les bâtiments, si est-ce que le temps
Œuvres et noms finalement à terre.

Tristes désirs, vivez doncques contents:
Car si le temps finit chose si dure,
Il finira la peine que j'endure.[51]

Ye sacred ruines, and ye tragick sights,
Which onely doo the name of *Rome* retaine,
Olde moniments, which of so famous sprights
The honour yet in ashes doo maintaine:

Triumphant Arcks, spyres neighbours to the skie,
That you to see doth th' heauen it selfe appall,
Alas, by little ye to nothing flie,
The peoples fable, and the spoyle of all:

And though your frames do for a time make warre
Gainst time, yet time in time shall ruinate
Your workes and names, and your last reliques marre.
My sad desires, rest therefore moderate:

For if that time make ende of things so sure,
It als will end the paine, which I endure.[52]

Du Bellay concludes his poem with thoughts like those of Horace on the comparative durability of built forms and poems. He argues, in Spenser's translation, "If under heauen anie endurance were / These moniments, which not in paper writ / But in Porphyre and Marble doo appeare / Might well haue hop'd to haue obtained it." But even now that they are "dead decayes," Du Bellay's ashes of "Poësie" will ensure that the ruins of Rome, and the poet's reputation, too, will survive "eternitie."[53]

Spenser's own poem, "The Ruines of Time," however, presents on the whole a far more bleak view of a landscape stripped even of its ruins, and it is time itself that is the inexorable force of destruction. His poem is a lament spoken beside the river Thames, not—as he first imagines—by a "nymph" of that place like the wailing nymph of van der Noot's *Theatre*, but by a ghostly old woman, who explains she is Verlame, spirit of the vanished Roman settlement of Verulamium. Like the sad and aged Roma of Fazio's *Dittamondo*, Verlame surveys the remains of the city she once knew. She speaks even of her own existence in the past tense:

I was that Citie, which the garland wore
Of Britaines pride, delivered vnto me
By *Romane* Victors, which it wonne of yore;
Though nought at all but ruines now I bee,
And lye in mine own ashes, as ye see:
Verlame I was; what bootes it that I was,
Sith now I am but weedes and wastefull gras?[54]

The poem describes the decay and disappearance of buildings and monuments:

High towers, faire temples, goodly theaters
Strong Walls, rich porches, princelie pallaces
Large streetes, braue houses, sacred sepulchers
Sure gates, sweete gardens, stately galleries
Wrought with faire pillours, and fine imageries
All those (O pitie) now are turned to dust . . .[55]

And where "a thousand nymphs" once played on the banks of the crystal-clear river Thames, only "moorish fennes and marshes" can be found.[56]

The collection of *Complaints* ends with three sequences of visionary sonnets. The "Visions of the worlds vanitie" suggests in closing: "And ye, that read these ruines tragicall, / Learne by their losse to love the low Degree."[57]

The final sequences, "The Visions of Bellay" and "The Visions of Petrarch," are taken respectively from Du Bellay's *Songe*—a sonnet sequence forming a dream vision of the mythology of Rome that Spenser had translated earlier for *A Theatre for Worldlings*—and from various scenes in Petrarch's *Canzone*. Spenser writes in his penultimate sonnet of "The Visions of Petrarch":

> At last, so faire a Ladie did I spie,
> That thinking yet on her I burne and quake;
> On hearbs and flowres she walked pensiuely,
> Milde, but yet loue she proudly did forsake:
> White seem'd her robes, yet wouen so they were,
> As snow and golde together had been wrought.
> Aboue the wast a darke cloude shrouded her,
> A stinging Serpent by the heele her caught;
> Wherewith she languisht as the gathered floure,
> And well assur'd she mounted vp to joy.[58]

The narrative recalls the demise of Eurydice—and, even more, stories of the Virgin Mary and infant Christ each stepping on, and crushing, a serpent representing Satan—and, given the fair lady's death, ends in an echo of the Assumption.

The City as Woman

In the *Hypnerotomachia* the proper names of the lovers, Poliphilus and Polia, as well as the place name, Poly, all indicate the Greek *poly*, or city. Poliphilus is the lover of the city; Polia a feminine version of *polias*, the city's guardian—the name given to Athena as guardian of Athens from the Acropolis. The Neoplatonic sublimation of Poliphilus's desire from sexual knowledge to a knowledge of the genius of antiquity follows the path of this etymology. The author echoes the sentiments of Chrysolaras, who, perusing Roman monuments, wrote in his *Comparison of Old and New Rome* in 1411, "And so, walking through the city, one's eyes are drawn from one work to another, just as lovers never have their fill of wondering at the living beauties and gazing intently at them."[59] Yet the humanist vision of the city, translated as well into an account of Elizabeth's court and kingdom, is haunted by another relation between cities and women. A pervasive, in many ways troubling, theme of the stories of destroyed cities that we have surveyed in the Hebrew scriptures links them to the binary of virgins and whores.

As the story of Jericho indicates, a woman could have agency and be rewarded for her good deeds, even if she were a harlot. But in the story of Lot's daughters, we find the far more common account of women under patriarchy: viewed as property, they could be exchanged as objects of value or compensation with no consideration of their own volition and consent—and their virgin status the basis of their value. In Exodus 22:16–17, for example, we find "And if a man entice a maid that is not betrothed, and lie with her, he shall surely endow her to be his wife. If her father utterly refuse to give her unto him, he shall pay money according to the dowry of virgins."

Ezekiel 16 outlines an extended allegory where Yahweh reminds Jerusalem that he raised her as an orphan and "I clothed thee also with broidered work, and shod thee with badgers' skin, and I girded thee about with fine linen, and I covered thee with silk. I decked thee also with ornaments and I put bracelets upon the hands, and a chain on thy neck. And I put a jewel on thy forehead, and earrings in thine ears, and a beautiful crown upon thine head" (Ezek. 16:10–12). He accuses her of adultery, of sacrificing and slaying the children she has borne him, and adds that "thou hast also unto thee an eminent place, and hast made thee an high place in every street. Thou hast built thy high place at every head of the way, and has made thy beauty to be abhorred, and hast opened thy feet to every one that passed by, and multiplied thy whoredoms" (Ezek. 16:24–25). He mentions specifically her "fornication with the Egyptians," "playing the whore with the Assyrians," and "fornication in the land of Canaan." (Ezek. 16:26–29). He threatens that in retribution he will "give thee blood in fury and jealousy" (Ezek. 16:48) and will "bring up a company against thee" who will stone her and "cut her with swords and burn her houses with fire" (Ezek. 16:40–41).[60]

Why do we continually find themes of virginity, nymphomania, and prostitution in ruins narratives?[61] The theology of the virgin in Western Christianity joins her to the God/man Christ and to countless stories of incorruptible saints as beings that cannot be ruined. Beliefs about virgins are a complex inheritance of a number of attitudes toward the materiality of women's bodies. As we have seen, the stories of the destruction of cities in the Hebrew scriptures, and their legacy in the literature of the Renaissance and the Reformation, abound with metaphors of virgins and prostitutes. And the notion that the downfall of cities is the consequence of promiscuity extends at least to the reflections of the first English visitor to describe the site of Troy: Thomas Coryat observed in 1612, "You may also observe as in a cleere Looking-glasse one of the most pregnant examples of Luxurie, that ever was in the World in these confused heapes of stones that lie before your eyes. For Adulterie was the principall cause of the ruines of this Citie." He concluded that contemporary London was "as much polluted and contaminated with extravagant lusts as ever was this old Troy."[62]

Coryat's analogy underscores a widely believed legendary genealogy that extends from Troy to Rome to London—the Trojan Aeneas fleeing his ruined city to found Rome and the Romans founding Londinium, or, alternatively, the Trojan Brutus, descended from Aeneas in some versions and not in others, himself battling giants to found London and then followed by Dunwallo Mulmutius and Julius Caesar. As early as Geoffrey of Monmouth's twelfth-century *Historia regum Britanniae* and as late as 1577, *Holinshed's Chronicles* cited the Brutus story as historical fact.[63] In book 2, canto 10 of *The Faerie Queene*, Spenser recounts this fabulous history from giants to Trojans to Romans to Saxons to the reign of Pendragon and Arthur and Tudors, weaving into it a line of "Elfin" rulers who will be predecessors to the fairy lineage of his virgin queen "Gloriana."

As Spenser was inventing his faerie queene, Shakespeare was exploring the relationship of founding to chastity in his version of the story of Lucretia. Shakespeare adapts the narrative of the rape of the chaste wife of Collatine (Collatinus) by the king's son Sextus Tarquinius from Ovid's *Fasti* (book 2, lines 721–856) and Livy's *History of Rome* (books 57–59). Ovid's Tarquin grows lustful via memories of capturing the city of Gabii through deception and violence. Shakespeare in turn describes the attack on Lucrece's "sov'reignty" as like the siege of a city: Tarquin, sword and flaming torch in hand, "scale[s]" the doors of her house, the curtains about her bed, and the "ivory wall" of her body, and her blue-veined breasts with "round turrets destitute and pale."[64] Ruined, Lucrece is haunted by images from a painting or tapestry that depicts the fall of Troy. She, too, thinks of Tarquin as a ruthless invader: she compares him to Pyrrhus as he enters the penetralia of Priam's palace. She is drawn to the portrait of despairing Hecuba: "In her the painter had anatomized / Time's ruin, beauty's wrack, and grim care's reign" and she condemns Helen, "the strumpet that began this stir." She sees in the treachery of Sinon an allegory of Tarquin's deception.[65]

The tautology of Lucrece's suicide is the exercise of an agency that has only itself available as an object, and her self-sacrifice is her only means to reverse the damage Tarquin has brought to her social status.[66] In Livy, Ovid, and Shakespeare alike, Tarquin threatens a scenario that will damage her beyond the suffering of the rape itself. As Ovid writes, "'It's no good,' he said. 'I'll take your life through accusations. I, the adulterer, will be false witness to adultery. I'll kill a slave, and it'll be said you were caught with him.' Overcome by fear for her reputation, the young woman yielded."[67] By destroying her body, Lucrece preserves her reputation. In a reclamation that underscores the terms of their initial exchange, her father and husband express a duet of grief:

> The one doth call her his, the other his,
> Yet neither may possess the claim they lay.
> The father says "She's mine" "O, mine she is,"
> Replies her husband: "do not take away
> My sorrow's interest; let no mourner say
>   He weeps for her, for she was only mine,
>   And only must be wail'd by Collatine."

"O," quoth Lucretius, "I did give that life
Which she too early and too late hath spill'd."
"Woe, woe," quoth Collatine, "she was my wife,
I owned her, and 'tis mine that she hath kill'd."
"My daughter" and "my wife" with clamours fill'd
　　The dispersed air, who, holding Lucrece's life,
　　Answer'd their cries, "my daughter" and "my wife."[68]

Her kinsman Junius Brutus, overlooking the scene, declares that Rome "herself in them doth stand disgraced" and he spurs his fellow Romans to revenge.[69] The story becomes an etiological legend about the founding of the Roman Republic, and Lucrece endures as an eternally allegorized figure of female chastity.

When women are considered to be objects of such transmission and exchange, virginity and chastity, on the one hand, and prostitution and promiscuity, on the other, are complementary aspects of the same frame for the materiality of their bodies. In Sextus Tarquinius's deliberations in advance of his crime, he imagines the only valid reason he could "work upon" Lucrece would be "Had Collatinus kill'd my son or sire." Lucrece summons her father and her husband at dawn to the scene of her "confession," demand for revenge, and self-sacrifice; the terms of their pact regarding her living body are translated into a new bond forged by her death.[70] Shakespeare follows Ovid and Livy in making the larger consequence of her death the male bonds that will found the new political order. He underscores that it is her blood that her kinsman Brutus, holding her dagger aloft, claims as the force generating the miraculous social cohesion that enables "the Romans" to overthrow the kingship of Tarquin, bringing about his "everlasting banishment."[71]

Virginity from a social standpoint is unspent exchange value while prostitution is exchange value in process. For the ancient Greeks, feminine virginity was not just a membrane, veil, or net which was or was not intact; it was of more importance as a biographical fact that would have to be stated negatively—by what one did not experience rather than what one actually underwent.[72] Even at the time of Hippocrates, women and their physicians were aware that a physician himself could perforate a membrane at the entrance to the womb in the course of an examination.[73] In his meditation on Lucrece, Augustine worries about virgins who might commit suicide in the face of violation, and he considers the case of "a midwife" who "trying a certain maid's integrity of the virginal part (whether for malice, or by chance, it is uncertain), spoiled it."[74] Ambrose and Augustine objected to the physical verification of virginity, holding that virginity was a moral or ethical state and not a physical one.[75] The usefulness of this position for explanations of the virgin birth of Christ is evident: a virgin mother, like the chaste spouse she becomes, remains uncorrupted so long as she possesses what Ambrose termed *mentis integritas*—integrity of the spirit.[76]

Is it merely because virginity has exchange value—a daughter's virginity is offered in exchange for the "bride price"—and, surrendered or awarded alike, that it can be "spoiled"? Each human being acknowledges, and invents understandings of, the unremembered period before birth and the unknown period after death. We ourselves are the evidence that our births existed, though our experience of it eludes us; our deaths, defined by the end of bodily experience, necessarily remain pure speculation: a certainty without particulars—our knowledge of the mother's body. The mythic suspended state of virginity, fetishizing not so much the originary space beyond the veil of the hymen as its penetration, has presented an enduring epistemological allegory in Western culture.[77]

Prototypes of virgin protectresses, the Roman vestal virgins safeguarded their environment as they safeguarded their own bodies. Six priestesses, chosen between the ages of six and ten, the women were bound to their virginity for a minimum of thirty years, after which they were free to marry. In their persons and their rituals they are symbols of purity, order, and continuity: all in the service of ensuring the preservation of the state. Horace's Ode 3, as we have seen, thinks of eternal fame as lasting "as long as the priest climbs the Capitol with the silent virgin." The vestal virgins appear within the context of the *pudicitia*, or modesty, demanded of the chaste Roman matron. Yet, as the classicist Mary Beard has emphasized, "Throughout all the ancient sources which deal with the priesthood great stress is laid on the physical virginity of the women and their total abstinence from sexual intercourse during their thirty years or more in the college. It is an element which is integrated into the mythologizing stories of early priestesses, several of whom saved themselves from the charge of unchastity by the performance of miracles aided by Vesta herself, and it recurs in the historical period when we see that serious crises in the state could give rise to suspicions of sexual activity among the Vestals." Severed from their families and hence from the patriarchal system of marriage exchange, the vestals were abstracted beings embodying the citizenry of Rome—their marginal and sacred status made them all the more likely to be taken as scapegoats at times of crisis.[78] Lapsed, or simply accused, vestals were killed by being buried alive in underground chambers provided with a lit lamp, milk, water, oil and bread.[79] The vestal Tuccia famously proved her innocence by carrying water in a sieve from the Tiber to the Forum.[80] The vestal Minucia was buried in 337 BCE when her chastity became suspect, and at times the Sibylline oracles were consulted to determine the vestals' sexual status.[81]

Like virgin nymphs, vestal virgins are associated with the free flow and safety of water. Their water rites included managing the ritual use of water in connection with sacrifice; administering water as a purificatory libation to the dead; washing the sacra; washing their domicile at the Forum, the *aedes*, and using water to make *muries*, a kind of brine. They could use only fresh, running water that had never touched the earth directly in these rites, and the water had to be gathered from the spring of Juturna, the goddess of streams, fountains, and wells.[82]

But the primary domain of the vestal virgin is the hearth and sacred fire which must be maintained perpetually within the *aedes* if Rome is to be protected from harm. Plutarch, in his *Life of Numa* (9) describes this obligation:

> If by any chance [the fire] goes out, . . . then they say it must not be kindled again from other fire, but made fresh and new, by lighting a pure and unpolluted flame from the rays of the Sun. And this they usually effect by means of metallic mirrors, the concavity of which is made to follow the sides of an isosceles rectangular triangle, and which converge from their circumference to a single point in the centre. When, therefore, these are placed opposite the sun, so that its rays, as they fall upon them from all sides, are collected and concentrated at the centre, the air itself is rarefied there, and very light and dry substances placed there quickly blaze up from its resistance, the sun's rays now acquiring the substance and force of fire.[83]

The vestals performed nine annual state rites. The first would be New Year's rites on the first of March, the last the women's mystery rites of Bona Dea in December.[84]

Water and fire, those forces of destruction, are transformed into elements of protective and purifying rites in the practices of the vestal virgins. Along with grain and products made of grain, the cult manipulates these elements. Accompanying the vestals are donkeys, who mysteriously appear in the Vestalian rites ornamented with loaves of bread. As animals that breed at any time and establish no particular bonds between coupling pairs, they are notorious in Latin literature, and world folklore, for their sexual proclivity.[85] Here donkeys serve the vestals by carrying their ritual implements, as the Gospels promise that Christ will arrive on a donkey and other accounts tell of donkeys bearing the Virgin Mother herself: the vagaries of animal lust are managed by sacred rule.

Yet the perfected, intact virginity of the vestal arose from the conditions of a dangerous marginality: severed from blood ties, the abstracted sexuality of the vestal nourished and sustained the state while the vestal herself remained a being with a body and could serve as well as an object given over to sacrifice. After the advent of Christianity, the vestals were in the precarious position of continuing to guarantee the preservation of the city and its inhabitants, and at the same time suffering the decline of pagan beliefs in general. In chapter 3 of his *De virginibus*, Ambrose criticizes the vestal virgins. He asks how virginity can be quantified by years of service and questions whether a woman can be a virgin for those defined years and then marry. He notes the low number of candidates for the position in his own time, claiming the extant vestals were recruited with difficulty.[86]

The Virgin Mary

It is telling that when the nymphs bring Poliphilo before three doors, in a reprise of a well-known motif of fairy tales and folktales, he must choose among the passages marked *Gloria Dei*, *Gloria Mundi*, and *Mater Amoris*. To the disdain of Logistica, he chooses the last door, bridging the gap between heaven and earth.

The Virgin Mary is a relatively late development in Christianity. The first mention of direct worship of her seems to be in the early fifth century. The cult of the Virgin first developed in Syria but eventually spread throughout the Greek-speaking church. Mary was given the title of *theotokos*, or "God bearer," at the Council of Ephesus in 431. Her perpetual virginity became established doctrine at the Fifth Ecumenical Council of 553. It was reaffirmed at the Lateran Synod in 649.[87] Against the Nestorian belief that Mary was mother only of the human aspects of Christ, the Council of Ephesus in 431 upheld the Monophysite contention that she was the mother of God. This emphasis upon the supernatural aspect of Mary's virgin maternity thus comes to stand in contrast to the belief that Mary is responsible for the human dimension of Christ. Unlike, for example, a nymph who will bear only mortals to mortals and immortals to immortals, Mary bears a hybrid being. Although she is human, she has qualities, such as her sinlessness, that distinguish her from other humans.[88]

Eve and Mary are both represented as virgins. Eve's fall, and consequently the fall of all of her descendants, is redeemed through the virginity of Mary as she sustains her perfection and innocence. Virginity emphasizes that the ideal world of Paradise gave way to one of a harsh and resistant materiality—a materiality underscored by the resistance of the world to human labor and the pain of childbirth.[89] Eve's children are flawed, born in pain and suffering from a murderous sibling rivalry; Eve's are sacrifices of first fruits and the blood sacrifice of animals. Eve is banished from Paradise into endless work and inevitable death. Mary's child, in contrast, is a sacrifice that Christians believe to be an endless redemption. Mary will not die the death of a mortal being—instead she is transported to heaven.[90]

In the multitude of accounts of the Virgin Mary, in the devotional writings of not only the Christian church, but also as Mary appears in the Qur'an and Muslim commentaries, the emphasis on sacrifice and sacramental culture[91] links her to the vestal virgins and other sacrificial virgins. As Giulia Sissa has noted in the context of a study of virginity from the Greeks forward, early Christianity continually joined its concept of virginal material integrity to metaphors of the *sigillo* (the seal or print), the closed door, the cloister, the septum or separating wall, and the hedge or boundary.[92] As the protection of the bodies and *aedes* of the vestal virgins, in an obvious symbolism, ensured that the larger walls of Rome were intact, in medieval writing the fortified tower became a metaphor for the figure of the celibate monk and virgin.[93] In devotional literature written for women, the symbolic rendering of virginity by means of the metaphor of the fortified place is also common, but, as in the Old English *Juliana*, in the form of an allegory of the castle of the body wherein the body's integrity safeguards the resident soul. In Hali Meidenhad, "the high tower of Jerusalem" typifies the state of virginity: the maiden stands and looks down upon those leading a less exalted life. There the high tower of Jerusalem is called "Sion," indicating both "exalted vision" and the elevated state of virginity.[94]

The Virgin Mary herself is designated by the early church fathers and ritual practice as the "Temple of the Temple." This imagery evolves through particular typological relations between the Hebrew scriptures and the Gospels as well. As "Temple of the Temple" and "Mother of the Church," she is associated with ancient Hebrew temple cults as retrospectively conceived in the Christian imaginary. An early hymn, "Kontakion for the Presentation of Mary in the Temple," describes her as "the temple most pure of the savior. / The bridal-chamber most precious, the Virgin / The sacred treasury of the glory of God." The historian of Mariology Cleo Kearns has described how, in the liturgy, Mary "enters into the temple of the Lord, bringing with her the grace of the divine spirit. Therefore, it is said, the angels of god sing to her: 'This is the heavenly tabernacle.'"[95] Gregory of Nyssa recounts the legend of Zechariah, the priest who was Mary's caretaker in childhood and who arranged that she could remain in the temple precinct reserved for preadolescent virgins between the court and the altar even after she came of age. Gregory writes of how Zechariah permitted Mary to remain because she represented "a new kind of generation" wherein a mother could be a virgin.[96]

Kearns describes the recurrence of this motif in further patristic writings. For Jerome, too, Mary is the temple of the "temple of God" in the specific sense that the Temple of Solomon served to house the ark of the covenant, itself a sacred enclosure. Jerome explains, "Only Christ opened the closed doors of the virginal womb, which continued to remain closed, however. This is the closed eastern gate, through which only the high priest may enter and exit and which nevertheless is always closed." Gregory of Nazianzus declares that "the God man was born from the Virgin's womb, which the Spirit of the great God formed, constructing a pure temple to house the Temple. For the Mother is the temple of Christ, while Christ is the temple of the Word."[97] In other legends and myths of the Virgin, she is described within this enclosed space, weaving or reading, at the time of the Annunciation, or leaving the precinct of temple and home to draw water from a well.[98]

A perfected and intact body finds its apt metaphor in such an enclosed space, just as the walls and turrets of Lucrece's sleeping form symbolized chastity. But the Roman ethos of the chaste woman remains physical and literal— Lucrece's ruin cannot be overcome by a transcendent or spiritual reframing.

With Christianity, the birth of the infant God, prophesied by the interruption and intrusion of the annunciating angel, marks a moment of transformation as another architectural metaphor for Mary's being, "the passable gate," is applied to the story of her (non)labor. Ezekiel 44:2 had declared of the gate of the Temple: "This gate shall be shut. It shall not be opened and no man shall enter in by it: because the LORD, the God of Israel, hath entered in by it." Interpreting this passage as a prophecy of the virgin birth, Amphilochius, the bishop of Iconium, declared in the fourth century, "As regards the virginal nature, the virginal gates were not at all opened; as regards the power of the Lord who was born, nothing is closed to the Lord."[99] In medieval England, the "passable gate" imagery appears in several Old English Advent Lyrics (2, 4, and 9) where Mary is viewed as the embodiment of the promised gate for God's passing into the city of humanity. Lyric 9 particularly says she is "the gate, unique, through which the Ruling Lord / into this earth journied forth."[100] In his anti-Semitic "Prioress's Tale," Chaucer drew on this imagery, having his clergeon sing the antiphon to Mary from the Advent to Candlemas. The hymn begins, "Alma redemptoris mater, quae pervia caeli / Porta manes, et stella maris . . ." (Nourishing mother of the redeemer, who / remains the passable gate of heaven and star of the sea . . .).[101]

The Shattered Image

In the fourth century, early Christians attacked and destroyed statuettes of Isis.[102] In a similar fashion, after the Reformation, and particularly during the frenzies of iconoclasm, representations of the Virgin were subjected to violence. As buildings were destroyed and tens of thousands of monks and nuns were dispersed, a 1535 proclamation declared that all "idols and false reliques" should be "utterly . . . abolished, eradicated and erased out." Six years later, zealous Protestants in Ely attacked the town's fourteenth-century Lady Chapel. They destroyed all the shrines, pictures, paintings, and "coverings" of shrines so that "there remain no memory of it." They also severely defaced the chapel, most often by "beheading"—smashing—all the statues. Local reformers rode their horses into the building's interior, decapitating and mutilating all the statues they could reach from their perches in the saddle.[103]

What does it mean to "behead" a statue? This violence wrought upon things can be viewed as a transposition of the archaic relation between virgin sacrifice and the safety of the state: whereas once the person must be sacrificed, now the image of the person must be destroyed, much as it was in the practice of *damnatio memoriae* by the ancient Romans. Yet here the erasure is not so much of the memory of the exalted person as an attack on representation itself. A powerful taboo continues across stories of a sacrificed virginity and a destroyed image: the taboo of the gaze, of seeing as a mode of possession and penetration.

The Roman Catholic virgin saints Katherine, Margaret, Barbara, Agnes, and others—so often subjected to spectacular and horrible deaths by torture—are also subject to the pain of exposure. When Agnes is stripped in punishment for rejecting the advances of the local prefect, her hair instantly grows to cover her and she is enveloped by light. Barbara is a virgin of great beauty, and her pagan father puts her in a tower to protect her virtue and keep her unseen. Lucy, patroness of the blind, removes her own eyes when they are the object of amorous admiration. These saints are venerated and sought after not only because of the heroic dramas they evoke but also because, like Mary and John the Evangelist, they are seen as sources of intercessory power. Virginity, as the concrete realization of spirit over body, was something to be tapped in moments of difficulty.[104]

Under the aegis of iconoclastic fervor, as shrines at Walsingham, Woolpit, Willesden, Penrhys, and Ipswich faded into ruins, stories and beliefs faded as well. The many "holy wells" associated with Marian shrines, including those at Woolpit and Walsingham, had been said to "spring up" from under the Virgin's feet as she walked in these sites. Wells were filled with rubbish as they also became "wishing wells," stripped of sacred significance yet retaining some of their magical powers.[105] A sixteenth-century poem, "The Stripping of the Altars," in the Bodleian Library sets out a desolate picture of post-Reformation Walsingham that eerily echoes the Old English "Ruin" poem. It describes the site's "sacred vines" "rooted up by the swine"; the grass growing over the walls; the towers "level with the ground"; and "no gates" where there were gates. It concludes:

> Owls do shriek where the sweetest hymns
> Lately were sung;
> Toads and serpents hold their dens
> Where the palmers did throng.
> Weep, weep, O Walsingham,
> Whose days are nights,
> Blessings turned to blasphemies,
> Holy deeds to despites.
> Sin is where Our Lady sat,
> Heaven turned is to hell.
> Satan sits where Our Lord did sway;
> Walsingham, O, farewell.[106]

The Afterlife of the Ruined Virgin

This dynamic between the eternal desire of the nymph and the perfected integrity of the virgin has had a long afterlife in the culture. It might make us wonder if the relation between the ruin of women and the stability of the world is a powerful cultural puzzle, rooted in the physiological ambiguity of paternity and the paradoxes that flow from a veneration of women that is tied to their denigration.

The *Hypnerotomachia* and *The Faerie Queene* share certain features: emblematic readings of text and imagery, themes of ruined worlds, a fascination with a virginal innocence, techniques that simulate the effects of dreams through the expansion of seemingly minor details; the omission of crucial elements of a plot; the incorporation of contradictions, repetitions, and obscure allusions. And these textual attributes are found as well in the illuminated works of William Blake. Blake, despite his aversion to allegory, several times expressed his enthusiasm for Spenser and found *The Faerie Queene* to be "full of vision."[107] But had Blake seen a copy of the *Hypnerotomachia*? Ben Jonson's copy of the Aldine edition was in Sir Hans Sloane's collection at the British Museum, where it remains today. Meanwhile, the 1546 and 1561 French versions and Dallington's 1592 version, with its vastly truncated selection of images, were available in private hands. As early as 1757, the British Library had copies of the 1546 and 1561 French editions.[108] But perhaps the most likely candidate for a copy that Blake might have seen was the Aldine first edition belonging to the physician William Hunter—a volume now in the University of Glasgow Library. Hunter's *Anatomy* was illustrated with engravings by James Basire, to whom Blake was apprenticed, and Blake ridiculed Hunter's surgeon brother John as "Jack Tearguts" in his satire *An Island in the Moon*.[109]

Among Blake's many established influences are the Hebrew scriptures and a collection of Old Master prints he possessed whose content we can only guess, for in the winter of 1819–1820 he sold them to the dealer Colnaghi, and the company's holdings and archives were destroyed in a later fire. Blake wrote of himself as a young man, "I Saw and I Knew immediately the difference between Rafael & Rubens," and he left a record of his great admiration for Albrecht Dürer and Maerten van Heemskerck.[110] Virginity and ruin are themes that suffuse his work, and he continually associated the process of printmaking with a descent into, and emergence from, processes of destruction. As he famously wrote in *The Marriage of Heaven and Hell* of the "infernal process" of etching with acids, "first the notion that man has a body distinct from his soul, is to be expunged: this I shall do by printing in the infernal method, by corrosives, which in Hell are salutary and medicinal, melting apparent surfaces away, and displaying the infinite which was hid. . . . If the doors of perception were cleansed everything would appear to man as it is: Infinite."[111]

Blake's lurid and replete imagination was accompanied by a desire for a natural innocence. It is not surprising that, as the *Hypnerotomachia* succeeds in presenting an eroticism burdened neither by mere lust nor by unthinking convention, Blake continually pursued a notion of virginity that could survive, even thrive, within experience. Some of his concept came from Spenser's view of chastity, particularly in book 3 of *The Faerie Queene*, where chastity is clearly distinguished from celibacy as a natural phase of life that could be carried over into wedded sexual experience as faithfulness. In Blake's 1793 *Visions of the Daughters of Albion*, Oothoon is raped by Bromion but asserts she is a virgin: "Innocence! honest, open, seeking / The vigorous joys of morning light; open to virgin bliss" and "a virgin fill'd with virgin fancies / Open to joy and to delight." She contrasts her state of metaphysical virginity to the "hypocrite modesty" of those who are mere physical virgins waiting to trade virginity for marriage—her love Theotormon remains fixated in jealousy by the loss of her physical virginity and is unable to recognize the "pleasures of [her] free born joy."[112] Here Blake was indebted to Mary Wollstonecraft, who had written in her 1792 *A Vindication of the Rights of Woman: With Strictures on Political and Moral Subjects* that "with respect to [women's reputation], the attention is confined to a single virtue—chastity."[113] Wollstonecraft deplored the demeaning of women's moral agency if their honor was based solely on that virtue.

Visions of the Daughters of Albion remains a kind of sketch for Blake's last works, wherein Albion is mired in materialism and convention, a Babylon awaiting redemption. Jerusalem will be built on the site of London only when the shackles of materialism, ceremony, and rational calculation are freed by a genuine Christian morality and the arts of poetry, painting, and music. Perhaps here is the greatest achievement of Blake's overpowering originality—his model of a wise innocence forged in, but ultimately transcending, the material exigencies of existence. In Blake's view, only through a necessary fall or collapse can Albion flourish. It is ruin and transformation that empower the "open seeking" achievement of joy and the generative possibilities of language and creation.

Blake's Oothoon is only one of his virgins and nymphs. Oothoon herself asks a marigold in Leutha's vale, "Art thou a flower! Art thou a nymph!" and "the golden nymph" tells her she can pluck the flower, for another flower will arise in its place. Blake here holds a Neoplatonic view of nymphs as spirits of generation—out of the matter of water, all life and thought will spring.[114] In his "Book of Thel" of 1789, the daughters of Mne Seraphim follow pastoral lives around a spring. They are content except for the melancholy youngest daughter, Thel, who holds conversations about her fleeting mortality with her fellow virgins "the little virgin of the peaceful valley" (a lily of the valley) and the "virgins of the skies" (a little cloud). They reveal the mutual ephemerality and purposiveness of their own lives and remind Thel that she will serve the important purpose of becoming the food of worms. The Cloud sends her to speak with the Worm, who reminds her that "we live not for ourselves" and declares that he simply lives and loves, beloved by God. The "matron Clay" then hears Thel's pitying tears and leads her to "enter with [her] virgin feet" the land of the Dead. There she sees her own grave plot and hears a voice that laments the misuse and waste of the senses—the human ear, eye, eyelids, tongue, ear, and nostrils. The voice ends by lamenting, "Why a tender curb upon the youthful burning boy! / Why a little curtain of flesh on the bed of our desire?" The virgin Thel leaps up and with a shriek returns to the spring of the vales of Har. In the end, Blake has made his way through a critique of virginity, revealed to his protagonist layer by layer, conversation by conversation, through these encounters of forms of life; the end of her innocence will be the beginning of her existence.[115]

We have explored some of the ways that "mountain ruin" and architectural decay are central to the themes of Goethe's interpretation of the Faust legend. He also turned in *Faust*, parts 1 and 2 alike, to themes of women's chastity and destruction. Two contrary, but intertwined, figures of ruin stand at the center of his work: the village girl Margaret, who worships the Virgin Mary and is found by the well with other adolescent girls, speaking of virginity and sexual initiation; and the familiar classical figure of destruction and beauty, Helen of Troy. It is Faust's dream of Helen as an idealized figure of woman, some time before he sees a vision of the actual Margaret/Gretchen, that prompts his own initial seduction by Mephistopheles. When Faust tempts Margaret with boxes of jewelry, the first box is confiscated by her mother and dedicated to the Virgin, via the rapacious local priests: Margaret's mother is sure that the Virgin will reward them with "Himmels-Manna" (manna from heaven).[116]

After the scene by the well, where girls gossip about their ruined peer, Barbara, Margaret puts fresh flowers in earthen jugs beneath a Madonna in a niche of the city wall and prays to the Virgin, asking her to save her from shame and death. When Gretchen is with the congregation in the cathedral, an Evil Spirit stands behind her, describing how trumpets are sounding, sepulchers quaking. The walls and pillars close in on her, and the vaulted ceiling comes crashing down. Faust acknowledges that he has brought about her ruin, comparing himself to a "wild waterfall":

> And as I passed—she, childlike, innocent,
> A hut, a meadow on the mountain-slope,
> A home like that, such sweet content,
> Her little world, her little scope!
> And I, whom God had cursed,
> Rocks could not satisfy
> My rage to rive and burst
> And wreck as I rushed by!
> I had to ruin her, to undermine
> Her peace; she was our victim, hell's and mine![117]

Faust is further tormented by Mephistopheles in the prose section "Gloomy Day. Open Country," who asks "Who was it who ruined her? I, or you?"[118] Part 1 ends with the quiet salvific reassurance of Gretchen's ascent to heaven.

In the phantasmagoria that is *Faust* part 2, the figure of Helen of Troy never expresses the simple realism of the Margaret/Gretchen persona. And

Helen's mythic status is underlined as other female figures appear—the witch-like Mothers who give Faust the magic to conjure up the shades of Paris and Helen, the many nymphs and nereids, the sirens, and the doomed women of Troy who accompany Helen back to her Spartan palace. The specter of Troy haunts the entire work, as Nereus sings in act 2, telling of his unheeded prophecy: "... I foresaw it: fire and smoke upstirred, / Bloodying the air, roof-timbers all aglow, / Slaughter and carnage down below; / Troy's ordeal, captured in a poet's spell."[119]

In part 2, the decline of Pan, the account of the Fall in the Hebrew scriptures, and the theme of salvation through the intercession of the feminine are not only taken up but also broadly extended: the final scenes reveal Faust saved from damnation by the Mater Gloriosa and a resurrected Gretchen. The last section of the work, "Mountain-Gorges, Forest, Cliff, Wilderness," is peopled by holy anchorites who live scattered on the mountainsides in the clefts of rocks. Faust, as a purified soul transmuted into the anchorite Doctor Marianus, sings a hymn to the Virgin and is accompanied by a chorus of penitent women, including Gretchen. The chorus proclaims in the work's last words, "Das Ewig-Weibliche / Zieht uns hinan" ("Eternal Womanhood / Draws us on high").[120]

Goethe's two sojourns in Rome—from November 1786 to February 1787 and from June 1787 to April 1788—were a spiritual and aesthetic resource to him for the rest of his life; his tremendous effort to reconcile a northern vernacular, a Romantic individualism, and classical concepts of beauty finds its lasting form in the final accomplishment of his *Faust*. Yet Goethe's relationship with Christiane Vulpius—after 1788, his mistress and later wife, who, like Margaret, was raised in a lower social class—expressed a sexual freedom and refusal of convention that he had practiced, in life and in his poetry, from the period of his Roman residency and the subsequent composition, between 1788 and 1790, of his *Römische Elegien* (*Roman Elegies*) forward. The sequence begins with the first elegy's imploring questions:

Saget, Steine, mir an, o sprecht, ihr hohen Paläste!
Straßen, redet ein Wort! Genius, regst du dich nicht?

Speak to me, stones, o say, you lofty palaces, tell me—
Streets, are you lost for a word? Spirit of Rome, are you mute?[121]

Yet despite the many allusions to Rome's monuments and to the classical love poets—Tibullus, Catullus, and Propertius—who are his models, Goethe's elegies continually return to the immediate experience of the room where he makes love with "Faustina," who may have been an Italian woman or an amalgam of several women formed during his process of composition. The last lines of the first poem proclaim:

Amors Tempel, nur sein, der den Geweihten empfängt
Eine Welt zwar bist du, o Rom; doch ohne die Liebe
Wäre die Welt nicht die Welt, wäre denn Rom auch nicht Rom.

Love's great temple, and I'll be its initiate then.
Rome, though you are a whole world,
Yet a world without love would be no world,
And if there were no love, Rome would not even be Rome.[122]

The entire sequence plays even more on two historical puns or, we might say, rhymes: first, the palindrome hidden in these lines about love and Rome: ROMA/AMOR; and second, the myth of the vestal virgin Rhea Sylvia, recounted in the third of the Roman elegies. Fetching water from the Tiber, Rhea Sylvia was raped by Mars and impregnated with the founders of the city—the twins Romulus and Remus. The vestal theme of a continually burning fire runs throughout the elegy sequence as the fire in the lovers' bedroom becomes the symbol of their ardor. In the long fifteenth elegy, Goethe rapidly retells the story of the rise of the city from simple huts to ruin, claiming that

Sahst eine Welt hier entstehn, sahst dann eine Welt hier in Trümmern,
    Aus den Trümmern aufs neu fast eine größere Welt!

This was the birth of a world, and you saw it then perish in ruins,
    But from the ruins perhaps something still greater arose.[123]

The poet's narrative is hurried, excited, for his lover has just told him, in symbols sketched in wine on a table, the hour for a nighttime meeting. In the ninth elegy he writes:

Herbstlich leuchtet die Flamme vom ländlich geselligen Herde,
    Knistert und glänzet, wie rasch! sausend vom Reisig empor.
. . . .
Morgen frühe geschäftig verläßt sie das Lager der Liebe,
    Weckt aus der Asche behend Flammen aufs neue hervor . . .

Now on the rustic welcoming hearth an autumnal fire glows,
    Kindled from crackling wood, brilliant with uprushing flame.
. . . .
Early tomorrow she'll busily rise from the bed of our loving;
    Quickly the ashes she'll stir, soon the bright flame she'll renew . . .[124]

Goethe in 1788 wrote in a letter that he would like his tomb to be under the shadow of the Pyramid of Cestius in the Protestant cemetery,[125] and his son was buried there in 1830. In Tischbein's well-known portrait of Goethe stretched, in his white coat and large-brimmed hat, on the ground across the remains of a fallen obelisk, a ruin stands in the distance on the horizon (see plate 4). Goethe is resting along the Via Appia, and the ruin is the tomb of Caecilia Metella, whom Goethe, following nineteenth-century guidebooks, would have known mistakenly as a notoriously "fallen" woman.[126]

Hamartia

In an arresting passage in his 1988 book *The Experience of Freedom,* Jean-Luc Nancy writes of ruin as a matter of choice between the freedom of existence and the reification of essence:

> Hasn't thinking decided, he says, at the most intimate point of its decision for decision, in favor of the "grace" of existence, and not of the fury of essence? (And moreover, since it is henceforth time to ask the following: can we speak of "grace" and "fury," of "healing" and of "ruin," without having allowed a decision to be made by language[?]) ... For if the existent can decide on ruin and on its own ruin, and if this possibility is inscribed in the very being of existence, such a decision is no less what also ruins the decision in its existential essence.[127]

The ruin of persons, unlike the passive destruction of inanimate matter and the suffering of animals, is informed by the autotelic potential of human action and the inevitable limits of human knowledge. Nancy is concerned, as Western thinkers have been since Aristotle, with the notion of *hamartia,* or tragic error. If we can choose our ruin—if we are free to err—we will suffer damage (losing power, riches, or health), but we will not lose our capacity for free will. Oedipus, Hamlet, and Lear err from ignorance or weakness, and their ruin is individual; it is what characterizes their histories and makes them significant.

The cliché we have been pursuing of the ruined woman, trapped within a sense of a woman's life as synonymous with her status as a reproducing organism, cannot be "corrected" by saying that such status "does not matter"—mattering is irreducible. Instead, any correction or countering must begin with an assumption of a woman's existence as an acting, thinking, agent, capable of her own ruination, even her own destruction, for only under such conditions could a chosen fate have meaning. Here is a difference between the passive suffering of Hecuba and Andromache and the willful errors of Medea and Antigone. Yet it is perhaps a deeper tragedy that these ancient models of free will are retrogressive: Medea and Antigone represent the "logic" of the old gods, of blood tie and chthonic sacrifice, and return us again to the materiality of women's being.

IV. Matrix

HUMANISM AND THE RISE
OF THE RUINS PRINT

Foreground/Background

The convention of placing ruins in the background of Nativity scenes spread from the fifteenth century forward from Italy to the North. By the early sixteenth century, particularly in the period following the Sack of Rome of 1527, northern artists began to visit Italy, and ruins images traveled back and forth from Rome to Antwerp, Prague, and other northern centers of artistic activity. By the seventeenth century, paintings of ruins underwent a change in function. Monsù Desiderio and Salvator Rosa introduced a moody landscape style that envisions ruins as occasions for artists to flaunt their skill with subtle color and effects of light. Architectural ornament is used as a design motif for the painting rather than as an index to identify specific buildings or celebrate the Christian precedence over the pagan past. Nicolas Poussin's heroic landscapes use classical ruins and fragments as part of their foregrounded narratives, with complete buildings in the distance like vivid memories.[1] His *Landscape with the Funeral of Phocion* shows the pallbearers moving through a path of stone fragments while an intact city looms far in the background. This mode of placing intact and broken elements adds to the great depth of field and feeling of movement in Poussin's narrative work.

The emerging sophistication in perspective views during the Renaissance was tied in the West to the archaeological rediscovery of Roman illusionist painting. And in representations of ruins we see that perspective—specifically the single-point-perspective grid—is what binds the ruin image as surely as scaffolding binds a collapsing building. Clouds and vegetation, which do not require the use of perspective lines, inevitably seem to serve as the counterpoint and complement to an image organized around planes and vanishing point.

We cannot speak of works of visual art that are no longer extant nor of those that lack any record, yet it is evident that the visual representation of ruins flowered after the advent of Christianity. The tradition of representing ruins in poetry, as we have seen, extends, so far as we know, from ancient

Egypt forward, and such poetry more often than not is compensatory—the level of descriptive detail counters the erasure and abstraction that ruination produces; the loss of the past often will involve a commitment to the future, or at least the inference of a moral that will be of eventual use. Petrarch wrote to his friar friend Colonna, reminding him of what he surely already knew, that the presence of ruins brings to the fore "that part of philosophy which deals with morals . . . and sometimes indeed we discussed the arts and their authors and rules."[2] As we saw in the late medieval frescos of Maso di Banco, a didactic function often accompanies the visual representation of ruins as well. And yet ruins come to play an important part, too, in the development of the descriptive arts of mapmaking and landscape representations. Stripped of their brilliant colors by time, they lend themselves to the black-and-white reproductions of drawings, engravings, and etching; losing their edges, they are captured by an art of outlines, flicks, and abrasion; porous to vegetation and decay, their clarity dissolves, as does that of the plate the more it is used; above all, formless forms, they suggest more than they denote.[3]

The theme of ruins became central to the emerging practice of printmaking, an art that could be multiple, portable, and widely disseminated. The fate of ruins and the fate of prints have been yoked from the early Renaissance into the present. This congruence of theme and medium begins with a homology between the printmaker's process and the evolution of ruins themselves. Printmaking is indeed a process of ruination. Using an engraving needle, burin, or other device to cut into wood, copper, tin, or, with the advent of lithography, stone to create the image, printmakers not only rely on unidirectional lines, they also use stippling and cross-hatching techniques that resemble effects of weather and geology. The etcher, as we say, "bites" the surface with acids and water and inks made of vegetable compounds. In the end, the printmaker inscribes a mineral surface with meaning and form. He or she uses many of the same processes that have resulted, in the case of ruins, in erasure—the production of images depends thereby, as we've observed, on the ruin of the plate.

We take for granted the conventions of foreground, middle ground, and background; figure and ground; vista, view, and zones of recession; yet these are aspects of two-dimensional representations that often depend on habits of perspective and techniques of organizing the visual field. What is to hand, what can be reached within a few steps, what we can walk to or glimpse in the distance, what is over the horizon, what is encompassed by our peripheral vision, what is intuited, or simply invisible? And how can any of these phenomena lend themselves to the graphic means available to us at any given moment in history? The, in retrospect, astonishingly rapid growth of the art of printmaking in the sixteenth century and its relation to poetry and painting is inseparable from the rise of humanism and the violent conflicts of culture and religion that characterize the period. When sixteenth-century scholars, painters, printmakers, and poets witnessed such conflicts, they saw them against a backdrop of Roman ruins that for the first time were viewed not only for the allusions they provided to allegory but also for the ambivalent aesthetic pleasures they offered.

Out of Rome

The Flemish painter Jan Gossart (aka "Mabuse"[4]) journeyed to Rome in 1508 or 1509. He was serving his patron, Philip of Burgundy, ambassador to Pope Julius II, under a commission to record and draw antiquities.[5] Gossart sparked an intense interest in the Italian art of his time as he also introduced Roman ruins into the architectural settings he had long used for his paintings. His *Adoration of the Kings*, of circa 1510–1515, painted after his return from his Roman sojourn, follows the tradition of representing the Nativity within ruined structures. His influential predecessor Hugo van der Goes used rough wooden beams and a single Gothic column to surround the holy family and their retinue; his contemporaries Albrecht Dürer and Albrecht Altdorfer chose, as we have seen, wood and brick structures chipped away and collapsing to decay. But Gossart's *Adoration* includes variegated marble columns, terra-cotta tiles, a mixture of dressed stone and brick buildings, and other details that seem to speak to the authenticity of his firsthand knowledge of the classical world (see plate 6), and he continued to work in tandem between "modern" late High Gothic and antique architectural styles.[6]

A drawing of the Colosseum that Gossart made around 1508 has a contemporary inscription: "Jennin Mabusen eghenen handt Contrafetet in Roma, Coloseum"—letting us know that Gossart made the image of the Colosseum himself, "with his own hand."[7] Gossart's journey was to inspire other artists to visit Rome and draw built forms and artworks, both ancient and contemporary, on-site. Their goal was the idealistic one of furthering a humanist education and a practical one of creating authentic backgrounds for their prints and paintings on classical and religious themes. Something of the confusion they must have felt in encountering the city as a panoply of unmarked forms and rubble is captured in the Latin poems on the decay of Rome written by Giovanni Vitale in the period and published by the mid-sixteenth century. A visitor from Palermo, Vitale took the pen name "Janus Vitalis"—his long life (1485–1560) intersected with that of his younger fellow poet Joachim Du Bellay and with Pope Leo X, of whom he was said to be a favorite. In his reflections on Rome, Vitalis wrote as a visitor and humanist of the unintelligibility of what lay before him. Here is the most well known of his sonnets:

> Qui Romam in media quaeris novus advena Roma,
> Et Romam in Roma vix reperis media:
> Adspice murorum moles, praeruptaque saxa,

Obrutaque horrenti vasta theatra situ.
Haec sunt Roma: Viden' velut ipsa cadavera tantae
Urbis adhuc spirent imperiosa minas?
Vicit ut haec mundum, nixa est se vincere; vicit,
A se non victum ne quid in orbe foret.
Nunc victa in Roma, Roma illa invicta sepulta est;
Atque eadem victrix, victaque Roma fuit.
Albula Romani restabat nominis index,
Quia fugit ille citis non rediturus aquis.
Disce hinc quid possit fortuna; immota labascunt,
Et quae perpetuo sunt agitata manent.[8]

The work was imitated by Du Bellay in his "Les Antiquités de Rome" within just a few years, and the poem eventually sparked imitations by Spenser and at least twenty-eight other Renaissance poets, living on in versions as recent as those by Ezra Pound and Robert Lowell. Here is a twentieth-century translation by J. V. Cunningham:

You that a stranger in mid-Rome seek Rome
And can find nothing in mid-Rome of Rome,
Behold this mass of walls, these abrupt rocks,
Where the vast theatre lies overwhelmed.
Here, here is Rome! Look how the very corpse
Of greatness still imperiously breathes threats!
The world she conquered, strove herself to conquer,
Conquered that nothing be unconquered by her.
Now conqueror Rome's interred in conquered Rome,
And the same Rome conquered and conqueror.
Still Tiber stays, witness of Roman fame,
Still Tiber flows on swift waves to the sea.
Learn hence what Fortune can: the unmoved falls,
And the ever-moving will remain forever.[9]

In Vitalis's "Qui Romam in media quaeris novus advena Roma, / Et Romam in Roma vix reperis media . . . ," Du Bellay's "Et rien de Rome en Rome n'apperçois," and Goethe's "Rome would not even be Rome" alike, we find an eloquent summation of the process of ruination and the problems of its representation. The difference between walls and rocks is a matter of the maker's intention, and Rome as a self-defining source of the discourse about itself is overcome by time. The poem's elegant shifts between passive and active forces—the conquered and conquering, the buried and burying—make what seems at first a still vista a problem of depicting motion and mapping it. The ever-moving Tiber paradoxically becomes the anchor, the fixed point from which all identities can be situated and as well the living proof of the transience of fate. Yet the poem's powerful repetitions, which Du Bellay would, in his Sonnet 3, adapt as "Et Rome Rome a vaincu seulement," underscore the difference between what is named and what is nameless. What were the visitors seeing? How did they know one entity from another? If Rome had collapsed within Rome, where does Rome begin and end?

A cast of a statue gives us much of its detail and envelops us in a sense of presence, but it doesn't explain its referent. A landscape painting or frescos on a mythological or historical theme, in contrast, may lead to rich associations of narrative and mood that take us beyond its particulars. When we look at the enormous *Fire in the Borgo* (*Stanza dell'Incendio*) frescos at the Vatican made by Raphael and Giulio Romano in the same year as Gossart's *Adoration of the Kings*, time collapses. Commissioned by Leo X to commemorate a miracle of 847 when his namesake Pope Leo IV put out a raging fire by making the sign of the cross, the frescos force our attention to pivot between the symmetrical, nearly still, order of the distant, blessing pope in the background and the chaos and frenzied motion of those fleeing the fire in the foreground. Prominent among the victims is a man carrying his aging father on his back: we are transported immediately to a memory of Aeneas fleeing a burning Troy, so often depicted carrying his father Anchises on his back and his child Ascanius in his arms. It is as if the same spark ignited both disasters.

Yet visitors to a city of vast and empty spaces, where walls made of stone turn to stones again, required maps and images with labels, captions, and measurements that would give forms articulation and place them within a field and discourse. Printmakers in Rome began to sell their wares to the thousands of pilgrims and travelers who came to the city each year, looking for Rome's "corpse of greatness." Reviving the medieval tradition of the *Mirabilia Urbis Romae*, the printmaker Antonio Salamanca produced images of classical Roman buildings as early as the 1530s, and by 1553, he had established a partnership with Antoine Lafréry (eventually also known as Antonio Lafreri), a younger Besançon printmaker who had set up shop in Rome to create and market such works as well. Their partnership dissolved after Salamanca's death in 1562, yet Lafréry remained so successful that he was the first printmaker to offer a catalog of his sheets for sale. In the mid-1570s, he published a title page inscribed *Speculum Romanae Magnificentiae*, or the *Mirror of Roman Magnificence*. His clients were invited to choose the prints they preferred and the set would be bound with this proud title sheet.[10]

Mainly interested in architecture, recording measurements in a hodge-podge of *palmi/pieds*, *unci/unces*, *minuti/minutes*, and, when Florentine buildings were noted, the *braccia fiorentine*, these early printmakers viewed their prints as aids to reconstruct the original forms of now ruined buildings.[11]

The title page of the *Speculum* promises that "nearly all" the monuments of the city, however small, some ancient and some modern, will be presented as *accuratiss[ime] delineate repraesentans*, or "accurately sketched." A Latin inscription in the lower center makes an even more ambitious promise: "Roma tenet propriis monumenta sepulta ruinis plurima, quae profert hic redivia liber. Hunc igitur lector scrutare benigni, docebit Urbis maiestas pristina quanta fuit" (Rome holds many monuments buried in their own ruins that this book presents restored. Therefore, kind reader, look at this book closely, for it will reveal the greatness of the magnificent former city).

What were these monuments? Delineated without any scenery aside from bulbous clouds made by quick imprecise strokes of the needle that form a counterpoint to the care brought to the architectural elements, the depicted monuments in extant copies vary. Yet they most often include the Foro Boario, Corinthian columns at the Forum (noted as being "fissuris . . . fractvris . . . deformes"), cutaway views of the Pantheon and Colosseum, the tomb of Caecilia Metella, the Septizodium, the Temple of Janus, the Mausoleum of Hadrian (Castel Sant'Angelo), and, among new buildings, the Tempietto and the dome of Saint Peter's.

The printmakers' work was surely encouraged by the humanist environment in Rome. The philologist Claudio Tolomei's *Accademia della Virtù* (aka *Accademia Vitruviana*) set out a plan in 1542 to revive knowledge of Vitruvius and to publish a comprehensive account of the ancient buildings and sculptures of Rome[12]—a call Salamanca already was answering. In 1559, Étienne Du Pérac, a few years younger than Lafréry, arrived in Rome to pursue the same fortune and joined the international group of engravers who worked in the printing establishment of his fellow Frenchman. He published, with Lafréry, successful plans of ancient Rome (1574) and modern Rome (1577) and in 1575 brought out his own bound survey of *I vestigi dell'antichità di Roma*.[13]

These sixteenth-century printshops were for the most part in the Via Parionis, the current Via del Governo Vecchio, which curves around the Piazza Navona, past the ancient statue of two effaced and intertwined figures known as the "Pasquino" that stands near the patch of ground where it had been unearthed at some point before 1500.[14] The effort to explore and record ancient structures and objects was not driven by an interest in their decay so much as speculation about their potential. A close look at the very small figures populating Lafréry's views of the Pyramid of Cestius or Trajan's column shows that they are conversing and gesticulating with one another—they wear cloaks and hats and go about their business carrying staffs. In an image of the Castel Sant'Angelo, men are fishing with nets while other figures are leaning over the Ponte and looking at the water; still others are tucked into the spaces of the Castel itself. In all of the prints, what might have been background—the ruined architectural forms—becomes both foreground and an object of attention to the figures within the scene.

Through these early prints, viewers learn how to see, how truly to envision and reconstruct, the history that stands around them. New buildings in an antique style, including the Tempietto, or under construction, including Saint Peter's, show the reversibility of processes of destruction and construction. Recording the dimensions and qualities of structures at a particular moment in time is here a practice oriented toward the future and one that repairs the gap in intelligibility between the ancient past and the present.

Treatises on architecture, including Sebastiano Serlio's *D'architettura* (*On Architecture*), published in installments between 1537 and 1575, and a 1556 edition of Vitruvius's work of the same title, underlined the relation between ancient and prospective buildings. The Vitruvius title page includes sundials, pieces of construction machinery, and measuring devices in a tangled presentation within a half-ruined frame.[15] Serlio includes in the title page of book 5 of his treatise, devoted to Roman antiquities, an imaginary ancient arcade in a state of ruin, cracked with weather and encroaching vegetation, a broken obelisk, and fragments of masonry and columns scattered on the ground. Hovering above the image is the inscription Serlio took from Francesco Albertini's *Opusculum de mirabilibus novae & veteris urbis Romae* of 1510, an update and "correction" of the medieval *Mirabilis*: ROMA QUANTA FUIT, IPSA RUINA DOCET (Even ruins can teach what Rome once was). It was a lesson about Rome's lessons that would be reinscribed in many later ruins images.

Northern Emblems

Nevertheless, the nature of the lesson was not at all clear and, as is true of all proverbs and aphorisms, the phrase's very ambiguity proves to be its most useful quality. In the same period, Flemish printmakers represented the same ruins in a quite different mode. Like the Spanish Salamanca and his French colleagues, they were necessarily strangers to the city and must have seen its built forms in all the raw and massive novelty of their monumentality and antiquity. After the 1527 Sack of Rome, a succession of northern artists arrived: the painter and draftsman Maerten (also known as Maarten) van Heemskerck was in residence between 1532 and 1537, and he was followed by the court painter of Louis X, Hermannus Posthumus, Titian's associate Lambert Sustris, the portrait painter Anthonis Mor, and Gossart's apprentice Lambert Lombard.

One of the now most well-known ruins paintings from this period, Posthumus's 1536 *Tempus edax rerum*, prominently displays at the center of its phantasmagoria of real and imaginary fragments, inscribed on a stone tablet, the motto from Ovid's *Metamorphoses* (15.234–36): TEMPVS EDAX RE / RVM TVQVE INVI / DIOSA VETVSTAS / O[MN]IA DESTRVITIS (Time devourer of things, and you envious age destroy all [see plate 5]). The painting shows a bearded artist wearing a turban, his sleeves rolled up, as he records measurements of a column base with a pair of dividers. Men with torches explore wall paintings at the Domus Aurea. Roughly evocative of the site of the temple at Tivoli, with incongruous allusions as well to the Castel Sant'Angelo, presenting recognizable fragments—including a pair of reclining river gods, the Juno Ludovisi, portions of the Torlonia Vase, an ancient marble sundial, and imaginary antiquities and assemblages—the painting is a tribute to the slow violence of time and invites artists and collectors to salvage the ensuing fragments. The painting as well gives evidence of collaboration and borrowing from Maerten van Heemskerck. The collection of Roman drawings known as van Heemskerck's sketchbook, now at the Kupferstichkabinett in Berlin, contains a number of drawings by another hand that has now been recognized as Posthumus's.[16]

Yet before these artists lay a landscape that also had been devastated by the ruin of sudden violence, punctuated with the recognizable landmarks of vanished Roman power. At some point during the following decades, van Heemskerck made a drawing of the Sack of Rome as an imaginative response to recorded events (see fig. 24). In this drawing we see the headlong fall and death of Charles, the Duke of Bourbon, principal of the army of the Spanish king and Holy Roman emperor Charles V. At the same time, the duke's Spanish and German (and largely Lutheran) troops, now out of control, can be seen attacking the Borgo; flames pour from the Castel Sant'Angelo where Pope Clement VII is imprisoned.[17] Printed in van Heemskerck's 1555–1556 series *The Victories of Emperor Charles V* and occasioned by Charles's abdication, the image includes, in its second and third printings, dual inscriptions in Spanish and French recording the consequences of the Duke of Bourbon's fall—in Spanish his death (*muerto*) is literally rhymed with the collapse of the city's walls (*muros*) and the violence of his fall with the total sacking of the city:

> Aquí fue Borbon muerto, y derribado
> Por los muros de Roma: pero entraron
> Los Soldados con ánimo efforçado
> Y ellos la ciudad toda faquearon.

> Here Bourbon died, brought down
> by the walls of Rome; but
> the soldiers entered with valiant zeal
> and they sacked the entire city.[18]

By the time of van Heemskerck's *Victories* series, thirty years after the sack, the now ailing emperor was about to surrender power and would die in 1558.

The printer, Hieronymus Cock, writes on the title page that he has published the work "by his own accord" and dedicates the sequence to the emperor's son and successor, Philip II, perhaps with every intention of pleasing him, given his reputation as a patron of the arts.[19] After Charles's victory against the

1 5 2 7.

BORBONE OCCISO, ROMANA IN MOENIA MILES
CÆSAREVS RVIT, ET MISERANDAM DIRIPIT VRBEM.

Aqui fue Borbon muerto, y derribado
Por los muros de Roma: pero entraron
Los Soldados con animo efforçado,
Y ellos la ciudad toda faquearon.   III

Soudain apres que Bourbon fut occis
Le tresvaillant Empereur feit emprife
D'affaillir Romme, & de fens trefraffis
En combatant en peu de tempz l'eut prinfe.

FIGURE 24. Dirck Volckertszoon Coornhert (after Maerten van Heemskerck), *The Death of Charles, Duke of Bourbon, and the Capture of Rome.* From *The Victories of Emperor Charles V* (Antwerp: Hieronymus Cock, 1555). British Museum, London.

Turkish advance in 1535, he had processed through the major cities of the Italian peninsula; in Rome he rode beneath the arches of the Forum, following the route of ancient emperors and giving the populace an opportunity to see him among the antiquities.[20] That van Heemskerck would choose to represent a moment that he did not witness, focused on the minute or two when the duke tumbled to the ground, says a great deal about the use and reuse of ruins images in the period by northern artists. Although we can glimpse the new Saint Peter's under construction in the upper right corner, this is not a depiction designed to represent the dimensions of Roman forms with architectural reconstruction in mind. In fact, by distorting the historical record in several places and exaggerating Charles's achievements, the series reconstructs the emperor's reputation.[21]

On the occasion of Philip's own triumphal progress through the major cities of the empire in 1549, ephemeral architecture "all'antica" was constructed to evoke Roman imperial predecessors as well. As the wealthiest and largest of the Netherland cities that Philip was inheriting, Antwerp created an elaborate *blijde inkomst*, or "joyous entry," for the imperial heir. Philip entered by a route that took him along the boundaries of the city, defining its thresholds, and past a mighty display of armed native citizens and the gallows field—where wagon wheels atop tall poles held the bodies of those who had been deemed criminals and denied burial. After these displays of liminality and potential violence, Philip and the city's representatives exchanged oaths in a ceremony conducted beneath an ephemeral temple that resembled Bramante's Tempietto. The constructed "architecture" that lined his route included a tableau that displayed Antwerp as a "beautiful young maiden" of "unblemished faithfulness." Inherent in the "surrender" of the virgin bride Antwerpia were a set of expectations that Philip must graciously and faithfully behave well toward the city.[22]

The northern concern with ruins stems from a range of motivations, from aristocratic Italophilia, to humanist interest in archaeology, history, and philology, to something like the retrospective and proleptic representation of trauma, for the Sack of Rome was only one incident in the ongoing violence of what became in the second half of the century the Eighty Years' War. Those armed Antwerpians would rise up against the Spanish occupation—perhaps the heavy rain that fell on the day of the procession was a harbinger of the ephemerality of the "marriage" itself. Thus northern artists creating ruins representations began by emphasizing landscape, but they went on to develop subjects on the themes of destruction and triumph, heresy and belief. They saw in the ruins of antiquity echoes of biblical accounts of destruction and reflections of the power relations and religious conflicts that marked their own circumstances. The *Victories* series, a relatively unusual contemporary historical topic, may have been commissioned, despite Cock's testimony to his own volition, by his patron, Antoine Perrenot de Granvelle, bishop of Arras, who was the chief minister of both Charles V and Philip II.[23] Among several contorted themes, the series' message of the emperor's defeat of the Protestants makes it an example of state propaganda more than a work of art alone.

In 1551, Cock first produced images of twenty-five views of Rome featuring the Colosseum and other Roman ruins under the title, *Praecipua aliquot romanae antiquitatis ruinarum monimenta, vivis prospectibus, ad veri imitationem affabre designata*.[24] "Vivis Prospectibus" implies that the ruins have been observed firsthand and has raised the still-unresolved question of whether or not Cock himself visited Rome, perhaps in the late 1540s. Cock made several drawings of ruins that are held in Cambridge and Edinburgh, yet they could be copies of sketches by others, especially the drawings of van Heemskerck, and it is not clear whether they were prefatory works for his prints on the same subjects or made after the prints.[25]

The publication of the first edition of Cock's ruins prints coincides with the onset of Granvelle's patronage of his printing house in 1551. Cock relied on a number of van Heemskerck's drawings, made in the 1530s, for his second edition of ruins prints, issued in 1561. Granvelle supported the entire cost of the series of depictions of the Baths of Diocletian after drawings by Sebastiaan van Noyen (1558), including funds for van Noyen's 1557 trip to Rome. And more than a dozen local and itinerant artists and engravers were employed by the firm over its nearly twenty years of activity. All in all, the work of these printing houses was a collaborative one at every level of production.[26]

The *Praecipua* begins with a dedication to Granvelle—accompanied by a quatrain written by the Antwerp humanist Cornelius Grapheus:

Barbaricus furor, annorumque horrenda vorago,
Sic Orbis Reginam, illam, lachrimabile, Romam
Vastarunt, fati nimirum, urgentibus: ecquae
Servandis r[e]liquis Usquam fiducia regnis?

Thus Barbarian rage and the terrible gulf of passing years
Laid waste with the indisputable urgency of fate, to Rome,
That queen of the world—How mournful! Are there any,
Anywhere, who have faith that her remains will be protected?[27]

A friend of Erasmus and Dürer, Grapheus was a young official of the state when he was arrested in 1522 for publishing heretical writings; he was jailed and forced to make a public recantation. By the time of the *Praecipua* he lived modestly as a schoolteacher and had become a well-known poet of Latin verses.[28]

What does he mean by "ecquae / Servandis r[e]liquis Usquam fiducia regnis"? The frail, vegetation-damaged, almost drooping images of Cock's prints in the *Praecipua* stand in stark contrast to the engineer van Noyen's twenty-seven images of the Baths of Diocletian, marked by careful notations of *palmi*, *digiti*, and *minuti*. Labeled parts in the Italian style of ruins notation are presented in intact, inferred, form, without any context—they could be based on a particularly elegant set of architect's blocks arranged upon a table and registered at eye level. The analogously precise work of Cock's employees, the brothers Lucas and Johannes van Doetecum, who had invented a mode of etching that resembled engraving in its smooth transitions of tone, translated van Noyen's images to the plate. Printing them could indeed be seen as a protective gesture.

Derived from the landscape painting tradition in which Cock had been trained before he became a printmaker, his prints, in contrast, are studies in the vagrancy of natural light and effects of ground and weather as much as they are representations of buildings. Yet ruins presented as landscapes and scenes continue to be a preoccupation throughout his career. Even the slightly more polished prints, etched as well by the van Doetecum brothers, in Cock's "Little Ruins Book," published more than a decade later in 1562 and extending the purview well beyond the city of Rome, display these qualities. The work's official title, *Operum antiquorum Romanorum hinc inde per diversas Europae regiones reliquias ac ruin[a]s saeculis omnibus supiciendas non minus vere quam pulcherrime deformatas libellus hic novus continet*, provides this explanation: "This new little book contains the remains and ruins of ancient Roman works of art scattered here and there over different regions of Europe to which all ages must look up in admiration, depicted as faithfully to life as splendidly."[29] The images convey an overwhelming effect of texture where the ground before the Capitol building seems made of small dunes of sand and the sky appears in rolling patches behind cottony clouds. An image of the Roman theater in Bordeaux has some of the sharp distinctions between light and shadow within colonnades that Cock employed in his images of the Colosseum from ten years before, and the light falls harshly on the sprouting edges of buttresses, emphasizing their broken more than their intact parts.[30]

Clients could purchase prints from Cock, too, in loose sheets or bound sets. Over time, like many printmakers, Cock published serial works on themes that were indeed serial: the four evangelists, the twelve months, the seven liberal arts. On the title print to the *Praecipua* he identifies himself as "pictor, typograph[us]," and in the 1562 series he writes his name as "Hironymus Cock, piktor." For virtual tourists who could only travel to Rome, the holy city and nominal center of the Holy Roman Empire, the prints provided a glimpse of structures authenticated by the publisher's claim that they were true to life. The *Praecipua*'s image of the ruins of the Basilica of Constantine in the Forum, for example, shows six male figures in sixteenth-century dress, wearing cloaks and carrying swords. Two are discoursing in the far left foreground, with the figure on the right lifting his arm in a deictic gesture toward the ruins. A small figure in the left background is bent over a piece of rubble in a posture that suggests he is puzzling over an inscription. Three figures in the center-left foreground take precedence. One standing, one sitting, two of them raise their arms in the same deictic pose, and the third, seated, props a tablet on his leg and sketches. The print invites its viewer to take up the same pose of noting and discoursing on the ruins and as well guarantees its authentic relation to its site (see fig. 25).

Even so, the viewer of the prints is not engaged only in a practice of turning pages and identifying structures. The new art of printmaking, with its precise delineations of surfaces and textures; its marks, stipples, plate color, and other effects of process; and its relation to inscription, writing, and aphorism also taught viewers to "read" in a new way. The encapsulation of various readers within the prints—the many figures pointing, exclaiming, drawing, discussing, and those travelers who are passing by, often on their way to work grounded in agriculture and herding—made the ruins backgrounds not

FIGURE 25. Hieronymus Cock, *Basilica of Constantine.* From *Praecipua aliquot romanae antiquitatis ruinarum monimenta* (Antwerp, 1551). National Gallery of Art, Washington, DC, Ailsa Mellon Bruce Fund. (Cock uses the common name for the structure, the "Temple of Peace.")

only to the past but also to the present. This division was already implicit in Alberti's *Della pittura* (*On Painting*; 1435–1436), wherein he explained the importance of having a commentator mediate the viewer's relation to the *istoria*, or narrative of the scene—someone who points to what should be observed and learned: a person who is admonishing, beckoning, and at times even menacing the viewer.[31]

As Cock labels actual ruins and at times places them among generic ruins, and as he emphasizes figures in contemporary dress, we are all the more aware of the forming gestures of the artist as he addresses the deformation of ruined structures. The importance of the moment of production is also evident when we look at an etching such as Cock's depiction of Saint Jerome amid ruins after Maerten van Heemskerck's 1547 painting on the same subject, labeled *Cock fecit, 1552.* The saint is crouching in the lower left corner of the image, with one hand on his traditional accouterment of a skull and the other held

FIGURE 26. Hieronymus Cock (after Maerten van Heemskerck), *Saint Jerome in a Land-scape with Ruins*, 1552. National Gallery of Art, Washington, DC, Ailsa Mellon Bruce Fund.

by an open book. Drawing his imagery from the painting, with slight adapta-tions, or perhaps from another image by van Heemskerck, Cock shows the saint surrounded above and in the distance by a vast landscape of truncated statues; sphinxes; tottering herms; a giant reclining river god; the she-wolf with Romulus and Remus; a pair of well-clothed contemporary men, pointing and gesturing; a collapsing, fantastic, version of a Flavian amphitheater; and minuscule figures driving camels and a donkey. In van Heemskerck's paint-ing, Jerome is looking intently at an illuminated version of the scriptures. If we in turn look closely at the volume the saint is examining in Cock's print, we find not the Bible but, in cursive script, the words "Martinus Heemskerck Inv" (see fig. 26).[32]

Of the many printing houses in Antwerp,[33] two came to particular prominence—their renown extending to all of Northern Europe through-out the sixteenth century: the first was Cock's own establishment, Aux Qua-tre Vents (At the Sign of the Four Winds), continued after his death by his wife and business partner Volcxen Diericx and known for publishing visual images. The second was De Gulden Passer (The Golden Compass), estab-lished by Christopher Plantin and his wife Joanna Rivière, and eventually run by his son-in-law Jan Moretus, and famous for publishing books and other printed texts.

The artists involved in ruins image production were constantly "trading places" as well as views: the itinerant Fontainebleau school artist Léonard Thiry was in Antwerp in the 1550s, and his colleague Jacques Androuet du Cerceau made a series of copies of Cock's prints. Aux Quatre Vents collaborated with and employed an international group of artists and printers: the Spanish cartographer Diego Gutiérrez contributed to a map of the Americas in 1562; the Mantuan Giorgio Ghisi, whose early prints had been published in Rome by Lafréry, worked between Antwerp, France, and Italy; Cornelis Cort worked in Italy with Barocci and Titian. The long-lived humanist sage and printmaker Dirck Volckertszoon Coornhert, another eventual member of Aux Quatre Vents, had been making prints since the 1540s, collaborating with Maerten van Heemskerck, from his shop in Haarlem; Coornhert's pupil Philip (aka Philips) Galle, also originally from Haarlem, would eventually establish his own Antwerp press, which was carried into the seventeenth century by his sons and sons-in-law. In the next generation, Galle's pupil, perhaps the greatest of Renaissance printmakers, Hendrick Goltzius, had also worked for both Cock and Cort. Goltzius eventually was to join the artists at the Catholic, art-loving court of Rudolf II in Prague, where Aegidius Sadeler II, a member of the itinerant printmaker family of that name, was court engraver. Born in Antwerp in 1578, Aegidius (also known as Egidio or Giles) came to Prague and stayed until his death in 1629 after living and working in Cologne, Munich, Antwerp, Rome, Verona, Venice, and Naples. The Antwerp brothers Jan and Rafael Sadeler, who worked for Christopher Plantin in the 1570s, would found a dynasty of more than ten Sadelers working as engravers in the Spanish Netherlands, Germany, Italy, Bohemia, and Austria.[34]

In 1561, the Venetian printmaker Battista Pittoni effectively pirated Cock's *Praecipua*, using twenty-four of the plates and, augmenting them, making copies directly taken from the *Praecipua* and even presenting them under the same title. He reworked the images from Cock in some places as he also added another ten plates that were either his own or taken from elsewhere. Cock's plates often are reversed, and Pittoni sometimes inserted, as Cock himself occasionally did, small narrative scenes, adding cloud formations and increasing the contrast between light and shadow.[35] Two decades later, Pittoni's copies were reprinted with Vincenzo Scamozzi's *Discorsi sopra l'antichità di Roma*. In his introduction to the work, Girolamo Porro suggested that ruins images were of interest as a resource for painters—"disegni di ruine . . . à questo tempo hanno potuto principalmente servire à quei pittori, che di fingere paesi nelle loro opere si dilettano"—and added that they could be useful to architects when they included commentaries.[36]

Influential as they were, Cock's ruins prints, so far as we know, never seem to have been used as direct models for freestanding single paintings, but when Philip Galle issued a new title page print in 1561 for the series, he, too, inscribed the work as "for the benefit of painters." And in 1562, Paolo Veronese

relied on Cock's ruins images for Palladio's Villa di Maser in the Veneto.[37] The
Antwerp painter Paul Bril, collaborating on the fresco cycles in Santa Cecilia
in Trastevere, also drew on Cock's ruins prints, and so the image of Rome cir-
cled back to its origin. Aux Quatre Vents issued more than a thousand prints
before its production fell sharply in 1565 as mounting enthusiasm for iconoclasm would explode into the riots of 1566.[38]

Placing ruins in the background as a means of reading history and myth
became commonplace. This inherent structure in Western visual art indicates
that the viewer otherwise would not know where to look: the background or
elements of the scene—the phenomenal world—is subordinate to the implicit narrative, which must be inferred. When the background is a ruin, the
viewer must be shown its significance; the story must be made intelligible.
Thus ruins are placed within a historical account that emphasizes the role they
have to play in the viewer's perception of the world.

The Transparency of the Present

Here, too, a considerable gulf exists between ruins prints designed as records
of measurement—either for recording details of the remains of the past or
using the ruins' dimensions for future building projects—and ruins prints
incorporating figures. Known as *staffage* in art history discourse, these figures traditionally have been seen to acquire significance only when they have
names. When they are discernible as figures from history or the scriptures,
they take place in a scene, their surroundings become a site, and the work itself
enters into the genre of history painting—the most esteemed mode of visual
representation from the Renaissance through the eighteenth century. In turn,
a genre painting or print might use anonymous figures to create a typical anecdote or allegory in the service of a theme, but within a work devoted to the
representation of landscape, the figures most often express scale and motion.

Nevertheless, in ruins prints, running from their origin in this period all the
way into the nineteenth century, such staffage figures rarely are contemporary
to the origins of the ruins themselves.[39] With the exception of images of biblical scenes, the prints of the artists of Aux Quatre Vents most often display
figures in sixteenth-century dress. Pilgrims are dressed in heavy cloaks and
flat woven hats that would provide protection from the sun[40]; shepherds and
workmen wear boots and short jackets, and sometimes cloche-like or otherwise soft-brimmed hats, carrying their bundles on their backs and their staves
in their hands; commanding figures often wear the short capes, swords, leg-
gings, small pointed beards, and helmets or caps of the occupying Spanish
forces. Hidden in the distant recesses of ruined classical spaces is a cast of
characters from the immediate and local present.

The viewer looking for the *istoria* necessarily sees his or her own history
against the backdrop of deep time and is led to speculate allegorically on the

outcomes of vanished and triumphant religions or the expansion and fall of empires and to engage as well with the immediate particulars of the depicted scene. We see artists sketching the ruins, pilgrims pointing to the features of structures or ignoring their surroundings as they trudge around and through the landscape. And we also see acts of violence, suppression, and figures hiding in the shadows and recesses of abandoned ruins. We might imagine that such figures were gratuitous, not meant to be especially noted, but we should remember that these prints were created in a milieu where new technologies of lenses were being developed, and it is likely that what seems obscure may be as important as what is evident.[41]

Prints were a medium considered privately; to view a print in detail, only one or two people could look at an individual work at a time. Underlying that individuation and private situation of viewing is a knowledge that the print is a multiple, produced out of what is literally termed the plate, or *matrix*—from the Latin *mater* (mother) and *matrix* (womb, source, origin, or female animal kept for breeding). Once the edition is complete, in a single run or over any length of time determined by the artist or contingency, the plate's destiny is to become worn with each consequent edition. The conditions of private, close, viewing, unrestricted by any particular conventions limiting the time spent with each view, and an awareness that one is viewing one of many impressions from a single plate and one of several similar images in a series, lend themselves inherently to attention to subtle detail, such allegorical or otherwise layered meanings, potential counterdiscourses, and a sense of hidden bonds to other viewers.

In other words, the surge of prints in the Netherlands during the sixteenth century is inherently bound up with the duality of the printmakers'—and print viewers'—religious and social history. When we look closely at Cock's ruins prints with figures, and at later copies of them, their multiplicity of meanings becomes remarkably complex, frequently evoking amid still scenes of ruined forms depictions of toil and leisured appreciation and dramas of sex and violence alike. His *Fifth View of the Colosseum* shows a man wrapped in a toga or cloak, holding what looks like a book in his arms and accompanied by a dog. In his etching of the Baths of Diocletian from his *Praecipua* of 1551, two men in cloaks are attacked by two armed men, one of whom seems to be in charge—whether they are robbers or soldiers or others is not clear (see fig. 27). Consider as well Cock's 1550 pen-and-(black)-ink drawing of a set of encounters at the Colosseum (see fig. 28). The drawing, from the National Gallery of Scotland, is related to his print on the same subject and to Battista Pittoni's 1561 copy.

Here, within the recesses of the outer concentric corridors of the Colosseum, we can see a standing anatomical male figure in a roughly sketched short cape with an extended sword reaching out to catch, by her long hair, a fleeing female figure in a long dress, who runs away from him with outstretched arms. To the viewer's left, in a posture of surprise, beneath a fornice, a barely discernable nude male figure is poised above and encircling a second, reclining, female figure who braces herself on a stone. In the engraving based on the drawing, the central male figure catching the woman is wearing more clothing—a short cape flaps in the air behind him and his legs are sheathed in pantaloons, his anatomy no longer visible. The couple to the left remain nude, though more clearly drawn as a man above a woman.[42] Is this apparent scene of multiple rapes, or a rape and a secretive coupling, an instance of pornography? An allusion to the brutality of the Sack of Rome or the Spanish occupation of the Netherlands? Is it an elaborate visual pun, in that the Latin *fornix*—an arch and consequently an arch-shaped oven—becomes the term for a brothel? Perhaps the well-known reputation of the fornices of the Colosseum as a locale for prostitution is presented here. Yet *fornication* also, at least since the writings of Tertullian, is associated with idolatry.[43] And so Cock's image could in fact be totally paradoxical: a graven image presenting an allegory of idolatry: a figure of the law apprehending a fornicator with two other fornicating figures looking on as commentators.

FIGURE 27. Hieronymus Cock, *Baths of Diocletian*. From *Praecipua aliquot romanae antiquitatis ruinarum monimenta* (Antwerp, 1551). National Gallery of Art, Washington, DC, Ailsa Mellon Bruce Fund.

FIGURE 28. Hieronymus Cock, *Colosseum* (interior), 1550. Pen and ink. National Galleries of Scotland, David Laing Bequest to the Royal Scottish Academy, transferred 1910.

Reflections of Destruction

In each of these cases, ruins are the backdrop to human ruination: women, whether victims or solicitors or both, remain protagonists in a narrative of sin. As we've recounted, the year before (1549) had marked Philip II's triumphal entry, accompanied by his father Charles V, into Antwerp—with its mutual declarations, or "marriage," of allegiance between the prince and the Antwerp authorities. As the city celebrated the oath giving by turning public spaces into stage sets with triumphal arches covered in allegorical reliefs and tableaux vivants celebrating the city's resources, four thousand local men paraded in battle array. Charles was compared to Atlas and Philip to Hercules: they were portrayed carrying the world on their shoulders. The processions and images of future harmony and merciful rule were designed by the citizens to impress upon Philip a model for his sovereignty.

The festivities ended, however, on an alarming note. A closing fireworks display was set up in the Grote Markt (the city's central marketplace) where so many of the triumphal displays had taken place. An artificial apple tree stood beside wooden figures of a nude Adam and Eve; in its branches a "large and terrifying snake," as Cornelius Grapheus recorded, was twined. What the admiring audience could not at first discern was that the bodies of Adam and Eve, the snake, and all the leaves and apples of the tree were filled with gunpowder. Eve's feet were set on fire and as the fire extended to her abdomen, the entire scene exploded with an enormous sound. Adam, the snake, and the tree blew up, and flames shot in every direction. The people were terrified and fled pell-mell away from the marketplace. The Genesis story of the Fall had taken a shortcut directly to Revelation, and the citizenry was reminded that the pageant's celebration of worldly wealth and glory was mere vanity. The ruin of Eve, for a people deeply immersed in a theology of mortal sin, held the seeds of the ruin of the world.

The Dutch historian Stijn Bussels concludes that this traumatic finale may be the prototype for Pieter Bruegel the Elder's 1562 depiction of a devastated Antwerp as the landscape for the end of the world—his *Triumph of Death* (see fig. 29).[44] There flames lick the sky behind the execution grounds at the city's periphery, an army of skeletons spreads death and destruction to king and peasants, old and young, sacred and secular figures alike; an apocalyptic horseman reaps the living with his scythe, and the populace flees in every direction.

We traced in chapter 3 some of the violence exercised upon statues of Isis by early Christians and the analogous destruction wreaked in the mid-sixteenth century upon images of the Virgin Mary. Nevertheless, attitudes toward images in earlier humanist circles were ambivalent but generally benign. As early as Gregory the Great, and especially during the Byzantine iconoclastic strife of the eighth and ninth centuries, theologians had argued how to interpret, and how much weight to give, the decalogue's instructions regarding the eschewing of carved idols, or what eventually came to be called in the King James version of the Bible "graven images." There we find "Thou shalt not make unto thee any graven image, or any likeness [*of any thing*] that [*is*] in heaven above, or that [*is*] in the earth beneath, or that [*is*] in the water under the earth" in Exodus 20:4–6. In Deuteronomy 5:8, we have the interdiction "Thou shalt not make thee *any* graven image, *or* any likeness *of any thing* that *is* in heaven above, or that *is* in the earth beneath, or that *is* in the waters beneath the earth." A strict interpretation argued that it was anathema to represent the divine, which by definition was immaterial. At the same time, the incarnation of Christ made material representations of divinity possible. Church leaders understood that visual images played an important pedagogical role; beliefs could be taught and preserved in memory by addressing such images in a concerted way.

Erasmus and Luther were critical of the abuse of images, especially condemning the church's overreliance on spectacle and costly ornament and

FIGURE 29. Pieter Bruegel the Elder, *The Triumph of Death*, ca. 1562. Oil on panel. Museo del Prado, Madrid.

the worship of statues and relics at the expense of the veneration of God and Christ. Yet they also understood that images could strengthen the memory and deepen religious understanding. Luther wrote in his tract "Wider die himmlischen Propheten von Bildern und Sakramenten" ("Against the Heavenly Prophets in the Matter of Images and Sacraments") of 1524–1525 that any destruction of images should be carried out by officials and in an orderly way.[45]

This was the Reformist and tolerant ideology of many of the humanist printers as well. The press of Christopher Plantin, as an official organ of the Spanish court, was printing Roman Catholic doctrine by day and, as a clandestine center for Protestant dissent, Reformation tracts by night. In the same year as Bruegel's *Triumph of Death*, three of Plantin's journeymen printers, perhaps without his knowledge, produced a thousand copies of the Calvinist tract *Briefve instruction pour prier* (*Brief Instruction for Prayer*). The edition was seized by the sheriff, but five hundred copies already were on their way to Paris and Metz. Small and, eventually, large groups met in secret by candlelight to pore over Protestant books.[46] Plantin was closely associated with Hendrik Niclaes, the founder of the "Family of Love," a Protestant sect that eschewed institutionalized religion, ornament, and sacraments and eventually became a precursor of the English Quakers. Niclaes and, after a schism of the sect in 1573, his fellow Familist Hendrik Jansen van Barrefelt attracted many members of Plantin's circle, including Philip Galle, who moved his engraving firm from Haarlem to Antwerp around the time of Cock's death in 1570.[47] De Gulden Passer itself was a hidden meeting place for the group.[48]

By 1566, the "Year of Wonders," when the state began to allow hedge preaching and open practices of reform, Protestantism surged. The summer of that year brought the *Beeldenstorm* (statue storm) of the iconoclastic riots. In Antwerp on August 18, onlookers insulted the image of the Virgin in the annual traditional procession. Calvinist preachers continued to denounce the image the next day, urging the destruction of all such representations. By the following day, rioters had begun to smash images in the Church of Our Lady, then turned to monasteries and religious structures, and gradually moved to institutions outside the city's walls.[49] The destruction was conducted by Calvinist hired workmen proceeding according to plan: in groups of ten, they wrecked the city's sacred images of the Virgin, saints, and apostles, pulling down statues, smashing altars, slashing paintings, and breaking up organs.[50]

The Duke of Alba was sent to counter political unrest, and he seized the book industry. Many printers were banished, and at least one was executed. Booksellers were prosecuted as well, and many books were added to the church's index of forbidden works. The Battle of Oosterweel, near Antwerp, in March 1567 resulted in the total defeat and execution of Calvinist rebels by a professional Spanish army and the start of the Eighty Years' War.

In a series of drawings made from 1564 to 1569 and printed by Cock in Antwerp and Galle in Haarlem, Maerten van Heemskerck depicted the destruction of the idols in stories from the Hebrew scriptures, drawing on narrative accounts in 3 and 4 Kings and the book of Daniel: the histories of Bel (Baal) and the Dragon; Ahad and Elijah; Athaliah; and Josiah. He found his imagery within the stories of Josiah's destruction of Jeroboam's altars with golden calves at Bethel and the ruin of Baal—the slaughter of its priests and the smashing of its idols; the moral failings of King Ahab and Queen Jezebel, confronted by Elijah, and King Cyrus, confronted by Daniel. Van Heemskerck called on imagery from his early studies of Roman structures as well as the built environment of wooden buildings that surrounded him.

Figures take hammers to statues while cities burn in the background; a building with the ceiling of the Pantheon hosts a scene of image smashing; graves are opened and tomb monuments destroyed.[51] By giving iconoclasm a biblical context, van Heemskerck provides it with some legitimation. Nevertheless, each of his images shows an iconoclasm undertaken at the command of legitimate kings and prophets, and his history of Josiah reminds his viewers that Josiah carried out the destruction of the worshippers and images of Baal in a particularly bloodthirsty and headlong way. The viewer would be left with a mixed message regarding the legitimation and abuse of iconoclasm. And as the presentations condense the destruction of pagan temples' idols by the Hebrew kings, the destruction of Solomon's temple by the Romans, the fall of Rome, and contemporary Protestant vehemence, the viewer encounters, rather paradoxically, the apparent historical recurrence, and perhaps inevitability, of iconoclasm—all thanks to a learned and skillful manipulation of visual images.

When, in October 1572, Orange forces seized Mechelen, Alba's commander let his men ignore a plea for peaceful surrender and go on to rape and pillage the city for three days. The duke reported to Philip that "not a nail was left on the wall."[52] This was the first of the so-called Spanish Furies; Zutphen and Naarden suffered further atrocity and devastation, and a policy of killing all rebels and executing citizens became the norm. In 1576, Spanish soldiers, particularly enraged by not receiving their pay, looted and burned Antwerp. Eight thousand citizens were killed, a thousand houses were burned, six million florins' worth of property torched. The city never recovered. Christopher Plantin was forced to pay ransoms nine times to keep his press from destruction.[53]

The historian Peter Arnade has recorded the fate of the Antwerp citadel during the sack and its aftermath. Sometimes referred to as "the Duke of Alba's Temple" because it was one of his most prestigious building projects, the Antwerpians also called the citadel "Madonna Castilla" (Madonna Castle). Their satirical songs described it wearing a "Catholic virgin's cloak" and registered that "everyone hates it" because of its association with the sack. In 1577, with the city's German garrison of mercenaries dispersed, Antwerpians armed with pickaxes and shovels took satisfaction in dismantling parts of the citadel for use in the city's walls—the "Madonna Castilla" was thus subjected to an act of enormous iconoclasm and eventually became the residence of the court of William of Orange.[54]

The Tower of Babel II

The sack of Antwerp resulted in a tragic loss of life and vast destruction of property: it also brought to an end Antwerp's vibrant and cosmopolitan status as a great trading port. The city's dualistic strife between a Spanish-sponsored Roman Catholicism and a panoply of largely underground reform movements belies the complexity of its cultural life, based in trade, its many and varied craft guilds, and its far-reaching export and import activities. Some foreigners became Antwerp citizens; others could reside in the city if they were involved in wholesale importing and exporting or finance: French, English, Italian, Portuguese, Hanseatic, and Spanish merchants were able to thrive. Portuguese "Marranos," or "new Christians," and Spanish "conversos," were subject to the whims of the Antwerp authorities, on the one hand, and the Roman Catholic Church and imperial state, on the other—at times tolerated and at other times put under severe restrictions. Admitted in 1540 as "accepted Christians," by 1549 most Marranos were expelled by imperial decree. A number of the dozen Portuguese Jewish families who remained were active in the Protestant reform movements to follow. African slaves had arrived with the Portuguese and through Dutch sugar ventures in Brazil, and they often worked as servants and court musicians.[55]

The polyglot world of the Antwerp port in the sixteenth century existed on the page as well as along its streets and in its warehouses. Its most important manifestation was burgeoning interest in multilingual sacred texts. Such works already had the sanction of the Roman Catholic Church in Spain, and at the same time they appealed to Reformist tenets of individual Bible reading and a continuing interest in the kabbalah on the part of Christian humanists. The first polyglot Bible, edited at Alcalà, known as the *Biblia Complutensis* (after the city's Latin name *Complutum*), was printed in 1514–1517 and published in 1520. The 1520 work included texts of the "Old Testament" in Hebrew, Greek, and Latin; the Chaldaic Targums, or commentaries, of the Pentateuch; and the New Testament in Greek with an interlinear Latin translation. Simultaneous to the creation of the Alcalà polyglot, in 1516, Agostino Giustiniani brought out the first European humanist polyglot—his Psalter, published in Genoa, with eight columns across each opening of two pages: the Hebrew text, a Latin translation, the Vulgate, the Greek Septuagint, an Arabic text, the Targum, a Latin translation of the Targum, and a column of scholia. The preface declared that plans were in store to produce the whole Bible in polyglot format. Erasmus edited a Greek New Testament, published in 1516, and his fourth edition of 1527 shows the influence of the Alcalà project.[56]

Christopher Plantin printed a Latin Bible in 1559, a Greek New Testament in 1564, and a Hebrew Bible at the end of 1566. He had established a Hebrew Press in 1563, ten years after the Inquisition had condemned the Talmud to destruction and all nonbiblical Jewish texts were burned in the Campo de' Fiori.[57] In the winter before the iconoclastic riots of the summer of 1566, Plantin wrote to the scholar of Hebrew and Arabic Andreas Maes (called "Masius"), asking for his help with Syriac and Hebrew texts in the production of a polyglot Bible. By December, his Calvinist business partners had fled, and he petitioned for Philip's patronage for the polyglot Bible, sending him printed sheets of his proposed text and hoping that the king, who himself spoke neither Dutch nor French,[58] would spare the press and the project. To his good fortune, the theologians of Alcalà supported the project, and Plantin acquired a particular champion in Benito Arias Montano, the king's chaplain and a scholar of Oriental languages. Permission was granted: the Bible came to be officially known as *Biblia sacra hebraice chaldaice, graece et latine, Philippi II regis catholici pietate et studio ad sacrosanctae Ecclesiae usum*, or the "Biblia Regia"—the King's Bible. Using the Alcalà texts as a foundation, the work would come to include an interlinear translation of the Hebrew, the Chaldaic Targums (with Latin translation) of most of the books of the Hebrew Bible following the Pentateuch, and the standard text of the Syriac New Testament with a Latin translation.

Montano was sent to Antwerp in 1568 to supervise the project. He became involved in the Family of Love and was close to the Antwerp printmakers,

FIGURE 30. Genesis *incipit*. From Biblia Regia (Antwerp Polyglot Bible; 1568–1573). Hill Museum and Manuscript Library, St. John's University, Collegeville, Minnesota.

including especially Philip Galle. By May 570, the scholarly work on the polyglot was completed, and within another six months, all of the texts were set for printing. The opening pages of the Latin Genesis included an ornamented incipit with a female figure turning pointedly back across the column margin toward the Hebrew text (see fig. 30).

Between 1570 and 1572, the work was subjected to examination by the Roman Catholic Church; Montano vigorously defended the endeavor against its numerous Spanish detractors, who were suspicious especially of the Jewish texts and the influence and citation of rabbinical writings. In deference to the king's role in its production, permission to print was granted in 1572, the same year as another brutal suppression by the Duke of Alba of Protestant reformists. Montaro was ordered to present a copy of the polyglot Bible on vellum to Alba himself. In 1575, Montaro went to Rome to defend the text directly to the Inquisition. By 1576, the Spanish Fury was unleashed on Antwerp despite Philip's protection of his great textual project. Montano returned to Spain, living as an ascetic and continuing his work in scholarship, particularly his interest in allegorical, at times mystical, readings of biblical architecture, above all the Temple of Solomon. Montano in fact had made a contribution to the eighth volume of the polyglot Bible of 1572, *Exemplar sive de sacris fabrics liber* (*Exemplar; or, Book on Sacred Edifices*): his portion presented a reconstruction of the Temple according to the Hebrew tradition with a tower above the porch and five stories in elevation. The illustration included tribal tents, the tabernacle replete with small cherubim, a reconstruction of Noah's Ark, and a topographical map.[59]

Here, then, we find a striking, if not necessarily mystical, link between the early Antwerp printmakers' interest in Roman ruins and the long Western

narrative that leads from the Roman destruction of the Temple of Jerusalem to the translation of the spoils from that event into the building of the
Colosseum and on to the Colosseum as the model for the Tower of Babel in
numerous Renaissance artworks. The construction of a polyglot monument
in the aftermath of another devastating period of material destruction and
spoliation only underscores the relations among languages, texts, building,
and ruins that had long been a trope of the period's intellectual and artistic
development.

In 1547, at the age of forty-two and six years before his death, the Amsterdam artist Cornelis Anthonisz., whose work was featured and sold in the
Antwerp printing houses,[60] created a drawing of a building in the process
of tumbling down that resembles the Colosseum (see fig. 31). Angels with
trumpets seem to be blasting down the seven stories of the building with the
sheer force of their heavenly noise. A large bat flies off into the sky bearing the
monogram of Anthonisz. himself. Figures in the foreground in contemporary
dress seem halted as they are carrying building materials, or thrown about,
anguished and stricken to the ground by what is transpiring. A festooning inscription reads ALST OP THOECHSTE WAS / MOST HET DOEN NIET VALLEN:
what it was at the highest, must it then not fall?[61]

The Antwerp painter and printmaker Hendrik van Cleve, who had traveled to Italy and made an extensive portfolio of Roman ruins prints, as well
produced a series of landscapes with the Tower of Babel in construction and
destruction, showing it at times as a Colosseum-shaped structure and at other
times as a circular building emerging from a square base.[62] From the time
of their flight from Antwerp during the iconoclastic fury into the 1590s, the
brother painters Lucas and Marten van Valckenborch, friends of Bruegel and
most likely Protestants, also painted numerous images of the Tower of Babel.[63] All of these images depict the tower as a port city with workers in contemporary dress: the landscape is far closer to Antwerp than to the biblical
plains of Shinar.

But it is Bruegel's own Tower of Babel images, one—lost—on ivory and
the remaining two paintings now at Vienna (1563) and Rotterdam (1568), that
most clearly address these congruent themes. The paintings follow Christopher Plantin's exile from Antwerp for eighteen months after 1562 and Bruegel's
own departure from the city for Brussels in 1563. In an insightful essay published in 1982, the art historian S. A. Mansbach has outlined the many ways
the two paintings address the situation of Reformist thought in the years of
Spanish rule.[64] The Vienna version (see fig. 32) shows the tower at the margins
of a city. Laboriously, Nimrod's workmen have used a stretch of bedrock by
the sea to provide the foundation for a massive stepped cone, a wedding-cake
Colosseum, made in the Roman style of bricks clad in stone. The ruler appears
in the left foreground, supported by armed men, his artisans humbled before
him on their knees in sixteenth-century clothing.[65] The Tower of Babel is ris-

FIGURE 31. Cornelis Anthonisz., *Tower of Babel*, 1547. British Museum, London.

ing beside a port with wharves. The somber Rotterdam Tower (see plate 7) is an ever-spiraling as well as incomplete construction, also alluding to the Colosseum and reaching into the clouds. It, too, is rising beside a port where seagoing vessels and barges appear, although the structure appears in a more pastoral landscape than the Vienna version.[66]

Acquainted personally with Rome's ruin and the devastation of the 1527 sack, ruled by a foreign king who spoke none of the living languages of their city, subjected to foreign military violence, and torn by local religious strife regarding representation, a number of the printmakers of the period were particularly drawn to this story of ruined human making and broken communication. At the same time, Antwerpians were producing their polyglot version of the Bible, drawing on Jewish, Roman Catholic, and Protestant traditions and secretly practicing a newly ecumenical form of religious devotion. These projects resonated to the humanist dreams of cooperation and mutually understood values that were also a message of the Tower of Babel narrative.

FIGURE 32. Pieter Bruegel the Elder, *The Tower of Babel*, 1563. Oil on oakwood. Kunsthistorisches Museum, Vienna.

Coornhert's Haarlem pupil Galle's first engravings had appeared with the Aux Quatre Vents workshop in 1557.[67] In 1569, six and seven years after Bruegel's towers, Galle engraved one of his many print series on the theme of human suffering. His *Clades Judaeae Gentis* (*The Disasters of the Jewish People*) were engraved in 1569 from drawings made between 1567 and 1568 by Maerten van Heemskerck, including a monumental self-portrait of van Heemskerck as the frontispiece.[68] Beginning with an image of Noah making a burnt sacrifice and another of Noah's drunkenness and exposure, van Heemskerck includes two images of the Tower of Babel. The first bears a Latin inscription explaining that "together" the people courageously gather their materials to the top of the clouds and stars, yet the image shows the ziggurat-shaped tower already beginning to fall in large pieces, apparently unnoticed by the figures on the ground.

The context here is a *vanitas* theme that frequently appeared with reference to the magnificence of ancient buildings, especially the wonders of the world. One of Martial's epigrams, for instance, says of the vault in Domitian's palace on the Palatine that the pyramids themselves would be a "small part of the Palatine hall": Domitian's vault "pierces heaven," and it is "hidden amid the lustrous stars."[69] The second image shows the building in ruins, with startling distortions of perspective and upside-down features underscoring van Heemskerck's talent in creating mass and depth in the image. Here the figures retreat toward the front of the plate while an oddly nonchalant Nimrod/Nebuchadrezzar figure leans on a sarcophagus. The inscription explains that high Babylon, built by many men, fell, shaking the earth and making the hearts of men tremble. The remainder of the series includes images of Lot and his family leaving burning Sodom; Lot committing incest with his daughter and hiding his face in shame; the destruction of Jericho (see fig. 33); the destruction of Ai and the stoning of Achan; the hanging of the king of Ai and his corpse brought to the gate of the city; Samson, released from prison, destroying the temple of the Philistines; the burial of Samson; the capture of Tirsah; the people of Israel divided between Tibni and Omri; Jehu destroying the temple and statue of Baal; Jehu adoring the golden calves; the Chaldeans carrying away the pillars of the Temple of Jerusalem; the Chaldeans carrying away the temple treasures; the birth of Christ and adoration of the shepherds; the adoration of the Magi; and, finally, the destruction of Jerusalem by Titus.

FIGURE 33. Philips Galle (after Maerten van Heemskerck), *The Destruction of Jericho*. Plate 7 from *The Disasters of the Jewish People* (1549). Museum Plantin-Moretus, Antwerp, collection Printroom.

In sum, the series is something like a protofilmstrip of the dominant images of ruin in the Hebrew scriptures and New Testament. The engravings, with their reliance on many of the same passages in Kings that had been emphasized in earlier depictions of iconoclasm, depict stories of religious violence and material destruction from the Hebrew scriptures by redeploying van Heemskerck's drawings of Rome: its arches, triumphs, *opus caementicium* basilicas, columns, statues, and, in the depiction of the Nativity, even the oculus of the Pantheon, through which a heavenly light comes down into the center of a simple awning stretched between ruined walls.

Three years later, in 1572, again employing drawings by van Heemskerck, Galle engraved a set of eight plates of the wonders of the world (the traditional seven with the Colosseum added as an eighth in the series) accompanied by Latin verses by Hadrianus Junius. Despite their grandeur, the enormity of the wonders of the world is not sufficient to lay claim to significance; it is the combination of magnificence with ingenious striving—creative powers— that made them of interest to early humanists including Chrysolaras, Alberti, and the author of the *Hypnerotomachia*, who had asked, on viewing an obelisk, "what bold invention of art, what power and human energy, what organization and incredible expense were needed to hoist this weight so high into the air, to rival the heavens[?] ... It was enough to silence every other structure, however large and incredible."[70] The wonders of the world often seemed to persist simply as the gauge for measuring more recent achievements. Saint Peter's was compared to the Temple of Diana at Ephesus, Brunelleschi's dome to the Temple of Artemis in the same city.

In van Heemskerck's series of the wonders, *The Walls of Babylon* are juxtaposed to *The Colosseum at Rome*: the former bears an inscription describing the tomb of Semiramis and mentioning that the walls are "bitumine," or pitch; the latter's inscription tells of the sacred and ludic uses of the Colosseum. The Colosseum alone is depicted in a ruined state and clearly borrows, as *The Disasters of the Jewish People* does, from drawings of more than forty years earlier. Juxtaposing these two series helps us distinguish between the intact, even if vanished or invisible, forms of the "wonders of the world," each of which remained integral through legends and traditional portrayals.

Van Heemskerck and Galle show the completed buildings, but they also depict, most often in the foreground, scenes of building: workmen chisel the columns of the Temple of Diana and sand and polish the gigantic face of the Colossus of Rhodes; a figure wearing a laurel wreath holds a two-dimensional drawing on a tablet for the Colossus, whose completed form towers in the middle distance. Time goes from left to right and foreground to background. Such structures are never less than wholes, which is how they endure as comparisons for measurements. Like the pagan gods themselves, they do not suffer decline—they disappear.

In something like the style of Poussin, time had moved from background to foreground in the prints depicting the ruined forms of *The Disasters of the Jewish People*. What was once whole was erased by sudden violence and blazing flames—even the birth of Christ is an eruption in the fabric of ancient structures. Yet, together, the two series—one properly a collection of landscapes arranged in loose chronology, the other made of narratives arranged in the "historical" order of the books of the Bible from Genesis to Matthew, with the addition of Titus's destruction of the Temple of Jerusalem after the birth of Christ—give the viewer a sense of the impermanence of sacred structures.[71] There is little sense of Christian triumph of the kind we found at Santa Croce.

Instead, Galle, a close friend of Arias Montano and most likely involved with the Family of Love, too, finds in his Latin inscriptions, and in his many other series depicting wisdom and morality (his series of the *Sibyls*, of *Exemplary Women*, and of *The Power of Women*, his portrait engravings of prominent humanists) an accommodating practice of belief. At the same time, his total oeuvre also includes images of classical gods and goddesses; his series of seventeen *Nymphs* from classical mythology shows nymphs of the sea holding tridents and resting on seashells; his nymphs of rivers and streams are shown by water, most often spilling more water from urns and basins.[72] Although he remained a Roman Catholic, even when the Calvinists dominated Antwerp in the 1580s, Galle apparently held to the heterodox morality of his mentor Coornhert into his old age. His biographer and editor Arno Dolders explains that Coornhert's position could be summarized as "strongly affirming man's own moral responsibility for his actions on earth, while also striving for perfection by following the moral and spiritual guidelines set by the life and Passion of Jesus Christ."[73] The humanism of van Heemskerck and Galle, like the classical outlook of the school of Fontainebleau, included a fascination with archaic pleasures. The function of ruins representations here is a reminder of the Fall, a means of reflection on experienced destruction, and, via serial production, a way to minimize the material status of images.

The *matrix* of the plate was a point of origin for reproduction and, once struck, an emblem of finitude. Even the most skilled printmakers provided the viewer with an experience more akin to reading than to the sensual apprehension of surfaces and forms. Printmaking incorporated its own shattered image; the plates were altered and worn down in the process of their fabrication, and their arrangement in series was conducive to using them for didactic and moralistic purposes. Out of the North came two dominant strains of ruins imagery—the landscape and the allegory—that stand in contrast to the archaeological and architectural functions that had dominated, and indeed continued to dominate, southern printmaking. Landscape and allegory were the dominant strains of northern Renaissance art per se, yet ruins imagery gave temporal poignancy to these modes in both painting and printmaking:

FIGURE 34. Dirck Volckertszoon Coornhert (after Maerten van Heemskerck), *Satan Smiting Job with Boils*, ca. 1548. British Museum, London.

for Protestants, the decay of materials and the continuity of human action appeared against a backdrop of vanished pagan mores, a humanist classical revival, and a critique of the Roman Catholic Church that became conflated with the imperial and pagan Rome it had itself superseded.

Inherent to the experience of allegory is a sense of the literal, the material, giving way and fading under the pressure of inferred meaning. Allegory is inherently iconoclastic in this sense—and allegorical readings of art carry with them a denigration of ornament and skepticism regarding the pleasures of aesthesis that would continue to perplex and challenge moralists and philosophers of the Enlightenment, contributing to the development of aesthetics as a philosophical field. Allegorical meaning is stored in the work in an overdetermined fashion; it compels private and repeated viewing; its use is both immediate and deferred and, once internalized, discarded. For northern humanist printmakers, ruins were evidence of the pastness of the past but increasingly viewed as continuing backdrops to the realm of present moral action.

Stories from the Hebrew scriptures, in a paradoxical inversion of the Roman obliteration of the Temple, took place in the looming and shadowed recesses of Roman structures, and, as we have seen, so did stories of contemporary violence during the Spanish occupation. The artist and viewer could be witnesses to history and to history's repetition. In the earliest ruins images by Cock and van Heemskerck, the field of representation was defined by the observing artist on the scene: eventually native figures were shown traversing the landscape, the artist himself might be presented in a self-portrait as he worked to depict, or studied, or gestured toward the features of the structure before him. Yet van Heemskerck also used his on-site sketches as backdrops to biblical scenes, as he does by situating the narrative of his 1548 *Satan Smiting Job with Boils*, engraved by Coornhert, within the frame of his 1532 sketch of the Forum of Nerva (see fig. 34).

Beyond their use as archaeological curiosities and souvenirs of experience or vicarious experience, northern ruins representations came to rely on a hermeneutic involving an acknowledgment of layers of time that were mirrored in the layering of the image—the ruined backdrop, the scene of ancient action, the analogy to contemporary circumstances. All were threaded by questions of theodicy: what was the legacy of the fall and redemption of humankind? Were women nymphs and daughters of Eve, agents of corruption; or, as daughters of the Sibyls and the sage women of the Hebrew scriptures, were they agents of redemption? Was contemporary religious violence an aftershock of the disasters of the classical and Hebrew worlds? These questions were founded upon the material existence of ruins and, in true dialectical fashion, quantities of such ruins prompted the qualities of immaterial speculation.

PLATE 1. Maso di Banco, *Saint Sylvester Sealing the Dragon's Mouth and Resuscitating Two Pagan Magicians*, ca. 1335. Fresco. Bardi di Vernio Chapel, Santa Croce, Florence. From *The Life of Saint Sylvester*.

PLATE 2. Sandro Botticelli, *Adoration of the Magi*, 1475. Tempera on panel. Uffizi, Florence. Cosimo, Piero, and Giovanni de' Medici are depicted as the Three Kings; the spectators include Giuliano and Lorenzo de' Medici and Botticelli himself in a self-portrait on the right.

PLATE 3. Albrecht Altdorfer, *Nativity* (*Die Geburt Christi*), ca. 1513. Oil on wood. Gemälde-galerie, Staatliche Museen, Berlin.

PLATE 4. Johann Heinrich Wilhelm Tischbein, *Portrait of Goethe in the Roman Campagna*, 1787. Oil on canvas. Städelsches Kunstinstitut, Frankfurt am Main. (Many viewers have noticed that Goethe seems to have two left feet.)

PLATE 5. Hermannus Posthumus, *Landscape with Roman Ruins*, 1536. Oil on canvas. Palais Liechtenstein, the Princely Collections, Vaduz-Vienna.

PLATE 6. Jan Gossart (aka Mabuse), *The Adoration of the Kings*, 1510–1515. Oil on wood. National Gallery, London; bought with a special grant and contributions from The Art Fund, Lord Glenconner, Lord Iveagh, and Alfred de Rothschild, 1911.

PLATE 7. Pieter Bruegel the Elder, *The Tower of Babel*, 1568. Oil on panel. Museum Boijmans van Beuningen, Rotterdam.

PLATE 8. Hubert Robert, *Vue imaginaire de la Grande Galerie du Louvre en ruines*, 1796. Oil on canvas. Musée du Louvre, Paris.

PLATE 9. Charles-Louis Clérisseau, *Stanza delle rovine*, 1766. La Chiesa della Trinità dei Monti, Rome.

PLATE 10. Joseph Michael Gandy, *Architectural Ruins, a Vision*, 1798. Watercolor on paper. Soane Museum, London.

PLATE 11. François Racine de Monville, Broken Column, completed 1782. Désert de Retz, Chambourcy, France.

V. Model

THE ARCHITECTURAL IMAGINARY

In contrast to the practices of these northern allegorists throughout the sixteenth century, other printmakers—especially in Prague and Rome—continued to create ruins representations of commemorative and archaeological interest. Two-dimensional representations of three-, and occasionally two-, dimensional phenomena, ruins prints played among the functions of drawing, schema, map, guide, and model. As transcriptions made at the time of observation, registries of ruins undergoing an ongoing ruination, they also served as historical records in themselves and could go on to influence forms yet to come. In his *Antiquités*, Joachim Du Bellay had written:

> Judge by these ample ruins View, the rest
> The which injurious Time hath quite outworne,
> Since of all Workmen helde in reckning best,
> Yet these olde fragments are for patternes borne:[1]

The historian of sculpture Malcolm Baker has emphasized the duality of models, particularly in the eighteenth century, as "models of" and "models for," asking how models intended for execution differ from those that follow existing works or artifacts.[2] As we have seen in the work of Sebastiano Serlio, Vitruvius, Étienne Du Pérac, and Antoine (or Antonio) Lafréry, ruins representations could be designed to function as "models for" future constructions in often entirely different sites and contexts. Indeed, even when ruins images are "models of"—in the archaeological or metaphysical sense alike—their context specificity has tended to erode, for they belong to vanished worlds and can be measured and copied only to the extent that their fabric and surroundings have survived. Perhaps for this reason, secular, nonallegorical, practices of printmaking tended to include measurements, descriptions, and details of the ruin's location. Yet, at the same time, artists of ruins come to experience an increasing freedom not only in their juxtaposition of disparate times but also in their manipulation of spatial relations and play with the physical constraints of their own mediums.

Trompe l'Oeil

As early as 1500, Pinturicchio (Bernardino di Betto) was painting images of actual vines twining and obscuring the vegetal ornaments of a ruined Roman building in his *Nativity* at the Baglione chapel of Santa Maria Maggiore in Spello.[3] This kind of play between organic forms and stone images of organic forms is particularly evident in the elaborate title pages printmakers created for works arranged in series from the mid-sixteenth century forward. Ruins prints come to be framed by the ornaments and motifs of Greek and Roman architecture. And since ruined buildings, especially Roman ones, frequently bear inscriptions themselves, representing inscription through inscription leads to a complex practice of trompe l'oeil.

Copying existing inscriptions and in turn inscribing the ruins with one's name dates at least to the seventeenth-century practice of the Roman traveler Pietro della Valle at Persepolis—where visitors can also read the names of generations of merchants, travelers, and adventurers responding with graffiti to the great inscriptions of the Achaemenid kings.[4] But inscriptions in literature and visual art began a century earlier to take their cue from ancient practices of inscription. Gaps and lacunae in time call for a supplemental speech or voice. In the sonnet tradition, this voice emerges in the use of closing, aphoristic lines, as a kind of written pediment that follows the twists and turns of earlier spoken lines. In visual art, this supplemental language most often introduces writing or carving into the scene.

Since ruined buildings often already come with inscriptions, a practice of trompe l'oeil develops here as well. To inscribe an inscription authenticates the relation between the present moment of writing and the inscribed object in a process akin to punning. Bound in folios for perusing, the prints function as a series of inscriptions, and an inscription becomes the "cover" of the ruin.

When Hieronymus Cock published his *Praecipua* in 1551, he made a title page (see fig. 35) that depicted an inscription for the work placed within an altar-like frame, which—beneath a pile of trophies (helmets, axes, swords, and shields), flanked by a herma and a herm, and standing above a garland of vegetables and fruits attached to the beards of matching flanking satyrs—was itself situated within a grotto.

Beneath the title he adds his claim as maker and lets the reader know where and when the work was produced: "Antuerpia per Hiro[nymus] Coc[k] MDLI [1551]." The privilege of King Philip (Caesar) appears in a medallion serving as a caption to a masklike portrait below. Aside from signaling a legitimacy derived from antique forms, particularly armorial displays on sarcophagi, the title page speaks to notions of boundary, threshold, accumulation, and fertility. Herms developed out of the use of piles of stones to mark boundaries in the ancient world; armorial trophies allude, as does the narrative of many contemporary cultural forms from theater to prints themselves, to triumphal displays; the satyrs and their produce to sexual pleasure and fertility.

FIGURE 35. Hieronymus Cock, title page from *Praecipua aliquot romanae antiquitatis ruinarum monimenta* (Antwerp, 1551). British Museum, London.

The engraved trompe l'oeil rusticated stonework frame, with its herms at slightly different angles and depths and its dizzying perspectives and planes, makes it difficult to determine what is prior and what is later on every level. A decade later, when the Venetian printmaker Battista Pittoni issued his revised edition of Cock's same prints, the herma appears on the left, the herm on the right, and Pittoni's name, and the privilege of the Venetian state, are placed where Cock's signature and the privilege of Antwerp had appeared.[5] Pittoni, in other editions, used a two-page spread as an opening page that welcomed the reader down a road of ruins, where he or she is invited to follow the gesticulating figures of other students of ruins and recognize the column of Marcus Aurelius, the columns of the Forum, the Castel Sant'Angelo, the Flaminian obelisk, and the distant Pantheon (see fig. 36). His print of an artist drawing in the Colosseum (see fig. 37) and another of someone sketching while boys tumble over a wall near the Septizodium (see fig. 38) give the reader further instructions in ruin appreciation. Whether Pittoni's version of the *Praecipua* was taken literally from the copperplates of Antwerp is doubtful since more than half are reversed and most have been reworked in their details.

The frames, inscriptions, and mottos of ruins prints continue to be important for the reception of the actual images throughout the Renaissance. They underscore the importance of allegorical readings and supplement

FIGURE 36. Battista Pittoni, plate 1 (title page spread) from *Ex variis rvinis pr Romanae*, n.d. Marquand Library of Art and Archaeology, Princeton University.

FIGURE 37. Battista Pittoni, *Draughtsman in Colosseum* (*Haec habet scenographiam secundorum porticuum colossei*). Plate 12 from *Ex variis rvinis pr Romanae* (n.d.). Marquand Library of Art and Archaeology, Princeton University.

FIGURE 38. Battista Pittoni, *Draughtsman, climbing boys, and figures near Septizodium*. Plate 5 from *Ex variis rvinis pr Romanae* (n.d.). Marquand Library of Art and Archaeology, Princeton University.

whatever attention has been devoted to realism, accuracy, and the firsthand view. Among the sixteenth-century engravers in Rome, Du Pérac went to particular pains to include elaborate frames around his images. As his work matured, he increased this practice in its detail and complexity. He clearly came to consider his individual prints as elements of larger series with repeated ornaments unifying the wholes. He adds inscriptions, sometimes using alphabetized keys, to the images themselves, including information about the most up-to-date status of the sites, but the frames, with their caryatids, grotesque winged heads, trompe l'oeil backgrounds of brickwork, and scrolls, bring the ruins into the realm of reverie as his readers are invited to compare actual and "reconstructed" views of each site.[6]

Therefore, as much as the prints speak to survivals, they also speak to decay: Du Pérac's customers at his shop near the church of Santa Maria della Pace could vividly picture the decline of each structure. At the same time, printmakers emphasize that theirs is an art made with lines on metals depicting lines on metals underscoring their wear and decay on the levels of both artistic practice and the thematic of the image. Giacomo de Rossi's 1660 reprint of the 1606 *Vestigi delle antichita di Roma, Tivoli, Pozzuolo et altri luochi* (*Vestiges of the Antiquities of Rome, Tivoli, Pozzuolo and Other Places*), "stampati"

FIGURE 39. Marco Sadeler (after Aegidius Sadeler), title page from *Vestigi delle antichita di Roma, Tivoli, Pozzuolo et altri luochi, come si ritrovavano nel secolo XV* (Prague, 1606). This photograph from the reprinted edition by G. J. de Rossi (Rome, 1660[?]). Marquand Library of Art and Archaeology, Princeton University.

(printed) in Prague at the court of Rudolph II "cum priviligio" of the "Caesar" as well as by Aegidius Sadeler and "excudit" (engraved) by Marco Sadeler, bears its inscriptions by many hands in trompe l'oeil spaces (see fig. 39). Here, too, herms flank the title inscription, which is incongruously carved into a splayed wolf's skin hung by pegs in an altar opening. Above their heads, braziers send out clouds of smoke. Flanking the herms are a triumphant angel on the left, perched on a pile of maps and bound volumes and holding aloft a trumpet, and a winged reaper with a scythe on the right, sitting atop broken columns and masonry ornaments that are scattered as well across the foreground. Arches behind each figure are open to an illusory neutral background. Reading from right to left, the grim harvest of ruins seems to be making its way into two-dimensional pages and maps. The triumph goes to the trumpeting angel.

Piranesi's Labor

In his first book, his *Prima parte di architetture, e prospettive*, published in 1743 when he was only twenty-three, Giovanni Battista Piranesi provided a similar trompe l'oeil title page but with a characteristic inventive difference: Piranesi's inscribed stone—announcing his title and dedication to his early patron and mentor, the Venetian builder Nicola Giobbe—appears lodged in a shadowed wilderness of weeds and fungi, branches and tumbling pediments, a tilted urn, broken columns and a portrait bust, funerary reliefs, and, framing the left side of the image, the worn surface of an obelisk (see fig. 40). The reader's view is not at all an encounter with a flat surface. Instead, we must find the stone by tacking upward from our *sotto in sù* (worm's eye) perspective. In this image, we find not only traces of Piranesi's preparation for his career as architect and engraver but as well the cultural attitudes that will underlie his entire oeuvre of more than one thousand plates.

FIGURE 40. Giovanni Battista Piranesi, frontispiece from *Prima parte di architetture, e prospettive invente incise da Giambattista Piranesi* (Rome: Nella stamperia di N.e M. Pagliarini librari a Pasquino, after 1748). Department of Rare Books and Special Collections, Princeton University Library.

Born in 1720 in Mogliano Veneto, near Mestre, Piranesi was the son of a stone mason and throughout his life described himself as a "Venetian architect." His maternal uncle Matteo Lucchesi served as chief architect for the "Magistrato alle acque," the waterworks authority of the Venetian Republic, a position that would have involved supervising the construction and upkeep of breakwaters, moles, and massive foundations. In addition to his knowledge of aqueducts and other forms of civil engineering, Lucchesi was engaged with the formulation of theories regarding architectural history as he and his architect colleague Tommaso Temanza joined the intellectual circle around the Franciscan friar, intellectual, and architectural theorist Carlo Lodoli. Lodoli favored a unifying, ultimately mathematical, logic as the underlying principle of all building. He further contended that the development of architecture was characterized by multiple points of origin—a view in sharp contrast to that of the Jesuit Abbé Marc-Antoine Laugier, with his influential account of the primitive hut as the source of all later architectural forms. Lodoli objected to the use of materials as anything other than themselves: hence, for example, he condemned the representation of wood in stone. The truth of architecture lay, he believed, in the intrinsic qualities of its materials.[7]

Temanza and Lucchesi themselves argued that all antique edifices were constructed according to a set of basic procedures as early builders employed blocks of stone and beams of timber. The first procedure used blocks of stones alone: the Egyptians relied on this technique and were followed by the Etruscans. The Greeks built their early structures in this "Egyptian manner" but introduced a second innovation as they created small timber houses with post-and-beam forms. Lucchesi and Temanza held that the Greeks went on to copy these timber forms using stone alone. However, since a stone architrave cannot span a large and high space, a further innovation was necessary. Relying on the arguments of Alberti in *De re aedificatoria*, the Venetians described how one beam was replaced by two forming a gable, and then further supports were added. The Romans added an arch to Etruscan stone walls and Greek trabeation; their "mixed manner" made it possible to build enormous forms—baths, amphitheaters, and the Pantheon.[8] Lucchesi and Temanza encouraged Piranesi to study architecture, and their valorization of Roman ingenuity would continue to inform his studies and endeavors—claims for Roman genius would lead him into a preoccupation with architectural polemics throughout his middle and late age.

Piranesi's fascination with stone and vaults, particularly on a "magnificent" scale, evolved from this early milieu of architectural speculation. His brother Angelo, a Carthusian monk, provided him with lessons in Greek and Latin and a knowledge of ancient history, studies that fired him with zeal for classical antecedents. And in his youth Piranesi was given instruction in perspective theory and engraving at the *bottega*, or studio/shop, of Carlo Zucchi. The *bottega*'s commissions for theatrical designs exposed Piranesi to the innovations of baroque scenography. He went on to study with the scene painters

Giuseppe and Domenico Valeriani at a time when stage design was radically reformed by Filippo Juvarra and, above all, by Ferdinando Galli-Bibiena and his son Giuseppe. Members of a Florentine/Bolognese family of theater designers, the Bibiena, over three generations, radically manipulated the possibilities of perspective, particularly in their practice of the *scena per angolo*—two-point perspective with asymmetrical placement of the flats.

The Bibienas' depictions of ruins, pyramids, obelisks, funeral halls, and prisons affected Piranesi's imagination not only through their content but also via their striking use of shadows, depth, and sharp recession.[9] Ferdinando Bibiena's 1711 treatise, *L'architettura civile: preparata su la geometria e ridotta alle prospettive* (*Civil Architecture: Composed with respect to Geometry and Reduced to Perspective*), was well known to Piranesi. There the scenographer particularly emphasizes views that exaggerate the monumentality of structures; they loom dramatically in ways that never could be visible when projected from the ordinary horizon line.[10] Yet the depth of the *scena per angolo* fills the stage in such a way as to produce effects not only of enormity but also of interiority. Because such a view is oblique and partial, the audience must complete the depicted forms by using their imaginations.

With his move to Rome in 1740 as a draftsman in the retinue of the Venetian Ambassador Francesco Venier, Piranesi could be found working in the *bottega* of Giuseppe Vasi by 1742, continuing to develop his skills as a printmaker. The year after the *Prima parte*, he explored the archaeological sites at Herculaneum. When, out of funds, he returned to Venice, he frequented the studios of Tiepolo and the engraver Giuseppe Wagner and eventually, in 1747, returned to Rome as Wagner's agent. In a period of less than a decade, he went on to publish his fantastic architectural images of the *Prima parte*, worked out plans for two drawing series, the *grotteschi* and the *carceri d'invenzione* (imaginary prisons), and began the production of his first set of *Vedute di Roma*.[11]

As we saw in the *Prima parte*'s title pages, the imagination can commit a view to memory and offer senses of time and space that cannot be realized. In his preface to his four-volume work of 1756, *Le Antichità Romane* (*Roman Antiquities*), Piranesi explains that he plans to re-create Roman space on paper: "When I saw the remains of the ancient buildings of Rome lying as they do in cultivated fields or gardens and wasting away under the ravages of time, or being destroyed by greedy owners who sell them as materials for modern building, I determined to preserve them forever by means of engraving."[12] In the course of the development of his work, he displays a vertigo-inducing facility for moving between the page and the architectural space. The very title of *La Tavola Monumentale* (ca. 1749) from the *grotteschi* (see fig. 41) evokes a kind of trompe l'oeil, indicating the word for the engraving plate itself, *la tavola*, as well as what might be considered to be the monumental central image it presents—the tabula rasa facade of a stone block framed by an egg-and-dart border on which rest, or are hung, several cameos of figures in ancient drapery. The block is flanked to its left, at a recession, by another, similar, stone

FIGURE 41. Giovanni Battista Piranesi, *La Tavola Monumentale*. From *Opere varie di archi-*
tettura prospettive grotteschi antichità sul gusto degli antichi romani. Inventate ed incise da Gio.
Battista Piranesi, architetto veneziano (Rome, 1750). Department of Rare Books and Special
Collections, Princeton University Library.

block. And yet it would be just as possible to believe we are looking at stone
blocks of varying proximities, against each of which rests a picture frame. Or,
perhaps more accurately, we could argue that it is only the title of the plate
that gives the "tavola" its centrality within a veritable cascade of images. The
work's feathery curving lines obviously owe a debt to Piranesi's exposure to
Tiepolo, and especially the older Venetian's 1743 capricci. Juxtaposed to the
copperplates of the *carceri* with their harsh deep engraved lines effecting a
resemblance to carved stone and hewn timbers, the copperplates of the *grot-*
teschi are marked with the lightest of etching strokes and nowhere more than
in the frothy effects of the *La Tavola Monumentale*.

What are we looking at when we look at *La Tavola Monumentale*? The first
answer we might pose is "a sheet of paper." That is, the print portrays on paper a sheet of paper, rippling at the bottom edge, scrolled slightly on the right
side, where it rests on a textured surface, and vanishes on the left side as the
border of the plate cuts it off. Perhaps only by imagining that we are looking
at a drawing of a drawing—or, more accurately, an etching of a drawing—can
we accommodate the jumble of objects we find here. We cannot be looking at

a space informed by gravity, landscape, or any other order of experienced perception. Instead we see something like a dreamscape. In the upper left corner
(see fig. 42), barely visible, is a stone tablet inscribed with illegible and legible
letters alike; those that are legible say CHE SIENO / ALLEGRAMENTE (roughly,
"that are merrily"). A draped hand holds a carafe or glass beside it, and just below is a barrel, supposedly a wine barrel, on its side. The letters, according to
an interpretation offered by Carlo Bertelli in 1976, represent a notation for the
price of wine—"otto quattri foglietta a i che sieno allegramente"—*otto* is the
number eight, a *quattrino* was a copper coin, a *foglietta* a half-liter measure.[13]

Returning to the larger plate (fig. 41), to the right of these images are ambiguous billowing forms from which emerge shields (one of which bears the
open-mouthed face of a Medusa) and escutcheons that seem lodged in clouds
and braided through by garlands and feathers—all floating above a large urn
fuming with smoke or steam. To the left of this cluster of plumes a trumpet
is suspended over the great stone block. In the foreground a sphinxlike head
protrudes from a vessel with vegetation sprouting from its edges; a petite,

FIGURE 42. Giovanni Battista Piranesi, *La Tavola Monumentale* (detail), 1750. (See fig. 41.)

FIGURE 43. Giovanni Battista Piranesi, *La Tomba di Nerone*. From *Opere varie di architettura prospettive grotteschi antichità sul gusto degli antichi romani. Inventate ed incise da Gio. Battista Piranesi, architetto veneziano* (Rome, 1750). Department of Rare Books and Special Collections, Princeton University Library.

though monstrous, flying basilisk, or a sculpture of one, sits, wings spread, before the fuming urn; a welter of stones and sticks and logs and what could be pan pipes; a stick in the embrace of a slender snake, or the remains of a caduceus; what could be a tumbled model of an ancient arcade; skulls, and more.

The overabundance of particulars and the paucity of identifiable wholes here put the viewer-reader in a quandary. It is not simply that forms are ambiguous but rather that things and the atmosphere in which they reside are in transformation; they emerge, recede, change shape, scale, and dimension; foreground and background and horizon, perspective lines and point of view (e.g., are we looking up or looking down?) are indeterminate. We are inhabiting a paper world with its own internal dimensions of time and space.

It is therefore not surprising that the four *grotteschi* plates—this, *La Tavola Monumentale*; the skull-littered architectural extravaganza of *Gli Scheletri* (*The Skeletons*); the tumbling sarcophagi, tombs, and cascades of water, threaded with curling serpents, of *La Tomba di Nerone* (*Nero's Tomb*; see fig. 43); and the architectural debris, chains, bones, sphinx, reclining figures, and herm of *L'Arco Trionfale* (*The Triumphal Arch*)—have been variously interpreted as allegories. The pathbreaking English-language Piranesi scholar John Wilton-Ely holds that Piranesi is likely to have executed the four plates as a contribution to the Accademia dell'Arcadia, the elite literary and artistic society that had its headquarters in the Bosco Parrasio on the Gianicolo. Wilton-Ely suggests that the newly elected Piranesi may have intended the plates to represent themes of renewal in concert with the Arcadian Academy's ambitions to renew the culture.[14]

Maurizio Calvesi has claimed that Piranesi's use of the noun *grottesco* and at times the adjective, as in *grottesca invenzione* and other applications of the notion, indicates not only the fantastic but also elements of the arabesque and the baroque and that such allusions are not merely decorative; they indicate the presence of meanings.[15] Among these is the Roman origin of the term, as we've seen, in the decorative paintings found in the subterranean vaults (the *grotte*) of the Golden House of Nero in the late fifteenth century. Calvesi finds as well throughout Piranesi's work a recurring set of allusions to the *New Science* of the Neapolitan philosopher of history Giambattista Vico, with the *grotteschi* particularly alluding to Vico's interest in the Mosaic tablets of the law and the labors of Hercules.[16] Calvesi believes that each of the *grotteschi* refers as well to one of the four seasons. More recently, Francesco Nevola has argued that whether or not the four *grotteschi* refer to Vico's four eras in his spiral of history—that is, the era of the Giants, the era of the Egyptians, the era of the Romans, and the era of the Moderns—the series is about "the passage of time." He goes on to give his own interpretation of the plates as a commentary on the ages of Gold, Silver, Bronze, and Heroes set out by Hesiod in his *Works and Days*.[17]

The temptation to allegorize presented by these prints underscores Piranesi's unsurpassed skill in re-creating temporal sequence by means of works in series as well as the hermeneutic difficulties of "reading" the fragments and detritus of history. Both the *carceri d'invenzione* and the *grotteschi* are vital for understanding Piranesi's relation to his "speaking ruins." Uncommissioned works, determined so far as we can know solely by the expressive, intellectual, and technical needs of the artist, these early works set out a paradigm for printmaking that engages the connections between words, images, and their referents at every level—not the least of which is the fertility of reproduction.

The vast machines of the well-known *carceri*, which seem designed to humiliate human powers of cognition and physical strength, are artifacts of a human hand; their enormous enclosed spaces the products of an even more enormous visionary mind. In the plate known as *The Giant Wheel*, numbered "IX" from the second edition onward, the cavernous architecture is intact, but the barely discernible figures—in torqued struggle along the rim, bowed in the foreground, or collecting in the distance—seem broken, nearly destroyed by some violence or suffering. A space above the wheel is evocative of sky, but is not sky—only adding to the feeling of claustrophobia and agoraphobia at once and so typical of the *carceri* as a group (see fig. 44).

In contrast, the gathered cultural debris of the *grotteschi*—their broken statues, columns, tombs, roundels, reliefs, herms, cornucopias, shells, fasces,

FIGURE 44. Giovanni Battista Piranesi, *The Giant Wheel*. Plate 9 from *Carceri d'invenzione* (*Imaginary Prisons*; 1749–1750). Metropolitan Museum of Art, New York; Harris Brisbane Dick Fund, 1937.

cameos, trumpets, bones, skulls, chains, mooring rings, and urns; their half-erased or faint inscriptions, rosettes, portraits, egg-and-dart moldings; their hazy skies, intimations of the sea, pines and palms, cascades, broken sticks and weeds, entwined with snakes and vines—is framed by illusionistic references, or metacommentaries, to the process of art itself. The image resolves, as it approaches the plate mark, to abstraction or a trompe l'oeil representation of the ground as paper. The lower right edge of *La Tomba di Nerone* (see fig. 45) shows a painter's palette lying on what seems to be the ground. And we find, sticking up through a hole in a fallen *enroulement*, or scroll-shaped ornament, a set of paintbrushes.

Viewed in relation to one another, the *carceri* and *grotteschi* are a brilliant exercise in the representation of emptiness and fullness. The vast and looming *carceri*, their stairs and ladders leading to nowhere, continually drawing the eye upward to where glimpses of "life" and light might appear, as they do to the inhabitants of Plato's cave, are defined by lack. We search in vain for exchange beyond pain, finding the inexorable fact of human limits within a silence that cries or screams would only echo and erase. The *grotteschi* are, by contrast, forests of symbols, dense with a kind of visual noise that demands the eye to keep searching particulars. The viewer is in the open—in this case, perhaps too free and confronted with an endless interpretive task.

FIGURE 45. Giovanni Battista Piranesi, *La Tomba di Nerone* (detail), 1750. (See fig. 43.)

All of Piranesi's early work manifests the tension between the closed actuality of material fact and the endlessly open possibilities tradition offers to invention. The ruin and disintegration of bodies and forms are transferred to the plate, but not simply to memorialize or capture them. Piranesi makes ruin the ground of a prolific reproduction.

The recent discovery that Piranesi used not only etching needles and several kinds of burins but also the more forceful *cisello profilatori*—a tool employed in metal sculpture—helps us understand the repertoire of lines he had at his disposal. Giovanna Scaloni writes that in the *carceri* Piranesi uses the burin (*bulino*) to bite into the metal with near "violence," accentuating the deep volumes of the images, adding to their strong aura of three-dimensionality.[18] Such a tool also requires gestures of stopping, lifting, and reinserting—quite the opposite of the fluid motion possible with the etching needle. The completely man-made world of the *carceri*, with their blocked, resolutely enclosed spaces, could not find a greater contrast to the fluid, organic motion created in the *grotteschi* via the etching needle. Mineral hardness and the soft vegetal imagery of vines, tendrils, and leaves are served respectively by the capacities of these tools.

Throughout Piranesi's imagery, these earthly phenomena are juxtaposed to objects of air and light: clouds and smoke. The revisions he made to his work rarely, if indeed ever, were technical corrections. Instead, any changes introduced new content or, above all, altered the effects of lighting. He seldom used cross-hatching, preferring instead to create more or less dense parallel lines.[19] The development of his work is tied to an increasing use of dark shadows, both deepening them and increasing them, and refinements in his presentation of clouds.[20] It is extremely difficult for a printmaker to evoke transparency, and the transparency of clouds without defined edges requires a very high level of mastery: between the *Prima parte* and a 1750 image of the fall of Phaeton, Piranesi learned to create effects of a mutable and moving sky.

The return to Rome strengthened the young would-be architect and engraver's connections not only with the Arcadians and their agenda of cultural renewal but also with the artistic circles of the French Academy, then housed in the Palazzo Mancini on the Via del Corso near his studio. Piranesi was attached enough to the French Academy that he signed some of his early prints: "Piranesi inv; incise, e vende in Roma in faccia all'Accademia di Francia."[21] When he issued the title page in later states of the *Prima parte*, he increased its deictic power by lightening the image of the inscribed stone, adding more cracks, rocks, and wear to the ruins and, vitally, placing tiny figures among them—their heads on a scale smaller than that of the funerary relief portraits in the foreground. Armed with staffs, their sleeves rolled up for climbing, these wiry explorers point to the title inscription. In states made after 1750 (including our fig. 40, shown earlier), Piranesi has added to his title "Architetto Vene-

FIGURE 46. Giovanni Battista Piranesi, frontispiece from *Prima parte di architetture, e prospettive*. In *Opere varie di architettura prospettive grotteschi antichità sul gusto degli antichi romani. Inventate ed incise da Gio. Battista Piranesi, architetto veneziano* (Rome, 1750). Department of Rare Books and Special Collections, Princeton University Library.

ziano" and an announcement of his new status as a member of the Arcadian Academy, "FRA GLI ARCADI / SALCINDIO TISEIO" (Among the Arcadians / Salcindio Tiseio). "Salcindio Tiseio" was the pastoral pseudonym Piranesi took upon his election. And at some point, for unknown reasons, he erased his initial dedication to Nicola Giobbe (see fig. 46).[22]

Piranesi was one of the approximately nine thousand members of the Accademia dell'Arcadia during the eighteenth century—many of them foreign, and particularly French, members. Founded in 1690, the academy encouraged a practice of the "sister arts" of painting and poetry, its devotees pursuing notions of a balance between nature and reason. The Arcadians refuted the extravagance of baroque aesthetics with a revival of classical knowledge and dedication to national and church-approved ideals. They took up Giovanni Pietro Bellori's doctrine of the "Idea" as a principle of concept-driven making, referring to their images and poems as *pensieri*. At the same time, they engaged in quite a bit of imaginative play: male members of the academy were known as *pastori*, and their female associates were called *pastorelle*—shepherds and shepherdesses. As we can see with "Salcindio Tiseio," they also took pastoral nicknames.[23]

Yet Arcadian neoclassicism involved more than costume drama. The poets, among them Gian Vincenzo Gravina and his pupil Paolo Antonio Rolli, rationalized the hendecasyllabic and paved the way for a revised lyric of freshness and originality intended to replace the metaphysics and elaborate conceits of the Marinists. Rolli, for example, who lived in England from 1715 to 1744, translating the works of John Milton and serving for a time as a librettist for George Frideric Handel (and described by Alexander Pope "with a feather behind his ear"), perhaps remains best known for his poem of a despairing lover seeking solace in a remote wood, "Solitario bosco ombroso." The work, published in 1727, begins:

> Solitario bosco ombroso
>   A te viene afflitto Cor
> Per trovar qualche riposo
>   Nel silenzio e nell'orror.[24]

> Solitary, shadowed wood
>   An afflicted heart comes to you
> To find some rest
>   Within your silence and terror.

The poem builds, from shadows, stones, sounds, and echoes, a scene of unrelenting melancholy.

Piranesi and Rolli, two Arcadians who could have met in the woods of the Gianicolo in the 1740s, had a profound effect on the Romantic reception of the Italian landscape. In *Dichtung und Wahrheit* (*Poetry and Truth*), Goethe explained that it was Rolli's song, performed by a "cheerful old Italian teacher named Giovanizzi" that, alongside his father's collection of engravings of Roman scenes, first gave him his dream of Italy.[25] When Goethe arrived in Rome forty years later, he wrote, "All the dreams of my youth have come to life: the first engravings I remember—my father hung his views of Rome in the hall. . . . Whenever I walk, I come upon familiar objects in an unfamiliar world; everything is just as I imagined it, yet everything is new."[26]

Rolli's poems with their amorous pastoral themes also involved the re-creation of the points of view of Cleopatra, Penelope, Medea, and other classical figures, bringing the legendary dead to life.[27] We can see that Piranesi's "speaking ruins" are rooted in this reanimating spirit that characterized such varied and imaginative Arcadian appropriations of the past. Nevertheless, developing his own motives for studying and representing the ancient monuments of the Romans, Piranesi went beyond Arcadian values.[28] From the start, Piranesi felt compelled to explain and justify his practice as an architect-engraver. He declares in his opening paragraphs to the *Prima parte* that, whether because of a decline in architectural practice or the absence of architectural patrons, no architect of the present could execute the "august majesty and Roman magnificence" of Roman relics. He finds "there seems to be no recourse than for me or some other modern architect to explain ideas through drawings . . . engrav[ing] them on copper."[29]

The twelve plates of Piranesi's 1743 edition in fact remain on the level of ideas: they are typical structures, imagined and projected, and indeed show the interface between imagination and projection. That interface is the source of all architectural creativity, yet in ingenious ways Piranesi displays "completed" or "intact" imaginary spaces: a "Large Sculpture Gallery," a "Dark Prison," a "Magnificent Bridge," a "Hall According to the Custom of the Ancient Romans," an "Ancient Capitol," "Stairways," a "Royal Courtyard," the "Vestibule of an Ancient Temple," an "Ancient Roman Forum," a "Doric Atrium," a "Group of Columns," an "Ancient Temple," and an "Ancient Mausoleum"—all of which are shown in perfected condition and inhabited by figures in contemporary eighteenth-century dress. And then he juxtaposes them to ruined forms in the process of being overcome by vegetation and weather: his "Remains of Ancient Buildings," "Ruins of an Ancient Tomb," and "Ancient Altar" are viewed in close-up and strewn with bones and skulls, and a "Sepulchral Chamber" is shown with exposed skeletons and upturned tombs and skulls.

In the recesses of Piranesi's ruined forms, the observer can see an occasional upper-class visitor in contemporary dress taking in a vista, but the structures are more often traversed by climbing figures of workmen, beggars, bent and weary-looking pilgrims—stooped figures in rags of the kind Piranesi later would hire as models off the Roman streets. These may in fact be realistic depictions of the poverty-stricken denizens, beaten down by life, of such local decayed structures. In the foreground of his view of the remains of the fountainhead of the Acqua Giulia, he prominently features a pair of women hanging up their ragged laundry—as if they needed the scarce sunlight in that part of the image to dry their clothing (see fig. 47).[30] Yet elsewhere—for example, in the figures leaning and balancing, trompe l'oeil style, on the "beam" of a caption in the foreground of his *Veduta del Sepolcro di Pisone Liciniano su*

FIGURE 47. Giovanni Battista Piranesi, *Veduta dell'avanzo del Castello, che prendendo una porzione dell'Acqua Giulia dal Condotto principale* (*View of Remaining Portion of the Fountainhead of the Acqua Giulia*). From *Vedute di Roma* (1760–1778). British Museum, London. The structure in the right background is the Villa Palombara.

l'antica via Appia, oltre gli acquidotti di Torre di mezza via d'Albano, Piranesi's pointing, conversing, and gesturing figures look like members of a troupe of commedia dell'arte characters who have found themselves stranded in the campagna (see fig. 48).[31]

The fact that ruined persons—the poor and homeless—often lived in the recesses of ruins is evidenced by many contemporary testimonies. To turn to two celebrated ones: William Beckford wrote in his 1780 *Travel-Diaries* of how, leaning late one day on a column of the Temple of Jupiter Stator, he saw that

> some women were fetching water from the fountain hard by, whilſt another group had kindled a fire under the shrubs and twiſted fig-trees which cover the Palatine hill. Innumerable vaults and arches peep out of the vegetation. It was upon these, in all probability, the splendid palace of the Caesars was raised. Confused fragments of marble and walls of lofty terraces, are the sole traces of its antient magnificence. A wretched rabble were roaſting their chestnuts, on the very spot, perhaps, where Domitian convened a senate. . . . The light of the flame caſt upon the figures around it, and the mixture of tottering wall with foliage impending above their heads, formed a ſtriking picture.[32]

FIGURE 48. Giovanni Battista Piranesi, A. *Veduta del Sepolcro di Pisone Liciniano su l'antica via Appia, oltre gli acquidotti di Torre di mezza via d'Albano: il cui lavoro è tutto di terra cotta. B. Sepolcro della famiglia Cornelia, spogliato de' suoi ornamenti. C. Rovine di altri antichi Sepolcri.* From *Vedute di Roma* (1760–1778). British Museum, London.

And in his *Italienische Reise* (*Italian Journey*), Goethe records a walk through Rome by the light of a full moon that, given the many years that passed between his experience and his writing of it, may be shaped by Piranesi or may, instead, give us some clue that Piranesi's figures are simply realistic. Goethe writes:

> Nobody who has not taken one can imagine the beauty of a walk through Rome by full moon. All details are swallowed up by the huge masses of light and shadow, and only the biggest and most general outlines are visible. We have just enjoyed three clear and glorious nights. The Colosseum looked especially beautiful. It is closed at night. A hermit lives in a small chapel and some beggars have made themselves at home in the crumbling vaults. These had built a fire on the level ground and a gentle breeze had driven the smoke into the arena, so that the lower parts of the ruins were veiled and only the huge masses above loomed out of the darkness. We stood at the railing and watched, while over our heads the moon stood high and serene. By degrees the smoke escaped through holes and crannies and in the moonlight it looked like fog. . . . This is the kind of illumination by which to see the Pantheon, the Capitol, the square in front of St. Peter's, and many other large squares and streets.[33]

Nineteenth-century guidebooks to Rome frequently recommend that visitors view the ruins by moonlight, as Goethe had. An early nineteenth-century collection of Piranesi's prints that had belonged to the English naturalist Frederick William Hope in the Ashmolean Museum is splashed with candle wax, indicating that at least some of Piranesi's viewers attempted to replicate such nocturnal visits.[34] Yet at the same time it is likely that the very idea of moonlit visits owes something to the tremendous popularity of Piranesi's prints throughout Britain and northern Europe.

Beckford and Goethe alike see the scenes before them with eyes well acquainted with the conventions of ruins prints: "wretched" figures, smoke, dramatic shadows, vegetation erupting through crumbling forms. Their accounts of particular details close with a sense of a "striking picture" and the abstractions of an illuminated view. Piranesi's own pronounced use of shadows and dramatic contrasts of light and dark areas and his placement of figures in recesses and shadowed spaces where the viewer must look closely to discern them builds into a strong sense of mood. Early on, he had explained that he used "perspective" to ensure that "some parts [are] seen before others."[35] This inherently temporal means of representing architectural space emerges from his training as a set designer and as well from his desire to re-create the lived experience of ruins as they come into view. The objective position of the Renaissance viewer of ruins prints, who may or may not identify with observers and draftsmen depicted within the landscape, is here shifted to a far more subjective experience of being drawn into a scene. There is no "natural" perspective frame for the representation of ruins in context, yet Piranesi deliberately sets out both to underline the enormity of ancient structures and to make visible their relevant archaeological features.

To understand how he does this, we might take a close look at one of his *vedute*, his large *Altra Veduta del Tempio della Sibilla in Tivoli* (see fig. 49).[36] Today, as we know from its nineteenth-century facsimile at the Parc des Buttes-Chaumont, this structure is called the Temple of Vesta (a smaller rectangular temple ruin now is known as Tivoli's "Temple of the Sibyl"). This ancient round temple had been "restored" in a much-lauded drawing by Palladio in his 1570 *Quattro Libri* (*Four Books*) and was the subject of previous engravings by Aegidius Sadeler in his 1606 *Vestigi delle antichita*; by Antoine Desgodetz,[37] who in 1682 also provided measurements and elevations; and by Piranesi's teacher Vasi; as well as in oil paintings by Adam Elsheimer and Claude Lorrain. Piranesi himself made at least two other views of the temple.

In this version, a trompe l'oeil document (see fig. 50), propped by a fallen tree limb and unscrolled in the lower left corner, provides the title of the work and the captions for two designated features: *1. Sustruzioni dell' aja del tempio dalla parte della cascata del Teverone. 2. Parte del Tempio supposto d'Albunea.* Below he has signed "Piranesi F[ecit]." The view depicts the temple in three distinct layers.[38] Viewed only on the level of the base of the pediment, the

FIGURE 49. Giovanni Battista Piranesi, *Altra Veduta del Tempio della Sibilla in Tivoli*. From *Vedute di Roma* (1761). Metropolitan Museum of Art, New York; The Elisha Whittelsey Collection; The Elisha Whittelsey Fund, 1956.

In the image, text reads:

Altra Veduta del
tempio della Sibilla
in Tivoli

1 Sustruzioni dell' aja del
tempio dalla parte della
cascata del Teverone.
2. Parte del Tempio sup=
posto d'Albunea.

Piranesi F.

FIGURE 50. Giovanni Battista Piranesi, *Altra Veduta del Tempio della Sibilla in Tivoli* (detail), 1761. (See fig. 49.)

approximately twenty-two-foot-high columns and their seven-foot base are in rough proportion to the gesturing figure who leans at the angle of a tree at the edge of the acropolis. Below the arbor depicted to the figure's right, two layers of cryptoporticos dug into the acropolis are viewed more or less from below—more in that we see the entire exposed ceiling of the vaulted opening on the right all the way to the back wall, but less in that we seem to be looking at a less steep angle up into the ceiling of the lowest level of vaults. There at the lower left we see the largest two of the print's sixteen figures. Whereas others are gesticulating to one another, pointing, seeming to converse, or climbing by themselves around and over the parts of the ruin, these two men in casual dress seem to have been plucking oak leaves like those they are wearing as wreaths in their hair. Our view thus is a slightly swooping *sotto in sù*—moving down and up, we must mine our perspective. The figures, with the exception of our two (oak-leaved) laureates, seem to be at a great distance from us and from one another. In the deepest recesses of the acropolis, below a lintel, a large-hatted male figure seems to be steering a small-hatted figure in either a dress or a coat with a long skirt out into the light. There another man, seated and leaning cross-legged against a wall, turns his head as if listening. Vast and empty as the recesses and the landscape itself may seem, the image of the temple is also humming with activity.

Piranesi is careful to distinguish among decaying surfaces of Roman brick, travertine, and flint, and he clearly delineates the inscription on the temple's architrave attributing the structure to its Roman builder Lucius Gellius (L GELLIO L F). Details of the Corinthian columns and bucrania and fruit garlands decorating the architrave itself are as clearly etched as if we were using a telescope: their significance goes beyond ornament since they give evidence of the mixed Roman style of combining bucrania with orders other than the Doric. Furthermore, Piranesi shows, accurately, that the bucrania here are fleshed oxen heads with eyes, thus correcting Palladio's mistake of depicting them as conventional bucrania formed in the likeness of empty skulls.[39]

What is the function of such a ruins image for Piranesi? As we can tell from the climbing and discoursing figures scrambling about the scene, the ruin is a site of discovery, valued intrinsically as an index to the building it once was, as a model for future building, and as evidence of a tradition. Rarely has an artist been able to combine rationality, measure, and science with a near-melodramatic theatrical sense of presentation as Piranesi has, and yet his work is drawn from important precedents. From the beginning of the sixteenth century onward, we have seen that ruins prints would often bear—in addition to the trompe l'oeil architectural imagery of their title pages—explanatory captions for each view. Maps of the period often included a separate key or legend providing a guide to the work; such keys were often framed by trompe l'oeil stone plaques or illusionistic leather straps "holding" them to the maps they described.[40] In the sixteenth century, Serlio and Palladio had sought precedents for their own work in ancient examples and taxonomies of classical orders, and, at the turn of the seventeenth century, Carlo Fontana, looking for precedents as well, drew reconstructions of ancient structures that took account of their historical contexts. Fontana further played an important role in the development of ruins imagery by recording both the modern, dilapidated, and the antique, reimagined and integral states of ruins.

Contemporary views required the presence of a viewer, and, as we saw in Gossart noting he had made his 1508 drawing of the Colosseum "with his own hand," artists esteemed the authority of work produced from the represented site itself. It was Piranesi's predecessor Desgodetz (1653–1728) who presented the definitive documentation of antique buildings. Commissioned by the French minister of finance, Jean-Baptiste Colbert, to go to Rome and produce a compendium of ancient structures, Desgodetz was captured by Ottoman pirates and spent sixteen months as a prisoner in Algiers. Colbert arranged for his release and he finally arrived in Rome. Desgodetz discovered, over a period of more than a year of field study, that Serlio, Palladio, and others had presented inaccurate accounts of Roman buildings. In 1682, he published his *Les édifices antiques de Rome, dessinés et mesurés très-exactement* (*The Antique Buildings of Rome, Drawn and Measured Very Exactly*).[41] The text was made up of 137 plates showing twenty-three Roman monuments, the Temple of Vesta/the Sibyl at Tivoli (see fig. 51), and Verona's amphitheater. In all fairness, he mentions that a number of the buildings were inaccessible because of their heights and others buried in the earth. He points out with regard to the Pantheon that Palladio's measurements are too low and Serlio's too high. He does not idealize the forms but rather shows the vegetation breaking through the stones and the transparent views available through arches to broken walls, where he often juxtaposes rubble and brickwork.

Throughout his career, Piranesi seems haunted by a perpetual self-inflicted competition with Desgodetz as the definitive authority regarding the dimensions, *très exactement*, of ancient buildings—we might even wonder if the prisons to which Piranesi continually returned, which were unlike any existing prisons in Rome, were somehow linked in his imagination to Desgodetz's biography. Piranesi's pupil the Scottish architect and antiquarian Robert Adam saw his own drawings of Roman monuments as corrections of Desgodetz's work and rubricated any of his measurements that were in conflict with the Frenchman's account. As late as 1760, Piranesi wrote to the English architect Robert Mylne a long letter sending him news and congratulating him on his design for the Blackfriars Bridge over the Thames. He then mentions that he had been on the scaffolding put up beside the "three Columns of the Campo Vacino" (now called the Temple of Castor and Pollux in the Forum), taking exact measurements there and copying the ornaments. At the time, he had been accused by a Frenchman, a Monsieur Morand, of having recorded less accurate measurements than Desgodetz had years before. Piranesi, in a typical quarrelsome state, explains to Mylne that he then invited a group of Englishmen to go up on the scaffolding with him and, with a copy of Desgodetz in hand, showed that Desgodetz had "varied all the ornaments" and "altered most of the measurements."[42]

The architectural historian Frank Salmon has explained that measurements made in 1991 indicate that Desgodetz was only five millimeters off the actual dimensions. Nevertheless, Desgodetz erred by twenty centimeters at the Hadrianeum and invented other measurements elsewhere in his work, and so Piranesi and his followers had some justification for their skepticism.[43] Salmon adds that, despite a contemporary obsession with accuracy, antiquarians "felt some uncertainty about the minutiae of measurements made on timber ladders 15m (50 feet) or so above the ground, where parallax distortion was likely to occur if the eye was not exactly level with the element being measured."[44]

The two aspects of the *Altra Veduta del Tempio della Sibilla in Tivoli* that Piranesi has decided to number and designate here orient the viewer in geography and history: by letting us know we are looking at the substructure on the side of the waterfall of the Teverone (now called the Aniene), he reveals the position of the image—away from the settlement and toward the ravine and waterfalls—and adds to the sense of precariousness of the ruined cliffside forms. With the second designation he points to the site of the temple of the

FIGURE 51. Antoine Desgodetz, *Du Temple de Vesta à Tivoli (Elevation and Plan).* From *Les édifices antiques de Rome, dessinés et mesurés très-exactement par Antoine Desgodetz architecte* (Paris: Chez Jean Baptiste Coignard, 1682). Marquand Library of Art and Archaeology, Princeton University.

sibyl Albunea, thereby underscoring his interest in the Etruscan goddess and her powers of prophecy.

A similar archaeological precision characterizes Piranesi's assemblages of capitals and architectural ornaments, his cutaway drawings of structures and their foundations, and his analyses of ancient engineering. Here the presentation of a scene is not the aim; rather, the ruin is broken down into a catalog of its parts; parts that are not so much Romantic, metonymic fragments of a lost whole as they are bits of evidence of Roman intention and ingenuity. Such evidence became increasingly important to Piranesi as he engaged in a series of passionate quarrels about the origins and transmission of ancient architectural styles and practices.

Disputed Origins

From the mid-1750s into the late 1760s, Piranesi plunged into debate—in treatises, drawings, etchings, and bound volumes—regarding the origins of Western architecture. Starting in 1748, the Scottish artist and architect James Stuart and his partner, the English architect Nicholas Revett, published their surveys of ancient Greek buildings. Known as "Athenian" Stuart, the Scotsman and his colleague acquired the sponsorship of the English Society of Dilettanti, a social club dedicated to classical enthusiasms. Its members hoped that Stuart and Revett could provide accurate accounts of Athenian remains. After a great deal of personal strife, their surveys appeared in a 1762 collection called *Antiquities of Athens*.[45] But in the meantime, their designs for interiors and drawings of Greek ornaments had a powerful impact on the Greek revival in British architecture.

In 1753 Laugier published his *Essai sur l'architecture* (*Essay on Architecture*), an additional argument for the importance of Greek design. Laugier claimed that the Greeks advanced architecture from wood to stone, with freestanding columns and trabeations of the most straightforward and simple sort their contribution to the possibility of a rational way of building, one in consonance with nature.[46] On the heels of Stuart and Revett, Julien-David Le Roy turned to Greece as the source of "the most beautiful monuments": his *Les ruines des plus beaux monuments de la Grèce* appeared in 1758 and argued for the superiority of Greek creative genius. Particularly galling to Piranesi was Le Roy's claim that the composite forms of Roman architecture were copies, lacking in the "male character" of the Greek orders.[47] And the German art historian and archaeologist Johann Joachim Winckelmann, who celebrated the austere and fundamental ideals of Greek architecture in his *Gedanken über die Nachahmung der griechischen Werke in der Malerey und Bildhauerkunst* (*Thoughts on the Imitation of Greek Paintings and Sculpture*) of 1755 and his study *Anmerkungen über die Baukunst der alten Tempel zu Girgenti in Sicilien* (*Remarks on the Architecture of the Ancient Temples at Agrigento in Sicily*) of 1762, enjoyed a growing influence. Winckelmann argued that the Romans had come to rely heavily on

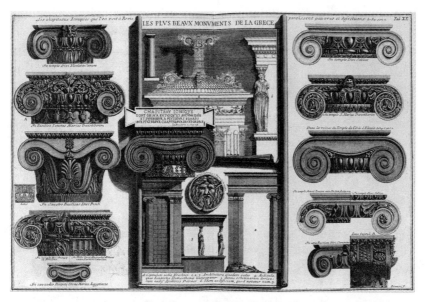

FIGURE 52. Giovanni Battista Piranesi, *Various Roman Ionic Capitals Compared with Greek Examples from* [Julien-David] *Le Roy, S. Maria in Trastevere, S. Paolo fuori le Mura, S. Clemente, etc.* From *Della magnificenza ed architettura de' romani* (*On the Magnificence and Architecture of the Romans*), tab. 20 (1761). Metropolitan Museum of Art, New York; Rogers Fund.

ornament and complexity, losing the beauty of proportion and simplicity that he admired in an earlier Greek practice.[48]

Piranesi, steeped in the notions of indigenous culture he had absorbed from Vico, and caught up in nationalist sentiments that looked to Etruscan engineering and building as an original and powerful predecessor for Roman innovation, took deep offense at the success and popularity of these "hellenophilic" theories. With support from his fellow Venetian, the new pope, Clement XIII (Carlo Rezzonico) and his family, Piranesi launched a counterargument about the importance of Etruscan and Roman buildings. His first polemic appeared in his 1761 work of more than two hundred pages, his *Della magnificenza ed architettura de' romani* (*On the Magnificence and Architecture of the Romans*), following in the footsteps of Cicero in attributing *magnificentiam* to practices of virtue and civic life.[49] Drawing on all the scholarship he could find regarding the Etruscans, he pointed to their austerity and clarity, as well as their feats of engineering. He claimed that these qualities were the literal foundation of Roman forms and that the Etruscan talent for stone building, as well as the simple Tuscan order, preceded the achievements of the Greeks. He created illusionistic collages of Le Roy's line engravings, "pasting" them into his own plates amid lush representations of Roman ornamental fragments. Mocking Le Roy's claims, he engraved an image of the "bocca della verità," or mouth of truth, from Santa Maria in Cosmedin below a passage from the *Monuments de la Grèce*, ready to bite the hand of his "lying" rival (see fig. 52).

Piranesi went on to publish a set of technical studies of the ruins of the castellum of the Aqua Iulia; a description of the emissarium of Lake Albano, with plans, cross sections, elevations, reconstructions, and perspective views; and further studies of the Cloaca Maxima, Castel Gandolfo, and the Etruscan site of Cura, known as Cora in Latin and Cori in Italian. His folio of the latter claims that the Etruscan influence on the structures is evident and argues that Propertius and Lucan write that Cora already is ruined in their own eras. Showing the ruins of ancient fortifications, he places among the rocks and mountains figures who are pointing and balancing themselves. Other figures look through openings: two bent old men converse; ragged walkers bend over staffs; and women stand before a column fragment that casts a shadow beyond the plate. He includes plates that feature ornamental details, including Corinthian-style acanthus and seashells embedded in leaves. The corners of the plates include small pendants of close-up views. The plates include measurements in "palmi romani" with representations of measuring sticks; the earth is cut away to allow for a key to dimensions, written on a trompe l'oeil ribbon of paper. The final plates of the volume are schematic profile drawings of parts of the temple. His view of the Lake Albano emissarium similarly invites the viewer to become an archaeologist: a trompe l'oeil page depicting the drainage outlet is designed to look like an overlaid drawing board— vistas, plans and elevations, cross sections and aerial views, both schematic and detailed, are placed and fixed over and under each other and traversed by a length of measuring string and its "shadow."[50]

Piranesi's fervent arguments for the importance of Etruscan contributions and Roman complexity reached their highest pitch in his *Il Campo Marzio della Roma antica*—a study of the history and importance of the Roman Campus Martius that he began in the second half of the 1750s and published as a folio in 1762. Here, too, a paper architecture becomes a paper archaeology—an often imaginary, and for the most part speculative, account of the long destiny of a Roman space, beginning with its most primitive origins along the banks of the Tiber and extending to the present view. Correlating literary references to the Campus Martius with information from what remained in the surviving fragments of the ancient Severan Plan, Piranesi set about recording what could be discerned at the site. The final product—an autodidact's assemblage of texts in Latin and Italian—was a hypothetical reconstruction, with details of plan, elevation, and perspective, of the entire area. The *Ichnographia*, or *Ground Plan*, is a six-plate map summarizing his findings, supplemented by thirty-seven plates of views and architectural surveys. Piranesi went on to include a set of aerial perspectives of parts of the *Ichnographia*. As a proposed totality, the work moved from archaeological and archival "evidence" excavated from the deep past to a final perspective from the air.

Desgodetz and others divorced ruins from their contexts, creating what was necessarily a schema, or what was known from the nineteenth century onward as a blueprint, that could serve as a plan for the future. Piranesi, however, was engaged, early on in the manner of Juvarra and the Bibiena, with the scenic and present-centered aspects of ruins; and later, as he threw himself into arguments about the importance of Etruscan and Roman precedents, he also sought to represent moments in time when past and future are visibly joined, each image indexing antiquity and its aftermath, each composition inviting the viewer to enter into the action of the scene or judge the merits of his evidence. The *vedute* bear an emotional, compelling, pull; the works of *Della magnificenza ed architettura de' romani* and the *Campo Marzio* folio give the reader a sensation of an eclectic totality, with every possible angle and detail replete with significance. Piranesi's engravings thus not only serve at once as evidence of the reality and dimensions of ancient architecture, and as mementos of, and testimony to, experiences of the grand tour; they also disseminate broadly, truly "seed," by means of their multiple reproductions, the reality of Roman magnificence far and wide.

The oral and two-dimensional transmission of architecture rescues it from material decay and site specificity, allowing for a kind of immortality that before was the exclusive domain of poetry and legend. Whereas Winckelmann had celebrated austerity, denigrating the Roman taste for ornament as a decline, in the end Piranesi came to celebrate an imaginative syncretism and freedom that he believed was the particular contribution of Roman antiquity. In his "Opinions on Architecture," written as a dialogue between "Protopiro" (adherent to the Greek side of the debate) and "Didascolo" (representative of Piranesi's views), Protopiro argues against ornaments, with adherence to a strict and rational convention "by comparison with the unbridled license that prevails in construction today," and Didascolo responds, "Show me designs by any of the rigorists . . . and I warrant he will look more foolish than the man who works to please himself—yes, more foolish—because the only way he could imagine a building without irregularities is when four upright poles with a roof—the very prototype of architecture—can remain entire and unified at the very moment of being halved, varied, and rearranged in a thousand ways; in short, when the simple becomes composite, and one becomes as many as you like."[51]

In the sole three-dimensional architectural commission that Piranesi received—additions to the church of Santa Maria del Priorato on the Aventine, which was awarded to him in 1764 and would in the end become, at his request, the site of his own tomb, the printmaker-architect's contributions to the project adhered largely to restoring the church and adding innovations to the facade and entryway.[52] The church and adjoining palace belonged to the Knights of Malta and had first been raised in 1568; the commission came to Piranesi through the current grand master of the Knights Hospitalers, Giovanni Battista Rezzonico, who was the nephew of Piranesi's patron, Pope Clement XIII. Piranesi's contributions are centered on the optical experience of the viewer; his designs for the *piazzale* that precedes the entrance and his invention of the elaborate ornaments and reliefs of the temple pediment create a dizzying experience of reading.

Rudolf Wittkower has written of Piranesi's "strange interpretation of individual motifs here: the sometimes confusing superimposition of architectural elements, the play with different planes, the unpredictable breaking up and reversal of familiar features, the willful combination of traditional ornamental detail and, indeed fascinating, his introduction of an ornamental language up till then unknown."[53] Wittkower does not go into more detail about the facade, but a closer look shows us that Piranesi is treating the experience of the *piazzale*'s monumental reliefs and the facade of the church as an assemblage of symbols and signs arrayed to be seen at various distances (see fig. 53, left facade; fig. 54, right facade; fig. 55, nautical detail; and fig. 56, panpipe detail). At the center of the pediment stands a relief of a crowned two-headed eagle, surrounded by a laurel wreath, a vast feathered wing, a serpent, a lyre, arms and hands holding trumpets, a skewed framed relief of the Rezzonico castle, panpipes, the Masonic symbols of ark and anchor, the Maltese cross, Roman helmets, seashells, medallions within which appear smaller iterations of the Rezzonico castle. These are displayed as if upended from a vast table where they had been piled as a triumphal assemblage. As symbols are layered and intersecting in space—the serpents, for example, weaving behind and before other images—they also are repeated at varied scales so that we are looking at images and images of images. The viewer is encouraged to look closely and from a distance—an experience underscored by Piranesi's famous "keyhole" at the site: a view through a keyhole that shows the dome of Saint Peter's in the far distance, today perfectly framed by a dense and receding arcade of greenery.

Part of the emotional force of Piranesi's engravings comes from these same peculiar combinations of effects of distance and proximity. Particularly with the *sotto in sù* view, the observer has access to tactile detail and a looming magnificence. As we have seen, *magnificenza* is indeed a word Piranesi often used to underscore the aesthetic value of very large *opus caementicium* structures—we remember that his first volume with a long polemical text was his 1761 *Della magnificenza ed architettura de' romani*. In his earliest work he paid little attention to the actual topography of the sites he represented; indeed, the *Prima parte* is made up of largely imaginary buildings assembled from his studies of existing structures and represented in colossal dimensions. In his later, and especially in his polemical, work, however, he became more and more interested in analyzing and detailing his subjects from an archaeological perspective and clarifying the relation between the past and the present.[54]

Capricci, grotteschi, vedute: the development of print genres, directly or indirectly influenced by firsthand experiences of ruins, vastly expanded the place of ruins in the European and British imagination. Piranesi had announced, in the *Prima parte* and in the *Della magnificenza ed architettura de' romani*, that

FIGURE 53. Santa Maria del Priorato, Rome (left facade relief), 1764–1766.

FIGURE 54. Santa Maria del Priorato, Rome (right facade relief), 1764–1766.

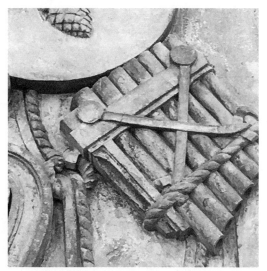

FIGURE 55. Santa Maria del Priorato, Rome (nautical detail), 1764–1766.

FIGURE 56. Santa Maria del Priorato, Rome (panpipe detail), 1764–1766.

he was practicing a kind of archaeological inventory—his images would be accurate and necessary as he made the case for the Etruscan antecedents to Roman architectural achievements. Yet by the 1760s, a ruin became, as Bernardin de Saint-Pierre implied, not merely an architectural remnant, or a source of forms, techniques, and ornaments for new architectural endeavors, but a projected state of mind.

With the *grotteschi*, Piranesi produced hybrid forms of ornament juxtaposed in an array without regard to single-point perspective. With the *capricci*, he brought disparate structures into a landscape that existed only within the borders of the plate.[55] Perhaps because of his early fidelity to accuracy and the long tradition of printmaking as a medium for the measured representation of antique forms, Piranesi's *capricci* take on a particularly fantastic aura. A set of drawn *capricci* from the mid-1750s from the collections of Robert Adam and his brother James show Piranesi assembling imaginary temples and tiered funerary monuments with small figures making their way up enormous flights of stairs. The assemblages spiral up into the clouds and evoke fantasies, if not of heaven, given the resolutely secular world of Piranesi's imagination, then of flight, ascent, and drawing without limit.

As early as 1746–1748, Piranesi made a frontispiece for his *Vedute di Roma* that he called a *Fantasy of Ruins with a Statue of Minerva in the Center Foreground* (see fig. 57). There real and imaginary ancient monuments are juxtaposed, rising from detritus in the foreground, amid foliage, clouds, and a ghostly architrave of spiraling columns in a fantasy landscape. The statue in the center is the *Dea Roma*, which we can find today, as Piranesi found it—

FIGURE 57. Giovanni Battista Piranesi, *Fantasy of Ruins with a Statue of Minerva in the Center Foreground.* From *Vedute di Roma* (1746–1748). Metropolitan Museum of Art, New York; Harris Brisbane Dick Fund, 1937.

FIGURE 58. Giovanni Battista Piranesi, frontispiece from *Le Antichità Romane*, vol. 2 (1756).

standing in the courtyard of the Palazzo dei Conservatori on the Capitoline. A version of the right foot of the fragmentary statue of Constantine, elements of the Arco di Portogallo, a tomb topped in the Etruscan style by a reclining couple, and other "antique" remains appear with real and imaginary inscriptions. Lilliputian figures stand precariously on an arched bridge, reading an inscription taken from Pliny the Elder celebrating the conquests of Pompey.[56]

We have seen how the trompe l'oeil effects of title pages and frontispieces became a convention of ruins volumes from the sixteenth century onward, and Piranesi had used them in the *Prima parte*. Yet it is incongruous to find that Piranesi begins his presentation of his *vedute*, posited as actual spaces, accurately represented, with such fantastic images. Perhaps the minute figures reading within the miasma of images give us some clue that what follows will not be merely real. His 1756 frontispiece to the second volume of *Le Antichità Romane* is a fantasia of the Via Appia packed with obelisks, urns, entablatures, and tombs, including his own imaginary tomb on the right and, below the she-wolf on the left, a tomb for the also living Scottish antiquaries Robert Adam and Allan Ramsay (see fig. 58). Nothing is factual in such an image except the context of the Via Appia and the inevitability of death, yet each element has been created and projected out of a deep knowledge of ancient remains. The fantasy is a kind of resurrection and tongue-in-cheek acknowledgment of mortality at once.

Piranesi's images of Rome continually involve viewing above and beyond and beneath their everyday appearances—dramatically lit, inhabited by shadows and mysterious figures, and magnificent in their enormity. The frontispiece to the fourth volume of his *Le Antichità Romane*, for example, is a *sotto in sù* view of Hadrian's Mausoleum. In the foreground is a scene of tiny fishermen casting poles from a promontory, boats, and beneath the bridges of the Ponte Sant'Angelo. A pile of cut rocks juts into the water; they are marked rather vaguely "T," "Rovine antiche" (ancient ruins). The worm's-eye view and miniature rocks and fishermen make the mausoleum seem to loom above the scene, and in the left background, contemporary buildings behind the structure seem similarly miniaturized. Piranesi carries the gigantism forward in the following "View of the Subterranean Foundations" of the mausoleum— minute figures climb over the colossal buttresses and walls, and Piranesi invents a jumble of enormous architectural fragments and rocks that spill over into his caption, adding to the tremendous effect of weight and monumentality. Other touches are more subtly exaggerated as he invents a fantastic foundation system for the mausoleum and the bridge and a system of voussoirs in the entry arch and barrel-vaulted corridor that apparently also did not exist.[57]

The Danish Piranesi scholar Bent Sørensen has carefully traced Piranesi's debt to printed sources in his earliest architectural images in the *Prima parte* and the *grotteschi*. He shows that, despite his fidelity to exact measurements and details, Piranesi copied and adopted images from engravings by many French and Italian seventeenth-century and earlier eighteenth-century artists. Sørensen deduces that Piranesi never reversed his sources and usually worked by eliminating detail as he copied, moving quickly. This is another sense in which Piranesi has produced a paper architecture, built from primary and secondary sources, altered by speed and new values. Indeed, Sørensen concludes that Piranesi must have drawn directly on the plate without intermediary preparatory studies—a remarkable skill earlier mentioned in Legrand's biography.[58]

William Beckford and other visitors to Roman sites noted the disparity between their first encounters with ruins and the versions they had known through artworks. Beckford wrote of his first glimpse of the Pantheon that he had "entered with a reverence approaching to superftition." But "the whiteness of the dome offending me," he closed his eyes and tried to imagine that the pagan gods were present—when he opened them, he saw only "St. Andrew with his cross, and St. Agnes with her lamb, &c, &c." He notes that he was "very near being disappointed, and began to think Piranesi and Giovanni Paolo Panini had been a great deal too colossal in their view of this venerable ftructure." Only the place's "venerable air, an awful gloom, breathed inspiration, though of the sorrowful kind."[59] Goethe wrote in his *Italian Journey* in an entry dated November 2, 1786, that as he first arrived in Rome, his memories of the engravings of the city in his father's hallway had come to life: "I now see in reality, and everything I have known for so long through paintings, drawings, etchings, woodcuts, plaster casts and cork models is now assembled before me."[60] But as his long-delayed reconstruction of his travels ends and his mood changes, he declares, in his late age, during his second Roman visit, in December 1787, that, even for the most artistically trained eye, the actual appearance of the Pyramid of Cestius and the ruins of the Baths of Caracalla could not live up to the rich and imaginary impressions that Piranesi had offered.[61] The effectiveness of Piranesi's scenes threatens to "prefabricate" the experience of the viewer, perhaps especially in memory.

In an influential account of Piranesi's work, the architectural theorist Manfredo Tafuri claims that Piranesi's "heterotopic" aim was to criticize the concept of place—his account of forms that break up, fall into distortion, multiply and disarrange themselves upsets any idea of a center or organic growth. Tafuri finds Piranesi from the beginning, even before the "negative utopia" of the *carceri*, engaged in "the capacity of the imagination to create *models*, valid in the future as new values and in the present as immediate contestation of the 'abuses of those who possess wealth, and who make us believe that they themselves are able to control the operations of Architecture.'"[62] Tafuri emphasizes the larger trajectory of Piranesi's work toward letting perspective overcome our limitations in quantitatively controlling space. Piranesi's use of a multitude of standpoints, the fluctuation he creates between two- and three-dimensional space, his employment of bird's-eye and worm's-eye vistas, his engagement with the syncretic progression of styles from Egyptian to Greek to Etruscan to Roman forms and his adaptation of all of them within *capricci* or fantasies of mixed modes: all are means of creating an architecture of "hypothesis" rather than "solution."[63]

This experimental practice was an enormous undertaking. Legrand, too, notes in his biography that Piranesi typically seemed to be working urgently directly on the plate, believing that to make the print from a finished drawing would be to produce a mere copy. The prolific Piranesi ironized: "Let's go slowly" and "make three thousand drawings at a time."[64] Embroiled in polemical quarrels with his fellow antiquarians and correspondents, Piranesi also struggled to find patrons. The unreliable Lord Charlemont, for example, was to find himself on the receiving end of Piranesi's own practice of *damnatio memoriae*. The fickle young Irish lord drifted away from his commitment to sponsorship of the 1756 volume of *Le Antichità Romane*. Piranesi visibly erased his name as the dedicatee there and published two letters excoriating him. Nevertheless, Piranesi's vast output relied upon a collective and commercial effort.[65] Like Samuel Johnson, he represents a cultural shift toward the artist as a person who is paid by the public that consumes his work. Piranesi's sons Francesco and Pietro and their older sister Laura collaborated in the production of his prints. Eventually Laura and Francesco, and to a lesser extent Pietro, became noted printmakers in their own right. Laura died in Rome at the age of twenty-nine but left several folios of ruins prints, which she signed in such a way that a viewer wonders about the burden of labor she undertook. At times, she signed with her own name (see fig. 59), at others with "Lavora Piranesi incise" (see fig. 60), which could have the double meaning of coming from the family workshop and, more specifically, "She works Piranesi." Ruins representations, and the artifacts and fragments attached to them, were radical means of knowledge and critique: they could reveal the dense particulars of the past and point to the hidden injustices of the present. But they also had become commodities, demanding an unending, if impossible, production of discoveries and reproductions.

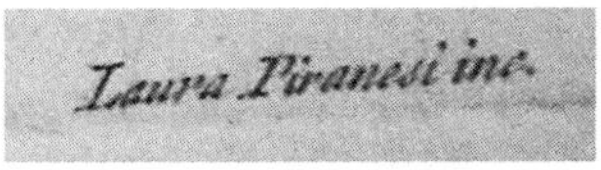

FIGURE 59. Laura Piranesi, autograph, ca. 1780.

FIGURE 60. [Laura] Piranesi, variant autograph, ca. 1780.

VI. Mirrors

THE VOYAGES AND FANTASIES
OF THE RUINS CRAZE

Finding Rome

In 1724 the twenty-five-year-old Welsh poet and painter John Dyer traveled to Italy intending to sketch the major classical monuments. He hoped his journey would provide a foundation for a career as an esteemed visual artist. He stayed for a year. When he returned, he produced, and became well known for, not his drawings or any account of his Italian ventures, but rather a topographical poem in couplets about a local prospect: "Grongar Hill." Nevertheless, at some point during or after his Italian sojourn, Dyer composed a 545-line blank verse account of a daylong visit to the Palatine that he titled "Ruins of Rome," finally publishing it in 1740. Both poems are moralizing topographical narratives of ascent to vistas of ruins. Yet "Grongar Hill" begins with a dedication to an unnamed and silent nymph and muse of painting[1] and remains vague in the details of its alternately shadowy and brightly lit scenes. "Old caſtles on the cliffs ariſe, / Proudly tow-ring in the ſkies!" The sides of the Towy river are described as "cloath'd with waving wood" while "... ancient towers crown his brow, / That caſt an awful look below; / Whoſe ragged walls the ivy creeps, / And with her arms from falling keeps ..." Trees and animals, including a poisonous adder hiding amid "ruins, moss and weeds," receive specific names, but Grongar Hill is a local place traversed by the solitary local wanderer—so familiar that it needs no landmarks, and the nearby castles, Dynevor (or Dinefwr) and Dryslwyn, remain anonymous and interchangeable.[2] Even the poem's anticourt and antiurban agenda remains unspecified. If the poem is painterly, it achieves this effect with its broad strokes of color and light and sustained single-point perspective. At the same time, Dyer also creates visual surprises—suddenly opening vistas and chiaroscuro effects emerging in time—that verbal art alone can convey.

"The Ruins of Rome: A Poem" bears a Latin epigraph (*Aspice murorum moles ...*) from Vitalis's sonnet "Qui Romam in media quaeris" that we encountered at an earlier moment of its popularity—lines asking the reader to behold the walls and rocks of Rome, where the corpse of the great city still breathes warnings. Dyer plunges into his own poem on Rome with the imperative, "Enough of Grongar!" He then quickly takes the reader over the Alps to Latium and the Tiber. In an obvious borrowing from John Milton's "Lycidas," Dyer stokes his inspiration by writing, "Yet once again, my Muſe, / Yet once again, and ſoar a loftier flight; / Lo the reſiſtleſs theme, imperial Rome," and he exercises an equally Miltonic resistance to rhyming. The soaring perspective soon comes down to earth: "Fall'n, fall'n, a ſilent heap; her heroes all / Sunk in their urns; behold the pride of pomp, / The throne of nations fall'n; obſcur'd in duſt; / Ev'n yet majeſtical." His actual sojourn through the ruins then begins with the sunrise, and he quickly sketches an overall view under the emerging light:

> the rising ſun
> Flames on the ruins in the purer air
> Tow'ring aloft, upon the glitt'ring plain,
> Like broken rocks, a vaſt circumference;
> Rent palaces, cruſh'd columns, rifled moles,
> Fanes roll'd on fanes, and tombs on buried tombs.

He will end with nightfall and a vision of storm clouds coming down from the Alps in an allegory of barbarian invasion.

Along the way, "the love of arts, / And what in metal or in ſtone remains / Of proud antiquity" leads him from site to site, and the poet is inspired by thinking of the founding of the Roman Republic. Like Petrarch and Colonna surveying the city from the healthy air and open views available at the heights of the Baths of Diocletian, Dyer seeks an overlook and finds that from the vantage of the Palatine he can view "most of the remarkable antiquities." From there he spies his own assemblage of significant, though decaying, monuments: the Colosseum, which he pauses to describe as a "mountainous pile" with a "capacious womb"; the Temple of Jove, the Capitol, the Pantheon, the Temple of Concord, the public granaries and aqueducts in the distance, the Campo Marzio, the Temple of Peace, the Pyramid of Cestius, the Baths of Caracalla, Trajan's column, Nero's tower (the Torre delle Milizie), the Palatine Library, and the Temple of Romulus and Remus. He also lists, without naming it, Bernini's Fontana dei Quattri Fiumi in the Piazza Navona, commenting on the fountain's associations with ancient rivers, although it is only seventy years old as he is writing and one of the rivers, the Rio de la Plata, is a relatively recent discovery in the New World. It is as if anything in Rome can receive credentials of antiquity, simply by being in Rome.

And, as he did in "Grongar Hill," Dyer looks everywhere for lessons and morals—demanding of the landscape that it reflect back to him some commentary on the present. Recounting the history of virtuous patrician Romans—Clelia, Cocles, Manlius, the Fabii, Decii, and Gracchi—as he reaches the highest point of the Palatine, he is inspired to dedicate himself to his own country:

> Me now, of thefe
> Deep-mufing, high ambitious thoughts inflame
> Greatly to ferve my country, diftant land,
> And build me virtuous fame; nor fhall the duft
> Of thefe fall'n piles with fhew of fad decay
> Avert the good refolve, mean argument,
> The fate alone of matter.

Later, musing on Catiline, he urges Britain to secure Liberty and shield her laws—others, he says, may delight in music, masques, and dance and make works of art, but Britons should "check the ravage of tyrannick fway," "quell the proud," "fpread the joys of peace," and engage in "ingenious trade." A mood of melancholy descends on the poet at sunset and leads him to review further the entire history of Rome from its founding to its decline and collapse: as the poem ends, past sunset, the barbarian hordes descend.

Dyer's lively and sweeping poetic survey gives us some sense, as Giovanni Battista Piranesi's repertoire of etching subjects for the *vedute* do, of the designation of major monuments at the beginning of the eighteenth century and of their actual appearance. The poem mentions the presence of "pendent goats" among the ruins and describes how pilgrims reciting their "oraisons" in the dead of night hear towers "tumbling all precipitate down-dash'd," indicating both Dyer's vivid imagination and how unstable the antique structures might have been at the time.

In a touching set of lines, Dyer describes his fellow artistic travelers: ". . . here advent'rous in the facred fearch / Of ancient arts, the delicate of mind, / Curious and modeft, from all climes refort, / Grateful fociety! With thefe I raife / The toilfome ftep up the proud Palatin." Salmon has written in his study of eighteenth-century British architecture that "between 1750 and 1840 every architect of note went to study in Rome." By the 1760s, Piranesi was a member of not only the Arcadian and French Academies but also the Academy of Saint Luke and found himself surrounded by numerous British and French architects, many of whom had won the four-year pensions of the "Prix de Rome." Among them were Mylne, Le Roy, William Chambers, Thomas Harrison, Marie-Joseph Peyre, Charles-Louis Clérisseau, and Laurent Pécheux. Others were wealthy travelers on tour, including the Adam brothers, who would become close associates of Piranesi and take his ideas back to Britain, implementing them in actual structures. Robert Adam, whose projected tomb we glimpsed in Piranesi's fantasy of the Via Appia (fig. 58, in chap. 5), took his grand tour to Italy in 1754–1757, and his younger brother James followed in 1761–1763. Their associate John Soane would also, in 1778, travel to Rome, arriving just five months before Piranesi's death.

Piranesi's circle of acolytes gathered at the Caffè degli Inglesi near the Spanish Steps, where the artist had provided the walls with decorations in the Egyptian style. Their conversation must have been a kind of improvisatory

creole of Italian, French, and English, for Piranesi wrote without apology to
Robert Mylne in Italian, and Robert Adam recorded, after his first meeting
with Piranesi, that his "disposition" "bars all instruction" and "his ideas in lo-
cution so ill arranged, [and] his expression so furious and fantastic, that a
Venetian hint is all that can be got from him, never anything fixed or well-
digested so that a quarter of an hour makes you sick of his company."[3] Nevertheless, he and Piranesi soon developed an abiding friendship. The albums
of one thousand drawings Robert and James Adam made during their Italian
sojourns, now at the Soane Museum in London, include Robert's work during
sketching trips undertaken with Piranesi to Hadrian's Villa at Tivoli, the Baths
of Caracalla, the Via Appia, and Lago Albano in the summer of 1755. Although
Robert Adam never took a deep interest in engaging in theoretical debate,
Piranesi found in him an ally committed to the inventive reuse of archaeological materials. Adam's monument in the fantasy of Appian tombs in the
1756 frontispiece to the second volume of *Le Antichità Romane* is inscribed:
DIS MANIB—ROBERTI ADAM SCOT—ARCHITECTI—PRAESTANTISS—
I.B.P.—FAC COERAVIT. And, in a more sober homage, Piranesi dedicated his
massive treatise of the Campo Marzio to Adam in 1762.[4]

Adam wrote in a letter of March 1755, "It is almost a month since my arrival. I have neither had time to Eat or Sleep in a manner, there is so much to
be Seen Such variety of Scenes to employ ones attention," and in July he reported, "I fancy my stay in Rome will be much longer than I imagined upon
going here, as the more I see the longer I find I must remain in order to digest
and see them to purpose."[5] Robert's letters to the family's financial agents in-
quire into the costs of duties on drawings in oils and crayons; he asks about
the arrangements for shipping marble and much else; and he describes his
increasingly burdensome luggage—"since I left Rome that it is impossible for
me to Lugg it about with me in Kind"—and says he needs another trunk.

Voyages

The *stranieri* had come to Rome to study and draw classical orders of the major monuments, and their work gradually extended beyond the city to other
locales.[6] A number of these architects and draftsmen sought to increase their
livelihoods through the production of large folios of ruins prints. Such an
undertaking required an initial patron: the Society of Dilettanti, as we have
seen, provided for James Stuart and Nicholas Revett in their voyage to Greece.
The society also gave funds for the journey to the Levant in 1750 undertaken
by Robert Wood, James Dawkins, and John Bouverie. The Comte de Cay-
lus sponsored the publication of Le Roy's parallel journey to Greece, which
had been funded by both the French Academy and the state.[7] Robert Adam
and Charles-Louis Clérisseau's five-week journey to Spalatro (now Split) in
Dalmatia in the summer of 1757 was partly funded by Adam's family and by
subscriptions. In his presentation copy to King George III, however, Adam

pointedly draws the king's attention to the Emperor Diocletian's sponsor-ship of architecture, "which excited the Masters of that Art to emulate in their Works the Elegance and Purity of a better Age,"[8] clearly making a plea for sub-stantial and continuing patronage. Perhaps in consequence of the competi-tion for funding, bitter disputes arose among these many voyagers, a number of whom, including Piranesi, supplemented their income from publications with the sale of fragments and specimens of antiquities. Polemics and scholar-ship aside, the denigration of one style meant the elevation of another.

Le Roy, who had swiftly followed Stuart and Revett and promptly brought out his own *Les ruines des plus beaux monuments de la Grèce*, found himself, as we saw in chapter 5, a target of Piranesi's wrath, his Greek examples accused of "vana leggiadra," a vain lightness or prettiness.[9] Stuart and Revett, spend-ing from 1750 to 1755 on their survey of ancient buildings of Greece and Pola, in turn waited until 1762 to publish their results; in the meantime Stuart bit-terly attacked Le Roy's *Les ruines* for what he saw as its inaccuracy. Stuart and Revett failed to have prolonged careers, and antipathy toward their estimation of Greek buildings continued throughout the second half of the eighteenth century. Sir William Chambers wrote in the 1768 edition of his *Treatise on the Decorative Part of Civil Architecture* of the "celebrated Trifles" they had pre-sented. Writing of the structure known by the various names of the Lantern of Demosthenes or Choragic Monument of Lysicrates or Temple of Hercu-les, he said, "Messrs. Steward and Ryvet [*sic*] have given twenty-six Plates of this Edifice well-drawn and well-engraved . . . represented with the utmost Accuracy and from an Inscription upon the Architrave it appears that this Monument was erected in the Days of Alexander the Great when the Grecian arts were at the highest Pitch of Excellence." He finds the work, however, as despicable as that of Borromini, the "most licentious and extravagant of all modern Italians."[10]

We might think that Chambers is supporting Piranesi's stance against the "hellenophiles" here, but in fact Piranesi was deeply influenced by Borromini's use of ornament and celebrates, in his "Opinions on Architecture," his great-ness as an heir to Roman practice.[11] In contrast to the critics of the Greek voy-agers, James Dawkins was amenable to Stuart and Revett and even arranged for Revett to design his tomb at Chipping Norton. Robert Adam praised Stu-art for "introducing the true style of antique decoration"[12] and then took up his Greek ornaments into the kind of hybrid style that Piranesi had proposed and that Stuart would have abhorred. Adam reserved his ire for Robert Wood, whose work he found coldly academic and lacking in context. He declared that Wood's taste was as "as hard as Iron & as false as Hell."[13]

The stakes of personal and professional animosity were high: journeys were dangerous and expensive, and any antiquities that were discovered and "acquired" were valuable. The sea presented dangers beyond storms: Robert Adam wrote home in August 1756, "It is to be hoped that at present we are Masters of the Mediterranean. But in spite of that, British ships have great hazards to run from Privateers." Once the travelers arrived, there were new cultures and new mores to navigate, not always successfully.

Stuart argued with a Greek consul and knocked him down; the antiquarian also was "nearly put to death" by some Turkish companions.[14] In a paragraph of his introductory "Epistle to the Reader" in his book *The Ruins of Palmyra*, Robert Wood mentions the dangers he and Dawkins and John Bouverie faced and then rather abruptly writes that "the death of Mr. Bouverie" (of a fever in Güzelhisar) was an "accident so highly distressing." He adds that "if any thing could make us forget that Mr. BOUVERIE was dead, it was that Mr. DAWKINS was living," and so they were able to "rescue from oblivion the magnificence of Palmyra."[15] In the preface to his *The Ruins of Balbec* (1757), Wood contends that "avarice is no doubt as much an Eastern vice as hospitality is an Eastern virtue" and concludes that the former was most often found in "men of power and public employment" and the latter in "private retired life." Refusing a request from an emir, Wood and his party are told by the ruler that they would be "attacked and cut to pieces in [their] way from Balbec." They decide to exchange presents as a peacemaking gesture, but then the emir is assassinated "by an emissary of [his] rebellious brother."[16]

A generation earlier, Desgodetz, too, had mentioned in his preface his capture by the Turks as he came to measure monuments in Rome. But Desgodetz was headed toward the center, not the periphery, and he could return repeatedly to the objects of his studies. As eighteenth-century travelers explored the farther reaches of the Roman Empire and its manifestations, they made elaborate preparations to "capture" what they saw, most likely in a onetime glimpse. Their goal, according to Wood, was to undertake "a voyage, properly conducted, to the most remarkable places of antiquity, on the coast of the Mediteranean, [that] might produce amusement and improvement to themselves, as well as some advantage to the publick." Wood suggests in "An Enquiry into the Antient State of Palmyra," his reflections on his journey to Palmyra, "It is the natural and common fate of cities to have their memory longer preserved than their ruins. Troy, Babylon and Memphis are now known only from books, while there is not a stone left to mark their situation. But here we have two instances of considerable towns out-living any account of them. Our curiosity about these places is rather raised by what we see than what we read, and Balbeck and Palmyra are in a great measure left to tell their own story."[17]

Wood is aware of the Roman origins of the structures he is seeing, but he notes that the local people believe that "Solomon built Tedmore [Palmyra] in the Wilderness."[18] He discovers inscriptions indicating that Diocletian erected some of the buildings there and indeed, today, this part of what remains of the Palmyra site is known as the *castra*, or camp, of Diocletian, a military encampment of the late third century CE after the suppression of the rebellion that had brought about the brief reign of Zenobia of the Palmyrene

FIGURE 61. After Giovanni Battista Borra, *View of the Temple of the Sun*. Plate 21 from Robert Wood, *The Ruins of Palmyra, otherwise Tedmor, in the Desart* (London, 1753). Marquand Library of Art and Archaeology, Princeton University.

Empire. Overall, Wood tells his reader in his preface to *The Ruins of Balbec*, even the "happiest precision of language" cannot convey the information provided by the plates: "It shall in this, as in the former volume [*The Ruins of Palmyra*] be our principal care to produce things as we found them, leaving reflections and reasonings upon them to others."[19]

The plates, however, are not his handiwork. The reader can see that they are signed "Borra.Arch/Delin," for they have been engraved after drawings on-site by Giovanni Battista Borra, the architect, engineer, and architectural draftsman who accompanied both expeditions and recorded what he saw in detailed close-up views of the ruins and images informed by conventions of contemporary genre and landscape paintings. Buildings are shown in their "present ruined state" and include figures in Arab dress, leaning on staves and conversing (see fig. 61). By now, a significant shift had occurred in the role of the draftsman and engraver—the folios are known by the names of the impresarios who organized the expeditions rather than by the artists who created their images. Accuracy and pure information, as well as the collecting and accumulation—in truth confiscation and robbery—of objects have replaced the theoretical and historical speculations of the antiquarians.

In his preface to his *Ruins of the Palace of the Emperor Diocletian at Spalatro in Dalmatia*, Adam generously cites the "splendours" of the ruins drawings of Dawkins, Bouverie, and Wood, albeit without mentioning Borra, and says "I was not, like these gentlemen, obliged to traverse desarts, or to expose myself to the insults of barbarians."[20] Wood relates of his Palmyra journey that "we set out from Haffia the 11th of March 1751 with an escort of the Aga's best Arab horsemen, armed with guns and long pikes, and travelled in four hours to Sudud, through a barren plain, scarce affording a little browsing to antilopes, of which we saw a great number." Sudud turns out to be a small and poor village inhabited by Maronite Christians. They go on to Howareen and Carietein and then Palmyra, where, he recounts, "Our caravan was so increased to about two hundred persons, and about the same number of beasts for carriage, consisting of an odd mixture of horses, camels, mules and asses."[21] He tells of the Arab horsemen conducting racing contests. In the panoramic view of the ruins, several sets of racing horsemen are shown crossing the scene.

Wood collected manuscripts, many from the Maronite churches of Syria, as well as marbles in Palmyra and shipped them back to England before he went on to Baalbek. He copied inscriptions in Baalbek and there, too, he "carried off the marbles whenever it was possible; for the avarice or superstition of the inhabitants made that task difficult and sometimes impracticable." He adds that "few ruins were so complete such as not to preserve very valuable fragments, especially as we had provided our selves with tools for digging and sometimes employed the peasants in that way, for several days, to good purpose."[22] He never questions the ethics of his thefts.

What was the use of these drawings beyond being valuable souvenirs of momentous journeys into hitherto unknown territories? Adam explains that "the buildings of the Ancients are in Architecture, what the works of Nature are with respect to the other Arts; they serve as models which we should imitate, and the standards by which we ought to judge." Borra would return with Wood to England. Working as an architect in London and Turin, he incorporated the forms and ornaments of the Palmyra and Baalbek structures into projects for Norfolk House on St. James's Square, into interior decorations and designs for the south facade and garden buildings of Stowe in Buckinghamshire, and to the Castello dei Racconigi and the Palazzo Isnardi di Caraglio.

The albums of Adam drawings at the Soane Museum from the period of Robert's grand tour are inscribed: "All the sketches that follow were drawn abroad."[23] Following a long-standing custom of traveler's sketchbooks, many of the drawings were made with pencil first and then inked. As he became more adept as a draftsman and especially under the influence of his teacher, Clérisseau, Adam began to use washes to add effects of light and shadow. Both Robert and James Adam selected elements from real buildings as their subjects, but they also copied existing prints and paintings. An early Robert

Adam drawing is a copy of a Salvator Rosa painting of a contorted tree in a gale. Robert wrote to his sister, once he was in Italy, "I want to be a hero of the picturesque"—an intriguing ambition, for it suggests he saw himself as a figure within a landscape as well as the agency behind its creation.

Despite the influence of archaeology, Robert Adam is often vague about historical detail. When he was making plans to voyage to Spalatro, he seems to have been confused about whether he was studying the Palace of Domitian or the Palace of Diocletian—a mere two hundred years off track. He only occasionally represents inscriptions, and when he does, he often uses squiggling lines rather than words. Winckelmann had put forward an influential opinion that color was an impediment to the perfection of form—a tenet that archaeological discoveries at Pompeii put to rest as excavations revealed the ancient use of colored ornament and colored stones for sculpture and sarcophagi. Jean-Baptiste Lallemand, the French academician who, like Clérisseau, also tutored Robert Adam in drawing methods, experimented with working on blue-gray paper with white chalk highlights—a technique that Adam in turn adopted. But more often, Adam and Clérisseau showed stone and brick-faced concrete structures in pen and brown or gray watercolors. They used golden-yellow washes for columns and sometimes showed blue skies. In his own occasional drawings, Piranesi had relied on ferrous gallnut ink and, at times, red chalk, and Clérisseau and the Adam brothers followed. Their work became the prototype for representing Roman ruins for generations of architectural draftsmen.[24]

Leonardo da Vinci had advised his fellow painters of classical and biblical scenes not to use contemporary dress.[25] We have seen that Piranesi's "staffage" figures ranged from the beggars and shepherds who actually inhabited the most broken-down regions of Roman ruins to playful representations of commedia dell'arte characters balancing in trompe l'oeil between the represented worlds and their captions, to quick glimpses of aristocrats, scholars, and artists pointing toward and studying features of ruins. In the folio drawings and images of Stuart and Revett, Wood, and Robert Adam and Clérisseau, figures in Western dress are juxtaposed to local natives in native dress; we also see ambiguous figures in "Turkish" or "Oriental" costume of the kind Lord Byron liked to wear as he went to the East. The final volume of Stuart and Revett's *Antiquities of Athens* captures their reunion with Wood and Dawkins as they met at the Monument of Philopappos in Athens in May 1751 (see fig. 62).[26] Stuart looks directly at the viewer, and he and Revett are dressed in native costume. Dawkins talks to Revett while Wood studies the monument, recording the inscription on a pilaster. Small figures—a goatherd, goats, and dogs—recede in the background, and in the foreground, as Stuart explains, "Our Janizary is making coffee, which we drank here; the boy, sitting down with his hand in a basket, attends with our cups and saucers."[27]

FIGURE 62. James Stuart and Nicholas Revett, *Antiquities of Athens*, vol. 3, chap. 5, plate 1 (London, 1794). Marquand Library of Art and Archaeology, Princeton University.

Robert and James Adam and their architect peers followed many of the conventions of ruins representation we have been tracing. They were attracted by what Piranesi had repeatedly deemed the "magnificence" of Roman buildings. Massive *opus caementicium* structures gave them an opportunity to deal with effects of mass and decay under changing light as they sketched them in person. Representing the local people going about their usual activities gave evidence that the travelers truly were in the presence of these forms. Scenes from the Spalatro folio include glimpses of inhabitants trading goods, tending animals, listening to proclamations, begging, picking pockets, and, as Wood recorded, racing their horses. At the same time, the picturesque placed quite different demands on the artist than those under which Desgodetz and Lafréry had produced their "exact measurements." Conventions of both landscape and genre painting overcome the strictures of archaeological record keeping. Piranesi showed the Adam brothers how to create emotional effects through lighting. Clérisseau was particularly adept at composing picturesque views, and he often removed any details from the scene that were postclassical.

Thus, although contemporary persons were allowed to remain in the scene, contemporary structures—indeed, anything after the Roman imperial era— were often erased. In a drawing of the Temple of Venus and Roma, Clérisseau takes out all the medieval elements; the Christian fittings of the cathedral at Spalatro also disappear to show its original state as a temple of Jupiter.[28]

FIGURE 63. James Adam, *British Order*, 1762. Pen and ink, wash and gouache. Metropolitan Museum of Art, New York; Harris Brisbane Dick Fund.

As any visitor to Spalatro can discern even today, the entire location has been stripped of its medieval and contemporary frame in Adam's great folio—the folio's dramatic views of the palace that stands directly on the Adriatic Sea surrounded by a vast empty plain belies the way the city grew up around the ancient forms, incorporating and reusing them.[29]

These emphases on large antique structures as essential elements of external landscapes stand in contrast to the practical use architect-travelers made of what they saw. Upon their return to Britain, the Adam brothers often pursued large projects—from James's hopes to redesign the Houses of Parliament to the final financial catastrophe of their "Adelphi" complex on the banks of the Thames, a set of buildings meant to allude to the dramatic south facade of Diocletian's palace on the sea.[30] Nevertheless, their strongest legacy was their creative application of ornaments. James went so far as to invent a "British order" that he proposed for his Parliament scheme: it was a Corinthian column incorporating a lion and a unicorn, the British crown, thistles and roses, and the collar of the Order of the Garter (see fig. 63). Realizing his native north also would need representation, he designed as well a "Scottish order" of entwined thistles above acanthus leaves topping a fluted column.[31]

Piranesi, in the voice of "Didascolo," praises James's invention in his "Opin-ions on Architecture," defending him against a criticism levied in an otherwise positive review of his work in the French *Gazette littéraire* that he could not truly create a new order "just by putting new ornaments on the capitals and on the other parts of a building." Piranesi/Didascolo argues that the funda-mental manner of architecture—the use of columns, pilasters, and continu-ous walls—is unvaried and that without variation in ornament, architecture would be degraded to a mere practice of copying. He admonishes his interloc-utor Protopiro, "by all means treasure the rationality that you proclaim, but at the same time respect the freedom of architectural creation that sustains it."[32]

If the new order never became a widely adopted convention, the "Adam style" nevertheless remains best known for the brothers' use of arabesques and scrolls of foliage, swags and ribbons, vases, tripods, gryphons, sphinxes, fes-toons of husks and bellflowers, framed medallions, flat panels of "grotesques" and pilasters—augmented with a delicate pastel palette of yellows, pinks, and greens. These characteristics of their work, details linking interiors to exteri-ors with composure and elegance, alluding to the Etruscans, Egyptians, and eventually even a notion of the Chinese, were far from the brutal irregularity of battered *opus incertum*. By 1769, as the Scottish brothers were steadily at-tracting patrons, Piranesi himself produced a final polemical folio of inventive and eclectic designs for interiors, his *Diverse maniere d'adornare i cammini*—a compendium of plans for chimneypieces, furniture, and interior ornaments. These fireplace designs would have a strong influence on subsequent interior commissions taken up by the Adam brothers. The Scots borrowed much of Piranesi's presentation style in the *Diverse maniere* for their own *The Works in Architecture of Robert and James Adam*, issued from 1773 onward. Piranesi perhaps had hoped to receive some British commissions himself, for as Sir William Hamilton wrote to him from Naples after viewing the prints, "I am delighted that you have done this work for it will be very useful in my country where we make much use of fireplaces. The ornaments will be found without end there. I admire the way you have arranged them, and only you are capable of giving the engraving such a strength and so much character."[33]

Fantasies

One project of the period, however, brought an unusual experience of ruins indoors into a three-dimensional, room-sized illusion. This was Clérisseau's 1766 commission from two learned Franciscans, members of the mathemati-cal Order of the Minims, Thomas Lesueur and François Jacquier, to make an interior room a "ruin room" in their monastery of Santa Trinità dei Monti at the top of the Spanish Steps (see plate 9). By this time, Clérisseau had been companion, employee, and drawing teacher to the Adam brothers since his meeting with Robert in 1755, and he, too, had been active in Piranesi's circle just down the steps from the monastery.[34] Lesueur and Jacquier would have been attracted to the idea of an illusionistic ruins room not only because of the zeitgeist brought about by *anticomanie*, but also because the Minims had long sponsored artistic projects based in mathematics, including the anamorphic frescos commissioned by their seventeenth-century predecessors Emmanuel Maignan and his disciple Father Jean-François Niceron.[35]

Clérisseau had been a student of Panini, who was "professeur de perspective" during Clérisseau's early and turbulent tenure at the French Academy. He was close to artists on every side of the debates on classical ruins—a friend to Le Roy and Winckelmann as well as Piranesi. His training in perspective theory served him well at Santa Trinità as he created illusions of receding arcades of pilasters, a coffered ceiling broken open to the sky, foregrounds of niches and urns and misty distant vistas, rustic wooden doors and gridded windows, and great sarcophagi. Whereas most ruins representations survey their landscapes from a vantage point, Clérisseau creates a repertoire of views—glimpsing, peeking, oscillating, and scanning. The viewer is truly surrounded by, and immersed in, ruins.

The room, closed in actuality, seems to open to infinity. A recent study of the space by Cristian Boscaro using three-dimensional laser camera technology reveals the precise measurements Clérisseau used to create his tumbling illusion with such verisimilitude. Today the room is called by the inhabitants of the Sacred Heart convent that now occupies the site, "la stanza del papagallo" (the room of the parrot), for Clérisseau painted a bright parrot perching on an exposed beam beneath the broken wooden planks of a wrecked ceiling.[36] The colorful bird draws us toward a consciousness that we are looking at paint and the powers of painting that have lasted by now for hundreds of years; at the same time, it gives a sense that we are present to the actual, within the brief moment when a living thing might perch on forms that are slowly breaking down and disappearing.

The trompe l'oeil ruins frescos of Giulio Romano's Palazzo del Te in early sixteenth-century Mantua and Domenico Piola and Andrea Seghizzi's similar seventeenth-century decorations at the Villa Balbi-Durazzo allo Zerbino in Genoa had reveled in much the same way in the illusionistic powers of perspective drawing. Yet such earlier works often used ruins as a backdrop to myth, telling narratives of Gigantomachy in the Palazzo del Te, and of Venus and Enone at the Villa Balbi-Durazzo, largely taken from Ovid's *Metamorphoses*. These works created vertiginous feelings of imminent collapse in their viewers. In contrast, Clérisseau places the viewer within a surround of vistas; the walls and ceiling and window frames seem to be hatching, breaking open to an imagined light. Clérisseau's ruins room indicates motion paradoxically through its still architectural reliefs and its "living" parrot. For many years the monks and consequently the nuns of Santa Trinità used the room as an infirmary, and its ruined forms no doubt gave some consolation to the imaginations of the bedridden, lending at least relief from boredom and at most a feeling of rebirth.

By the second half of the eighteenth century, ruins had become autotelic; at this point they are about their own forms and details and the artist's powers of representation. Piranesi's first collection of ruins images in the *Prima parte* is made up of inventions, and over the course of his career, within his ever-evolving philosophy of artistic freedom, he contended that the draftsman can begin with the motifs of classical forms and end wherever he or she likes. Clérisseau, however, clearly felt that such imaginative forays had to be based on a deep knowledge of actual details. Robert Adam wrote, soon after their initial meeting in Florence, "Clérisseau preaches to me every day to forbear invention or composing either plans or elevations till I have a greater fund, that is, till I have made more progress in seeing things and my head more filled with proper ornaments and my hand more able to draw to purpose what I would incline." He complained that he was burdened with "laboring at perspective and doing cornices with modillions, viewed from an angle of a building, which has its own difficulties."[37] During his work for the Adam brothers, Clérisseau frequently improved Robert Adam's drawings, and toward the end of the brothers' sojourn in Italy, their relationship with the talented French artist soured.

Clérisseau clearly believed his own progress was sufficient to be radically playful in his depictions. In the Palace of Diocletian folio we find he often reproduces reliefs—a subject for engravings that inherently plays, as drawing moves to plate and print, between two- and three-dimensional mediums representing two- and three-dimensional images: for example, *Another View of the Temple of Aesculapius* juxtaposes a relief of stone horses on a sarcophagus to a boy leading an actual horse around a corner, an angle that emphasizes motion and depth of field (see fig. 64). In his view of the interior of the Temple of Jupiter, he shows a man in Western dress drawing the scene while a person in native dress looks on—in the center of the picture a group of figures in Western and native dress are assembled while a disabled man clothed in rags is being pulled, with great effort, on a cart by a barefoot attendant.[38] Just a few years later, Denis Diderot noticed a similar play of surfaces and moving figures in the ruins work of Hubert Robert. He suggested, however, turning back in time, "Painters of ruins, if you include a relief fragment, let it be of the finest workmanship, and have it always depict an interesting action from a period antecedent to the flourishing peak of the ruined city. You will thus produce two effects: you'll transport me that much further back into the past, and you'll awaken within me all the more veneration and sorrow for a people that had brought the fine arts to such a degree of perfection."[39]

Ruins become an allusion to themselves, fragments and souvenirs of an amorphous notion of the past that gradually came to include what the neoclassical at first excluded: the Gothic. By the late eighteenth century, the genres of ruins paintings and prints became even more specialized: *vedute essate* were meant to record the actual features and dimensions of extant ruins; *vedute ideate* presented recognizable buildings and ruins in picturesque

FIGURE 64. Charles-Louis Clérisseau, *Another View of the Temple of Aesculapius* (detail). From Robert Adam, *Ruins of the Palace of the Emperor Diocletian at Spalatro in Dalmatia* (London, 1764). Department of Rare Books and Special Collections, Princeton University Library.

settings, often including other structures and monuments and so juxtaposing the present context to the ancient form; and *vedute di fantasia* involved the free handling of existing buildings and the introduction of imaginary forms, often mixing elements from various sites. The very existence of such a range of approaches to representation signifies the many roles that ruins images came to play in the culture. *Vedute essate* carried over the demands of both archaeology and architectural practice, providing reliable measurements and details about ancient building types. *Vedute ideate*, which could include both older medieval buildings and later baroque forms, provided a set of juxtaposed time frames that would necessarily highlight historical differences. And *vedute di fantasia* offered near-hallucinatory occasions for meditation and imaginative play. The remarkable ascendance of ruins during this period of *anticomanie*, where so many painters, draftsmen, and engravers took ruins as their principal artistic subject and specialty, is only slightly less surprising when we consider this extensive range of purposes for representing ruins.

Following seventeenth-century experiments with amalgams of classical building types placed in the same scene, Panini gathered real ruins into fictional contexts in his *capricci*. As Clérisseau and Piranesi absorbed his influence, so did his protégé Hubert Robert, who would emerge as the foremost French painter of ruins, coming to be known eventually as "Robert des ruines." Robert furthered Panini's predilection for mixing real and imaginary scenes and, under the influence of Piranesi, came to rely on the theatrical staging of perspective and shadows. Nevertheless, these assemblages and dramatic vistas were perhaps not merely artistic conventions. Goethe's first impressions of the city give us some hint that an artist's practice of "moving" ancient buildings closer to one another in a kind of "greatest hits" assemblage was not merely a matter of whim but rather an attempt to register what it is like to first encounter the city. Goethe observed, "As I rush about Rome looking at the major monuments, the immensity of the place has a quietening effect. In other places one has to search for the important points of interest; here they crowd in on one in profusion. Wherever you turn your eyes, every kind of vista, near and distant, confronts you—palaces, ruins, gardens, wildernesses, small houses, stables, triumphal arches, columns—all of them often so close together that they could be sketched on a single sheet of paper."[40]

Such a tendency to think of vistas of the city in terms of specific ancient touchstones has a long provenance. Between 1534 and 1536, Pope Paul III, a native Roman, was faced with the task of preparing the city for the triumphal visit of Charles V. He appointed his fellow humanist Latino Giovenale Manetti as the first papal commissioner of antiquity, and they set about clearing ancient monuments of ivy, wild fig, and other invasive vegetation. They dismantled the vineyard at the base of the Septizodium and demolished medieval buildings and ordinary houses and shops around the structures in the Forum in an effort to create a panorama of magnificent structures that would, they hoped, capture the imagination of the Holy Roman emperor.[41] Renaissance mapmakers often set to the task of representing Rome by laying out the major monuments—the Arch of Constantine, the Pantheon, the Colosseum, the Baths of Caracalla—and then filling in the spaces between with paradigmatic forms, a method that had been suggested as early as Leon Battista Alberti's advice to surveyors in his *Descriptio Urbis Romae* (*Delineation of the City of Rome*).[42]

This type of preservation of the structure at the expense of the context has its corollary in the tremendous energy Piranesi, the Adam brothers, Clérisseau, Robert, and many of their compatriots invested in imaginary ruins as they assembled actual classical structures and ornaments to manufacture buildings that never existed. We have found such idiosyncrasies masked as the typical in Piranesi's *Prima parte* and his frontispiece of a fantastic Via Appia, and his acolytes followed with Robert Adam's *Fantastic Scenes* and *Fantastic Buildings in a Landscape*, Clérisseau's extravagant images of *Architectural Ruins* from 1771 and his *Architectural Fantasy* of 1773,[43] and numerous masterpieces by Hubert Robert, including the four paradigmatic paintings of fictive ruins—*The Ancient Temple, The Obelisk, The Fountains*, and *The Landing Place*—that he made in late life for the wealthy financier and entrepreneur the Marquis Jean Joseph de Laborde for his château at Méréville near Étampes.

Here all the literal building blocks of ruins images—deeply shadowed arches, coffered vaults open to the sky, niches with vaguely familiar renditions of Roman statuary, majestic stairways leading off the bottom of the canvas or through the perspective lines into a distant horizon—tower over small figures going about their ordinary tasks as usual, their realism and specificity in contrast to the looming oneiric structures that hover about and above them.[44]

The time travel that such dreamlike ruins images suggested was also employed, by the turn of the eighteenth century into the nineteenth, in a novel form of proleptic ruins imagery. In 1782, the aristocratic philosophe, Constantin-François de Chasseboeuf, the Comte de Volney[45] undertook a journey to Syria and Egypt to learn Arabic and study "oriental" cultures. Seven years later he would publish his *Les ruines, ou méditations sur les révolutions des empires* (*The Ruins; or, Meditations on the Revolutions of Empires*). There he looks to the rise and fall of Babylon, Egypt, Ethiopia, and Palmyra, and to the religions of "the Indians, Persians, Jews, Christians, and Musselmans" to survey the underlying sources of power and principles of worship at work in human history and "what concerns the happiness of mankind in a state of society."[46] Writing in visionary, near-hallucinatory prose, Volney introduces his subject as he meditates on the desert ruins of Palmyra. "Here, said I to myself, an opulent city once flourished; this was the seat of a powerful empire. Yes, these places, now so desert, a living multitude formerly animated, and an active crowd circulated in the streets which at present are so solitary. . . . These heaps of marble formed regular palaces, these prostate pillars were the majestic ornaments of temples, these ruinous galleries present the outlines of public places." He reviews the intervening centuries and comes to "the last step of the comparison":

> Reflecting that if the places before me had once exhibited this animated picture: who, said I to myself, can assure me, that their present desolation will not one day be the lot of our own country! Who knows but that hereafter, some traveller like myself will sit down upon the banks of the Seine, the Thames, or the Zuyder sea, where now, in the tumult of enjoyment, the heart and the eyes are too slow to take in the multitude of sensations; who knows but he will sit down solitary, amid silent ruins, and weep a people inured, and their greatness changed into an empty name?[47]

Stepping from the shadows, an "Apparition," in "grave and solemn accents" declares, "Unjust man! If you can for a moment suspend the delusion which fascinates your senses, if your heart be capable of comprehending the language of argumentation, interrogate these ruins! Read the lessons which they present to you!" Astonishingly, the apparition in turn addresses the "sacred temples!" "venerable tombs!" and "walls once glorious!" and calls on them to participate in the "tribunal" that will determine the human causes of human suffering. Then, by supernatural means, the apparition lifts Volney into space, where, touching his eyes, "they became more piercing than those of an eagle": aloft, Volney can see all of the planet, and as well the ruined buildings, barren landscapes, moldering columns, and empty ports of what had once been civilizations. The apparition narrates the glorious pasts of these locations and goes on to provide an account of the revolutions inherent in the processes by which members of societies acquire power, make distinctions, and breed internecine hostilities.

Volney draws a secular vision of human frailty, a fall into social ills from the *amour de soi*, or love of being that we share with animals and forgo as we develop societies—a notion, despite the numerous philosophical differences between Volney's and Jean-Jacques Rousseau's views regarding a state of nature, that is clearly indebted to Rousseau's *Discourses on Inequality* from the 1750s. Volney takes no pleasure in the return of human effort and intention to an ever-encroaching nature of desert, jackals, and vegetation, nor, in his intense anticlericism, does he look to the "mysticism" of religion for help or find in the extant "savage" peoples he encounters in his journeys in the Middle East and North America an inherent nobility. Instead, in an assertion that would later have a profound effect on the thinking of William Godwin, Thomas Jefferson, and Percy and Mary Shelley, he proposes an agenda of building: humankind must "investigate the laws of nature" that are true "for the whole without exception" and "form an authentic and immutable code": "be the legislators of the human race as ye are the interpreters of their common nature."[48]

Volney's *Ruines* famously were begun in conversation with Benjamin Franklin,[49] and the era of revolutions induced many such reflections on the inevitability of cycles of history. The rise and fall of the Roman Empire, so memorably traced by Edward Gibbon in the propitious year of 1776, was only one "lesson" to be read. As early as his *Salon of 1767*, as he responded to the ruins paintings of Hubert Robert, Diderot surmised:

> Another thing that would make ruins still more effective is a strong image of transience. Well, well, the powerful men of the earth who believed they built for the ages, who erected such superb residences for themselves, and who in their folly anticipated an uninterrupted series of descendants, heirs to their names, their titles, and their opulent way of life, nothing remains of their work, of their enormous expenditure, of their grand visions but debris serving to shelter some of the most indigent and unfortunate members of the human race, much more useful as ruins than ever they were in their initial splendor.[50]

Diderot's depiction, like Robert's actual paintings, is clearly indebted to Piranesi's predilection for revealing ruined persons in the shadows of ruined structures.

FIGURE 65. Hubert Robert, *Project for the Disposition of the Grande Galerie of the Louvre*, 1796. Oil on canvas. Musée du Louvre, Paris.

Volney's dream of immanent ruin—a vision not of ruins giving us a clue to an intact past but rather a glimpse of future ruin viewed through an intact present—becomes in this period a trope of paired works. Hubert Robert produced in 1796 a set of pendant paintings of the Louvre. The first painting projects an image of the near future—a *Project for the Disposition of the Grande Galerie of the Louvre* (see fig. 65), showing Robert's suggested plan for the transformation of the former palace into a new national museum. He depicts well-dressed visitors, including young women and fashionably dressed young men seated in chairs and on the floor copying works, a child tugging at his adult companion's arm, strolling through the galleries and stopping to point and admire the paintings and sculptures in niches and on display. And he paints a self-portrait: the sixty-three-year-old Robert is shown hunched and wizened, sitting in a ladder-back chair, copying Raphael's *Holy Family*, as light streams through the high skylights and the Serlian bays recede without limit.

The second painting, *Imaginary View of the Ruins of the Grande Galerie of the Louvre Palace* (see plate 8), shows the museum reduced to a set of bare classical elements—columns, entablatures, arches, and fragments, broken open to the sky. In the left foreground, three figures, a woman and two men—one of whom seems to be in ancient dress, while the others are in contemporary clothing—tumble over one another as they lean down to examine the helmeted, yet severed, head of a broken statue. At the center of the scene, a young man concertedly, obliviously, draws the sole standing identifiable sculpture—the Apollo Belvedere. In the space between and behind the sculpture and the artist, two peasant women, perhaps laundresses, hover near a cauldron. Robert has juxtaposed the near and distant futures of the museum where he served as both commissioner and curator. He envisions the yet-to-be-completed space as a novelty, presenting a lively sunlit democratic scheme for the display of public art. And he also paints it as a shadowed antiquity of the kind he studied during his eleven years in Rome. Both of his views are "imaginary"—one a mirror of his hopes, another a mirror of his fears. He brings his personal past into the present as he projects a future for the Louvre that literally returns neoclassicism to the fate of a ruined classicism.[51]

By the summer of 1796, Napoleon's invasion of the Italian peninsula had begun. The scene at the Caffè degli Inglesi, which had continued to be a gathering place for visiting British architects and artists in the decades after Piranesi's death, became poisoned by malicious gossip and political maneuvering. The English architect Joseph Gandy, staying in Rome on his grand tour, found himself perilously caught up in these pro- and anti-Jacobin disputes. Drawn to the ideals of the American Revolution and at the same time fearful of "mobs," he expressed his admiration for the stability of monarchy in letters to his father. In the same period that he was the subject of gossip and suspicion for his political views, all of his sources of patronage from home had vanished. He was forced to sell his drawings and collections; receiving some emergency credit from the friend of a friend, he escaped to Florence and went on to London.

Before Gandy left, he witnessed the sacking of antiquities and artworks, writing that "the French Commissioners are now in Rome taking their choice of the best pictures and statues," adding sarcastically, "I wonder they never thought of taking the Egyptian Obelisk which was brought to Rome by the Emperors as trophies to their victories. I cannot help telling you that in the sermons the priests mentioned the taking away of the pictures and statues. 'Rome,' said they, 'will always be Rome, the French cannot carry away the Pantheon or Colosseum.'"[52] The terms of the Treaty of Tolentino in 1797–1798 "legalized" these instances of appropriation, allowing French administrators to confiscate, and send to the Louvre, any work of art they chose—the terms first applied only to works in the Vatican and then, within a year, to works anywhere in occupied Italy.

This plundering was attacked by the architectural theorist Antoine-Chrysostome Quatremère de Quincy in a series of letters to General Francisco de Miranda, the Venezuelan revolutionary who fought beside the Girondists and during the Reign of Terror had reverted to supporting the royalists. With these *Lettres sur le préjudice qu'occasionneroient aux arts et à la science, le déplacement des monuments de l'art de l'Italie, le démembrement de ses Écoles et la spoliation de ses Collections, Galleries, Musées, etc* (*Letters on the harm caused to the arts and to science, the displacement of Italy's works of art, the dismantling of its schools, and the spoliation of its collections, galleries, museums, etc.*), issued as a pamphlet and eventually known simply as *Lettres à Miranda* (*Letters to Miranda*), Quatremère argued fervently against the dislocation and decontextualization of Italian sculptures and architectural forms. He held that all of Italy is "a museum," one not simply made up of objects but as well constituted by its places, sites, mountains, quarries, roads, ruined villages, geographical relationships, and their entire contextualization in the memory of the people. His objection was moral: he pointed to spoliation as theft and underscored his belief that all of Europe should be united in a "spirit of liberty" contrary to a "spirit of conquest."[53]

Gandy would, upon his return, begin to work as a draftsman for the firm of John Soane, who had returned to London after visiting the dying Piranesi in the spring of 1778. Gandy would never complete more than a few architectural commissions; his melancholy and easily irritated temperament impeded his career, and his taste tended toward the sepulchral; he would die in misery in a Devon insane asylum in 1843 and be buried in an unmarked and unregistered grave.[54] Yet, like "Robert des ruines," he has left a well-known proleptic vision of ruins: his commissions from Soane, in 1798 and then again in 1830, of the Bank of England in ruins. Soon after joining Soane's office in 1798, Gandy created two views of Soane's renovation of the Bank of England rotunda. The first, *View of the Bank of England Rotunda as Built* (see fig. 66), with crisp details and streaming light and a clock with Roman numerals registering the time at 10:17 a.m., shows a still and empty space with blue skies and cumulus clouds visible through the skylights. The second, *Architectural Ruins, a Vision* (also known as "Bank of England in Ruins") (see plate 10) shows the rotunda broken open, with gathering clouds in the distance and bright light falling into the interior where treasure seekers are camped by a fire. Vegetation sprouts all around and about the crumbling masonry, and the fallen pieces of the heavily damaged structure are piled in a heap in the right foreground.

In 1830, Gandy created *A Bird's-Eye View of the Bank of England* that resembled a painting of a damaged model—the facade is mostly intact, but the courtyards, offices, and vaults of the bank are open to the sky, looking worn and desolate, with brick stripped of its facings, and columns broken from their ornamental capitals. In the left foreground the street falls away to reveal a dramatic escarpment where the bank's foundation vaults are exposed. In the right foreground, contrary to the picture plane, Gandy has gathered broken fragments of sculptural ornament and capitals—the material that seems to have been stripped from the image of the bank itself—in a compressed *sotto in sù*

FIGURE 66. Joseph Michael Gandy, *View of the Bank of England Rotunda as Built*, 1798. Ink and watercolor. Soane Museum, London.

view. The drawing overall, with its slanting light and ghostly images of the intact city around the bank standing far below its position, gives an uncanny sense of flying and climbing at once, as if we are in a world of reversals as quick as the blink of an eye.

Gandy's several images of the Bank of England in ruins were displayed in 1832 at an exhibit for the Royal Academy titled *Architectural Ruins, a Vision*. The specter of natural disasters and financial collapse became there an allegorical theme for ideas of sublimity and social catastrophe alike.[55] Soane, meditating upon "the ravages of all devouring time and the convulsions of Empire," quoted from *The Tempest* in his catalog: "The cloud-cap't towers, the gorgeous palaces, / The solemn temples, the great globe itself, / Yea, all which it inherit, shall dissolve."[56]

Between 1809 and 1814, despite the conscience of Quatremère, the French excavated myriad ruins with abandon. They moved trees and demolished houses in the Forum, swept away the Convent of Santa Francesca Romana, detached the Arch of Titus and the Temple of Saturn from the buildings where they were embedded, and cleared the three columns of the Temple of Castor and Pollux to their bases. Massive amounts of earth were removed from the Basilica of Maxentius, exposing the pavement and south portico, and from the Temple of Vespasian. Pieces of columns, capitals, and entablature that had been merely protruding from the ground were hoisted, cleared, repaired, and straightened.[57] The loggia of the Villa Medici still bears the inscription today: "*A Napoléon le Grand, les arts reconnaissants.*" Yet in fact it was not the arts that recognized, or paid homage to, the invader here so much as the invader who recognized, in the collection and display of ruins and their artifacts, artistic forms of treasure.

This plundering overlaps exactly with the parallel enterprise of Lord Elgin between 1801 and 1812 in Greece. Byron became Elgin's Quatremère, writing in *Childe Harold's Pilgrimage*:

> Let such approach this consecrated land,
> And pass in peace along the magic waste;
> But spare its relics—let no busy hand
> Deface the scenes, already how defaced!
> Not for such purpose were these altars placed:
> Revere the remnants nations once revered:
> So may our country's name be undisgraced,
> So may'st thou prosper where thy youth was rear'd.
> By every honest joy of love and life endear'd!

In an appendix to the Second Canto, from which this passage is taken, Byron added, "At this moment (January 3, 1810), besides what has been already deposited in London, an Hydriot vessel is in the Pyraeus to receive every portable relic. Thus, as I heard a young Greek observe, in common with many of his countrymen—for, lost as they are, they yet feel on this occasion—thus may Lord Elgin boast of having ruined Athens."[58] Byron points out that the French Consul, too, is trying to lay hands on the relics.

We have seen Gandy suggesting, as he quotes the local Roman clerics, that at least the French could not remove the Colosseum and the Pantheon, but Byron points to the tremendous scale of the spoliation he was witnessing in Athens. He records that while Elgin's agent, an Italian painter named Lusieri, and his patrons "confine themselves to tasting medals, appreciating cameos, sketching columns, and cheapening gems, their little absurdities are as harmless as insect or fox-hunting, maiden-speechifying, barouche-driving, or any such pastime; but when they carry away three or four shiploads of the most valuable and massy relics that time and barbarism have left to the most injured and most celebrated of cities; when they destroy, in a vain attempt to tear down, those works which have been the admiration of ages, I know no motive which can excuse, no name which can designate, the perpetrators of this dastardly devastation." He, too, argues that the plundering means the ruin of national reputation: "[I] do not think the honour of England advanced by plunder, whether of India or Attica."[59]

As early as the 1720s, Dyer had noted with some equivalence in the "Ruins of Rome" that visitors were stealing marbles and using them to decorate their halls and grounds:

> the traveller
> Such antique marbles to his native land
> Oft hence conveys; and ev'ry realm and ſtate
> With Rome's auguſt remains, heroes and gods,
> Deck their long galleries and winding groves;
> Yet miſs we not th'innumerable thefts,
> Yet ſtill profuſe of graces teems the waſte.[60]

In the years since Wood readily had recorded filling his pockets with ancient artifacts and hiring local laborers to use pickaxes to pry up architectural fragments, the scale of plundering had only grown. The establishment of the great imperial museums brought it to a pitch. Yet at the same time, an archaeological conscience, a sense that the meaning of objects arises from their contexts of production and place in an entire way of life, and moral qualms regarding the injustice of war spoils created a growing awareness that appropriation corrupted the appropriator.

Gardens of New Ruins

In a moment when the patronage system weakly persisted and artists needed to find new audiences for their work, ruins images offered a subject that could be both visceral and mysterious. Ruins no longer were viewed primarily within Christian allegories, or arguments regarding classical architecture, or theories of cultural styles; more often than not, they became instruments of mood, as they had been for the melancholy Dyer: objects of private meditation and subjective pleasure. The British aesthetician Henry Home, Lord Kames, who became a close friend of Robert Adam, wrote in his *Elements of Criticism* of 1762 of the differing consequences of studying medieval and ancient ruins: "Whether should a ruin be in Gothic or Grecian form? In the former, I think; because it exhibits the triumph of time over strength; a melancholy, but not unpleasant thought; a Grecian ruin suggests rather the triumph of barbarity over taste; a gloomy and discouraging thought."[61]

We also have some evidence of the multivalent reception of ruins at the end of Goethe's second visit to Rome in December 1787, when, as we have seen, his mood had changed. Reflecting on his sadness at the illness of a young

Milanese to whom he became attached, at that point "prematurely wasted and pale from mental and physical suffering," he writes:

> I looked at the ancient monuments and saw only that, after many centuries, they had been reduced to shapeless masses; I looked at buildings of a later date, magnificent and intact, and they spoke to me only of the decline of many great families; I looked at things which were alive and blooming and, even there, I thought only of the secret worm within which would in time destroy them. . . . Just as a happy mind will invest even crumbling walls and scattered masonry with new life, like a fresh, perennial vegetation, so a melancholy mind robs a living creature of its most beautiful adornment and reduces it, in our eyes, to a bare skeleton.[62]

From his youthful experience with stage sets to his development of dramatic effects of light, shadow, and recession, Piranesi had led the way in imagining ruins as projections or scenes. As actual ruin fragments were made portable and "new" ruins were fabricated, artists—including Clérisseau, the Adam brothers, and Hubert Robert—often doubled as garden or landscape designers. They created ruins as destinations and points of view within parks designed for walking and meditating or, in the case of aristocratic pavilions in the period just before the French Revolution, established for amorous rendezvous. Whereas actual ancient ruins were encroached upon by vegetation, these practices turned that process inside out as they inserted new mineral forms within arrangements of plants. What is decaying and what is growing, what is old and what is new, become a matter of often playful exchange.

The first instance of an artificial ruin established as a focal point for a garden seems to have been Girolamo Genga's vanished Barchetto in Pesaro, built for the Duke of Urbino, Francesco Maria della Rovere, in the 1530s. The design incorporated a "casa in forma di ruina."[63] By the second half of the seventeenth century, Gian Lorenzo Bernini incorporated a ruined bridge at the right side of the Palazzo Barberini in Rome. This Ponte Ruinante (Ruined Bridge) includes a partially collapsed arch and another arch with stones suspended, as if about to fall, from the vault. Structurally sound, the bridge gave access from the palace to the upper section of the gardens and is still visible today (see fig. 67).

English gardeners, designing large open landscape parks, turned to both Gothic and classical ruins, sometimes within the same space. In 1709, Sir John Vanbrugh made an appeal to the Duchess of Marlborough that the medieval ruins of Woodstock Priory be retained as a vista to be seen from the newly constructed Blenheim Palace: he argued that the ruins would be set "like a painted canvas" and the viewer "could step through a picture frame into a living scene." The duchess instead had them completely demolished.[64] Yet even before William Gilpin's "picturesque" made Vanbrugh's logic a commonplace,

FIGURE 67. Gian Lorenzo Bernini, Ponte Ruinante, Palazzo Barberini, Rome, 17th century.

Batty Langley would suggest in *New Principles of Gardening* (1728) that it was a good idea to consider "Views of *the Ruins of Buildings*, after the *old Roman man-ner*, to terminate ſuch Walks that end in *diſagreeable Objects*."[65] William Kent built a Temple of Ancient Virtue (an intact peripteral temple) and a Temple of Modern Virtue (a ruin) on the estate of Lord Temple at Stowe, making a pun and producing something of the effect of the forms simultaneously intact and ruined that Hubert Robert and Joseph Gandy had envisioned.

In 1746, William, the Duke of Cumberland, built the Windsor Great Park by manufacturing the lake he called Virginia Water. Eighty years later, accord-ing to a design by the royal architect Jeffry Wyatville, a set of ancient columns that had been shipped from Leptis Magna were erected there next to new columns that had been distressed to match them. Elsewhere, Thomas Wright of Durham and William Chambers produced artificial triumphal arches—Wright at Shugborough in Staffordshire in 1749 and Chambers at Kew on the outskirts of London in 1760. Wright's arch is based on the drawings and measurements made by "Athenian Stuart" of the Arch of Hadrian in Athens. Chambers's structure was "aged" with ivy and stone fragments arrayed at its base—a detail still curated today. In 1751, Chambers had also proposed a de-sign for a mausoleum for Frederick, Prince of Wales, as a ruin.[66]

On the continent in the same period, Frederick the Great situated his "Ru-inenberg" on a hill at his pleasure palace Sans Souci in Potsdam; it can be viewed either as a destination or serve as a point of view in the manner Van-brugh had imagined unsuccessfully for Blenheim. The Marquis de Girardin, patron to Jean-Jacques Rousseau, commissioned a sequence of monuments at Ermenonville that were laid out in 1765–1778. He was advised by Hubert Robert, the architect Jean-Marie Morel, and the Abbé Delille in the construc-tion of these artificial ruins known as "fabriques." The park, now the site of Rousseau's tomb, includes a grotto of naiads, a stone column, a rustic kiosk, and a temple of modern philosophy. Inspired by Hubert Robert's painting of the Temple of the Sibyl at Tivoli, which we last saw in Piranesi's etching and re-created at the Parc des Buttes-Chaumont, the marquis evoked a sense not of structures long inhabited and decayed but instead of the arrested and crum-bling development of incomplete projects. Three tombs—those of Rousseau, the painter Georges-Frederick Mayer, and an unknown Romantic who died by suicide—punctuate the landscape and add to the symbology of unfulfilled hopes and plans.

An hour by car southwest of Ermenonville, abutting the Forest of Marly in the commune of Chambourcy, stands one of the most remarkable, and today least visited, eighteenth-century gardens of "fabriques": the Désert de Retz constructed by François Nicolas Henri Racine de Monville on the eve of the French Revolution, between 1774 and 1789, as a private pleasure garden. On a relatively small one hundred acres, dotted with ancient trees, Monville placed twenty "fabriques": two imitations of classical "ruins" (a Temple of Pan based on the Temple of the Sibyl at Tivoli, and a towering Broken Column); an imitation of a medieval ruin (a Gothic church, which included the walls and arched window from the actual thirteenth-century church of the village of Retz); an imitation of an intact classical temple (a Temple of Repose, with rusticated columns flanking a wooden door); a Chinese pavilion made of Indian teak, with interior paneling of mahogany and Chinese silk hangings; a Tartar tent (made not of cloth but of painted tin); an obelisk (also made of tin and painted to resemble stone); a pyramid (a four-sided stone structure inspired by the Pyramid of Cestius, and used as an icehouse); a tomb, a rustic bridge, a thatch-roofed cottage, a hermitage, a dairy, an open-air theater, and a grotto with an entrance of rusticated stone resembling the massive foundation represented in Piranesi's *Giant Wheel* (see fig. 44 in chap. 5)—all flanked by two tin satyrs holding torches.[67]

The most original and striking of the "fabriques," the Broken Column, was in fact a pavilion or residence—its round form rises to fifty-five feet, with a width of fifty feet, and seems to be a remnant of the architecture of a giant (see plate 11).[68] Its jagged top and deep "fissures" are in fact ornaments—not signs of penetration by wind, rain, and weather but instead applications to the fundamental structure and thereby three-dimensional illusions. From inside, the visitor could travel on a circuit from one oval window to another and discover a 360-degree view of the park. The Broken Column is an organized, if reversible, panopticon; the experience of being inside it ends the wandering that the Désert itself prompts—there is no particular order or circuit to the placement of the "fabriques." One moves without regard to ancient, medieval, or "modern" time, without regard to Greece, Rome, Tartary, or China. An atmosphere of whimsy and serendipity undermines even the somber enormity of the Broken Column.

Everywhere, as the foremost English-language expert on the Désert de Retz, Diana Ketcham, has suggested, the park suggests elusive, incomplete, narratives—childlike, erotic, foreign, and ancient at once: "The gardening enterprise aimed at an ambitious form of emotion management. Views were created resembling paintings or recalling events from myth or literature with the aim of producing desired states of feeling in the observer."[69] Visitors—from Thomas Jefferson and Maria Cosway to King Gustavus III of Sweden, Marie Antoinette, Madame du Barry, the Duc d'Orleans, Hubert Robert, and the myriad mistresses Monville is said to have entertained there—could be not only seduced by the immediate pleasures of such a playground but also taken by an impulse for imitation. Jefferson borrowed from the Broken Column for his floor design of the rotunda at the University of Virginia, as Gustavus borrowed the form for his own gardens at Haga and Drottningholm, and Marie Antoinette used the Désert as the prototype for her English gardens at the Petite Trianon.[70]

Between the 1700s and the 1980s, the Désert survived in an increasingly neglected state: an artificial ruin became an actual ruin. Its restoration still incomplete, today it stands somewhere between the states of authentic and artificial ruin, remaining in quandariness as a challenge to "authentic" restoration. It was perhaps the cultural syncretism of the "fabriques" of the Désert— its Chinese house indebted to the fantasies of William Chambers at Kew, its Tartar tent indebted to the Eastern European pavilions that the exiled Polish king Stanislas built at Lunéville and the Tartar tent installed at La Bagatelle, its mixture of Gothic and classical, Christian and "pagan forms"—that led to the popular interpretation of the Broken Column as a Tower of Babel. Monville, despite his aristocratic friendships and an accusation of "sybaritisme" by the Revolutionary Tribunal, survived the Terror. He died in 1797 in his own bed at his Boullée-designed townhouse on the Rue d'Anjou.

VII. The Unfinished

ON THE NONFINALITY
OF CERTAIN WORKS OF ART

Non Finito

The Tower of Babel in the Old English Junius manuscript is described as *samworht*, or unfinished. Bruegel's towers, too, are still on their way, densely detailed with workmen at a dramatically small scale; it is up to the viewer to remember that they will be abandoned when those workmen no longer can communicate with one another. Companion of the ruin, the unfinished is not the sign of a damaged form but the sign of a damaged intention. Yet the damage extends to the receiver as well: Pliny had lamented, in his *Natural History*, that unfinished works deprived their viewers of experiencing their completed forms. At the end of his treatise on the art of painting, *De Pictura*, Alberti also advised that individual works should be completed: "When you begin a work make it complete in every part. I have seen some painters and sculptors, and even rhetoricians and poets . . . [who have] devoted themselves to a work with zealous eagerness. Then their intellectual ardour cools off and they leave the rough and scarcely begun work to take up new things with renewed eagerness."[1] Vasari, however, contended that the *non finito* of Michelangelo's works was to be admired: works left unpolished—the Boboli slaves and the sculptures of the New Sacristy of the Medici Chapel in San Lorenzo, for example—became tied to those projects that for external reasons Michelangelo could not finish. The "incomplete" by whatever means came to bear an extraordinary psychological power; the *non finito* could be viewed as ever-emerging, moving not toward closure but toward, as Leopardi would suggest so eloquently, the *infinito*.[2]

Whenever a work of visual or verbal art is deemed unfinished, the question of cause comes to the fore: is the work unfinished by plan or contingency? If the former, what led the maker to intend the work to be unfinished? And, if the latter—short of death—what drove the artist's attention and energies away from the urge toward closure? A host of consequent problems arise: when unfinished works are abandoned on the way to completed works, do they become "studies" for the finished piece? Should an unfinished work be curated? Does it differ from a fragment? What are the consequences when an unfinished work is left to decay and thereby becomes a ruin? Who decides that a work is finished and where does that certainty reside—in signatures, submissions, and declarations by artists? In the judgments of critics, viewers, and readers? And how do we make aesthetic judgments without the satisfactions of completion?

After all, Immanuel Kant's critique of judgment proposes that, in the presence of beautiful phenomena, we suspend our drive toward closure. The imagination and the understanding see-saw, unresolved and unresolving. This playful abeyance key to Kant's judgment of the beautiful nevertheless is anchored in the sure bounds of finality of form.[3] In unfinished works, where finality of form is not present, we are thrown back into the context of the work's production, asking all the questions regarding intention and reception we otherwise might hold at bay. If the work is completed both metaphorically and literally by the single artist's hand, the claim of immortality is ironized by the fact of death. Not only will the individual artist die; the work, too, is vulnerable to disintegration—if it is curated, its material form, like any, will require commitments that may or may not outlast it.

Here we find a great difference between unfinished works of visual art and unfinished works of verbal art. For, unlike visual art, verbal art and literature are rooted in a vernacular tradition that by definition is made up of unfinished works: the stories and songs, riddles and proverbs of folklore are modified by each person who performs them. With some forms, such as ballads, these ongoing modifications make so many works parts of other works that, within one genre, a multiplicity of hybrid forms has emerged. The partial, fragmented, pieces that have survived in medieval manuscript books of oral traditions— poems, saints' lives, and *enigmata*—were not intended to be incomplete, but they remain so.

In the mid-eighteenth century, Thomas Percy and other early ballad scholars would send remnants of songs they had discovered via manuscripts or renditions by local performers to literary friends, asking them to provide new endings where endings had disappeared.[4] Today we have more than two hundred ancient manuscripts of the *Iliad* and ninety-two versions of "Barbara Allen": scholars must make the case for the authority of any particular text over others on the basis of whatever evidence can be gathered.[5]

Once an oral genre takes on a life in writing, however, the form itself projects its own requirements for completion. The paradigmatic case is the epic, which, with its twelve books and dactylic hexameter line, provides a template for closure. Virgil, returning to Rome from Greece and dying of a fever at the port of Brundisium, asked, according to the "vita" of Donatus, that the manuscript of the *Aeneid* be destroyed, for he considered it unfinished. Thanks to

the contravening orders of Augustus himself, the epic exists in the full traditional twelve books, yet the work includes fifty-seven lines that are "half-
lines." Since Donatus records that Virgil wrote the *Aeneid* first in prose and
then translated it into verse, we must ask whether Virgil intended to return
to these half-lines as he completed his revisions. There are in fact no incomplete lines in his *Eclogues* or *Georgics*. Even so, could the half-lines be strategic
pauses, often appearing at parenthetical moments, and underscoring inter-
ruptions in the narrative?[6] In later eras, the twelve-book convention shaped
the intention Edmund Spenser brought to his *Faerie Queene*. Dying in 1599
in his midforties, Spenser completed only half of his plan to register "all the
moral vertues, assigning to every vertue, a Knight to be the patron and de-
fender of the same."[7]

Beyond the epic, some literary works provide other clues to their completion or incompletion. Three *cantiche*, each divided into thirty-three *canti*—
and adding an introductory *canto*, and so totaling one hundred *canti* in all,
make up the great matrix of Dante's *Commedia*, a work that incorporates its
own closure from its first uncertain steps to its final glimpse of heaven. Dante's
admirer Boccaccio built his *Decameron* through an overarching allegorical
frame tale, with one hundred stories told over ten days. Such elegant structures indicate that these works are finished forms. But Chaucer's *Canterbury
Tales*, in its eighty-two versions and sprawling intersections, has long been
considered unfinished.[8]

Poets discovered perhaps the most flexible and ingenious use of the closed
and open principles of numerical composition in the sonnet sequence. Invented by Sicilian poets of the thirteenth century, the sonnet's fixed form of
twelve to sixteen—but most often, fourteen—interlocking lines, shaped into
an octave and sestet or later stanza divisions of three quatrains and a couplet,
with a crucial *volta*, or turn, provided the satisfactions of a completed argument or case. Yet from Petrarch forward, the sonnet often appeared in a sequence indicating an ongoing narrative or development that may or may not
come to a close. Michelangelo himself was devoted to practicing this form as
a way of condensing, aphoristically, his thoughts on art making and his emotions regarding aging and the breakdown of bodily form. The resulting order
justifies, yet formally stands in contrast to, the ambiguities of his sculpture.[9]

Shakespeare's 154 sonnets are more of a collection than a sequence, yet
within the assemblage we can discern incomplete narratives that lead us to
view some of the poems as clustered; the enduring fascination of these sonnets depends at least in part on this relation between shining examples of
poetic closure and an unresolved external form. Perhaps because of these
tensions between closure and disintegration, sonnet writers reintroduce the
Horatian themes of material fragility and the enduring memory of the literary.
As Shakespeare wrote in Sonnet 55:

Not marble, nor the gilded monuments
Of princes shall outlive this pow'rful rhyme;
But you shall shine more bright in these contents
Than unswept stone besmear'd with sluttish time.
When wasteful war shall statues overturn,
And broils root out the work of masonry,
Nor Mars his sword, nor war's quick fire shall burn
The living record of your memory.
'Gainst death, and all oblivious enmity
Shall you pace forth, your praise shall still find room,
Even in the eyes of all posterity
That wear this world out to the ending doom.
So, till the judgment that yourself arise,
You live in this, and dwell in lovers' eyes.[10]

Horace believed, as we have seen, that so long as the silent virgins and the Pontifex climbed the steps of the Capitol, he would not "fully" die, for his poetry will keep him "fresh [thanks to] future praise." Shakespeare, with his typical ambivalence toward antiquity and his committed emotional realism, here reminds us that human artifacts are destroyed by human as well as natural forces; if a final judgment is destined to wipe out the world and resurrect the virtuous dead, his poems will be lasting, necessary, and sufficient alike in the meantime.

Throughout the eighteenth century, artists continually worked between a polished completion and a veneration of the fragment—those broken residues that, little in themselves, spoke volumes about their missing integrity. We have only to compare the neoclassical imitation to the Gothic revival to understand the dialectical interdependence of wholes and parts in an age that began with the clockwork perfection of Alexander Pope's "Rape of the Lock" and grew into the wild uneven spaces of the picturesque and the soaring abstractions of the great Romantic odes. Indeed, the contrast between the fleeting particulars of sensual apprehension and the hope to derive moral certainties from experience drove the very invention of aesthetics in the mid-eighteenth century. As we have seen, artists who practiced the picturesque eschewed the smooth surfaces of the beautiful and favored, as William Gilpin suggested, the tactile appeal of rough and uneven surfaces.[11] In eighteenth-century narrative forms, writers as well turned from "finish" to the notion of *bildung*, or development, that became the central valence of the novel.

The poet's life span gradually became the measure of the great work. Consider the lives of two of our foremost authors of ruins texts: Johann Wolfgang von Goethe's relation to his *Faust* stretches from the unfinished *Ur-Faust* of the 1770s, which Samuel Taylor Coleridge and Wordsworth perhaps knew, to the great carnival of *Faust: Part Two*, published posthumously in 1832, the year of his death. Although the narrative arc of Faust's life and death was completed, Goethe continued up until his final months to make revisions.[12] Byron's picaresque cantos in *Don Juan* stop at canto 17, the placeholder at his death; his plans for the story had no clear shape, and the work's near-manic ottava rima stanzas apparently could go on so long as he was pleased to write them. At the beginning of the eighteenth century, Giambattista Vico had imagined an endless spiraling cycle of ages as the fate of human history. By century's end, the contemplation of ruins itself had led Volney to picture history as a cyclical pattern of revolutions.[13]

In Britain, the dissolution, and often consequent decay and destruction, of monasteries, abbeys, and other religious buildings followed in the aftermath of King Henry VIII's acts of supremacy and suppression between 1534 and 1541. As we saw in the poems of John Dyer and the musings of Lord Kames in chapter 6, the ruins of Britain were typically Gothic as well as prehistoric and Roman. In his thoughts on "picturesque travel," William Gilpin, too, noted the specifically Gothic forms of British ruins, remarking that "the picturesque eye is perhaps most inquisitive after the elegant relics of ancient architecture, the ruined tower, the Gothic arch, the remains of castles and abbeys. These are the richest legacies of art. They are consecrated by time, and almost deserve the veneration we pay to the works of nature itself."[14] The unexplained, perpetually mysterious, remains of Neolithic, Celtic, and other early inhabitants, the barely intelligible and often buried or half-buried signs of Roman habitation, the few surviving brick and stone forms—often based on Roman models and using Roman fragments—from the Anglo-Saxon period, and the visible decay of the later medieval abbeys, monasteries, and castles that could have taken a century or more to be built made Britain a particularly likely ground for the aesthetics of the fragment to encounter the aesthetics of the unfinished.[15]

Blake's Eternal Forge

This syncretic sense of antiquity powerfully shaped William Blake's repertoire of images and attitudes toward tradition. In the late 1790s, Blake wrote in a letter that, aligning his values with those of his friend George Cumberland, the "purpose for which I alone live . . . is in conjunction with such men as my friend Cumberland to renew the lost art of the Greeks." Nevertheless, from an early age, he felt distaste for the Society of Dilettanti's style of genteel antiquarianism and for the refined collecting practices of aristocrats abroad even as he was, as a very young art student at Henry Pars's Drawing School, surrounded by the patronage and influence of this kind of antiquarian. It was his apprenticeship with James Basire that exposed him not only to classical antiquarians but also to other, more nativist scholars who looked to Rome as the foundation of local British traditions that were in turn Gothic and Christian.

Blake was drawn to claims that the Hebrew scriptures—and God himself—were the source of all traditions. He wrote in his *Descriptive Catalogue*: "Grecian, Hindoo and Egyptian [art] are the extent of the human mind . . . the gift of God, the Holy Ghost." By 1818, he was arguing that the Laocoön came from Solomon's temple and was merely copied by "three Rhodians."[16]

In his early work, as Blake addressed the ruin of women and the material estimation of virginity, he reframed the terms of the issue: as we've seen, rather than "restoring" the ruined subject, he critiqued the social values that could demean persons in the first place. By the time of his last prophetic book, *Jerusalem, or the Emanation of the Giant Albion*, composed between 1804 and 1820, with further later emendations, he was still railing against chastity as a commodity. *Jerusalem*, in all its complexity, seeks to restore the fallen figures of male Albion, or England, and its female Emanation, or formed creation, Jerusalem—City of Peace and representation of Liberty.[17] Blake describes how Jerusalem, despairing in the Mills of the textile industry, incessantly turning the wheels of a machine, is trapped in "a Religion of Chastity & Uncircumcised Selfishness."[18] The Divine Voice shows her a vision of Joseph and Mary as Joseph first rails against Mary's "adultery" before weeping and embracing her in forgiveness. Mary bursts into song and "flowed like a River of Many Streams . . . Like many waters, and Emanating into gardens & palaces . . ." all the way back to the rivers near the garden of Eden. Jerusalem declares, "Am I become lovely as a Virgin in his sight who am / Indeed a Harlot drunken with the Sacrifice of Idols . . . If I were Pure I should never / Have known Thee; If I were Unpolluted I should never have / Glorified thy Holiness, or rejoiced in thy great Salvation."[19]

Throughout *Milton* and *Jerusalem*—these last, most ambitious poems, composed between 1804 and 1820—and in his illustrations to Dante and to Young's *Night-thoughts*, we also find Blake concerned with the story of the fall of the Tower of Babel, its builder Nimrod, and the Unholy City of Babylon as the counterpart to the Holy City of Jerusalem. These familiar subjects of early ruins prints inform the most complex and difficult of Blake's long works. They are steeped in his private mythology as they allegorize elements of the Bible and history and address the rise and fall of empires and lost worlds.

Yoking his own metalwork to the tasks of Los the blacksmith, Blake develops in *Jerusalem* a vision of art making as the forging of new means of life. He suggests that if human communities were freed of materialism, commercial gain, and human-generated violence, liberty and creativity would thrive in an unending process of self-forming and reforming. In a letter to William Hayley in May 1800, Blake had declared that "the Ruins of Time build mansions in Eternity."[20] As Harold Bloom has summarized the poem, "Blake stands on the ruin 'Of old Jerusalem, of Druid Britain, of Rome, and of modern British freedom,' and works at his poem, menaced not only by all his enemies, but more seriously by the Spectre within himself."[21]

Jerusalem is built from a vast universe of allusions that, as Bloom indicates, cannot be readily separated into past, present, and future. Blake finds his moment shot through at once with archaisms reaching back to the Hebrew scriptures, classical Greek and Rome, and the Druids, and new myths moving forward via proper names that he has invented. Continuing the themes and sometimes the exact language of his earlier *Milton* and *The Four Zoas*, the poem puts Blake's own vatic, constellated, narrative system into motion: the destruction described in Ezekiel; figures of fairies, nymphs, and giants; contemporary Edinburgh, York, and, above all, London; the Roman city of Verulam(ium) that we met in Spenser's "Ruines of Time"; attacks on Deism, the mechanism of Newton, and the humanism and primitivism of Voltaire and Rousseau. The conclusion to the poem merges the available traditions of Blake's time, a rough unity forged in the "City of Golgonooza." This place is Blake's allegorical "serpent Temple," an allegory of artistic making which exemplifies a perpetual work in progress. Here time opens to, is perforated by, eternity. He writes:

> Where is the Covenant of Priam, the Moral Virtues of the Heathen
> Where is the Tree of Good & Evil that rooted beneath the cruel heel
> Of Albions Spectre the Patriarch Druid! Where are all his Human
>   Sacrifices
> For Sin in War & the Druid Temples of the Accuser of Sin: beneath
> The Oak Groves of Albion that coverd the whole Earth beneath his Spectre
> Where are the Kingdoms of the World & all their glory that grew on
>   Desolation
> The Fruit of Albions Poverty Tree when the Triple Headed Gog-Magog
>   Giant
> Of Albion Taxed the Nations into Desolation & then gave the Spectrous
>   Oath
> Such is the Cry from all the Earth from the Living Creatures of the Earth
> And from the great City of Golgonooza in the Shadowy Generation
> And from the Thirty-two Nations of the Earth among the Living
>   Creatures[22]

Jerusalem's temple is built from the works of Blake's own forge: the one hundred plates that make up the work itself. The four parts specify their addressees: "To the Public"; "To the Jews"; "To the Deists"; "To the Christians." In this account of art as the means of reconstituting a fallen peace and liberty, Blake makes religion and a critique of religion his theme. Introducing "To the Jews," he claims that Albion was "the parent of the Druids": "All things Begin & End in Albions Ancient Druid Rocky Shore."[23] And he asks if Jerusalem was and is the Emanation or creation of the Giant Albion—if so, then everyone on earth belongs to one religion, which he claims as the Religion of Jesus, derived from the patriarchal Hebrews: "Jerusalem is taken! . . . London is a stone in her ruins; Oxford is the dust of her walls! Sussex & Kent are her scatterd garments: Ireland her holy place! And the murderd bodies of her little ones are Scotland and Wales . . . her palaces levelld with the dust." But "the Voice Divine" declares, "Fear not O little Flock I come! Albion shall rise again."[24] Like poetry and thought, religion cannot be ruined, only vanished or replaced—the poet-blacksmith's gestures of continual forging and making, like the manipulation of time Blake finds in Christ's powers of forgiveness, are unending—and worthwhile to him because they are unending.

It may be, as W. J. T. Mitchell suggests in his pioneering study of Blake's "composite art" of word and image, that *Jerusalem* will remain forever unintelligible and inexplicable in any hierarchical or completed sense. Mitchell writes, "It may well be impossible to 'approve' every word and image in *Jerusalem*, not just in the sense of commending its truth or beauty but in the more fundamental sense of 'proving' or demonstrating the meaning of every particular in a practical way. Blake asks us . . . to read in a spirit of faith and forgiveness as well as demonstration, and not to repeat the error of Albion by making these two into antithetical habits of mind."[25] These seemingly negative qualities of an unfinished apprehension could be as well a sign of the work's utopian potential.

Wordsworth and Vernacular Ruin

As Geoffrey Hartman has memorably explored, William Wordsworth, who composed much of his work in thought and speech alone, was also drawn to practices of inscription informed by such ancient traditions and beliefs that future generations would sustain their legibility. Carving his words and lines into the actual surfaces of rocks and trees, depicting writing in the landscape, designing gardens, Wordsworth long meditated upon the function of inscriptions and epitaphs.[26] These were surely practices designed to be stays against forgetting. Yet Wordsworth made a significant intervention in the tradition of ruins representations in several ways. Many of his most well-known poems are concerned with the ruin of structures, persons, and places in his own time. "Lines written a few miles above Tintern Abbey, on revisiting the Banks of the Wye during a Tour, July 13, 1798"—more familiarly known simply as "Tintern Abbey"—was composed in its lengthier title's year; "The Ruined Cottage" exists in fifteen extant manuscripts dating from 1797 to 1804; and "Michael: A Pastoral Poem" was written at the end of 1800.[27]

As we have seen, any English poet born, as Wordsworth was, in 1770 could find himself or herself immersed in ruins imagery. Druid and Anglo-Saxon remains, damaged abbeys, churches and monasteries, castles, and Gothic mansions had become commonplaces from the seventeenth century onward.

FIGURE 68. Jacob van Ruisdael, *Ruined Cottage*, ca. 1655. Black chalk and gray wash on white paper. The Morgan Library and Museum, New York; Thaw Collection, 2017.229.

We can construct a repertoire of ruined structures in Wordsworth's work that go back to his earliest poems in imitation of the pastoral imagery of Moschus, Theocritus, and especially Virgil in the eclogues—an early Wordsworth idyll on a dog describes a moonbeam that "Pace[s] like a Druid." And "The Vale of Esthwaite," written when he was seventeen, describes a Gothic mansion with a rusted door that "shield[s] from death the wandering poor."[28] Wordsworth's 1797 fragment poem, "Incipient Madness," haunted his work for the rest of his life. The work begins by describing a moonlit visit, not to a decayed palace or mansion but instead to the barest remains of a ruined hut:

> I crossed the dreary moor
> in the clear moonlight; when I reached the hut
> I entered in, but all was still and dark,
> Only within the ruin I beheld
> At a small distance, on the dusky ground
> A broken pane which glittered in the moon
> And seemed akin to life . . .[29]

During the seventeenth century, a northern tradition of representing such humble ruined vernacular buildings had emerged. In 1655 Jacob van Ruisdael portrayed a ruined cottage (see fig. 68), as did Rembrandt in a series of rustic cottage prints. Yet Gothic and classical imagery continued as well.

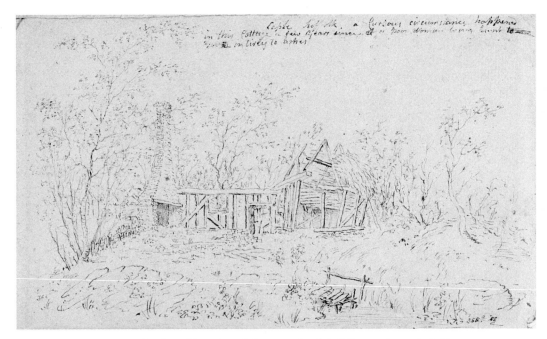

FIGURE 69. John Constable, *A Ruined Cottage at Capel, Suffolk*, 1796. Pen and ink. Victoria and Albert Museum, London.

By the late eighteenth century, picturesque ruins imagery had become for-
mulaic, and J. M. W. Turner, John Constable, and other artists began to use
a looser hand and wider field of vision. In 1796, Constable rendered a ruined
Suffolk cottage with its falling timbers and freestanding chimney wall (see fig.
69). The place drew his attention because it was reputed to have been inhabited by a local witch. The inhabitant was rumored to have burned to death
while everything else inside the house was undamaged. Johann Heinrich
Roos's numerous seventeenth-century prints of sheep and goats amid castle
ruins remained popular through the Romantic period (see fig. 70) and were
expressly admired by Goethe.[30] Goethe's own *Der Wanderer*, which was first
in print in English in August 1798 in a translation by William Taylor, describes
an encounter between a wanderer and a woman whose family lives in the ruins of an ancient temple. She at first thinks he is a peddler, but he explains that
he has come in search of something to drink. He recognizes that the nearby
stones are fragments of an ancient temple of Aphrodite.

These images often invite explanatory narratives. Like stories of miraculous appearances, from the gods appearing to Philemon and Baucis to Christ's
post-Crucifixion visits to his disciples to vernacular legends of ghosts and
witches, they involve the simultaneous appearance of impossibly disparate
time frames, the "cameo" of figures from the past erupting into the fabric of
the present, bringing solace or disorder alike. Ruined places are often haunted,
and learning to read them involves managing encounters with their resident
spirits.

FIGURE 70. Johann Heinrich Roos, *Sheep at the Base of a Column*, between 1663 and 1671. National Museum of New Zealand, Te Papa, Tongarewa.

Such problems of describing and drawing meaning from ruined structures extend to a tradition of topographical poems addressing actual and allegorical ruins. Among the poems that we know Wordsworth knew well was John Denham's *Cooper's Hill*, from 1642, a poem that addresses the decaying remains of Chersey abbey lying in what is otherwise a typical English landscape. Denham reflects, "May no such storm fall on our times / where ruin must reform," sensing that the scene carries a warning.[31] Following the success of Dyer's "Ruins of Rome," by the mid-eighteenth century the genre became especially popular. In 1777, Thomas Warton the Younger composed an "Ode written at Vale-Royal Abbey in Cheshire" that was typical of the form: prospects expand philosophically as the poet, in gloaming light, turns to contemplation "amid the wavering ivy-wreaths" and the "shards" of pitchers and alms dishes.

He describes how the abbey's ruins lie in a "bounded valley," with thistles, nettles, and pastured animals dotted across the site. Nevertheless, he concludes optimistically that new glories and new, more useful institutes will rise from these deserted places, with "manners enlarg'd and new civilities"—the poet proclaims "on fresh foundations build the social plan."[32]

In his early poems, ruins are not of interest to Wordsworth as architecture so much as synecdoches for vanished hospitality and shelter. As *hospitem* signifies both "guest" and "host," he takes up the standpoints of wanderers and tragic occupants alike. Often Wordsworth juxtaposes the scale of these structures within a frame of diminished expectations: in *The Borderers*, Herbert and Idonea, exhausted by their wanderings, describe their experience on a dismal moor—Idonea says "the bewildering moonlight / Mocked me with many a strange fantastic shape! / I thought the Convent never would appear; / It seemed to move away from us . . . And midway on the waste ere night had fallen / I spied a covert walled and roofed with sods— / A miniature" which she speculates may have been raised by a "Shepherd-boy" in a "nothing-doing hour." In the Salisbury Plain poems, a similar shift in scale is worked between the enormity of both Stonehenge and the distant spire of a church, evoking Salisbury Cathedral, and the diminished "loose walls" of the spital, or "dead house"—the abandoned hospital dedicated to the Virgin Mary, where the female vagrant and the sailor find refuge.[33]

Tintern Abbey was, like Warton's Vale-Royal, a Cistercian monastery. Lying in the valley of the Wye River near the English border with Wales, the abbey was looted and dismantled, with even the roof lead sold, in the autumn of 1536. For the next two hundred years, the gutted remains stood exposed to the elements, as they do today. Dr. Sneyd Davies's poem and travel record, "A Voyage to Tintern Abbey in Monmouthshire from Whitminster in Gloucestershire, August 1742," concentrates on the journey more than the abbey itself. And Gilpin's best-selling tourist publication, *Observations on the River Wye*, published forty years later, brought new visitors to the site who attempted to match the book's illustrations to the reality before them (see fig. 71).

William and Dorothy Wordsworth first made this journey to Tintern Abbey in 1793, bringing Gilpin's guide with them.[34] At that time they explored the abbey ruins. Gilpin had recommended that visitors come to such scenic places more than once to fix them in their memories—and an ambivalent desire to revisit the past dominates the poem. As David Bromwich and Nicholas Roe each have emphasized, the poem is shot through with Wordsworth's memories of France's immediate postrevolutionary period and the more recent events of the Reign of Terror in 1792 and 1793.[35]

As early as Gilpin, visitors to the abbey have mentioned the presence of poor inhabitants—itinerant workers and others employed in a local wire-making facility or ironworks, homeless people, hermits, and agricultural

FIGURE 71. William Gilpin, *Tintern Abbey*. From *Observations on the River Wye, and Several Parts of South Wales, &c. relative chiefly to Picturesque Beauty, made in the summer of the year 1770* (London: R. Blamire, 1782). Department of Rare Books and Special Collections, Princeton University Library.

laborers such as those Wordsworth infers from the smoke sent up in the distant woods. Gilpin had written, "Among other things in this fcene of defolation, the poverty and wretchednefs of the inhabitants were remarkable. They occupy little huts, raifed among the ruins of the monaftery; and feem to have no employment, but begging." He goes on to tell how a poor woman came to show them the dwelling she had made in what remained of the monk's library: "She could fcarce crawl; fhuffling along her palfied limbs, and meager, contracted body, by the help of two fticks. She led us, through an old gate, into a place overfpread with nettles, and briars; and pointing to the remnant of a fhattered cloifter, told us, that was the place. . . . I never faw fo loathfome a human dwelling. It was a cavity, loftily vaulted, between two ruined walls; which ftreamed with various-coloured ftains of unwholefome dews. The floor was earth; yielding, through moifture, to the tread." He provides more details of her miserable habitation and adds that when "Tintern-abbey" is described "as a solitary tranquil fcene," then "it's [*sic*] immediate environs only are meant," for within a half mile, the visitor would have encountered noisy and bustling ironworks.[36]

Wordsworth has been chastised by twentieth-century critics for failing to represent fully such figures. And these critics in turn have been chastised

FIGURE 72. Francesco Piranesi (after Louis-Jean Desprez), *View of the Tomb of Mamia among the Ruins of the Ancient City of Pompeii* (*Veduta del Sepolcro di Mamia negl'avanzi dell'antica Città di Pompei*), 1789. The Arthur Ross Collection, Yale University Art Gallery.

for chastising Wordsworth.[37] Putting aside the absurd insistence that poets represent the totality of their experienced perceptions, many aspects of "Tintern Abbey," and many cruxes of interpretation and style that have troubled readers, flow directly from a legacy of ruins representations, including the recurring presence of small, barely visible figures—most often shepherds, agricultural workers, and wanderers—in ruins landscapes. We have found these figures in the earliest ruins prints and seen, especially in chapter 5, the important role they play in the work of Piranesi as well. They continue into the early nineteenth century. Shepherds and antiquarian tourists climb the Temple of Isis in Pompeii in a 1789 print by another foreign enthusiast of the French Revolution: Piranesi's son Francesco (see fig. 72). J. M. W. Turner follows the same "labor and leisure" convention in his almost exactly contemporaneous Tintern images, made between 1792 and 1794 when he was in his late teens. We can see abandoned agricultural tools in the foreground and finely dressed visitors in the background of several of his views. We glimpse a roller and a bucket on wheels in one of his watercolors (see fig. 73) and an abandoned wheelbarrow in the foreground of another (see fig. 74).

FIGURE 73. Joseph Mallord William Turner, *Tintern Abbey*, ca. 1794. Watercolor. British Museum, London. The image shows the west front of the ruined abbey, overgrown with vegetation. A figure enters carrying a book; at left is a cottage with figures standing in front, in the foreground a roller and watering-can.

FIGURE 74. Joseph Mallord William Turner, *Tintern Abbey*, ca. 1794. Watercolor. British Museum, London. The image shows the transept; four figures amid the ruins garlanded by vegetation, a wheelbarrow and broom in the foreground.

Gilpin had published in 1768 *An Essay on Prints* outlining conventions for visual representations: artists should create faintness in the background, vividness in the foreground; no more than three subjects should appear in any image; a quiet atmosphere of repose is preferable, and even "clownish figures"—he means here rural people—should exemplify a "picturesque grace"; shadow should produce tone, perspective should provide the outline, and proportion should be observed with respect to near and distant objects.[38] For Gilpin, who titles his first chapter, "The principles of painting confidered, as far as they relate to prints," prints are akin to watercolor and other means of painting and often are derivative of these forms. As their oval frames indicate, his prints are made by using a Claude glass and sketching; there is little influence from the sophisticated mark making of Piranesi or the self-sufficiency of sixteenth- and seventeenth-century prints.

Despite Wordsworth's own expressed distaste for popular prints,[39] it is not difficult to trace an ekphrastic theme and practice in his "Lines" on visiting Tintern Abbey. Starting with this first word of the full title, the theme of lines and impressions runs through the opening of the poem and reappears at its close: the lines of water, the scenes that "impress," the "hedge-rows, hardly hedge-rows, little lines of sportive wood run wild," and "sensations sweet, / Felt in the blood, and felt along the heart."[40] The swooping details and high perspective suggest a moving bird's-eye view. Perhaps under the influence of Milton, Wordsworth was notably drawn to such elevated vistas. He particularly enjoys showing the ways, inversely, a bird's-eye perspective reveals how earthly landscapes can resemble the heavens: in 1800 in "Michael," then twenty-three years later in his "Description of the Scenery of the Lakes in the North of England," and as well in a poem he worked on for fifty years, "On Nature's Invitation Do I Come," which eventually became incorporated into *The Recluse*. There he writes of Lake District cottages as "clustered like stars" and "like separated stars with clouds between."[41]

In "Tintern Abbey," verbs of seeing and beholding dominate as the external landscape is held midpoem in memory. Wordsworth uses the word *landscape* repeatedly, mentioning "the landscape connected to the quiet of the sky," "the green and simple hue of the wild green landscape," "the landscape to a blind man's eye," "this green pastoral landscape." Yet perhaps the most relevant of the connections the poem has to contemporary conventions of topographical, picturesque, and landscape art lies in another category of Gilpin's aesthetics, and that is his notion of "keeping"—the artist's establishment of an overall frame. Gilpin defines this as "different degrees of strength and faintness, which objects receive from nearness and distance. A nice observance of the gradual fading of light and shade contributes greatly towards the production of a *whole*. Without it, the distant parts, instead of being connected with the objects at hand, appear like foreign objects, wildly introduced, and unconnected. Diminished in *size* only, they put you in mind of Lilliput and Brobdingnag united in one scene."[42] (In this pastoral domain of representation, it is relevant, too, that a "keeping" is also a herd of sheep, which must be maintained as individuals and as a group.)

Wordsworth seems to have had a lifelong interest in techniques of encapsulating a view: in *The Prelude* we find the well-known passages on the reflected stars on the surface of the ice where he skates and the reflections and visible objects glimpsed through water as he leans from the side of a boat. The "Elegiac Stanzas on Peele Castle" include the calm reflected image of the castle in the sea presented in contrast to Sir George Beaumont's stormy depiction of the same scene. "Keeping" can be done mechanically, as Gilpin himself does with his Claude glass. But Wordsworth in the end uses the notion of "keeping" imaginatively and resourcefully, nowhere more than in his concern in "Tintern Abbey" with establishing the relation between the near and distant worlds of 1789 and 1793 and in the force of the poem's closure, where a reversed perspective turns to Dorothy as the vicarious agent of his memory.

Here Wordsworth creates a deep coherence between his poetic genre— the turns, counter-turns, and stands of the ode—and his action in the world of returning to and countering his earlier self before he turns, in the end, to the future. The closing reverse perspective borrows from the same gesture at the end of Thomas Gray's "Elegy in a Country Churchyard," but Gray's poem seems suffused by the poet's anxiety that he will not in fact be remembered by the community of rural swains—those poor spellers conveying the oral tradition—who may have witnessed his wanderings. In the twenty-eight-year-old Dorothy, here envisioned as an eager child, Wordsworth hopes to have some of Horace's confidence in the future memories, and praise, of virgins.

The poem says nothing about the actual ruins of "Tintern Abbey," but it generates a comparison between open expansive structures, such as the topographical poem, the daydream, and the Pindaric, and the enclosed forms of confinements. In its own way, the poem converts the prison of the Bastille into the pacified Field of Mars. Wordsworth solves the central problem of the eighteenth-century landscape poem: that is, the refusal of description to yield in itself moral and social significance. James Thomson could end his 1730 version of his "Winter" stanzas in *The Seasons* with an assertion that "*The social tear* would rise, the social sigh; / And, into clear perfection, gradual bliss. / Refining still, the social passions work."[43] We have seen that in 1777 Thomas Warton's own ode on an abbey concluded with a commitment to building a "social plan" on "fresh foundations."[44]

Yet Wordsworth looks for remedies for suffering, isolation, and forgetting in the passage of time itself. The compensation the memory of Tintern Abbey has afforded Wordsworth while he has been pent up in lonely noisy rooms of towns and cities comes from the broad, musical qualities of the scene. Eschewing the Claude glass, Wordsworth breaks frame not only by evoking what can be seen alone in the mind's eye but also by expressing the sublimity of an infinite line extended as human memory and values. The poem makes the final case for the poetic over the visual and relies on the particularity of one individual interlocutor to stand for everyone.

To consider Wordsworth's simultaneous attraction to, and distance from, contemporary visual conventions in his poems on ruins and ruined persons, we can turn, as well, to the opening to "The Ruined Cottage." We are given a painterly description of a scene that could have been informed by Gilpin's guidelines for the picturesque—it lays down the broad brushstrokes of light and shade that would be preliminary to any landscape work. And yet this depiction turns out to be a displacement. It is never clear who can see it except for the narrator in "his mind's eye." From the B version:

> Twas Summer; and the sun was mounted high,
> Along the south the uplands feebly glared
> Through a pale steam, and all the northern downs
> In clearer air ascending shewed their brown
> And [ ] surfaces distinct with shades
> Of deep embattled clouds that lay in spots
> Determined and unmoved, with steady beams
> Of clear and pleasant sunshine interposed;
> Pleasant to him who on the soft cool grass
> Extends his careless limbs beside the root
> Of some huge oak whose aged branches make
> A twilight of their own, a dewy shade
> Where the wren warbles, while the dreaming man,
> Half conscious of that soothing melody,
> With sidelong eye looks out upon the scene,
> By those impending branches made
> More soft and distant. Other lot was mine . . .[45]

"Other lot was mine": the narrator, unlike this pleasant dreamer, has made his hot and parched way across a "bare wide Common on slippery ground" and cannot find anywhere to rest or to escape the insects and the tedious noise of bursting gorse crackling around him. He sees a group of elms and within them finds the ruined cottage, "four clay walls / That stared upon each other."[46] Wordsworth's frame-breaking, counterturning picturesque awakens us from our habitual ways of seeing; lingering for a time in the conventional and explicit, he lands in the invisible, renewing our powers of picturing negative spaces.

"The Ruined Cottage" will depict a ruined structure, but reaching back to "An Evening Walk" and the Salisbury Plain poems, it also depicts a woman and her infant destroyed in time. We witness earlier the physical and mental breakdown of Margaret's husband as well, and we learn of her vanished older son. Half the family is destroyed, and the other half, suspended by the narrative, disappears. The cottage and its environs are overcome by weeds and untended animals—signs of the surrender of human will and the ruin of human efforts.[47]

As we saw in chapter 3, in the long tradition of Western ruins representations, the ruined woman is most often either a virginal sexual victim or a prostitute. The destroyed cities of the Hebrew scriptures described as fallen whores; legacies of ancient stories of nymphs found near sources of water, especially wells and fountains; the vestal virgins, guardians of Rome's integrity, maintaining the sacred fire and drawing water from the Juturna spring next to their house at the foot of the Palatine; the promiscuous nymphs and classical fountains of the *Hypnerotomachia Poliphili*, the woman of Samaria at the well; the prostitutes in the recesses of the Colosseum: these cameos of ruined women amid ruins endure throughout the eighteenth and into the nineteenth century and beyond. Indeed, at the onset of modernism we will find Thomas Hardy's Tess meeting her doom at Stonehenge.

Coleridge was a student at Göttingen when Goethe's *Ur-Faust* was published as a fragment in 1790; Henry Crabbe Robinson left an account of Coleridge's familiarity with it. And Robert Southey's "The Ruined Cottage," number 6 of his English eclogues—a poem so dull it seems to exist to underscore the genius of Wordsworth—begins with the speaker saying, "I have seen . . . Many a fallen convent reverend in decay, / And many a time have trod the castle courts / And grass-green halls, yet never did they strike / Home to the heart such melancholy thoughts / As this poor cottage." The cause of this ruined house is the death of a virtuous old woman, destroyed by sadness when her only daughter has lost her virginity. Southey relates, "I saw the cottage empty, and the weeds / Already crowding the neglected flowers. / Joanna by a villain's wiles seduced / Had played the wanton, and that blow had reach'd / Her mother's heart."[48]

In light of Southey's sentiments, we can observe the fact that Wordsworth's female figures are virgins or chaste mothers. His female vagrants face starvation, exhaustion, and exposure to the elements, but, with the exception of the unfounded accusation of Herbert's motive toward Idonea in "The Borderers," there seems to be no hint of sexual predation. This absence is particularly obvious in the scene where the sailor comes upon the sleeping female vagrant in the spital on Salisbury Plain and their mutual terror dissolves into kind greetings and conversation. The unanticipated violence of the sailor's earlier act of murder stands in contrast here to the symbolism of the Virgin Mary and, later, the Philemon and Baucis-like hospitality of the peasant cottagers who provide a refuge for the sailor's dying wife. Despite the many kinds of suffering lying in wait for his poor female and male characters alike, Wordsworth does seem to have repressed or at least overlooked the possibility of sexual ruin.

In Wordsworth's poetry, ruin most often arrives as contingency, from outside rather than through any form of hamartia. The vivid psychological and political reasons for his concerns with homelessness, vagabondage, and the abandonment of the infirm and old long have been considered and are the subject of entire books by James Averill and, more recently, Quentin Bailey.[49] Yet Wordsworth's preoccupations with the suffering and deaths of mothers and children, the dislocations of shepherds and farmers, and the tragedies of returning veterans in the line of Virgil's eclogues all have formal consequences as well, for he must structure narrative time and provide clues to invisible causes.

The dying mother of "An Evening Walk," the female vagrant of the Salisbury Plain poems in her many incarnations, and Margaret of "The Ruined Cottage" all have husbands who enlist in the army; the mates of Margaret and the female vagrant do so under the compulsion of poverty. Margaret's husband never returns to her; the husbands of the other women die. All three are left to fend for themselves and their children. Margaret never becomes, however, like the other women, a homeless wanderer. Wordsworth shows her by the well, pitcher in hand, and describes the "cool refreshment" she draws there for passersby. Margaret is rooted by her futile hope of her husband's return. As the close of the poem says, the bench and the road are "fast rooted at her heart."[50] Yet it is possible, Wordsworth shows, to be lost in place: Margaret wanders more and more in the adjacent fields, she neglects her garden—like the weeds and truant sheep who come ever nearer the house, she goes astray.

Wordsworth's characters often suffer mental torment imposed from without as well. In the figure of Margaret's husband Robert, Wordsworth depicts the breakdown of an artisan/maker, showing how the cottager's weaving, carving, and child-rearing talents have decayed. The female vagrant in Salisbury Plain says, with a belying self-consciousness, "what afflicts my peace with keenest ruth / is that I have my inner self abused."[51] The Salisbury Plain sailor is a murderer by circumstance and not by action. When Margaret says she has wronged herself and her babe, in that order, no reader can quite blame her.

In fact, Wordsworth steadily drives home the problem of representation itself when conveying ruined persons and their environments. Reaching back to Spenser and, closer in time, to William Collins, Wordsworth is able to allegorize his figures as he also individuates his allegories. He is well aware that representation can be a kind of violence exercised upon the living. Based as they are on local events and legends, his stories of ruin remain both particular in their level of imaginative and sympathetic detail and typical in their fictiveness. It is as if Wordsworth is at perpetual work in the creation of an extended family resemblance between all contemporary forms of suffering—his is a process art and not a practice of reified portraiture.

Consider, for example, how he interrupts his narratives of "The Ruined Cottage" and "Michael" with an emotion near anguish regarding the telling itself. At the midpoint of "The Ruined Cottage," which coincides with noon, the hour of Pan—the speaker and the peddler, Armytage, come to a kind of narrative impasse as they reflect upon the ethics of telling stories of others' destruction.

He [Armytage] said, "Tis now the hour of deepest noon.
At this still season of repose and peace,
This hour when all things which are not at rest
Are cheerful, while this multitude of flies
Fills all the air with happy melody,
Why should a tear be in an old Man's eye?
Why should we thus with an untoward mind
And in the weakness of humanity
From natural wisdom turn our hearts away,
To natural comfort shut our eyes and ears,
And feeding on disquiet thus disturb
The calm of Nature with our restless thoughts?"[52]

In an exact symmetry, the second part begins with the speaker, whom we remember earlier suffered from heat and thirst, now chilled—a turn to trivial
conversation is "tasteless" to him, and he asks Armytage to begin his story
where he left off—as he says, "for my sake." Armytage replies:

It were a wantonness, and would demand
Severe reproof, if we were men whose hearts
Could hold vain dalliance with the misery
Even of the dead, contented thence to draw
A momentary pleasure never marked
By reason, barren of all future good.
But we have known that there is often found
In mournful thoughts, and always might be found,
A power to virtue friendly; were't not so,
I am a dreamer among men—indeed
An idle dreamer. 'Tis a common tale
By moving accidents uncharactered,
A tale of silent suffering, hardly clothed
In bodily form, and to the grosser sense
But ill adapted, scarcely palpable
To him who does not think.[53]

These passages on either side of noon work through a central problem of
eighteenth-century thought—the aberrant relation between perception and
cognition that will necessitate the invention of aesthetics itself as a means of
negotiating the relation between sense particulars and universals. Here, as in
Warton's Ode, sense and reason are juxtaposed. Natural wisdom is learned
from the natural world. We are shown the indifferent happy buzzing of those
flies that accompany all decay. And, in the second speech, Armytage insists

upon the necessity of bringing reason and thought to any dalliance with, any recounting of, misery. The B version ends simply with Margaret's death, but the D version draws out the moral:

> Amid the uneasy thoughts which filled my mind,
> That what we feel of sorrow and despair
> From ruin and from change, and all the grief
> The passing shews of being leave behind,
> Appeared an idle dream that could not live
> Where meditation was . . .[54]

The two in the end take to the road again and before dark arrive at "a rustic inn, our evening resting-place." Thus the initial problem of hospitality is solved by the discovery of the well and the final arrival at an inn. And the more serious problem, expressed midpoem, of the ethical ends of narratives of suffering is once again addressed by meditation or thought.

"Michael" similarly is halted by overarching questions of the reasons for speaking of the suffering of others. In an echo of the problem of "keeping" that we found in the final prayer of "Tintern Abbey," the speaker says of this story:

> although it be a history
> Homely and rude, I will relate the same
> For the delight of a few natural hearts,
> And with yet fonder feeling, for the sake
> Of youthful Poets, who among these Hills
> Will be my second Self when I am gone.[55]

The poem promises to be a delight, somehow edifying, yet the economy—the very domestic *oikos*—of its story seems out of balance. We wonder why the speaker mentions certain disturbing details: for example, that Michael loves his son more than his wife, that he wants Luke to know he has been both mother and playmate to him in early childhood, and that he believes children "By tendency of nature needs must fail."[56]

At several moments the speaker exhibits a half-embarrassed self-consciousness about the level of detail he is presenting, saying,

> why should I relate
> That objects which the Shepherd lov'd before
> Were dearer now?[57]

As he describes the lamp that hung near the cottage mantel, he feels he must justify mentioning it:

Not with a waste of words, but for the sake
Of pleasure, which I know that I shall give
To many living now, I of this Lamp
Speak thus minutely; for there are no few
Whose memories will bear witness to my Tale.[58]

Like the missing figures in "Tintern Abbey" and the missing child and father in "The Ruined Cottage," the missing son in "Michael" belies the fact that the shepherd has lived out a full span of eighty-four years: the deficit here lies in the life span of Isabel, who, twenty years younger, has outlived Michael by only three years.

Many critics have emphasized how the sacrifice of Luke alludes to the notion of covenant and the sacrifice of Isaac. The poem suggests other sacred allusions as well: foremost the story of Joachim and Anna—like Isaac and Sarah, parents in late age who give birth to a child of whom greatness is expected. Joachim had found that his sacrifice was refused by God because he was childless. But when he retreated to his sheepfold, he had a dream promising that he and Anna would have a child. In the scriptures, Joachim and Anna are rewarded and Isaac is saved.[59] In stark contrast, Michael's covenant is broken— ruined at the very level of genre, for just as "The Ruined Cottage" ends with a garden invaded by truant sheep and a potter's ass, the pastoral herding landscape of "Michael" has been in the end run through with a plow. The cottage known as "The Evening Star" is destroyed, and the sheepfold promised by the covenant between father and son is never built.

The Cathedral

In his 1971 preface to his edition of Wordsworth's poetry, Hartman concluded, "Perhaps Wordsworth never did emerge to an assured sense of self or a decisive poetry. There is something peculiar in the way his text corrupts itself: the freshness of earlier versions is dimmed by scruples and qualifications, by revisions that usually overlay rather than deepen insight."[60] Although this practice of self-corrupting revision sometimes has led Wordsworth scholars to place his work in the Romantic fragment tradition, Wordsworth rarely practices mimetic acts of decontextualization. To the contrary, he constantly is striving for a reintegration that may be, as Hartman indicates, in error. His task involves at once both spoliation and restoration. Much of what have been viewed as problematic practices—his repetitions, incessant revisions and reworkings, and his staging of scenes of unintelligibility between speakers—can be understood as solutions to the paradoxes of representing damaged persons and their worlds. Wordsworth demonstrates the constant reabsorption and reframing that is the carrying forward of language itself. By exercising a kind of right of return, admitting to change and endless interpretability, Wordsworth trans-

The Recluse ('the body of a gothic church')

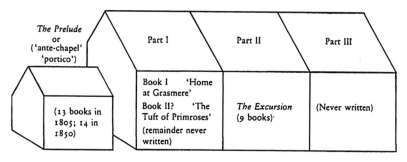

1797–99	The First Drafts: 'The Ruined Cottage', 'The Old Cumberland Beggar', 'The Discharged Veteran', and 'A Night-Piece'	1,300 lines
1798–99	The Two-Part *Prelude*	1,000 lines
1800	The Beginning of 'Home at Grasmere'	500 lines
1800–02	'Prospectus' to *The Recluse*	100 lines
1803–05	Main Composition of *The Prelude*	8,000 lines
1806	Completion of 'Home at Grasmere'	400 lines
1808	'The Tuft of Primroses', 'To the Clouds', and 'St Paul's'	700 lines
1809–12	*The Excursion*, Books II–IV	3,200 lines
1812–14	*The Excursion*, Books V–IX	4,700 lines

NOTE   Line totals are very approximate, and some dates are almost equally so. 'The Ruined Cottage' became Book I ('The Wander') of *The Excursion*; 'The Discharged Veteran' concludes Book IV of *The Prelude*; the two-part *Prelude* forms the bulk of Books I and II of the finished *Prelude*; the placement of 'The Tuft of Primroses' is conjectural.

FIGURE 75. "Wordsworth's Work Plan." From Kenneth R. Johnston, *Wordsworth and "The Recluse"* (New Haven, CT: Yale University Press, 1984).

forms our sense of what a poet's task might be and of the powers of poiesis beyond individual works.

Kenneth Johnston has created a diagram describing Wordsworth's goals as he worked to build what he called "The Gothic Cathedral of *The Recluse*" with its antechapel: *The Prelude* (see fig. 75). We can see in this scheme the background to the fate of the 1797 "Incipient Madness" fragment as it became the source of six lines in "The Ruined Cottage," which would itself be retold in book 1 of *The Excursion* of 1814, which was in turn meant to be incorporated into *The Recluse*. Wordsworth constantly is reinscribing, reusing, and rebuilding his life's work, using *The Prelude* as just that, a process of continuing beginnings.[61]

What makes a bit of glass akin to life is its capacity to reflect. Throughout Wordsworth's poems of ruined structures and persons, he breaks the narrative frame to introduce passages of reflection and self-consciousness. He left us some sense that he intended "Tintern Abbey" as an ode and hoped it succeeded, but how can we describe the species of composition, if not the genre, of the blank verse of "The Ruined Cottage" and "Michael"? "The Ruined Cottage" survives in many versions and in many works with other titles and itself emerges from earlier work. "Michael," too, exists in nine extant texts. And, as Johnston's diagram indicates, like all of Wordsworth's poems, these were intended to appear in *The Recluse*. Thus what seem to be fragments are in fact building materials, and Wordsworth's work as a whole reveals the ways that the unfinished or incomplete work of art is the reverse of a ruin, even though there is a moment, a hinge, when the building coming down and the building going up are impossible to tell apart.

As Maerten van Heemskerck shows us in his drawing of the Old Saint Peter's coming down as the new Saint Peter's goes up (see fig. 76), a construction site resembles a ruin, and at the same time works that are unfinished are the opposite of ruins—they are moving toward integrity, not toward disintegration, and the only means we have of distinguishing them is time itself. Michael's heap of stones returns us to the destruction of Ai from Joshua 8:28–29, a passage that we encountered earlier: "And Joshua burnt Ai, and made it an heap for ever, even a desolation unto this day. And the king of Ai he hanged on a tree until eventide: and as soon as the sun was down, Joshua commanded that they should take his carcase down from the tree, and cast it at the entering

FIGURE 76. Maerten van Heemskerck, *Northern Dome Support of the New Saint Peter's and the Rest of the Cross Arms of the Old Basilica, New Saint Peter's, and Constantine's Basilica on the Left*, ca. 1532–1536. Pen and brown ink. Gabinetto dei Disegni e delle Stampe, Uffizi, Florence.

FIGURE 77. Sheepfold at Sour Milk Ghyll, Cumbria.

of the gate of the city, and raise thereon a great heap of stones, that remaineth unto this day." Or it might follow from the story Wordsworth tells in "Rural Architecture," a poem that recounts how three schoolboys built a giant, the Magog of Legberthwaite Dale, from stones they collected on-site. When the wind blows down their creation, in the manner of William Blake, they go back and build another.

Dorothy Wordsworth records in her journal that there was an actual sheep-fold that became the site of "Michael" and that it was in the shape of an un-equal heart, perhaps resembling contemporary Cumberland sheepfolds (see fig. 77). She writes that the roofless structure is both the place where William composed the poem and a metonym for the poem itself: as she says, "William had been working at the sheepfold"—meaning he was there and also work-ing on the poem.[62] As the poem closes, Michael dies, but his labor remains incomplete:

> The length of full seven years from time to time
> He at the building of this sheep-fold wrought,
> And left the work unfinished when he died.[63]

Here the unfinished work in stone is both eroded and sustained by the continuity of poetic language—its source is the everyday iambic pentameter and flowing throughout William Wordsworth's work like a river, a stream, or at times a boisterous brook. This is why the poet/maker can take heart in knowing that whether or not works of art are completed, the task of art itself is ongoing and unending. A Wordsworthian poetry of thinking expressed by actual persons talking to other actual persons demands something more than finality of form and holds within it a critique of a materialist approach to art. This is a critique that remains both inspiring and unfinished—and perhaps most inspiring because it is unfinished.

VIII. Resisting Ruin

THE DECAY OF MONUMENTS
AND THE PROMISES
OF LANGUAGE

Wastelands

The long duration of ruins as they survived the gestures of force that shaped them has become a model for the artwork as monument and masterpiece—as the most treasured of made things, waiting to be received and reshaped, for better or worse, by one generation after another. Yet poets and artists of ruins also give us a sense not only that the material resists meaning but also that materiality at times cannot bear up under a surplus of meaning, that what seems to have been finished has not yet met its day, and that form cannot express everything it is and has been, especially once it loses its finality. These aspects of the ruin are tied to the inherent violence of all representation, which reifies or fixes its object, making living things dead and bringing dead things to life.

Ruins poems and images intervene in our common frames for thinking of the history of organic and mechanical means of reproduction, and they contribute to our understanding of certain formal predilections. These works often begin in multiples and evolve toward singular forms in a progression from drawings and prints to paintings and from poem fragments to at times unfinished wholes. And our taste for sketches, broken lines, caesuras, fragment poems, collage, and, more recently, earthworks and works made by explosions descend from this ruins tradition. The representation and repetition of fragmentation alleviates the problem of vanished cause and sets aside certain problems of agency and finality of form.

One of the best-known English poems in the tradition of the Romantic ruin, Percy Shelley's sonnet "Ozymandias," was written in 1817 on a lark. Shelley and a friend had read an account of the British Museum's acquisition of a fragmented head and torso from a statue of the thirteenth-century BCE Egyptian ruler Ramesses II and decided to compose competing sonnets on the object. (Among his accomplishments, Ramesses had completed the work known as the "Flaminian obelisk," now standing in the Piazza del Popolo, that we met earlier as fig. 12 in chap. 2.) Shelley uses his sonnet to invent an encounter with a witness to the statue's ruined form:

I met a traveller from an antique land,
Who said—"Two vast and trunkless legs of stone
Stand in the desert. Near them, on the sand,
Half sunk a shattered visage lies, whose frown,
And wrinkled lip, and sneer of cold command,
Tell that its sculptor well those passions read
Which yet survive, stamped on these lifeless things,
The hand that mocked them, and the heart that fed;
And on the pedestal, these words appear:
My name is Ozymandias, King of Kings;
Look on my Works, ye Mighty, and despair!
Nothing beside remains. Round the decay
Of that colossal Wreck, boundless and bare
The lone and level sands stretch far away."[1]

The witness, and the poet as imagined witness to the witness, and the reader who then receives the fragment thirdhand, are alike admonished to remember how the mighty fall, and how works decay, and that, beyond the resulting fragments, there is only "lone and level sand." The witness speaks, in medias res, yet goes on to convey the exact words of an inscription and to describe the erasure of context. Indeed, where one would expect the final aphorism of a sonnet, we find only empty, continuing description. The poem, in an act of self-consumption, tells us that total ruin results in negation pure and simple—the nonbeing of pure matter: an expanse of endless grains of sand. And it also underscores how, encountering a ruin, we are meeting presence on its way to absence. We become aware of the transience in time that is ours as well.

Shelley's poem was written during a period of conflict and famine when, as we saw in chapter 6, the plundering and commodification of ancient fragments and structures flourished. The poet emphasizes the varying degrees of unintelligibility that ruins present: through the efforts of archaeologists, the statue of Ramesses II can be identified, and through the efforts of museum curators, it can become the locus of future encounters, but it cannot appear within a restored context. "Ozymandias" has a near-nihilistic cast in the way it keeps its object at an ever-increasing distance. There are no commitments beyond the command to look and despair; the rest dissolves into desert. We are reminded again that ruins need a name and a knowing witness.

Beginning in 1921, in the wake of World War I, T. S. Eliot composed "The Waste Land," the most well-known ruins poem—perhaps the most well-known poem of any kind—of the twentieth century. Everything about the work is fragmented, except perhaps the unifying concept of fragmentation.[2] The poem's collaged or patched mode of composition invites us to view it not only as it unfolds in time but also as a kind of array. If we consider its opening and closing as shaping the whole, we find concerns regarding tautological violence and the conditions of ruined fertility running throughout its parts. Eliot takes his opening epigraph from Petronius's account of the Sibyl of Cumae in her cricket cage, tormented by boys; she desires to die as she is condemned to an eternal, more and more incommunicable, life. At the end of the work, we find the unattributed "I" that occasionally speaks throughout the poem saying, "These fragments I have shored against my ruins." That summarizing close is undermined by the immediate appearance (with no punctuation between lines) of a voice echoing Thomas Kyd's 1587 play *The Spanish Tragedy*: "Why then Ile fit you. Hieronymo's mad againe."³ Kyd's line, provided as a reference by one of Eliot's numerous half-serious, half-parodying footnotes to the poem, refers to the subtitle of his tragedy—*Hieronymo's Mad Againe*—which in turn refers to the work's revenge plot wherein Hieronymo kills his son's killers through feigning a court masque and afterward kills himself.

Begun when Eliot was thirty-three, the death year of Christ in Christian legend and in consequence the significant organizing number of Dante's *Commedia*, "The Waste Land" is thereby ornately and allusively framed. The epigraph on the Sibyl is followed by a tribute to Ezra Pound, who edited the poem, and parrots the compliment Guido Guinizelli affords Arnaut Daniel in Dante's *Purgatorio* as he calls him "Il Miglio Fabbro," the better maker. Eliot then adds a part title referring to the Anglican ceremony of burial. When the poem appeared in book form for the first time, Eliot also provided an opening footnote explaining that the symbolism of the poem borrows from the accounts of fertility myths ("vegetation ceremonies") and the resurrected gods Adonis, Attis, and Osiris, in Jessie Weston's *From Ritual to Romance*—a work on the anthropology of ritual concerned with the legend of the Holy Grail.⁴ In Weston's account, this tradition records the travails of an archaic "fisher king" who seeks to renew his drought-ridden kingdom, restoring its water and forms of life.⁵

Beyond these opening and closing devices, the poem is formed by five asymmetrical sections made up of the speech of voices—both named and unidentified, both male and female—and fixed texts excerpted from a vast array of sources: the Bible; Virgil's *Aeneid*; Ovid's *Metamorphoses*; Richard Wagner's *Tristan und Isolde, Parsifal*, and *Götterdämmerung*; Shakespeare's *The Tempest, Antony and Cleopatra, Coriolanus*, and *Hamlet*; Baudelaire's *Les Fleurs du mal*; Dante's *Inferno* and *Purgatorio*; numerous Jacobean revenge melodramas; *Paradise Lost*; the lyrics of popular songs; the Fire Sermon of Buddhism; Spenser's *Prothalamion*; Marvell's "To His Coy Mistress"; John Day's *The Parliament of Bees*; the myth of Tereus and Procne; poems by Sappho and Robert Louis Stevenson; Oliver Goldsmith's "When Lovely Woman Stoops to Folly"; Augustine's *Confessions*; records of the Shackleton expedition to the Antarctic; Hermann Hesse's *Blick ins Chaos*; Fyodor Dostoevsky's *The Brothers Karamazov*; the Upanishads; and nursery rhymes.

Anyone who follows the footnotes to the poem can make such a list—the work, long before the age of Google, relies on the possibility of its reader "looking things up." Yet Eliot may have created these notes for the most part

to extend to book length a poem that otherwise, at nineteen to twenty manuscript pages after a period of severe editing on the part of Pound and the
poet himself, was not long enough.[6] The "high culture" of the work is thereby
brought into the realm of ruin from the start by the oddly truncated status of
its references. It is, as the second stanza of the poem suggests, difficult, if not
impossible, to discover the "roots" and "branches" of "stony rubbish." We are
presented with "a heap of broken images" held together by the insistence of
voices whose motivations and connections to one another are difficult to discern.[7] Furthermore, these voices are monologues—their implied listeners remain mute. The reader becomes haunted by the convergence between speaking to one's self and speaking to those who are absent or dead.

The locations traversed by the poem unfold through each of its cited texts.
At the same time, the poem is situated within the "unreal cities" with "falling
towers" that are the traditional scenes of Western myth: Jerusalem, Athens,
Alexandria, Vienna, and, particularly, London. When Eliot writes "Unreal
City," he also is alluding to the financial district above the north end of London Bridge. There stand the Bank of England (not, as Joseph Gandy depicted
it, in ruins), the Royal Exchange, and other major commercial banks, including Lloyds, Eliot's employer from 1917 to 1925.

The time of the poem moves erratically from the morning of a winter dawn
to nightfall and timelessness. The work is as well punctuated by nocturnal encounters and trompe l'oeil effects of ceiling paintings and reliefs ("withered
stumps of time / Were told upon the walls") that displace the ground of reality, framing narrations within narrations. Throughout the poem, we find much
of the recurring imagery of the history of ruins representations: a chorus of
nymphs associated with the Thames and (Wagner's) Rhine; the controversial
status of the "Virgin Queen" Elizabeth I; "mountains of rock without water";
the "broken images" of iconoclastic fervor; and, above all, the degraded, the
dying, and the dead—victims of cruelty, lust, and violence. A description
of Dido in her palace at Carthage includes an image of the "seven-branched
candelabra" of a menorah surrounded by jewels and treasures. It is as if Eliot
had been reading Procopius on Gizeric's Carthaginian stash of the Jerusalem
spoils.

In the poem and the material of its notes, we encounter voyeurism (Actaeon
and Diana, Sweeney and Mrs. Porter), rape and seduction (the Duke of Florence seducing Bianca in Thomas Middleton's play *Women Beware Women*;
the rape of Philomel by Tereus; the encounter of a typist and a clerk in her
rooms; the seduction of Olivia by Squire Thornhill in Goldsmith's *The Vicar
of Wakefield*), murder (Apollo's killing of Hyacinth; Hamlet's killing of Polo-
nius; Hagen's murder of Siegfried; Maremma's murder of La Pia in *Purgatorio*,
canto 5; the Crucifixion of Christ; Coriolanus killed by the Volscians; Ugolino starved by Ruggiero in *Inferno*, canto 33), attempted murder (Romelio's
stabbing of Contarino in John Webster's play *The Devil's Law Case*), murder-

suicide (the Archduke Rudolf and his mistress; unsuccessfully, Tristan and Isolde; the deaths of *The Spanish Tragedy*), suicide (Dido, Cleopatra, Ophelia, Brünnhilde), fratricide (Flamineo murdering Marcello and Vittoria's attempt to murder Flamineo in Webster's play *The White Devil*), infanticide (the killing of Itys by Procne; Ruggiero's starving of the children of Ugolino), cannibalism of progeny (Tereus eating Itys; Ugolino eating his children's corpses), and abortion (by Lil, wife of the "demobbed" soldier Albert). Such a parade of pain owes an obvious debt to the travails of Dante's *Commedia*, yet Eliot's poem does not enter into the afterlife. Its literary allusions to human evil and suffering are woven into the experiences of the living—if history is not exactly being reenacted, it is framing our understanding of the events before us.

Who is speaking and who is listening in "The Waste Land"? We find the inscribed voices of texts and the animated voices of named and unnamed "characters." Of those with proper names, the first is a woman, "Marie," remembering her childhood and the lakes and mountains of Munich and based on an actual encounter Valerie Eliot claims her husband had with the disgraced Countess Marie Larisch von Moennich. "Bin gar keine Russin, stamm' aus Litauen, echt deutsch," she says, "no Russian," "a true German"—that is, paradoxically, a Lithuanian. Madame Sosistris, "famous clairvoyante," reads imaginary and real tarot cards. Mr. Eugenides, the Smyrna merchant, whose presence alludes to the contemporary genocide of the Christians of Izmir by the Turks, appears as a figure in someone else's first-person narration. The voice of the raped and tongueless Philomel, turned into the nightingale's cry, sings, "Jug Jug." Tiresias, who has powers of inhabiting the perspectives of men and women as well as powers of prophecy, delivers a monologue as he "perceives the scene" and has "foretold the rest" of the typist's passive surrender to rape by the "carbuncular" young clerk. The corpse of drowned Phlebas the Phoenician issues a warning to "Gentile or Jew / O you who turn the wheel and look to windward, / Consider Phlebas, who was once handsome and tall as you."[8] Eliot's reader must take the place of the missing interlocutors, making a concerted effort to listen, to hear, to furnish missing contexts; the work proceeds by means of a kind of aural archaeology.

The Tower of Babel III

As a poem of ruin, "The Waste Land" powerfully raises questions of theodicy and the relations between fallen persons and fallen worlds. And in this mosaic riddled with many kinds of prophets and prophecies, Eliot has proved to be strikingly prescient in his concern with the disappearance of water, fertility, and renewable sustenance in the modern era. Yet the problems of intelligibility that "The Waste Land" raises bring it under another aspect of ruins discourse: the relation we have found repeatedly between ruins and cultural syncretism—that connection between multilingualism and the story of the Tower of Babel. Eliot's original title for his poem in manuscript, "He Do the Police in Different Voices," refers to the depiction of the orphan Sloppy in Charles Dickens's *Our Mutual Friend*, who reads the police blotter in the newspaper in various dramatic voices to his adopted mother Betty Higden.[9] This notion of voicing also echoes the close of *The Spanish Tragedy*. As Hieronymo sets out the court masque that will bring about the revenge he hopes for, he insists that the murderers speak their parts in mutually unintelligible languages:

> Each one of us must act his part
> In unknown languages,
> That it may breed the more variety.
> As you, my lord, in Latin, I in Greek,
> You in Italian, and for because I know
> That Bel-imperia hath practisèd the French,
> In courtly French shall all her phrases be.

The theme appears elsewhere in the initial claim of Marie to be Lithuanian because she is a pure German, in the "demotic French" of the seducing Mr. Eugenides, and in the poem's many tongues: Latin, French, German, medieval Italian, Sanskrit, what we might call the demotic English of Cockney speakers, and even in the imitation of birdsong and water sounds.[10]

"The Waste Land" is yet another polyglot monument arising in the aftermath of war and devastation. Like Dante and Wordsworth before him, Eliot animates the vernacular—here "mother tongues" expressed in urgent testimonies—to awaken the culture. His efforts to write a critique of Western forms of desire and violence find their culmination in his "translation" of the fable of the meaning of the Thunder from the Brihadaranyaka—Upanishad 5.1. The Thunder's sound of "DA" is extended to three related terms: *datta, dayadhvam, damyata*—meaning, respectively, "give," "have compassion," "restrain yourself." These imperatives each pose a remedy for the many narratives of greed, lust, and savagery assembled in the poem: "a flash of lightning. Then a damp gust / Bringing rain." Eliot's final note explains that the poem's thrice-repeated final word *shantih* is "a formal ending to an Upanishad. 'The Peace which passeth understanding' is a feeble translation of the content of this word." Significantly, he speaks the Sanskrit word and not Philippians 4:7.[11]

A Dream of Monumentality

What can escape the oblivion of time passing? The answer, from the time of Sarenput's restoration of ancestral tombs, has been the establishment of a monument, most often accompanied by the writing and recording of an inscription that will underscore the intent of the monument maker. It is as if each generation unlearns and relearns the lesson of the inevitable inter-twining of monumentality and ruin. As the twentieth century was a period of accelerated ruin, with technologies of destruction far outstripping the powers of ordinary human will and consciousness, it also was a period marked by a fevered desire to create monuments: monuments above all to those damaged and destroyed by those same technologies of destruction.

Consider the case of the monuments of Berlin, a city known for its monu-ments and the focus today of many controversies regarding their purposes and legacies. Along with the rest of the Western world, Berlin has inherited the tradition of making and preserving monuments descending from the Egyptians and Romans that we have followed here. Indeed, the Latin noun *monumentum* indicates physical objects, such as tombs, and written records alike; as we have noted, the word comes from the verb *monere*, to remind or warn. Yet the ever-present potential for forgetting is what prompts a monu-ment in the first place. And the contrast between a monument's finite physi-cal form and the unending, erring, abstractions of memory leads to an often tragic relation between objects and the memories they evoke. We have seen Horace's hope for "a work outlasting bronze / And the pyramids of ancient royal kings." He declares that "The North Wind raging cannot scatter it / Nor can the rain obliterate this work."[12] Shakespeare claimed, "Not marble, nor the gilded monuments / Of princes, shall outlive this powerful rhyme."[13] "The Waste Land" brings its own readers into an endless hermeneutic process de-signed to keep the poet's concerns in view. Poets dream of making artworks that will not be vulnerable to the erosion that weather and time can wreak upon even the greatest of built human structures. Even so, the anxiety that their words, too, might not endure is palpable.

To survive as a physical form, a monument needs care and restoration. For its meaning to survive, it needs the continual engagement of institutions. There is no guarantee, however, that those institutions themselves will last. Within less than a hundred years, Karl Friedrich Schinkel's neoclassical mas-terpiece the *Neue Wache* (*New Guardhouse*) was known as a "Memorial of the Prussian State Government," as the site of the Nazi *Heldengedenktag* (Re-membrance Day) services, as a "Memorial to the Victims of Fascism and Mil-itarism," and, in its current incarnation, as a "Central Memorial of the Fed-eral Republic of Germany for the Victims of War and Dictatorship." Even if a monument endures, changes of regime and the succession of generations are likely to transform what it means. Christian Daniel Rauch's commanding mid-nineteenth-century equestrian statue of Frederick the Great and his retinue still stands at the heart of the city on Unter den Linden. With its twenty-four male figures and hovering goddesses representing the sovereign's virtues, it has outlasted monarchy and mounted armies alike. Its many inscriptions are increasingly useful as clues to its message, but it is the rare pedestrian who stops to read them.

And every landmark is not a monument. A monument imposes itself upon you and asks, or warns, you to remember it. For historians and architects of monuments today, Berlin is a well-known laboratory for designating sites of attention and memory. Hans Stimmann, former building director of Berlin, declared in 1991, in response to the collapse of the Berlin Wall, that his task was one of "critical reconstruction"[14]—a process that came to be based in a largely invented Berlin architectural "tradition" emphasizing nineteenth-century-style facades, relatively low eave heights of twenty-two meters (about seventy-two feet), and uniform materials of sandstone, limestone, and brick. At the same moment, other officials and various groups of citizens sought, and continually seek, to sustain and further discussion of still vivid memories of the recently lived past. Albert Speer's absurdly pompous "theory of ruins" contended that National Socialist buildings would impress viewers with their might for a thousand years.[15] Today only a few of those buildings, such as the deteriorating Olympic Stadium, are visible at all. Meanwhile, immediate knowledge of World War II and its consequences will vanish as the survivors of the war reach their late age. The events of the war are known through first-hand narratives by the next generation. For a new generation, these soon will be secondhand narratives.

Within the built environment of contemporary Berlin, many approaches to remembering the war and its victims can be found. Each monument has its own relation to space and time and weather. On the smallest, but far from least effective, scale, the Cologne sculptor Gunter Demnig has created and situated by today more than fifty thousand *Stolpersteine*, cobblestone-sized concrete cubes that carry brass plates recording the name and birth, deportation, and death dates of the victims of Nazi persecution. The stones are placed next to the most recent places where the victims resided or worked. The term *Stolperstein* refers to "stumbling stone" or "stumbling block"—the small memorial is meant to stop the pedestrian or observer in his or her tracks and help its readers orient themselves to the place and time of the victims.

On a larger scale, the ongoing reconstruction from the ground up of the sixteenth-century Stadtschloss projects a utopian image of the past into the future along the lines of Stimmann's tenets, eliding the twentieth century. The 2,711 stelae of Peter Eisenman and Richard Serra's *Denkmal für die ermordeten Juden Europas* (*Monument for the Murdered Jews of Europe*) already are beginning to show signs of deterioration. The remaining ruin of the Kaiser Wilhelm Gedächtniskirche, which was bombed during World War II, and its spire have now been stabilized (see fig. 78). The church stands—like its counterpart, the stabilized ruins of Coventry Cathedral in England (see fig. 79)—like a perpetually open wound, a testament to its own destruction and the suffering of war.

FIGURE 78. Ruins of Kaiser Wilhelm Gedächtniskirche, Berlin.

FIGURE 79. Ruins of Coventry Cathedral.

When Riegl put forward his theory of "age value," he explained that what endures in a ruin is not necessarily integral or intelligible and the signs of wear accrue their own independent value. The patina on the *Stolpersteine* indicates they have been read; the worn surfaces of the *Denkmal* stelae bring the work's enormity to the scale of eye and hand. In the Stadtschloss project, with its nostalgia for origin, and the Gedächtniskirche, with its sculptural form underscoring its own vulnerability, we find a vivid contrast: the reconstructed palace will remain an unreachable ideal; the fossilized church, incorporating its history into its form, has acquired an additional purpose.

Monuments are among the most controversial of built forms, and their controversy always lies in their inadequacy and in the inevitability of their failure. We pose impossible goals for them when we expect them to last forever, to convey permanent meanings, to manifest all of our beliefs and ideas about the dead. Unlike the "perpetual" meaning posed by the Gedächtniskirche, the classical heritage includes known vanished buildings, such as the Septizodium, and myriad unknown structures: those that remain are constantly returning to a state of nature and remind us that neither our bodies nor our buildings can transcend time.

The starkly compelling German word for "monument," *Denkmal*, indicates a pause in the flow of existence given over to acknowledging and pondering a designated place. Yet we live in time and therefore must find means of memorializing in time. We face the unending, and very expensive, task of conveying to each new generation our knowledge of the past. We can put up monuments, assuming their messages will cohere, or pull them down, assuming their meanings will disappear. The neglect of monuments can indicate a revived attention to ethics, as it is in the abandonment of Soviet-era military monuments across Eastern Europe and the dismantling or relabeling of statues validating the "Confederate States of America" of the US Civil War period. There is a homology between the reification of monumental forms and the unquestioning acceptance of ideology.[16] Yet explicit negotiation always threatens to bring new, unwanted, and even admiring attention.

In vivid contrast, Berlin's most precious living monument may be the deep allegiance of its citizens and government to the continuity of musical traditions. Invisible, music demands an ongoing commitment to its manifestation—to its production, performance, and reception. As mere sound can bring down the walls of a city, music can encircle and sustain it; yet without an ongoing and passionate engagement, music vanishes into silence and forgetting. This ever-present potential of music to appear and disappear, to continue through acts of performance and interpretation, gives us an alternative model of monumentalizing. If we can commit ourselves to judging together, out of the vast raw material of human achievements and errors, what is ethical and worthwhile, beautiful and good, useful and true, the fragility of materials is inconsequential. A monument can be a temporary means of teaching the living about the past. But it is only in the continual transmission of our values, in the life of thought, language, and critical reconsideration, that we can find any permanence. The universal and transparent language dreamed of in the Tower of Babel resembles music, to which, insofar as it hopes for immediacy and intelligibility, all translation aspires.

Further, the possibility of creolizing mother tongues and re-forming concepts via other languages and traditions underscores a basic truth: such intelligibility is always possible, for language itself cannot be ruined. Actual speech may be degraded, incoherent, or used to lie or harm, but our human capacity for language cannot be irreparably damaged so long as human life endures with an intent to be understood. Like water, language flows on, absorbing and healing itself, integrating, shaping, and changing whatever it encounters. It exists prior to our individual being and opens room for us in the world. We make our mark with it and contribute to it with each utterance we form. Yet the powers of language are continued only by means of a collective volition. Language is essential to the task of anthropomorphizing ourselves. The uses to which we put it are fundamental to our values as they change in time. If we surrender its powers to nonhuman agents, we will self-destruct. In an information age, given to churning all value into quantifiable "bits," the fragility and poverty of the merely material is all the more evident.

The study of ruins and ruins images reveals how deeply our hermeneutic vocabulary is, as Freud understood very well, indebted to architectural and archaeological terms. We do not have to be devotees of deconstruction to claim that we dig below or scratch the surface, open meanings, explore depths, follow or clear paths, reveal underpinnings and underlying structures, or peel away mere rhetoric and ornament. Are these spatial models of hidden or damaged meaning in some way masking a deeper, and perhaps less esoteric, dimension of the relation our understanding has to time? Plans to lift veils, to penetrate the noumenal, to reach the source or origin, on the one hand, and to control destiny, on the other, represent impossible desires to master the past and the future and to reconcile human mortality with both animate and inanimate nature.

If we believe an unconscious is buried somewhere within us and that what arises from the past is a desire about the future, we would also have to ask ourselves why we are so captivated by ruination—why, for example, do we pursue novelty at the expense of sustainability? Why, in advertising and many aspects of our popular culture, do we continue to find the juxtaposition of extreme deprivation and refined elegance picturesque? Western tradition both underscores and denigrates matter—a duality more than evident in the history of subjugated persons: those unconsenting women, children, slaves, and aboriginal peoples who have been viewed as mere property and all others who have been merely used by others, rather than beheld as thinking, desiring agents. In our greed for power and novelty, is there anything that might escape the inevitable obsolescence of use? Once our labor, our health, our traditions and knowledge, our emotions, our very thoughts become commodities, they are stripped of life and growth.

Nature is no longer the backdrop to human creation; our human world has become the backdrop for things of nature. Will we bear witness to the ruined forms of what we have known as the natural world with the same aesthetic pleasure and equivocation with which we look on these ruins images? In and for itself, as minerals and chemicals, the natural world will survive humankind. Whether it will re-create the means of life necessary to our species, or to beings resembling our species, is not within our ken. The environmental catastrophe we think of as the ruin of nature is in fact the ruin of human nature, the end of our sustainable life on earth. Perhaps, beyond disaster, we might discover in this history of ruins something ephemeral that is both significant and beautiful, something, as Wordsworth once said, "akin to life" that can guide us on to life. The this-worldly life of time and natural processes: the green weed breaking through the stone.

Acknowledgments

During this long period of studying and writing, I have benefited deeply from the generosity, and often the expertise, of my family—Daniel Halevy, Jacob and Sam Stewart-Halevy, Maria Sidorkina, and Anika Schwarzwald—and from the encouragement and inspiration of many friends and colleagues: Brunella Antomarini, Pia Candinas, Peter Flaccus, Ann Hamilton, Susan Howe, Robert Harrison, Kelly Zinkowski, Daniel Heller-Roazen, Lucia Allais, Eve Aschheim, Fabrizio Falconi, the late Pietro Zullino, Starry Schor, Hal Foster, Chris Heuer, Froma Zeitlin, Mary Harper, Janet Richards, Tacita Dean, Sarah Whiting, and Kevin Hart. I owe a special debt to John Pinto, Arthur DiFuria, and Edward Wouk, who offered learned and helpful suggestions for sections of the text. I have been fortunate to have the editorial support of Randy Petilos at the University of Chicago Press and the wisdom of Alan Thomas, long my prose editor, who, as always, introduced me to new perspectives on the manuscript and offered practical help as I assembled its images.

Between 1987 and 1997, I cotaught an annual graduate seminar in aesthetics at Temple University's Tyler School of Art in Rome—this book had its origins in that experience, and I remain grateful to Alan Singer and to our colleagues Jan Gadeyne, Peter Rockwell, and the late Franca Camiz for our work together. An invitation in 1997 from Lewis Hyde to write a memoir/essay, which came to be called "Our Ruin," for a special issue of the *Kenyon Review* titled "American Memory/American Forgetfulness," led me to think about the vast differences between the European and North American experiences of ruins.

In 2012, Shirley Tilghman invited me to speak in her Presidential Lecture Series at Princeton University, where I first presented a preliminary view of this research, and I remain grateful for discussions of the project then and at many other venues as my work continued in the ensuing years: the Getty Center for the History of Art and the Humanities; the Silberberg Lecture at the Institute of Fine Arts at New York University; the George H. Ford Lecture

FIGURE 80. Reading Room, Istituto centrale per la grafica, Rome.

at the University of Rochester; the Finzi-Contini Lecture at Yale University; the Berkeley Center for the Study of Values in the Humanities; the Alexander Lecture at the University of Toronto; the American Academy in Berlin; the English Departments of Princeton and Yale; the Humanities Institute at Ohio State University; the comparative literature program at Stanford University; the School of Architecture at Rice University; and the Society of Fellows in the Liberal Arts at Princeton. An invitation from the Metropolitan Museum of Art to write on the concept of "the Unfinished" for its spring 2016 exhibition on that topic contributed to my thoughts on the relations between ruin and incompletion here.

I am indebted to the Barr Ferree Publication Fund of the Department of Art and Archaeology at Princeton for a subvention supporting the book's publication. I remain grateful to Brian Gingrich and Andrew Ferris for checking numerous references; to Kate Clairmont, Tara Broderick, John Orluk Lacombe, and Karen Mink for help securing permissions for images; and to Lori Meek Schuldt and Christine Schwab at the press for their copyediting and production assistance. Zoë Slutzky helped proofread and June Sawyers created the index.

I have listed numerous specific debts to scholars, librarians, and curators in my notes, but I would like to acknowledge the staffs of the many institutions that aided my research: Princeton's Marquand Library of Art and Archaeology; the Department of Rare Books and Special Collections at Princeton's Firestone Library; the Pennsylvania Academy of Fine Arts, where study in techniques of copperplate etching with Tony Rosati helped me understand what I was seeing; Yolanda Korbe, librarian of the American Academy in Berlin, and the academy itself, which sponsored a fellowship in the spring of 2014 that allowed me to explore materials at the Kupferstichkabinett in Berlin, the Museum Plantin-Moretus in Antwerp, the Désert de Retz at Chambourcy, Goethe's Wohnhaus and Gartenhaus in Weimar, and the Palace of Diocletian at Split; Stephen Astley at the Soane Museum; the British Library and the British Museum; the rare book librarians of the American Academy in Rome; Valerie Scott and her colleagues at the British School in Rome; and the curators at the Istituto centrale per la grafica di Roma, who allowed a glimpse of Piranesi's copperplates and graciously welcomed me many times to the great study room behind the Trevi Fountain (see fig. 80).

Notes

Introduction

1. Frederick II: 1194–1250; Petrarch: Francesco Petrarca, 1304–1374; Francesco Colonna: 1433–1527; Raphael: Raffaello Sanzio da Urbino, 1483–1520. Names are a complex manner in this book peopled by figures who moved between languages. Many had Latin names, nicknames, names at once translated into French and Italian, German and Dutch, and, like Raphael, names associated with their places of origin in addition to the birth names. Throughout, I will provide alternative names at first mention and thereafter use the most common names. I follow the spelling of primary texts with the exception of several eighteenth-century prose texts, where for ease of reading I have emended the long *S* (ſ) to *s*.

2. G. B. Piranesi, *Prima parte di architetture, e prospettive* (Rome: Stamperia de' Fratelli Pagliarini, 1743).

3. Aristotle, Iamblichus, *Protrepticus* 49.3–51.6, Pistelli in *Complete Works of Aristotle*, ed. Jonathan Barnes, "Fragments" (Princeton, NJ: Princeton University Press, 2014), 2:2404.

4. Propertius, *Elegies*, ed. and trans. G. P. Goold (Cambridge, MA: Harvard University Press, 1990), bk. 2.31, p. 199; bk. 3.11, p. 261; bk. 3.13, pp. 269–71; bk. 2.31, p. 199; bk. 3.13, p. 269.

5. Exegi monumentum aere perennius
   regalique situ pyramidum altius,
   quod non imber edax, non Aquilo impotens
   possit diruere aut innumerabilis
   annorum series et fuga temporum.
   Non omnis moriar multaque pars mei
   vitabit Libitinam; usque ego postera
   crescam laude recens. Dum Capitolium
   scandet cum tacita virgine pontifex,
   dicar, qua violens obstrepit Aufidus
   et qua pauper aquae Daunus agrestium
   regnavit populorum, ex humili potens,
   princeps Aeolium carmen ad Italos
   deduxisse modos. Sume superbiam
   quaesitam meritis et mihi Delphica
   lauro cinge volens, Melpomene, comam.

   I have cited David Ferry's translation, *The Odes of Horace* (New York: Farrar Straus, 1997), bk. 3, ode 30, 254–55. For a commentary on the meaning of *situ* in this ode, see Greg Woolf,

"Monumental Writing and the Expansion of Roman Society in the Early Empire," *Journal of Roman Studies* 86 (1996): 22–39. It is intriguing that Horace and Propertius never mention one another by name, which seems a practice of proleptically ruining each other's reputation.

6. In his seminal *Civilization of the Renaissance in Italy*, Jacob Burckhardt notes this theme. He draws particular attention to a discussion in Poggio Bracciolini's famous reflection on the ruins of Rome in his 1431–1448 *De varietate fortunae*. Poggio's companion Antonio Lusco characterizes the city as the fount of an entire culture and laments the ruins of "hanc urbem . . . ex qua rei militaris disciplina, morum sanctimonia et vitae, sanctiones legum, virtutum omnium exempla et bene vivendi ratio defluxerunt." As a counter, Poggio says that being able to read age-worn inscriptions can help one date the buildings and acquire an intact picture of the ancient city (29–31). Burckhardt notes as well that the altars and sepulchers of Francesco Colonna's *Hypnerotomachia Poliphili* "speak their own stories of love and suicide through inscriptions which . . . call out to the passerby—'viator'—or the occasional 'lector' to delay and read their tales" (34–35).

7. Leon Battista Alberti, *On the Art of Building in Ten Books*, trans. Joseph Rykwert, Neil Leach, and Robert Tavernor (Cambridge, MA: MIT Press, 1988), 204–5. See the discussion of Alberti's "lettered" imagination in Mario Carpo, *Architecture in the Age of Printing: Orality, Writing, Typography, and Printed Images in the History of Architectural Theory*, trans. Sarah Benson (Cambridge, MA: MIT Press, 2001), 124.

8. Lucretius, *De Rerum Natura*, trans. D. Rouse (Cambridge, MA: Harvard University Press, 1989), 3:xxviii–xxx.

9. This feeling can be compared to Kant's claim that experiences of sublimity also require distance and safety. From *Critique of the Power of Judgment*, ed. Paul Guyer, trans. Paul Guyer and Eric Matthews (Cambridge: Cambridge University Press, 2001): "Bold, overhanging, as it were threatening cliffs, thunder clouds towering up into the heavens, bringing with them flashes of lighting and crashes of thunder, volcanoes with their all-destroying violence, hurricanes with the devastation they leave behind, the boundless ocean set into a rage, a lofty waterfall on a mighty river, etc., make our capacity to resist into an insignificant trifle in comparison with their power. But the sight of them only becomes all the more attractive the more fearful it is, as long as we find ourselves in safety" (144). He adds that towering mountain ranges, deep ravines holding torrents, and "deeply shadowed wastelands inducing melancholy reflection" also produce feelings of sublimity insofar as the viewer knows himself or herself to be in safety (152).

10. I have consulted the 1836 edition, *Études de la nature par Jacques-Henri-Bernardin de Saint-Pierre, avec des notes par M. Aimé-Martin*, vol. 2, *Étude douxième* (Paris: Chez Lefevre, 1836), 51–57. Citations here are taken from the translation of Henry Hunter, *Studies of Nature. By James-Henry-Bernardin de Saint-Pierre*, vol. 4 (London, 1796), study 12, 28–38. For contemporary debates regarding the dates of the Arch's construction and the meaning of its inscriptions, see James C. Anderson Jr., *Roman Architecture in Provence* (Cambridge: Cambridge University Press, 2012), 81–93. Anderson argues that such a triple-fornix arch is unlikely to have appeared before the second century CE.

11. Georg Simmel, "Die Ruine," in *Philosophische Kultur: Gesammelte Essais* (Leipzig: Klinkhardt, 1911), 137–46. See esp. 140–41.

12. Percy Shelley to Thomas Love Peacock, December 22, 1818, in *Letters of Percy Shelley*, vol. 2, *Shelley in Italy*, ed. Frederick Jones (Oxford: Oxford University Press, 1964), 59. In the period of this first visit to Rome, in November 1818, Shelley wrote a prose text, "The Coliseum: A Fragment," that offers a sketch of a dialogue between a young woman and her old blind father within the Colosseum. Their conversation is overheard by a stranger, "forever alone,"

who, though deeply learned, avoids contact with the locals of all classes and who views "these mighty ruins [as] . . . more delightful than the mockeries of a superstition which destroyed them." As the piece begins, the stranger vehemently chastises the elderly man for not realizing he is in the ruins of the Colosseum. The daughter explains, in turn, that the old man is blind. As she goes on to describe the ruins in answer to her father's questions about the scene, the Colosseum is gradually transformed from "a great circle of arches upon arches and shattered stones" to a place of "flowers . . . weeds, grass . . . and creeping moss . . . younglings of the forest . . . caverns such as the untamed elephant might choose, amid the Indian wilderness. . . . A nursling of man's art, abandoned by his care, and transformed by the enchantment of Nature into a likeness of her own creations, and destined to partake of their immortality!" The stranger seeks out their friendship as the piece closes; his earlier pedantry, including his knowledge of the ruin's name and function, is replaced by an appreciation of the "communion" of such "intelligent and affectionate beings." Percy Shelley, "The Coliseum: A Fragment," in *The Complete Works of Percy Bysshe Shelley*, ed. Roger Ingpen and Walter Edwin Peck (London: Ernest Benn, 1926–60), 6:299–306.

13. Rodolfo Lanciani, *The Destruction of Ancient Rome: A Sketch of the History of the Monuments* (New York: Macmillan, 1899), 123n1.

14. Sigmund Freud, *Civilization and Its Discontents*, trans. and ed. James Strachey (New York: Norton, 1961), 16–20.

15. It is useful to compare native North American archaeology to the situation in Mexico, for example. In her comprehensive book on state policy toward restoration there, Christina Bueno notes the Olmecs, Maya, and especially the Aztecs collected and preserved objects made by earlier peoples, the Teotihuacanos and the Toltecs, whom they wanted to emulate. Christina Bueno, *The Pursuit of Ruins: Archaeology, History, and the Making of Modern Mexico* (Albuquerque: University of New Mexico Press, 2017). The travel records—and lithographs and daguerreotypes—of the nineteenth-century US diplomat John Lloyd Stephens and the artist Frederick Catherwood as they explored Maya ruins brought the sites to the attention of the North American and European public. See the catalog of the September–November 2015 exhibition at Dumbarton Oaks, *Stephens and Catherwood Revisited: Maya Ruins and the Passage of Time* (Washington, DC: Dumbarton Oaks Research Library and Collection, 2015).

16. Richard B. Parkinson, *Reading Ancient Egyptian Poetry: Among Other Histories* (Oxford: Blackwell, 2009), 24–25. My guide to the values associated with Egyptian ruins has been Janet Richards, who kindly directed me to Parkinson's work and generously offered her expert thoughts and comments.

17. Detlef Franke, *Das Heiligtum des Heqaib auf Elephantine* (Heidelberg: Heidelberger Orientverlag, 1994), stele no. 9, pp. 155–57. This translation from Franke's German and all subsequent translations in this book, unless otherwise attributed, are my own.

18. The often anthologized New Kingdom "Song of the Harper" from ca. 1160 BCE introduces an *ubi sunt* theme and also underscores the continuity of legend and knowledge of oral traditions, even if material forms have vanished:

As for these builders of tombs,
Their places are no more.
What has become of them?
I have heard the words of Imhotep and Hardedef,
Whose maxims are repeated intact as proverbs.
But what of their places?
Their walls are ruins

And their places are no more,

As if they had never existed.

William Kelly Simpson, ed., *The Literature of Ancient Egypt: An Anthology of Stories, Instructions, Stelae, Autobiographies and Poetry*, trans. Robert K. Ritner, Vincent A. Tobin, and Edward Wente, 3rd ed. (New Haven, CT: Yale University Press, 2003), 332–33. Imhotep and Hardedef were a Third Dynasty architect and a Fourth Dynasty prince, respectively.

19. Michael Alexander, ed. and trans., *The Earliest English Poems*, 3rd ed. (London: Penguin, 1991), 2–3.

20. Michael Swisher, "Beyond the Hoar Stone," *Neophilologus* 86 (2002): 133–36.

21. Bede, *The Ecclesiastical History of the English People; The Greater Chronicle; Bede's Letter to Egbert*, ed. Judith McClure and Roger Collins (Oxford: Oxford University Press, 1999), 286.

22. *Beowulf*, ed. and trans. R. M. Liuzza, 2nd ed. (Peterborough, ON: Broadview Press, 2013). Line numbers are shown parenthetically in the text.

23. Alexander, *Earliest English Poems*, 48–51.

24. R. M. Liuzza, "The Tower of Babel: The Wanderer and the Ruins of History," *Studies in the Literary Imagination* 36, no. 1 (Spring 2003): 1–35 (poem and translation, 1–3).

25. Robin Fleming, *Britain after Rome: The Fall and Rise, 400–1070* (London: Penguin, 2011), 28.

26. R. Fleming, *Britain after Rome*, 36.

27. Seneca, *Epistles 93–124*, trans. Richard M. Gummere (Cambridge, MA: Harvard University Press, 1925), 90–91: "Habeamus in commune; nati sumus. Societas nostra lapidum fornicationi simillima est, quae casura, nisi in vicem obstarent, hoc ipso sustinetur."

28. Alberti, *On the Art of Building*, 5.

29. Vincenzo Scamozzi, *Discorsi sopra l'antichità di Roma* (Venice: Appresso Francesco Ziletti, 1582), 15, table 15 (The Colosseum). The plates in this volume are by Battista Pittoni.

30. For an account of a quite different tradition of ruins, and one that emphasizes the ruined tree or organic form, see Wu Hung, *A Story of Ruins: Presence and Absence in Chinese Art and Visual Culture* (Princeton, NJ: Princeton University Press, 2012).

31. See, for example, Jun'ichirō Tanizaki, *In Praise of Shadows* (New York: Vintage, 2006), trans. Thomas J. Harper and Edward Seidensticker, 18, 32, and 47, for a discussion of the aesthetics of patina.

32. Alois Riegl, "The Modern Cult of Monuments: Its Character and Its Origin," trans. Kurt Forster and Diane Ghirardo, *Oppositions* 25 (1982): 21–51, at 32.

33. Riegl, "Modern Cult of Monuments," 24.

34. Riegl, "Modern Cult of Monuments," 32.

35. Riegl, "Modern Cult of Monuments," 24.

36. Riegl, "Modern Cult of Monuments," 31.

37. William Gilpin, "On Picturesque Beauty," in *Three Essays: On Picturesque Beauty; On Picturesque Travel; and On Sketching Landscape; to Which Is Added a Poem, on Landscape Painting* (London: R. Blamire, 1792), 3–33. It is worth noting that Gilpin, expressing dissatisfaction with a series of reasons as to why roughness is preferable to smoothness (it offers more variety, it is closer to nature, etc.), gives up on explaining the pleasures of roughness, claiming that "inquiries into first principles . . . go on without end and without satisfaction" (25, 30–33).

38. *Encyclopédie Diderot et D'Alembert* ([Paris]: Classiques Garnier Numérique, 2016), s.v. "ruine," s.f. "grammaire," https://www-classiques-garnier-com.ezproxy.princeton.edu/numerique -bases/index.php?module=App&action=FrameMain.

39. Denis Diderot, *Salons*, ed. Jean Seznec and Jean Adhémar (Oxford: Oxford University Press, 1975–1983), 3:235.

40. Gilpin, "On Picturesque Beauty," 7.

41. Bernardin de Saint-Pierre, *Studies of Nature*, 29.

42. Viollet-le-Duc, *Dictionnaire raisonné de l'architecture française du XIe au XVIe siècle* (Paris: Édition Bance-Morel, 1854–1868), 8:14: "Restaurer un édifice, ce n'est pas l'entretenir, le réparer ou le refaire, c'est le rétablir dans un état complet qui peut n'avoir jamais existé à un moment donné."

43. John Ruskin, *The Works of John Ruskin*, vol. 8, *The Seven Lamps of Architecture*, ed. E. T. Cook and Alexander Wedderburn (London: George Allen, 1903), 244.

44. The influence of Riegl on restoration theory is discussed in detail in Brigitte Desrochers, "Ruins Revisited: Modernist Conceptions of Heritage," *Journal of Architecture* 5 (Spring 2000): 42–43. A useful historical survey of approaches to restoration and conservation, and of the willed destruction of cultural monuments in World War II, can be found in Miles Glendinning, "The Conservation Movement: A Cult of the Modern Age," *Transactions of the Royal Historical Society* 6th ser., 13 (2003): 359–76; see his discussion of Viollet-le-Duc, Ruskin, and Morris at 363–64.

45. Robert Eisner, *Travelers to an Antique Land: The History and Literature of Travel to Greece* (Ann Arbor: University of Michigan Press, 1991), 33. See also Rose Macaulay, *Pleasure of Ruins* (New York: Barnes and Noble, 1953), 151–65, for a survey of Greek ruin appreciation.

46. Synesius of Cyrene, *The Letters of Synesius of Cyrene*, trans. with introduction and notes by Augustine FitzGerald (Oxford: Oxford University Press, 1926), 126.

47. Macaulay, *Pleasure of Ruins*, 154–55.

48. Macaulay, *Pleasure of Ruins*, 227–28.

49. Eisner, *Travelers to an Antique Land*, 40.

50. Augustine of Hippo, *Confessions*, trans. R. S. Pine-Coffin (London: Penguin, 1961), 24.

51. Augustine of Hippo, *City of God*, trans. Henry Bettenson (London: Penguin, 1972), 12. He then went on, however, to remark on the barbarians' strange clemency in putting those who were spared inside basilicas for protection and attributed this divergence from the practice of war to Christ's influence.

52. Henry James, *Italian Hours* (1909; repr., New York: Ecco Press, 1987), 165. If James is right, our culture could be becoming more heartless and perverse, for a great many books on ruins recently have appeared. Among the most noteworthy works in English surveying the aesthetic and cultural role of ruins are Macaulay's pathbreaking and compendious *Pleasure of Ruins*, cited earlier; Paul Zucker's study of ruins in art history, *Fascination of Decay: Ruins; Relic—Symbol—Ornament* (Ridgeway, NJ: Gregg Press, 1968); Robert Harrison's study of Roman melancholy and the ends of literature, *Rome, la pluie, a quoi bon la littérature?* (Paris: Flammarion, 1994); Christopher Woodward's *In Ruins* (New York: Pantheon, 2001), a survey of ruins as sources of inspiration to British artists, writers, architects, and archaeologists from the gardens at Virginia Water to the effects of World War II and the London Blitz; Robert Ginsberg's *Aesthetics of Ruins* (Amsterdam: Rodopi, 2004); Julia Hell and Andreas Schönle's collection of essays on ruins and twentieth-century culture, *Ruins of Modernity* (Durham, NC: Duke University Press, 2010); Hell's new study, *The Conquest of Ruins: The Third Reich and the Fall of Rome* (Chicago: University of Chicago Press, 2018), where she discusses the long legacy of imperial fascination with ruins, from the Roman preoccupation with the story of Troy and the erasure of Carthage to the "neo-Roman" frames of the Hapsburg conquests and twentieth-century fascism; Brian Dillon's edited volume of ruins meditations, *Ruins* (Boston: MIT Press, 2011), a collection linked to his curatorship of a far-ranging and suggestive recent show, *Ruin Lust*, at the Tate Gallery in London in the spring of 2014 which surveyed artistic interest in ruins from the seventeenth century to the present; and Robert Harbison's medita-

tion on the aesthetic uses of fragmentation, *Ruins and Fragments* (London: Reaktion Books, 2015).

53. Edward Gibbon, *The Autobiographies of Edward Gibbon*, ed. John Murray (London: John Murray, 1896), 302.

54. Patrick Leigh Fermor, *Mani: Travels in the Southern Peloponnese* (1958; repr., New York: New York Review, 2006), 140.

Chapter One

1. Hans Jonas, "Jewish and Christian Elements in Philosophy: Their Share in the Emergence of the Modern Mind," in *Philosophical Essays: From Ancient Creed to Technological Man* (Englewood Cliffs, NJ: Prentice Hall, 1974), 38. The original essay appeared in German as "Judentum, Christentum und die westliche Tradition," *Evangelische Theologie* 28 (December 1968): 613–29.

2. John Milton, *Paradise Lost*, ed. Scott Elledge (New York: W. W. Norton, 1975). All citations of the work refer to this edition.

3. Exodus 20:34 (AV). All biblical citations in this book are from *The Bible: Authorized King James Version* (Oxford: Oxford University Press, 1998).

4. Tertullian quoted in William Reeves, ed. and trans., *The apologies of Justin Martyr, Tertullian, and Minutius Felix, in defence of the Christian religion, with the Commonitory of Vincentius Lirinensis concerning the primitive rule of faith, translated from their originals with notes, for the advantage chiefly of English readers, and a preliminary discourse upon each author, together with a prefatory dissertation about the right use of the Fathers* (London: A. and J. Churchill, 1709), 1:219.

5. Lactantius, *Divine Institutes*, ed. Anthony Bowen and Peter Garnsey (Liverpool: Liverpool University Press, 2004), 414.

6. See Augustine, *City of God*, 142–44, on the "tiny gods" and greater gods of the pagans, and, 494, on "the utterly unchangeable mind of God, which can embrace any kind of infinity and numbers all the innumerable possibilities without passing them in sequence before its thought."

7. Simon Schama discusses medieval beliefs in dragons inhabiting mountains and the eventual transformation of attitudes toward mountain climbing in the eighteenth century in several chapters of his *Landscape and Memory* (New York: Knopf, 1995), 411–23 and 447–513. On p. 512 he discusses Ruskin's association of mountains with ruined forms of architecture.

8. William Camden, *Britain, or A chorographicall description of the most flourishing kingdomes* [. . .] (London: Printed by F. K[ingston,] R. Y[oung,] and I. L[egatt] for George Latham, 1637), 620. This passage originally came to my attention through Gordon Davies, *The Earth in Decay: A History of British Geomorphology, 1578–1878* (London: Macdonald, 1969), 20–21.

9. Stuart Piggott, *Ruins in a Landscape: Essays in Antiquarianism* (Edinburgh: Edinburgh University Press, 1976), 113.

10. The Ode, in 1606 designated "Ode 7," is appended to the end of "the 26th song" in *The Works of Michael Drayton*, ed. J. William Hebel (Oxford: Basil Blackwell and Mott, 1961), 4:530–34.

11. Thomas Hobbes, *The Moral and Political Works of Thomas Hobbes of Malmesbury* (London: n.p., 1750), 679.

12. John Donne, *The Variorum Edition of the Poetry of John Donne*, vol. 6, *The Anniversaries and the Epicedes and Obsequies*, ed. Gary A. Stringer et al. (Bloomington: Indiana University Press, 1995), pp. 13–14, lines 300–302.

13. Marvell writes:

Here learn ye Mountains more unjust
Which to abrupter greatness thrust,
That do with your hook-shoulder'd height
The Earth deform and Heaven fright,
For whose excrescence ill-design'd,
Nature must a new Center find,
Learn here those humble steps to tread
Which to securer Glory lead.

Andrew Marvell, *The Poems and Letters of Andrew Marvell*, ed. M. Margoliouth, rev. Pierre Legouis with the collaboration of E. E. Duncan-Jones (Oxford: Clarendon Press, 1971), pp. 60–62, lines 9–16.

14. John Wilkins, *The Discovery of a World in the Moone; or, A Discovrse Tending to Prove That 'Tis Probable There May Be Another Habitable World in That Planet* (London: E. G. for Michael Sparke and Edward Forrest, 1638). Alexander Wragge-Morley discusses Wilkins and others with a phobia of mountains in "A Strange and Surprising Debate: Mountains, Original Sin and 'Science' in Seventeenth-Century England," *Endeavour* 33, no. 2 (June 2009): 76. Gabriel Gohau writes of Burnet and "The Fear of Mountains" in his *Histoire de la géologie*, translated by Albert V. Carozzi and Marguerite Carozzi as *A History of Geology* (New Brunswick, NJ: Rutgers University Press, 1990), 49–51. There he quotes John Evelyn's late seventeenth-century diary with its description of mountains as "strange, horrible, and frightful." Evelyn contended in 1646 that "nature has swept all the rubbish on Earth into the Alps"; mountains "had shattered and collapsed one on top of the other" (50).

15. Gabriel Plattes, *A Discovery of Subterraneall Treasure, viz. Of all manner of Mines and Mineralls, from the Gold to the Coale* (London: by I. Okes for Jasper Emery, 1639; repr. in facsimile for the Institute of Mining and Metallurgy, Ilkey, UK: Scolar Press, 1980), 5.

16. Ray's posthumous 1713 volume of *Three physico-theological discourses* [...] (1693; repr., London: William Innys, 1713) is discussed in Davies, *Earth in Decay*, 20–21. Davies's pathbreaking study again has been my guide here.

17. Quoted in Wragge-Morley, "Strange and Surprising Debate," 76–78.

18. Burnet's 1681 edition is in Latin, the 1684 in English. See also Thomas Burnet, *The Theory of the earth: containing an account of the original of the earth, and of all the general changes which it hath already undergone, or is to undergo, till the consummation of all things* (London: R. Norton, for Walter Kettilby, 1691), 145; discussion of the useful and beautiful on 144. The classic book on Burnet and his influence on British Romanticism and the rise of eighteenth-century notions of sublimity, as well as the association of mountains with both disaster and solitude, is Marjorie Hope Nicolson's *Mountain Gloom and Mountain Glory: The Development of the Aesthetics of the Infinite* (Ithaca, NY: Cornell University Press, 1959).

19. Davies, *Earth in Decay*, 242. Hutton's sense of geology as a "circulation of matter" is discussed as well in Gohau, *Histoire de la géologie*, 111–23. In a compelling study of the relations between human culture and landscape, Paul Shepard traces a countertradition of exalting mountains, beginning with Augustine's admonition that men "forget their own selves" in the presence of "lofty mountains and broad seas" and other features of nature, and continuing to Petrarch climbing Mount Ventoux, the naturalist Konrad von Gessner writing in 1541 that he would commit himself to study plants on "high mountains . . . very worthy of profound contemplation" and on to the aesthetics of sublimity and the revival of the Gothic that developed in the late seventeenth and eighteenth centuries. Paul Shepard, *Man in the Landscape: A Historic*

View of the Esthetics of Nature (1967; repr., College Station: Texas A&M University Press, 1991), 160–68.

20.   Michael Jakob, "On Mountains: Scalable and Unscalable," trans. Timothy Attanucci, in *Landform Building: Architecture's New Terrain*, ed. Stan Allen and Marc McQuade (Zurich: Lars Müller, 2011), 145.

21.   Michael Jakob, "On Mountains," 148–49.

22.   Greg Woolf, ed., *The Cambridge Illustrated History of the Roman World* (Cambridge: Cambridge University Press, 2003), 162.

23.   Andrew Ayers, *The Architecture of Paris: An Architectural Guide* (Stuttgart: Edition Axel Menges, 2003), 266–67. The original measurements of the Tivoli temple were made by Antoine (aka Antonio) Desgodetz, among the most prominent early engravers of ruins.

24.   Johann Wolfgang von Goethe, *Faust: Part One* and *Faust: Part Two*, trans. David Luke (Oxford: Oxford University Press, 2008). Page numbers throughout the text discussion refer to this edition of the work.

25.   Other legends suggest that the Raven Stone glows, for it is illuminated by the remains of the eyes of executed criminals, picked and dropped by the crows circling above. See Ernst Moritz Arndt, "Der Rabenstein," *Märchen und Jugenderinnerungen* (Berlin: G. Reimer, 1843), 2:348–49.

26.   William Gilpin, *Observations on Several Parts of the Countries of Cambridge, Norfolk, Suffolk, and Essex* [. . .] (London: T. Cadell and W. Davies, 1809), 119–23.

27.   According to the *Oxford English Dictionary*, a *vestige* is "a. A mark, trace, or visible sign of something, esp. a building or other material structure, which no longer exists or is present; a piece of material evidence of this nature; something which remains after the destruction or disappearance of the main portion. In the singular freq. in negative phrases." *Oxford English Dictionary*, s.v. "vestige," accessed February 25, 2019, http://www.oed.com/view/Entry/222911. The first recorded use of *vestige* in English refers to the remains of the Arch of Septimius Severus in a pro–Roman Catholic work by the Scottish theologian and spy John Colville from 1602. J. Colville, *Parænese To Ministres*, sig. v. ii: "Not . . . farder . . . not vnto ye vall of Septimius Seuerus . . . vharof the vestiges yit Remane."

28.   Urban T. Holmes, "Mediaeval Gem Stones," *Speculum* 9, no. 2 (April 1934): 197.

29.   Johannes Rohleder, "The Cultural History of Limestone," in *Calcium Carbonate from the Cretaceous Period into the 21st Century*, ed. Wolfgang Tegethoft (Basel: Springer, 2001), 55–135. The discussion of Egyptian, Minoan, and Greek quarrying and stonecutting extends throughout pp. 59–82; the softness of marble as a sculptural material is discussed on pp. 103–5.

30.   The quote is found in Suetonius, *Divus Augustus* 28.3. See Suetonius, *Suetonius: Julius, Augustus, Tiberius, Gaius, Caligula*, trans. J. C. Rolfe (Cambridge, MA: Harvard University Press, 1914), 1:193. For a discussion of its possibly questionable authenticity and afterlife, see Kathleen S. Lamp, *A City of Marble: The Rhetoric of Augustan Rome* (Columbia: University of South Carolina Press, 2013).

31.   Rodolfo Lanciani, *The Ruins and Excavations of Ancient Rome* (1897; repr., New York: Benjamin Blom, 1967), 32–44.

32.   Lanciani, *Ruins and Excavations*, 467.

33.   J. Clayton Fant, "Rome's Marble Yards," *Journal of Roman Archaeology* 14 (2001): 180.

34.   See the discussion of the qualities of marbles in Rohleder, "Cultural History of Limestone," 83–85, 111, 126.

35.   Fant, "Rome's Marble Yards," 171.

36.   Rohleder, "Cultural History of Limestone," 114, 122–23.

37.   Lanciani, *Ruins and Excavations*, 43–46. *Opus reticulatum* appears in three chronologically distinct styles: the oldest has small prisms and slightly irregular intersecting lines. The second

has larger prisms and perfectly straight "netting." The angles of the walls of the second type are strengthened with rectangular pieces of tufa that look like bricks. The house of Germanicus is Lanciani's example. The final style, which extended from Trajan to the first Antonine emperors, involves angles and arches made of bricks and the wall strengthened by the brick material. The network is thereby divided into panels.

38. For a survey of these examples and others, see Ernest Nash, "Hidden Visual Patterns in Roman Architecture and Ruins," in *Vision and Artifact*, ed. Mary Henle (New York: Springer, 1976), 95–103.

39. Fabio Metelli, "The Perception of Transparency," *Scientific American* 230, no. 4 (April 1974): 91.

40. Fabio Metelli, "What Does 'More Transparent' Mean? A Paradox," in Henle, *Vision and Artifact*, 19.

41. Metelli, "What Does 'More Transparent' Mean?," 20.

42. Interview regarding Kahn's never-built plans for an American Consulate in Luanda, Portuguese Angola, in Louis Kahn, "Kahn," *Perspecta* 7 (1961): 9.

43. Ernst Gombrich, "The Evidence of Images," in *Interpretation: Theory and Practice*, ed. Charles Southward Singleton (Baltimore: Johns Hopkins University Press, 1969), 57.

44. Leonardo da Vinci, *A Treatise of Painting, Translated from the Original Italian, And adorn'd with a great Number of Cuts* (London: Senex and Taylor, 1721), 34. The passage seems to have inspired the work of the innovative late eighteenth-century painter of "ink blots," Alexander Cozens, who quotes it in his *A New Method of Assisting the Invention in Drawing Original Compositions of Landscape* (London: J. Dixwell, 1785).

45. Homer, *Iliad*, trans. Robert Fagles (New York: Penguin, 1990), 229.

46. Homer, *Iliad*, 229.

47. Homer, *Iliad*, 325–26.

48. Homer, *Iliad*, 326. Ruth Scodel links the story of the destruction of the Achaean Wall to stories from the Hebrew scriptures of divine pride in construction and punitive floods. See Ruth Scodel, "The Achaean Wall and the Myth of Destruction," *Harvard Studies in Classical Philology* 86 (1982): 33–50. There she traces the relation of the Achaean Wall to Deluge myths of the Near East: "The destruction of the Achaean Wall by a nine-day's rain and the turning of primeval rivers is entirely appropriate. The passage on the wall is unlike any other in the Homeric corpus in its description of the heroes as a γένος of men born of partly divine parentage, and the importance attached to the wall suggests that it stands for something beyond itself: the achievements of its builders . . . Poseidon fears for his κλέος, complaining that the Achaean Wall will be famed beyond the one he built for Troy [7:451–53]. The heroes before the Biblical flood are the 'famous men,' and the theme of 'fame' recurs shortly after the Deluge in connection with a building which, like the Achaean Wall, arouses divine anger, the Tower of Babel (Gen. 11:1–9), whose builders seek to make a name for themselves and not be scattered (Gen. 11:4). If a distant echo of this myth is at work in the *Iliad*, it might help explain why the flood theme is transferred to a wall, and why the context emphasizes dispersal as much as destruction."

49. Plutarch, "Romulus," 11, in *Lives*, vol. 1, *Thesus and Romulus; Lycurgus and Numa; Solon and Publicola*, trans. Bernadotte Perrin (Cambridge, MA: Harvard University Press, 1914), 118–21; Livy, *The Rise of Rome: Books I–V*, trans. T. J. Luce (Oxford: Oxford University Press, 1998), 52–53.

50. Plutarch, "Romulus," 118–19.

51. In later periods, the space was marked by white stones called *cippi*; they marked the dimensions of the extension of the pomerium by the Emperor Claudius, whose reign from 41 to 54

CE was characterized by many building projects. See Mary Beard, John North, and Simon Price, eds., *Religions of Rome: A Sourcebook*, vol. 2 (Cambridge: Cambridge University Press, 1998), 4.8c, p. 95.

52. Ovid, *Ovid: Metamorphoses*, trans. A. D. Melville (Oxford: Oxford University Press, 1986), 376.

53. This is modern-day Albania. *Epirus* means "mainland," and in this it negates the violence of "the islander" Neoptolemus, who held both Andromache and Helenus in slavery.

54. Virgil, *The Aeneid of Virgil: A Verse Translation*, trans. Rolfe Humphries (New York: Charles Scribner's Sons, 1951), 73–78.

55. Charles Baudelaire, "Le Cygne," in *Oeuvres complètes* (Paris: Éditions Gallimard, 1961), 81–83, at 81.

56. Baudelaire, "Le Cygne," 82.

57. Baudelaire, "Le Cygne," 82.

58. Lucan, *The Civil War*, trans. J. D. Duff (Cambridge, MA: Harvard University Press, 1928), 577.

59. Lucan, *Civil War*, 577–79; Housman quotation at 579n3.

60. For an introduction to Mesopotamian City Laments, see Donna Lee Petter, *The Book of Ezekiel and Mesopotamian City Laments* (Fribourg, Switz.: Academic Press, 2011), 7–33.

61. This list and summary are taken from Michael D. Coogan, *The Old Testament: A Historical and Literary Introduction to the Hebrew Scriptures*, 3rd ed. (Oxford: Oxford University Press, 2014), 316. Coogan provides further arguments that the "oracles against the nations" in Amos follow Assyrian precedents as they also are a kind of propaganda proclaiming Yahweh's all-powerful wrath as extending to Israel's neighbors as well as Israel itself.

62. Coogan, *Old Testament*, 199.

63. According to David Grene's translation of Herodotus, *The History* (Chicago: University of Chicago Press, 1987), 1.14, p. 665n, a common cubit is 18.2 inches and a royal cubit 20.5 inches.

64. Stephanie Dalley argues convincingly on the basis of textual and archaeological evidence, in her recent book *The Mystery of the Hanging Gardens of Babylon* (Oxford: Oxford University Press, 2013), that it is unlikely that Nebuchadrezzar built such gardens in Babylon and that in fact the magnificent terraced gardens were more likely to have stood hundreds of miles away in Nineveh.

65. Coogan, *Old Testament*, 384. See also Hansjörg Schmid, *Der Tempelturm Etemenanki in Babylon* (Mainz, Ger.: P. von Zabern, 1995), plan 10.

66. Herbert Abraham, *Asphalts and Allied Substances* (Princeton, NJ: D. Van Nostrand, 1960), 23.

67. Béatrice André-Salvini, "Das Erbe von Babylon," in *Babylon: Mythos und Wahrheit*, ed. Joachim Marzahn and Günther Schauerte (Berlin: Hirmer Staatliche Museen; Munich: Hirmer Verlag, 2008), 2:36. These stepped structures are continuous with the terraced method of gardening; the Babylonian approach to verticality involved the construction of mud brick ziggurats sheathed in more mud and gardens that were most likely made of stone—for the necessary watering of the garden would erode rather quickly any structure made of mud brick. See also Coogan, *Old Testament*, 35.

68. André-Salvini, "Das Erbe von Babylon," 36. Herodotus gives an account of the temple as well, calling it "the bronze-gated temple of Zeus Belus" in his *History*, 115.

69. George Barton, "Shinar," and Samuel Fuchs, "Hammurabi," in *Jewish Encyclopedia*, ed. Cyrus Adler and Isidore Singer, 12 vols. (New York: Funk and Wagnalls, 1906), 11:290–91, 6:198–200. Hammurab(a)i is not mentioned directly in the Hebrew scriptures but is identified with Amraphael, who appears in Genesis 14:1.

70. Herodotus, *History*, 114–15.

71. Abraham, *Asphalts and Allied Substances*, 22. Abraham discusses Babylonian building techniques with bitumen; see 23, 32, 34, and 42. Babylonian asphalt is mentioned in Strabo,

Geography, trans. H. C. Hamilton and William Falconer (London: Henry G. Bohn 1857), vol. 3, bk. 16, chap. 1, p. 145; asphalt at the Dead Sea in Diodorus Siculus, *The Library of History*, trans. C. H. Oldfather (Cambridge, MA: Harvard University Press, 1935), vol. 2, bk. 2.48, pp. 42–45; Flavius Josephus, *Jewish Antiquities*, vol. 1, trans. St. J. Thackeray (Cambridge, MA: Harvard University Press, 1930), bk. 1, pp. 8–9, bk. 10, pp. 295–96; and Flavius Josephus, *The genuine and complete works of Flavius Josephus, the celebrated warlike, learned and authentic Jewish historian*, trans. William Whiston (Dublin: Thomas Morton Bates, 1796).

Chapter Two

1. Herodotus, *History*, 33.
2. J. I. Porter, "Sublime Monuments and Sublime Ruins in Ancient Aesthetics," *European Review of History: Revue européenne d'histoire* 18, no. 5/6 (2011): 686. Porter's position is curiously the reverse of the claim made in Roland Mortier's survey, *La poétique des ruines en France* (Geneva: Librairie Droz, 1974), 9, that "la ruine" is "curieusement inexistante pour les Grecs" (curiously nonexistent for the Greeks). He suggests that for the "Latins" it was only of interest as a material image of destiny—"elle n'est pas une présence, mais une *absence*, ou un *vide*, le témoignage d'une présence disparue, la marque *négative* de la grandeur détruite." Rather than being an object of horror, admiration or sadness, it conveys "la ville morte"—the dead city, razed to its foundations, as in the case of Troy and Carthage and where there no longer exists a sign of its extent (15–16).
3. Eisner, *Travelers to an Antique Land*, 30–31.
4. Discussed in Porter, "Sublime Monuments," 686. Porter takes this quote from J. G. Frazer, *Pausanias's Description of Greece* (1898; repr., Cambridge: Cambridge University Press, 2012), 551. See also Pausanias, *Guide to Greece*, trans. Peter Levi (London: Penguin, 1971), 1:409, where Parapotamia is included in a list of cities Phokis has taken and razed to the ground; Pausanias writes: "Their names were age old, and famous if only through the verses of Homer."
5. This aspect of Pausanias's travels is emphasized by a number of essays in Susan E. Alcock, John F. Cherry, and Jaś Elsner, eds., *Pausanias: Travel and Memory in Roman Greece* (Oxford: Oxford University Press, 2001). See Mario Torelli, "Reflections on Context," 54, on the political and cultural values informing Pausanias's choice of views; David Konstan, "The Joys of Pausanias," 57–60, on the importance of the *Periegesis* as a "min[e] of information" to be learned and remembered; and James I. Porter, "Ideals and Ruins: Pausanias, Longinus and the Second Sophistic," 62–63, on the text as a means of remembering ideas of freedom.
6. Ovid, *Ovid: Metamorphoses*, 379.
7. *Non didici geometrias critica et alogas naenias, sed lapidarias litteras scio, partes centum dico ad aes, ad pondus, ad nummum.* In William Arrowsmith's translation, "I never learned geometry or criticism or hogwash of that kind, but I know how to read words carved in stone and divide up to a hundred, money, measure, or weights." Petronius, *The Satyricon of Petronius* (Ann Arbor: University of Michigan Press, 1959), 65.
8. Woolf, "Monumental Writing," 22–39.
9. Woolf, "Monumental Writing," 23, 28.
10. See Millard Meiss, *Andrea Mantegna as Illuminator: An Episode in Renaissance Art, Humanism and Diplomacy* (New York: Columbia University Press, 1957), 56–60; Armando Petrucci, *Public Lettering: Script, Power, and Culture*, trans. Linda Lappin (Chicago: University of Chicago Press, 1993); and Stanley Morison, "Early Humanistic Script and the First Roman Type," *Library*, 4-24, no. 1/2 (September 1, 1943): 18.
11. Yourcenar imagines Hadrian going on to say "my epitaph will be carved in Latin on the walls of my mausoleum beside the Tiber; but it is in Greek that I shall have thought and lived."

Marguerite Yourcenar, *Memoirs of Hadrian*, trans. Grace Frick in collaboration with the author (New York: Farrar, Straus and Giroux, 1963), 36.

12. Ramsay MacMullen, "The Epigraphic Habit in the Roman Empire," *American Journal of Philology* 103, no. 3 (Autumn 1982): 246.

13. Don Fowler, "The Ruin of Time: Monuments and Survival at Rome," *Roman Constructions: Readings in Postmodern Latin* (Oxford: Oxford University Press, 2000), 193–217, argues that the Virgilian/Augustan position regarding writing was that material forms are permanent. Yet the need to claim that they are, and the desire to live on in oral tradition that we find in Horace and Ovid, might seem to indicate a sense of anxiety about such permanence. Fowler's point is girded, however, by features of the inscriptions themselves—for example, the prevalence of abbreviations speaks to a confidence in shared knowledge and future intelligibility. See the list of Greek and Latin abbreviations in Tyler Lansford's delightful and useful book, *The Latin Inscriptions of Rome: A Walking Guide* (Baltimore: Johns Hopkins University Press, 2009), xxvii–xxix. I am grateful to Kelly Zinkowski for the gift of a beautiful recent guide to the literary associations of Roman monuments: Adrianus Van Heck, *Breviarium Urbis Romae Antiquae* (Leiden, Neth.: Brill, 2002).

14. Woolf, "Monumental Writing," 27; on the materials of monuments, 30.

15. MacMullen, "Epigraphic Habit," 239.

16. MacMullen, "Epigraphic Habit," 246: "in not bothering any more to record on stone their names or any other claim to attention, perhaps they expressed their doubts about the permanence or importance of that world."

17. *Damnatio memoriae* is a modern term used to encompass the many ways that postmortem sanctions were brought against a condemned person's memory, representations, and monuments. Ancient writers would combine the verbs *damnare, condemnare, accusare, abolere,* or *eradere* to describe processes of historical censure. See the discussion in Eric R. Varner, *Mutilation and Transformation: Damnatio Memoriae and Roman Imperial Portraiture*, Monumenta Graeca et Romana, vol. 10 (Leiden, Neth.: Brill, 2004), 2. The most extensive study of the larger phenomenon of memory sanctions and the many subtle ways that memories of persons could be destroyed, distorted, and restored can be found in Harriet Flower, *The Art of Forgetting: Disgrace and Oblivion in Roman Political Culture* (Chapel Hill: University of North Carolina Press, 2006). She reminds us that sanctions "could also go on to shape the image of those who had invented or approved them" (282).

18. Woolf, "Monumental Writing," 32.

19. Codex Theodosian, 9.40.17. Translated in Jaś Elsner, *Imperial Rome and Christian Triumph* (Oxford: Oxford University Press, 1998), 56.

20. Lansford, *Latin Inscriptions of Rome*, 56–57, reproduces a defaced inscription to Stilicho on the Column of Phocus in the Forum.

21. See Dale Kinney, "Spolia," in *St. Peter's in the Vatican*, ed. William Tronzo (Cambridge: Cambridge University Press, 2005), 25. Kinney writes that *spolia* are "artifacts made for one physical and cultural context, and reused in another." In an earlier essay, "Spolia: Damnatio and Renovatio Memoriae," *Memoirs of the American Academy in Rome* 42 (1997): 117–48, Kinney traces the emergence of the term more specifically in Renaissance practices and further shaping of the notion by art historians (only) since the 1970s, when it began to attract intensive study. My concern is not with all reused artifacts but rather with artifactual remains of the built environment used in other structures.

22. Anthony Vidler, "X Marks the Spot: The Obelisk in Space," in *The Scenes of the Street and Other Essays* (New York: Monacelli Press, 2011), 221–32.

23. The Egyptian inscription appears on p. 13, the Roman one on p. 37, of the important survey of obelisks, Brian A. Curran et al., *Obelisk: A History* (Cambridge, MA: Burndy Library/MIT

Press, 2009). The authors note that Augustus put an identical inscription on the obelisk of Psammetichus, known as the Solarium or Horologium obelisk, now in the Piazza di Montecitorio.

24. Procopius, *History of the Wars*, trans. B. Dewing, 7 vols. (Cambridge, MA: Harvard University Press, 1916). The sack of Alaric (3.2.24) is in vol. 2, p. 17. The 507 attack on the Goths by Clovis and his army (5.12.36–45) is recounted in vol. 3, p. 129.

25. For the sack of Gizeric (3.4.9), see Procopius, *History of the Wars*, 2:4–11, 281. The most detailed and thorough account of the Jerusalem spoils, including their possible later transfer to Carcassonne, can be found in Pier Luigi Tucci, *The Temple of Peace in Rome* (Cambridge: Cambridge University Press, 2017), 228–31.

26. Helen Rosenau, *Vision of the Temple: The Image of the Temple of Jerusalem in Judaism and Christianity* (London: Oresko, 1979), esp. 19–31, "Antiquity, Destruction, and Spiritual Survival."

27. Kinney, "Spolia: Damnatio and Renovatio Memoriae," 123. Kinney notes that some modern archaeologists have questioned this account, but it has a substitutional logic that makes it of interest even as a legend.

28. Kinney, "Spolia: Damnatio and Renovatio Memoriae," 126.

29. Richard Stoneman, *Palmyra and Its Empire: Zenobia's Revolt against Rome* (Ann Arbor: University of Michigan Press, 1992), 183–85.

30. Kinney, "Spolia," 26. This is the Flaminian obelisk shown in figure 12. It is the inspiration for a Roman copy on a smaller scale that now looks down upon the original from S. Trinità dei Monti.

31. For a broad argument that practices of medieval *spolia* borrow from rhetoric, literature, and theology, and specifically the use of metaphor, see Maria Fabricius Hansen, *The Eloquence of Appropriation: Prolegomena to an Understanding of Spolia in Early Christian Rome* (Rome: L'Erma di Bretschneider, 2003). Hansen does not address the many ways that *spolia* can be silenced when their references vanish from cultural knowledge, nor the differences between *spolia* relying upon such living knowledge for their significance and *spolia* that bear on their surfaces inscriptions or images directing viewers how to frame them. Contemporary debate on the intention and interpretations brought to spolia of many kinds are discussed in Richard Brilliant and Dale Kinney, eds., *Reuse Value: Spolia and Appropriation in Art and Architecture from Constantine to Sherrie Levine* (Farnham, UK: Ashgate, 2011).

32. Beat Brenk, "Spolia from Constantine to Charlemagne: Aesthetics versus Ideology," in "Studies on Art and Archaeology in Honor of Ernst Kitzinger," special issue, *Dumbarton Oaks Papers* 41 (1987): 103–5. Brenk cites the contrary opinions of F. Deichmann, in *Die Spolien in der spätantiken Architektur*, and Richard Krautheimer, *Three Christian Capitals*, regarding *spolia*, with Deichmann arguing they were used because of economic necessity and Krautheimer claiming they are signs of a revival of interest in classical antiquity. For Brenk these are untenable positions, for he argues that using *spolia* was more expensive than relying on new construction and that *spolia* were designed to underscore an aesthetic of *varietas* rather than a revival of older canons of building.

33. Brenk, "Spolia from Constantine to Charlemagne," 104. Brenk writes of forty-two *verde antico* shafts in the cathedral as a whole. For the two ancient Numidian columns in the organ loft, see Amanda Claridge, Judith Toms, and Tony Cubberley, *Rome: An Oxford Archaeological Guide* (Oxford: Oxford University Press, 1998), 349.

34. Discussed in Kinney, "Spolia: Damnatio and Renovatio Memoriae," 127. Kinney notes that in the eighteenth century, they were believed to have been taken from the mausoleum of Hadrian. Later scholars suggest other buildings in the nearby area.

35. Kinney, "Spolia," 36–37.

36. Kinney, "Spolia," 16–24.

37. Giorgio Vasari, *Le vite de' più eccellenti pittori, scultori, e architettori nelle redazioni del 1550–1568*, ed. Rosanna Bettarini (Florence: Sansoni, 1967), 2:15: "E che ciò sia vero è manifesto, che il tempio del Prencipe degl'Apostoli in Vaticano non era ricco se non di colonne, di base di capitegli, d'architravi, cornici, porte et altre incrostature et ornamenti, che tutti furono tolti di diversi luoghi e dagl'edifizii stati fatti inanzi molto magnificamente."

38. Brenk, "Spolia from Constantine to Charlemagne," 105.

39. Joseph Alchermes, "*Spolia* in Roman Cities of the Late Empire: Legislative Rationales and Architectural Reuse," *Dumbarton Oaks Papers* 48 (1994): 167–68, discussed in Kinney, "Spolia: Damnatio and Renovatio Memoriae," 121.

40. Brenk, "Spolia from Constantine to Charlemagne," 107–8.

41. See Kinney, "Spolia," 27.

42. *La faccia sua mi parea lunga e grossa / Come la pina di San Pietro a Roma, / E a sua proporzione eran l'altre ossa.* Dante Alighieri, *The Divine Comedy of Dante Alighieri: Inferno*, trans. Allen Mandelbaum (New York: Bantam, 1982), canto 31, lines 58–60.

43. Kinney, "Spolia," 24, on the Emperor Constans II, and 35, for Hermann of Fritzlar.

44. Augustine of Hippo, *On Christian Doctrine*, trans. D. Robertson Jr. (Indianapolis: Bobbs-Merrill, 1958), 75.

45. Christian Kleinbub has described the convention of depicting pagan idols at the top of columns in Christian art, writing that their "very height dramatizes the epochal nature of their destruction." Christian K. Kleinbub, "Bramante's Ruined Temple and the Dialectics of the Image," *Renaissance Quarterly* 63, no. 2 (Summer 2010): 422.

46. Lansford, *Latin Inscriptions of Rome*, 506–11.

47. Robert Wood, *The Ruins of Palmyra* (London, 1753), 2.

48. William St. Clair, *Lord Elgin and the Marbles: The Controversial History of the Parthenon Sculptures*, 3rd rev. ed. (Oxford: Oxford University Press, 1998), 100.

49. William Smith, *A Smaller Dictionary of Greek and Roman Antiquities* (London: J. Murray, 1868), 347–48.

50. David Karmon, *The Ruin of the Eternal City: Antiquity and Preservation in Renaissance Rome* (Oxford: Oxford University Press, 2011), 123–24. There Karmon explains, "While this name [*coscia Colisei*] is of uncertain origin, it may have referred to the strange appearance of the newly exposed internal core of the monument following this collapse. Stripped of its classical travertine veneer, the coarse brick and concrete viscera of the monument now resembled an organic growth more than an architectural structure. Thus the name *coscia Colisei* may be derived from *coxae*, or the boreholes created by sea mollusks burrowing into stones." In this absorbing and thoughtful account of Renaissance preservation theory and practice, Karmon upends many of our present-centered assumptions about past conservation efforts.

51. See R. B. Parkinson, trans., *The Tale of Sinuhe and Other Ancient Egyptian Poems 1940–1640 B.C.* (New York: Oxford Classics, 1998). In "The Dialogue of Ipuur and the Lord of All," for example, the speaker writes that "they have fallen into ruin. / Look, all the craftsmen no longer work," going on to note that the recorder of harvests is ignorant of the harvest, the "lord of the fields" is ignorant of plowing, and more (181).

52. The entry for "Ruins" in *The Index of Medieval Art* (Princeton, NJ: Index of Christian Art, Princeton University), https://theindex-princeton-edu.ezproxy.princeton.edu, lists the following manuscript illustrations of ruins before the frescos of Maso di Banco in the mid-fourteenth century: The Lincoln Apocalypse, Lincoln College Library University of Oxford, UK (showing three birds, including two ravens, and a hybrid cock perched on the ruins), with a paneled background from 1320–1329, Lincoln College Ms. no. Lat.16 fol. 171r; a Caesarius the Physician scene, showing the earthquake at Antioch (which occurred in 526) from Gregory

Nazianzen, *Homilies*, ca. 800–899, 78 mss. number E. 49-50 of the Biblioteca Ambrosiana, Milano; another scene of the Antioch earthquake, depicting several fallen men from John Chrysostom, *Homilies*, mss. no 211, fol. 87r, from the National Library of Greece, ca. 880–899; a scene from the Burckhardt-Wildt Apocalypse of three birds (ravens or crows) biting beasts while an owl perches amid the ruins, mss. 119802 of the Cleveland Museum of Art (the illustration was originally from Metz, Lorraine, France), ca. 1290–1299; a scene of the departure from Sodom with Sodom in ruins showing two daughters and wife, veiled, following Lot, ca. 800–899, Biblioteca Ambrosiana, Milano, mss. E. 49059; another scene of Sodom in ruins, from the Trinity College Library, University of Cambridge, Sodom in ruins, ca. 1220–1230, fol. 10r; a scene of the walls of Jericho falling before three soldiers, ca. 1250–1254, from fol. 69v of the Bibliothèque de Arsenal, Paris, found in the France/Arsenal Old Testament, with the Acre Bible as the location of origin, and found as well in the Louis de Grolé Bible. Each of these drawings depicts falling bricks and stones of contemporary building types, as does the depiction of the ruined city in the fresco representing the effects of bad government by Maso's contemporary Ambrogio Lorenzetti for the Palazzo Pubblico of Siena in 1338–1339. Unlike Maso's frescos, these images do not juxtapose the classical or biblical past to the subjects at hand.

53. An interpretation of the *Legenda aurea*'s recounting of Sylvester's conversion of Constantine and miracles beyond the defeat of the dragon—and a discussion of the adjacent frescos and other representations of Sylvester's life—can be found in the appendices to David G. Wilkins's published dissertation, *Maso di Banco: A Florentine Artist of the Early Trecento* (New York: Garland, 1985). Color plates of the frescos are available in *Maso di Banco: La Capella di San Silvestro*, ed. Cristina Acidini Luchinat and Enrica Neri Lusanna (Milan: Electa, 1998). The editors include a brief essay discussing the placement of the architectural details in relation to the narrative, drawing connections to Masaccio's representation of the "Tribute Money" in the Brancacci Chapel of Santa Maria del Carmine.

54. *The Marvels of Rome: Mirabilia Urbis Romae*, ed. and trans. by Francis Morgan Nichols, 2nd ed., with new introduction, gazetteer, and bibliography by Eileen Gardiner (1889; repr., New York: Italica Press, 1986), 28–29. Nevertheless, the piazza before the Lateran today is marked by the oldest obelisk in the city, set up by Domenico Fontana in 1588—a red granite form covered in hieroglyphs, taken originally by Constantius II in 357 from the Temple of Ammon at Thebes and destined to be an ornament to the Circus Maximus.

55. *Marvels of Rome*, 41.

56. Jacobus de Voragine, *The Golden Legend: Readings on the Saints*, trans. William Granger Ryan, with introduction by Eamon Duffy (Princeton, NJ: Princeton University Press, 2012), 65.

57. Burckhardt, *Civilization of the Renaissance in Italy*, 179.

58. Tilmann Buddensieg, "Gregory the Great, the Destroyer of Pagan Idols: The History of a Medieval Legend Concerning the Decline of Ancient Art and Literature," *Journal of the Warburg and Courtauld Institutes* 28 (1965): 48. See also Leonard Barkan, "Rome," in *The Classical Tradition*, ed. Anthony Grafton, Glenn Most, and Salvatore Settis (Cambridge, MA: Belknap Press of Harvard University Press, 2013), 839–50. Barkan outlines the transition from Theodoric to the Frankish kings who "revivified Rome's place in the European imaginary as a seat of empire. . . . Pieces of Rome consequently acquired a talismanic value" (844).

59. The standard English-language biography of Petrarch remains E. Wilkins, *Life of Petrarch* (Chicago: University of Chicago Press, 1961). See also Albert Ascoli and Unn Falkeid, eds., *The Cambridge Companion to Petrarch* (Cambridge: Cambridge University Press, 2015), 13–38; and the introduction to Petrarch, *Petrarch's Lyric Poems: The "Rime sparse" and Other Lyrics*, ed. and trans. Robert M. Durling (Cambridge, MA: Harvard University Press, 1976), 1–33,

in which the coronation as laureate is discussed at 2. Andrew Hui's recent book, *The Poetics of Ruins in Renaissance Literature* (New York: Fordham University Press, 2017), broadly surveys the enduring influence of Petrarch's metaphor of the vestige in Renaissance poetry. Hui contends that the corresponding metaphors of *cendres* in the work of Joachim Du Bellay and *moniments* in Edmund Spenser follow from Petrarch's concern with the ephemerality of memory and, consequently, the transience of literary fame.

60. The relatively little-known text was not published until the 1390s, with a first critical edition appearing in 1926: Francesco Petrarch, *L'Africa: Edizione critica per cura di Nicola Festa* (Florence: G. C. Sansoni, 1926).

61. *Epistolae Familiares*, bk. 6, letter 2, in Francesco Petrarch, *Letters on Familiar Matters I–VIII*, trans. Aldo S. Bernardo (New York: Italica Press, 2005), 1:293.

62. *Epistolae Familiares*, bk. 6, letter 2, in Petrarch, *Letters on Familiar Matters I–VIII*, 1:291. The "trigemini" was the well-known battle, during the war between Rome and Alba Longa, between two sets of fraternal triplets (*trigemini*): the Roman Horatii and the Alban Curiatii (ca. 672–642 BCE).

63. *Epistolae Familiares*, bk. 6, letter 2, in Petrarch, *Letters on Familiar Matters I–VIII*, 1:294.

64. *Epistolae Familiares*, bk. 24, letter 8, in Petrarch, *Letters on Familiar Matters I–VIII*, 3:332–33, at 332.

65. See discussion in Buddensieg, "Gregory the Great," 48–50, of Boccaccio's *Genealogie Deorum Gentilium Libri* and the *Dittamondo*.

66. Fazio degli Uberti, *Il Dittamondo di Fazio degli Uberti*, ed. Vincenzo Monti (Milan: Giovanni Silvestri, 1826), 36–37.

67. From the discussion and translation of Chrysoloras in Christine Smith, *Architecture in the Culture of Early Humanism* (New York: Oxford University Press, 1992), discussion 150–70; translation of the *Comparison of Old and New Rome*, 199–215, citations here from 200–201.

68. Poggio Bracciolini, *De varietate fortunae*, critical edition with introduction and commentary by Outi Merisalo (Helsinki: Suomalainen Tiedeakatemia, 1993), 94.

69. Angelo Mazzocco, "Petrarca, Poggio, and Biondo: Humanism's Foremost Interpreters of Roman Ruins," in *Francis Petrarch, Six Centuries Later: A Symposium*, ed. Aldo Scaglione (Chapel Hill: Department of Romance Languages; Chicago: Newberry Library, 1975), 353–57.

70. Alberti presented a completed version of *De re aedificatoria* to Pope Nicholas in 1450; Alberti, *On the Art of Building*, xvi. He writes of faults needing "correction" in ancient buildings: "The saying 'Time conquers all things' refers to some of them; the batteries of old age are dangerous and very powerful; the body has no defense against the laws of Nature. . . . We feel the sun burn or the shadows freeze; we feel the power of ice and wind. The working of this engine can crack and crumble even the hardest flint; vast storms will tear away and thrust out huge rocks from the highest cliff, so that they will crash down along with much of the mountain. Then there is damage caused by man. God help me, I sometimes cannot stomach it when I see with what negligence, or to put it more crudely, by what avarice they allow the ruin of things that because of their great nobility the barbarians, the raging enemy have spared; or those which all-conquering, all-ruining time might easily have allowed to stand for ever" (320).

71. The "History" page of the Vatican Library site says that this collection of Latin and Greek manuscripts numbered 1,500 at the time of Pope Nicholas V's death: https://www.vatlib.it /home.php?ling=eng&pag=storia. In the catalog for the 1993 Library of Congress exhibition *Rome Reborn: The Vatican Library and Renaissance Culture*, ed. Anthony Grafton (New Haven, CT: Yale University Press; Washington: Library of Congress; Vatican City: Biblioteca Apostolica Vaticana, 1993), Anthony Grafton writes that in 1455, Nicholas's collection was "some 1,160 books, 353 of them in Greek" and that by the death of Sixtus IV, fifty years later, the library had more than 3,600 manuscripts (34–35).

72. Arthur White, *Plague and Pleasure: The Renaissance World of Pius II* (Washington, DC: Catholic University of America Press, 2014), 148–49. White discusses Biondo's relationships with papal patronage: out of favor with Nicholas V, Biondo nevertheless continued his work for his geographical and antiquarian survey, *Italia illustrata*, and went on to enjoy the support of Pius II. Pius II's efforts at collecting manuscripts focused on his personal library, which would become the basis for the Libreria Piccolomini at the Cathedral of Siena. Charles L. Stinger, *The Renaissance in Rome* (Bloomington: Indiana University Press, 1998), 286.

73. Mazzocco, "Petrarca, Poggio, and Biondo," 361–62.

74. Karmon, *Ruin of the Eternal City*, 18–19; Catherine Edwards, *Writing Rome: Textual Approaches to the City* (New York: Cambridge University Press, 1996), 6–8.

75. The *grotteschi* there continued to inspire artists in the ensuing period. Nicole Dacos notes that graffiti recording the visits of northern artists in the 1530s are still visible there in an inscription registering:

HEMKERC

HER.POSTMA

LAM AMSTE

In other words, Maerten van Heemskerck, Hermannus Posthumus, and Lambert Sustris. Nicole Dacos, *Roma Quanta Fuit: Tre pittori fiamminghi nella Domus Aurea*, trans. Maria Baiocchi (Rome: Donzelli Editore, 1995), 17. Dacos wrote as well an important earlier study of the *grotteschi* and their discovery: Nicole Dacos, *La découverte de la Domus Aurea et la formation des grotesques à la Renaissance*, Studies of the Warburg Institute, vol. 31 (Leiden, Neth.: Brill, 1969).

76. Leonard Barkan, *Unearthing the Past: Archaeology and Aesthetics in the Making of Renaissance Culture* (New Haven, CT: Yale University Press, 1999), 33.

77. Chrysolaras, *Comparison*, in C. Smith, *Architecture in the Culture of Early Humanism*, 204–5.

78. Buddensieg, "Gregory the Great," 52.

79. Buddensieg, "Gregory the Great," 44. The early fifteenth-century Paduan scholar Sicco Polenton formulated the idea that as a learned person, Gregory would have known there was no blasphemy in Livy. And the biographer of popes, Bartolomeo Platina, argued that Gregory, as a pope of ancient Roman ancestry, could not have destroyed the edifices of his beloved patria. Francis Haskell writes of "the long-held legend that in the sixth century Pope Gregory the Great had ordered the utter destruction of all surviving 'heathen idols'—a legend that had hitherto been handed down with little evident disapproval—[Ghiberti] nevertheless attributed the devastation to the Emperor Constantine and his contemporary Pope Sylvester. As early as the fourth century Eusebius had praised Constantine for his destruction of the cult statues of the pagans." Haskell adds that the idea may have been suggested to Ghiberti by Maso's fresco cycle in Santa Croce. Francis Haskell, *History and Its Images* (New Haven, CT: Yale University Press, 1993), 114.

80. Albrecht Dürer, *Literary Remains of Albrecht Dürer*, ed. William Martin Conway (Cambridge, 1889), 178.

81. Vasari, Proem to *Le vite de' più eccellenti pittori, scultori, e architettori*, 9–30, at 16–17.

82. Ingrid D. Rowland, *The Culture of the High Renaissance: Ancients and Moderns in Sixteenth-Century Rome* (New York: Cambridge University Press, 1998), 226–27.

83. Letter cited in Anna M. Kim, "Creative Iconoclasms in Renaissance Italy," in *Striking Images: Iconoclasms Past and Present*, ed. Stacy Boldrick, Leslie Brubaker, and Richard Clay (Burlington, VT: Ashgate, 2013), 77. Kim's translation is based in Raffaello Sanzio, *Tutti gli scritti*, ed. E. Camesasca (Milan: Rizzoli, 1956), 52. For discussions of the Raphael/Castiglione

letter and the text, see Adolfo Venturi, *Storia dell'Arte italiana* (Milan: Hoepli, 1926), vol. 9, part 2, pp. 45–54; and Raphael Sanzio da Urbino, *Raffaello gli scritti*, ed. Ettore Camesasca (Milan: Biblioteca universale Rizzoli, 1994), 257–61. The standard edition of Raphael's writings is *Raffaello nei documenti*, ed. Vincenzo Golzio (Vatican City: Pontificia insigne accademia di belle arti e lettere dei virtuosi al Pantheon, 1936). For a discussion of the contribution of Castiglione and the place of the letter in Raphael's appreciation for Vitruvius and developing stances on architectural history, see Rowland, *Culture of the High Renaissance*, 226–33. Rowland, finding the Golzio text and others inaccurate, has published a transcript of the Munich version of the letter in "Raphael, Angelo Colocci, and the Genesis of the Architectural Orders," *Art Bulletin* 76, no. 1 (1994): 81–104.

84.   Karmon, *Ruin of the Eternal City*, 91 and 158. Raphael himself seems to have fallen for the appeal of this teacher and kinsman's techniques since, according to Karmon, he acquired Bramante's Palazzo Caprini in his later years (160).

85.   Pietro Angèli da Barga, *De privatorum, publicorumque aedificiorum urbis Romae eversoribus epistola* (Florence: Sermartellius, 1589), 44–45, Bayerische StaatsBibliotek, http://reader.digitale-sammlungen.de/resolve/display/bsb11211092.html.

86.   Bonnie Effros, "Monuments and Memory: Repossessing Ancient Remains in Early Medieval Gaul," in *Topographies of Power in the Early Middle Ages*, ed. Mayke de Jong and Frans Theeuws (Leiden, Neth.: Brill, 2001), 94.

87.   Effros, "Monuments and Memory," 98.

88.   See Lawrence Nees, "Theodulf's Mythical Silver Hercules Vase, Poetica Vanitas and the Augustinian Critique of the Roman Heritage," *Dumbarton Oaks Papers* 41 (1987): 443–51.

89.   Effros, "Monuments and Memory," 111–12. See also Roger White, "Scrap or Substitute: Roman Material in Anglo-Saxon Graves," in *Anglo-Saxon Cemeteries: A Reappraisal*, ed. Edmund Southworth (Stroud, UK: A. Sutton, 1991), 125–52.

90.   Voragine, *Golden Legend*, 38–39. Alexander Nagel and Christopher Wood provide a discussion of Apollo's prophecy in relation to Renaissance nativity scenes in *Anachronic Renaissance* (New York: Zone Books, 2010), 302.

91.   See Marilyn Aronberg Lavin, "Piero's Meditation on the Nativity," in *The Cambridge Companion to Piero della Francesca*, ed. Jeryldene M. Wood (Cambridge: Cambridge University Press, 2002), 67. Lavin also notes that one of the shepherds in the scene is carrying a cylindrical staff held like a scepter. She contends that this is an allusion to a well-known statue type of the emperor Augustus, who was shown a vision of the Madonna and Child by the Tiburtine Sybil on the day of the winter solstice—an answer to the question he had posed as to whether there would ever be born a greater man than he (71).

92.   See Zucker, *Fascination of Decay*, 36–37; Erwin Panofsky, *Early Netherlandish Painting* (Cambridge, MA: Harvard University Press, 1953), 134–37, writes that Altdorfer contrasted the Old and New Dispensations through ruins versus intactness or Romanesque versus Gothic forms. He mentions that the same element of ruins underlies the imagery of Egypt in Altdorfer's 1510 *Rest on the Flight into Egypt*, where ruined classical and vernacular wooden buildings stand in the background. See also Larry Silver's extensive discussion of Altdorfer's Bremen and Berlin nativities in "Nature and Nature's God: Landscape and Cosmos of Albrecht Altdorfer," *Art Bulletin* 81, no. 2 (June 1999): 194–95. In *Anachronic Renaissance*, Nagel and Wood discuss ruins in nativity paintings in relation not only to the legends of the Temple of Peace but also to their frequent use of triumphal arches and other classical forms in decay. They include the following reading, based more in an approach to architectural history than in the religious symbolism of the works: "In fifteenth-century paintings of the Nativity and Adoration the process of architectural substitution, the succession of buildings, was submitted to analysis

through self-reflexive representation. . . . Advanced architecture has been laid low, and the history of architecture is cycled back to its beginnings in sheds, huts, and lean-tos. . . . The clock is stopped and restarted. The Nativity shed is the reverse image of the hut of Romulus; not surrounded by the masonry that has superseded it but propped on the castigated ruins of a whole era's worth of stone architecture. The pictures ask: Will the process begin again, or has the occasion for substitution been missed?" (301–19, 303). We will see that a consideration of the architectural metaphors of the Virgin birth illuminates further aspects of "the momentous event as passageway" (302).

93. Edwards, *Writing Rome*, 33. See her chapter "The City of Memories," 27–43, which focuses on the *casa Romuli* and another hut on the Palatine attributed to Evander.

Chapter Three .

1. Scholars differ as to whether the Samaritan references in the New Testament are historical. One view is that the historical Jesus had no contact with Samaritans; another is that the accounts go back to Jesus himself. In Acts 1:8, Jesus promises the apostles that they will be witnesses to the Samaritans. See Gerhard Kittel, Gerhard Friedrich, and Geoffrey Bromiley, eds., *Theological Dictionary of the New Testament*, trans. Geoffrey Bromiley (Grand Rapids, MI: Eerdmans, 1985), 999.

2. Rodolfo Lanciani, *Ancient and Modern Rome* (New York: Marshall Jones, 1963), 8.

3. Jennifer Larson, *Greek Nymphs: Myth, Cult, Lore* (Oxford: Oxford University Press, 2001), 3. Larson writes that, like Artemis herself, these figures "are mythopoetic representations of the Greek maiden at adolescence . . . they are representative of the social rituals by which females come of age and take their place in society [and not objects of cult themselves]" (109–10). The reality of adolescent girls' lives sadly continues into the present to be yoked to mystical and often misogynistic ideas about female sexuality.

4. Larson, *Greek Nymphs*, 4–5.

5. Bonnie MacLachlan, "Women and Nymphs at the Grotta Caruso," in *Mystic Cults in Magna Graecia*, ed. Giovanni Casadio and Patricia A. Johnston (Austin: University of Texas Press, 2009), 206–7.

6. Discussed in MacLachlan, "Women and Nymphs," 207. See also Peter T. Struck, "Allegory and Ascent in Neo-Platonism," in *The Cambridge Companion to Allegory*, ed. Rita Copeland and Peter Struck (Cambridge: Cambridge University Press, 2010), 60–61.

7. Callimachus, *The Poems of Callimachus*, trans. Frank Nisetich (Oxford: Oxford University Press, 2001), 140–41. See also Paolo Caputo, "Aegyptiaca from Cumae: New Evidence for Isis Cult in Campania; Site and Materials," in Casadio and Johnston, *Mystic Cults*, 245. Caputo also mentions that the shell decorations often found at nymphaea are associated with ideas of death and rebirth and are joined to the cult of Egyptian deities or, more generally, to that of mystery deities.

8. Discussed in both Larson, *Greek Nymphs*, 4, and MacLachlan, "Women and Nymphs," 209–11. At Locri, votive tablets displaying figures of Aphrodite have been read as a record of the vow taken by the Locrians in 476 BCE to designate a number of their virgins as prostitutes in the Temple of Aphrodite in order to avert a war. Yet their lore has also been read as a discourse on the broad range of erotic experience of Locrian women, from coming of age to marriage and motherhood.

9. Other early presentations of Roman ruins include images of the Palatine and Lateran by Paolino da Venezia in his *Compendium* (*Chronologia Magna*) of 1320; Pietro del Massaio's 1471 *Roma*; and Hartmann Schedel's *Liber cronicarum* (*Nuremberg Chronicle*) of 1493. These,

however, are cartographic and historical representations designed to show plans of Rome and not works underscoring the theme of ruin itself as we find in Maso's frescos and the *Hypnerotomachia Poliphili*.

10. Giovanni Pozzi has described the images as having either a narrative function (these contain figures and further the plot) or a descriptive function (presenting a material, often literal, image of the information in a textual passage). *Hypnerotomachia Poliphili*, ed. and with commentary by Lucia A. Ciapponi and Giovanni Pozzi, 2 vols. (Padua, It.: Editrice Antenore, 1980), 2:12–13.

11. Orthogonal projection was first adapted around 1499, the year that the *Hypnerotomachia Poliphili* appeared. Therefore, some scholars have believed the work must have been the creation of an expert architect, most likely Leon Battista Alberti, given that many of his innovations in representing buildings are carried over into the text: see Liane Lefaivre, *Leon Battista Alberti's Hypnerotomachia Poliphili: Re-cognizing the Architectural Body in the Early Italian Renaissance* (Cambridge, MA: MIT Press, 1997). Questions about the identification of the author also appear in Piero Scapecchi, *"L'Hypnerotomachia Poliphili e il suo autore,"* *Accademie e biblioteche d'Italia* 51 (1983): 286–98. He argues that Francesco Colonna is the dedicatee and the author Fra Eliseo da Treviso. Roswitha Stewering suggests the Paduan humanist Niccolò Lelio Cosmico in *Architektur and Natur in der "Hypnerotomachia Poliphili" (Manutius, 1499) und die Zuschreibung des Werkes an Niccolò Lelio Cosmico* (Hamburg: LIT, 1996), 159–245. Stewering presented these findings in her address "Who Wrote the 'Hypnerotomachia Poliphili'? Arguments for a New Author," at a July 4, 1999, congress in Einsiedeln, published in M. Mosser, W. Oechslin, and G. Polizzi, eds., *La réception européenne du Songe de Poliphile: Littérature, jardin et architecture* (Einsiedeln: Stiftung Bibliothek Werner Oechslin, 1999). Joscelyn Godwin surveys the arguments regarding authorship in *The Real Rule of Four* (New York: Disinformation Books, 2004), 69–104. Marcel Françon has contributed two essays on the influence of the *Hypnerotomachia* on Rabelais. In "Francesco Colonna's Poliphili Hypnerotomachia and Pantagruel," *Italica* 31, no. 3 (September 1954): 136–37, he discusses the geometrical characteristics of the fountains in Rabelais as being inspired by those in Colonna: two empirical methods for the building of polygons. In "Francesco Colonna's 'Poliphili Hypnerotomachia' and Rabelais," *Modern Language Review* 50, no. 1 (January 1955): 52–55, he argues that the calculation of Rabelais about the proportions of the buildings of the Abbey are a larger influence than any actual buildings (55). Stewering, in "Architectural Representations in the 'Hypnerotomachia Poliphili' (Aldus Manutius, 1499)," *Journal of the Society of Architectural Historians* 59, no. 1 (March 2000): 9, claims that unlike Bernardus Silvestris's *Cosmographia*, Alanus de Insulis's *De planctu naturae* and *Anticlaudianus*, or Guillaume de Lorris and Jean de Meun's *Roman de la Rose*, Colonna's text uses architecture and landscape settings to give a nuanced visual articulation to the relationship between Poliphilo and Polia—most obviously in the ruins associated with failed lovers and the shining splendor of new and precious building materials representing the lovers' happiness. She points out the use of dream perspective, resembling a bird's-eye view and being inconsistent with temporal logic (14). Tamara Griggs, in "Promoting the Past: The Hypnerotomachia Poliphili as Antiquarian Enterprise," *Word and Image: A Journal of Verbal/Visual Enquiry* 14, no. 1/2 (January–June 1998): 17–39, notes that Poliphilo is good at description but needs help from figures such as Logistica when he wants to interpret (20).

12. Francesco Colonna, *Hypnerotomachia Poliphili*, trans. Joscelyn Godwin (London: Thames and Hudson, 1999), 31. See *Hypnerotomachia Poliphili*, ed. Pozzi and Ciapponi, 2:23, f. b3v: "Non sento tanti in me di sapere che perfectamente la potesse et assai discrivere, praecipuamente che nella nostra aetate gli vernaculi, proprii et patrii vocabuli et di l'arte aedificatoria

peculiari sono cum gli veri homini sepulti et etincti. O execrabile et sacriligie barbarie, come hair exspolianda invaso la più nobile parte dil pretioso thesoro et sacraria latino et l'arte, tanto dignificata, al praesente infuscata dal maledicta ignorantia perditamente offensa?"

13. Colonna, *Hypnerotomachia Poliphili*, trans. Godwin, 2.

14. Colonna, *Hypnerotomachia Poliphili*, trans. Godwin, 11.

15. Colonna, *Hypnerotomachia Poliphili*, trans. Godwin, 30–31, 59.

16. Colonna, *Hypnerotomachia Poliphili*, trans. Godwin, 117, 138–39.

17. Rosemary Trippe, "The 'Hypnerotomachia Poliphili,' Image, Text and Vernacular Poetics," *Renaissance Quarterly* 55, no. 4 (Winter 2002): 1222–58, explains that elements of Polia's description come from books 9 and 12 of Boccaccio's *Commedia delle Ninfe Fiorentine (Ameto)*, a pastoral (written in 1341–1342 and printed twice before 1500), hence that Colonna made a composite of Boccaccio's nymphs (1223).

18. Larson, *Greek Nymphs*, 65.

19. Colonna, *Hypnerotomachia Poliphili*, trans. Godwin, 143.

20. Colonna, *Hypnerotomachia Poliphili*, trans. Godwin, 142–49.

21. Colonna, *Hypnerotomachia Poliphili*, trans. Godwin, 236, emphasis added.

22. Colonna, *Hypnerotomachia Poliphili*, trans. Godwin, 236–37, 242.

23. Colonna, *Hypnerotomachia Poliphili*, trans. Godwin, 242.

24. Colonna, *Hypnerotomachia Poliphili*, trans. Godwin, 469.

25. Alberto Pérez-Gomez, "The Hypnerotomachia Poliphili by Francesco Colonna: The Erotic Nature of Architectural Meaning," in *Paper Palaces: The Rise of the Renaissance Architectural Treatise*, ed. Vaughan Hart and Peter Hicks (New Haven, CT: Yale University Press, 1998), 86–104. He writes, "architectural meaning is not something intellectual, a 'formal' question of proportional relationships or abstract aesthetic values, but rather originates in the erotic impulse itself, in the need to quench our physical thirst" (92–93).

26. In *England's Helicon: Fountains in Early Modern Literature and Culture* (Oxford: Oxford University Press; 2007), Hester Lees-Jeffries argues that images of fountains are key to the structure of the narrative, and she traces the influence of the book, particularly Robert Dallington's 1592 translation, on works by Sidney, Spenser, and Jonson (41–102).

27. Gregory of Nyssa, "On Virginity," in *Saint Gregory of Nyssa: Ascetical Works*, ed. and trans. Virginia Woods Callahan (Washington, DC: Catholic University of America Press, 1967), 3–76.

28. Burckhardt, *Civilization of the Renaissance in Italy*, 111–12.

29. Certain paradoxes of virginity—that it is best exemplified by the dead and, according to Gregory of Nyssa and others, that virginity "outwits" and is stronger than death to the extent that it represents the incorruptible body—are explored by R. Howard Bloch in "Chaucer's Maiden's Head: 'The Physician's Tale' and the Poetics of Virginity," *Representations* 28 (1989): 113–34, esp. 120 and 131n44.

30. Henri Zerner, *L'école de Fontainebleau: Gravures* (Paris: Arts et Métiers Graphiques, 1969). Sebastiano Serlio had been a resident artist and consultant on the antique at Fontainebleau, yet the First School developed an abiding interest in mythical, aestheticized, and fantastic renditions of classical forms. Luca Penni's images of hunting and chase scenes with classical period dress and allusions to Diana, and Léonard Thiry's sequence of a dozen prints on the abduction of Persephone, from which figures 22 and 23 in the present volume are taken, are good examples of such dreamlike narratives. Their work was often engraved by the skilled and mysterious figure "Le Maître L.D.," whose identity is fervently contested and has not, to my knowledge, been discerned. One theory is that L.D. is Léon Davent and he is sometimes listed as the artist for works based on drawings by Thiry. See the discussion in Zerner, *L'école*

de Fontainebleau, xxi. Margaret McGowan, *The Vision of Rome in Late Renaissance France* (New Haven, CT: Yale University Press, 2000), discusses how Jacques Androuet du Cerceau, the architect of Fontainebleau, relied on maps and prints from the workshops of Antwerp and Rome for his designs and drawings. She discusses how he "adapted ruins to fill the central space of his designs. According to the size required he drew palaces, baths, obelisks, columns or church towers" (157).

31. Anthony Blunt has traced the influence of the *Hypnerotomachia* on later French culture in "The *Hypnerotomachia Poliphili* in 17th Century France," *Journal of the Warburg Institute* 1, no. 2 (October 1937): 117–37.

32. Paracelsus, "A Book on Nymphs, Sylphs, Pygmies, Salamanders, and Other Spirits," in *Four Treatises of Theophrastus von Hohenheim called Paracelsus*, trans. Henry E. Sigerist (Baltimore: Johns Hopkins University Press, 1941), 223–53.

33. The place of these beliefs in the theory and practice of the image in Western art is explored in Giorgio Agamben's treatise, *Nymphs*, trans. Amanda Minervini (New York: Seagull Books, 2013), translated from his *Ninfe* (Turin: Bollati Boringhieri editore, 2007).

34. Kathleen Wren Christian, *Empire without End: Antiquities Collections in Renaissance Rome, c. 1350–1527* (New Haven, CT: Yale University Press, 2010), 178–79.

35. George Gordon [Lord Byron], *Byron's Poetry and Prose*, ed. Alice Levine (New York: Norton, 2010), 229–30.

36. L. E. Semler, "Robert Dallington's *Hypnerotomachia* and the Protestant Antiquity of Elizabethan England," *Studies in Philology* 103, no. 2 (Spring 2006): 219–20.

37. Edmund Spenser, *The Faerie Queene*, ed. Thomas Roche, with the assistance of C. Patrick O'Donnell (London: Penguin, 1978), 16.

38. Spenser, *Faerie Queene*, 384.

39. The essays in Karen Bamford and Naomi J. Miller, eds., *Maternity and Romance Narratives in Early Modern England* (Oxford: Routledge, 2016), are suggestive regarding cultural attitudes toward sex and maternity and contemporary notions of physiology. See especially two essays on Spenser in this volume: Susan C. Staub, "While She Was Sleeping: Spenser's 'Goodly Storie' of Chrysogone," 13–32; and Anne-Marie Strohman, "Deferred Motherhood in Spenser's *The Faerie Queene*," 33–48.

40. Richard A. McCabe, "The Masks of Duessa: Spenser, Mary Queen of Scots, and James VI," *English Literary Renaissance* 17, no. 2 (1987): 224–42.

41. Quoted in McCabe, "Masks of Duessa," 227–28.

42. Walter Ralegh, "A Vision Upon This Conceipt of the Faery Queene," in Spenser, *Faerie Queene*, 19.

43. The virginal Una as a figure for Elizabeth is discussed in Robin Headlam Wells, *Spenser's "Faerie Queene" and the Cult of Elizabeth* (London: Barnes and Noble, 1983), 29–51.

44. Evidence for a London Isis temple is based upon a first-century flagon at the Museum of London, inscribed "LONDINI AD FANVM ISIDIS" (London at the Temple of Isis), and archaeological remains uncovered in Southwark. I thank the curators at the Museum of London who answered my query regarding this artifact.

45. Gary Waller, *The Virgin Mary in Late Medieval and Early Modern English Literature and Popular Culture* (Cambridge: Cambridge University Press, 2011), 182. See also Lees-Jeffries, *England's Helicon*, 117.

46. Spenser, *Faerie Queene*, 381.

47. Spenser, *Faerie Queene*, 138.

48. Spenser, *Faerie Queene*, 742.

49. Jan van der Noot, *A theatre wherein be represented as wel the miseries & calamities that follow*

the voluptuous worldlings [. . .] (London: Henry Bynneman, 1569), 10–13, p. 7 of Epistle (unpaginated), p. 10 of Epistle (unpaginated).

50. Anne Janowitz's *England's Ruins: Poetic Purpose and the National Landscape* (Cambridge: Basil Blackwell, 1990) remains a useful introduction to the relation between the works of Spenser and Du Bellay.

51. Joachim Du Bellay, *Les regrets; suivi de Les antiquités de Rome, Le Songe / Du Bellay*, ed. and annotated by François Roudaut (Paris: Librairie générale française, 2002), sonnet 7.

52. Edmund Spenser, "Ruines of Rome: by Bellay," in *The Poetical Works of Edmund Spenser*, ed. J. C. Smith and E. De Selincourt (London: Oxford University Press, 1912), 510.

53. Spenser, "Ruines of Rome," 514.

54. Spenser, "The Ruines of Time," in Spenser, *Poetical Works*, 472.

55. Spenser, "Ruines of Time," 472.

56. Spenser, "Ruines of Time," 473.

57. Spenser, "Visions of the worlds vanitie," in Spenser, *Poetical Works*, 524.

58. Spenser, "The Visions of Bellay," 523–25, and "The Visions of Petrarch," 525–26, verse quotation at 526, both in Spenser, *Poetical Works*.

59. C. Smith, *Architecture in the Culture of Early Humanism*, 202. Smith's analysis of the text of Chrysolaras's *Comparison* is in her chap. 8, 150–70; her translation of the entire work is included as an appendix, 199–215.

60. Ezekiel 23 is an analogous allegory of two whores: Aholah (Samaria) and Aholibah (Jerusalem). Since Aholah committed whoredom with the Assyrians, he has them destroy her; in turn, Aholibah prostituted herself with the Assyrians and, after seeing their striking images in stone, the Babylonians, and he raises both groups of lovers up against her with the same sequence of punishments by stones, swords, and fire.

61. Thinking of the ways that virginity always is tied to a process of transmission, Jacques Derrida suggested, "The always intact, the intangible, the untouchable (*unberührbar*) is what fascinates and orients the work of the translator. He wants to touch the untouchable, that which remains of the text when one has extracted from it the communicable meaning (a point of contact that is, remember, infinitely small), when one has transmitted that which can be transmitted, indeed taught . . . intact and virgin in spite of the labor of translation, however efficient or pertinent that may be. Pertinency has no bearing here. If one can risk a proposition in appearance so absurd, the text will be even more virgin after the passage of the translator, and the hymen, sign of virginity, more jealous of itself after the other hymen, the contract signed and the marriage consummated. Symbolic completion will not have taken place to its very end and yet the promise of marriage will have come about—and this is the task of the translator, in what makes it very pointed as well as irreplaceable." Jacques Derrida, "Des Tours de Babel," in *Difference in Translation*, ed. and trans. Joseph F. Graham (Ithaca, NY: Cornell University Press, 1985), 214.

62. The original Coryat passage, dating to his travels in 1612, was printed in Samuel Purchas, *Hakluytus Posthumus, Or Purchas His Pilgrimes*, vol. 10 (1905; repr., Cambridge: Cambridge University Press, 2015), 409. See also See Michael Strachan, *Thomas Coryat* (Oxford: Oxford University Press, 1962), 171.

63. See the note citing largely Carrie Anna Harper, *The Sources of the British Chronicle History in Spenser's Faerie Queen* (Bryn Mawr, PA: Bryn Mawr College, 1910), in Spenser, *Faerie Queene*, 1129.

64. William Shakespeare, *Rape of Lucrece*, in *Complete Sonnets and Poems*, ed. Colin Burrows (New York: Oxford University Press, 2002), lines 36, 440–41, 464.

65. Shakespeare, *Rape of Lucrece*, lines 1450–51, 1471.

66. The social status of Lucrece is indeed her only status, as both Ovid and Livy recognize. When Saint Augustine, believing from a Christian perspective that suicide is wrong and seeking a means of explaining that Christian martyrs who are violated in body are not violated in soul, condemns Lucrece for being "covetous of glory" and ruled by secular morals, he cannot grasp the circumstances of her world. See Augustine, *City of God*, 1.23–25.

67. Ovid, *Fasti*, trans. Anne Wiseman and Peter Wiseman (Oxford: Oxford University Press, 2011), 38–39.

68. Shakespeare, *Rape of Lucrece*, lines 1793–1806.

69. Shakespeare, *Rape of Lucrece*, line 1833.

70. Shakespeare, *Rape of Lucrece*, lines 232, 235.

71. Shakespeare, *Rape of Lucrece*, line 1855; see also Ovid, *Fasti*, 119.

72. Joan Breton Connelly explains that "virginity was viewed as a temporary state for ancient Greek priestesses. Indeed, the Greeks defined virgin (*parthenos*) status quite differently from how we do today. For them, it was the condition of a maiden who had passed through puberty but was not yet married. Emphasis was not focused on a state of intactness, which the modern definition requires." *Portrait of a Priestess: Women and Ritual in Ancient Greece* (Princeton, NJ: Princeton University Press, 2007), 18.

73. Giulia Sissa, "La verginità materiale: Evanescenza di un oggetto," *Quaderni Storici*, n.s., 25, no. 75.3 (December 1990): 745.

74. Augustine, *City of God*, 22.

75. Sissa, "La verginità materiale," 740.

76. Sissa, "La verginità materiale," 740. Sissa goes on to explain that whereas the early church fathers claimed that the Christian concept of virginity was unlike the purely physical and factual definition of virginity applied to the Roman vestals, in fact, Plutarch had argued that chastity was a feature of "the body and comportment, the body and the life."

77. Roland Barthes writes of related concepts in *The Neutral*, trans. Rosalind Kraus and Denis Hollier (New York: Columbia University Press, 2007), 21–22: Whereas *tacere* in Latin means verbal silence; *silere* means "stillness, absence of movement and of noise.... Used for objects, night, the sea, winds." "*Silere* would refer to a sort of timeless virginity of things, before they are born or after they have disappeared (*silentes* = the dead)."

78. Mary Beard, "The Sexual Status of Vestal Virgins," *Journal of Roman Studies* 70 (1980): 12–27, and her consequent "correction": "Re-reading (Vestal) Virginity," in *Women in Antiquity: New Assessments*, ed. Richard Hawley and Barbara Levick (New York: Routledge, 1995), 166–77. Beard's early work emphasized the vestals as figures who breached the categories of matron, virgin, and man—a view she came to recognize as underemphasizing the vestals' status as strictly virginal. Later studies, including Ariadne Staples, *From Good Goddess to Vestal Virgin* (London: Routledge, 1998), and Holt N. Parker, "Why Were the Vestals Virgins? or the Chastity of Women and the Safety of the Roman State," *American Journal of Philology* 125, no. 4 (2004): 563–601, emphasize the anthropological and legal status of the virgins—their role in "magically protecting" Rome and the importance of their virginity.

79. Robin Lorsch Wildfang, *Rome's Vestal Virgins: A Study of Rome's Vestal Priestesses in the Late Republic and Early Empire* (New York: Routledge, 2006), 60. Parker's "Why Were the Vestals Virgins?" discusses "witch hunts" and killing of Roman matrons.

80. M. Beard, "Sexual Status of Vestal Virgins," 16n32, gives as the source of this story Dionysus of Halicarnassus, *Antiquitates Romanae*, 2.69 (available in Loeb edition, translated as *Roman Antiquities* by Earnest Cary [Cambridge: Harvard University Press, 1937]: the story of Tuccia is in this section, 513; further discussion of the vestals and their customs are in sections 65–69, and 499ff.) See Tertullian, "Tertullian's Apologetick for the Christians," in *The apolo-*

gies of Justin Martyr, Tertullian, and Minutius Felix, in defence of the Christian religion, with the Commonitory of Vincentius Lirinensis concerning the primitive rule of faith, translated from their originals with notes, for the advantage chiefly of English readers, and a preliminary discourse upon each author, together with a prefatory dissertation about the right use of the Fathers, ed. and trans. William Reeves, 1:135–388 (London: A. and J. Churchill, 1709), at 274, note "b" on the feats of vestal virgins: Tuccia carried water in "a Sieve and Claudia dragg'd along a Ship founder/d in the Tyber by the Strength of her Girdle"; and Augustine, *On Christian Doctrine,* x, 16. Wildfang's *Rome's Vestal Virgins* outlines the available sources of information about the vestal virgins: Cicero, Livy, Dionysus of Halicarnassus, Plutarch's *Lives,* Ovid's *Fasti,* Varro, Valerius Maximus, Festus, and Aulus Gellius, and brief references also in Suetonius, Tacitus, and Juvenal (2). With the exception of Cicero and a few minor references in Varro and other antiquarians, all of the literary sources date to Augustus or after. Therefore, the sources are approximately seven hundred years after the cult's supposed founding at Rome.

81.   Alan Cameron, *The Last Pagans of Rome* (Oxford: Oxford University Press, 2011), 505–6.

82.   Wildfang, *Rome's Vestal Virgins,* 10. In a note to this passage, Wildfang explains, "The simplest and perhaps earliest explanation for the priestesses' use of this spring is that it was the source of water closest to them. Archaeological evidence in fact suggests that in the earliest period the shrine of Juturna was part of the precinct of Vesta. . . . Another possible explanation can be found in the Romans' belief that this spring was particularly health giving" (19n36). She notes that Staples in *From Good Goddess to Vestal Virgin,* on p. 150, argues that the vestals made use of the water from the spring of Juturna because it was located in the area where the *ancile,* a shield symbolic of Rome's power—was found. See also Georg Wissowa, "Vesta," in *Ausführliches Lexikon der griechischen und römischen Mythologie,* W. H. Roscher (Leipzig: B. G. Teubner, 1884–1937), vol. 6, cols. 241–72. Juturna, goddess of springs and fountains, received her divinity as compensation for Jupiter taking her virginity.

83.   The rites and duties of the vestals and Numa's role in their establishment are discussed in Plutarch, *Lives,* vol. 1, 339–46. Both Seneca the Elder and Pliny the Elder note that if the fire somehow went out, the vestals would drill a hole in wood until it caught fire—a technique viewed as evidence of the antiquity of the cult (according to Wildfang, *Rome's Vestal Virgins,* 9) and a ritual of obvious phallic symbolism.

84.   Wissowa, "Vesta," cols. 266–67, and discussion in Wildfang, *Rome's Vestal Virgins,* 22.

85.   Otto Jahn, *Über Darstellungen des Handwerks und Handelsverkehrs Auf Antiken Wandgemälden* (Leipzig: Hirzel, 1868), 315: "at the festivals of Vesta, adjacent to a mill, donkeys were decorated with garlands of flowers and as well strings of bread; the donkeys were sacrificed for a good harvest." He bases these conclusions on passages in Ovid (*Fasti,* bk. 6, ll. 310 and 347) and Lactantius (bk. 1, "False Religion"). Lactantius describes asses crowned with bread and sacrificed in rites of Priapus to appease the god after a donkey's bray thwarted his attack on Vesta. Lactantius, *Divine Institutes,* trans. Anthony Bowen and Peter Garnsey (Liverpool: Liverpool University Press, 2003), 110–11. See also Wildfang, *Rome's Vestal Virgins,* 60. Wildfang speculates that perhaps the milk included in the provisions for vestals in their burial chambers was donkeys' milk. Donkeys are also associated with Dionysus; see Roberto Calasso, *The Marriage of Cadmus and Harmony,* trans. Tim Parks (New York: Knopf, 1993), 42. A prophecy in Zechariah 9:9 proclaims that the Messiah will arrive on a donkey: "Behold, your King is coming to you; He is just and having salvation, Lowly and riding on a donkey, A colt, the foal of a donkey!" Whereas both the New Testament books of Matthew and John narrate the arrival of Jesus on a donkey, it is only in the apocryphal Protoevangelium of James, chapter 17, that the story of Mary arriving in Bethlehem on a donkey is told: "The day of the Lord shall itself bring it to pass as the Lord will. And he saddled the ass, and set her upon

it; and his son led it, and Joseph followed." *New Testament Apocryphal Writings*, ed. James Orr (London: J. M. Dent, 1903), 14. The donkey becomes an unremarkable commonplace of later iconography, as we found in the braying donkey singing with the angels of Piero's Nativity.

86.   Quoted in Cameron, *Last Pagans*, 41nn27–28.

87.   This summary comes from John Bugge, *Virginitas: An Essay in the History of a Medieval Ideal* (The Hague: Martinus Nijhoff, 1975), 142.

88.   Cleo McNelly Kearns, *The Virgin Mary, Monotheism and Sacrifice* (Cambridge: Cambridge University Press, 2008). See also Anna Jameson, *Legends of the Madonna as Represented in the Fine Arts* (London: Longman, 1857), xx–xxi. And see Julia Kristeva, "Stabat Mater," trans. Leon S. Roudiez, in *The Kristeva Reader*, ed. Toril Moi (New York: Columbia University Press, 1986), 162: "Thus Christ, the Son of man, when all is said and done is 'human' only through his mother—as if Christly or Christian humanism could only be a materialism. . . . And yet, the humanity of the Virgin mother is not always obvious . . . in her being cleared of sin, for instance, Mary distinguishes herself from mankind." The early development of the cult of the Virgin Mary is discussed in Marina Warner's comprehensive and far-reaching survey, *Alone of All Her Sex: The Myth and Cult of the Virgin Mary* (1976; repr., Oxford: Oxford University Press, 2013), 54–55.

89.   Bugge, *Virginitas*, 9, explores the impact of a tenet of virginity upon the interpretation of the Fall.

90.   Hilda Graef, *Mary: A History of Doctrine and Devotion* (London: Sheed and Ward, 1965), writes, "As Eve introduced death through her sin and was condemned to give birth in sorrow and pain, it is fitting that the Mother of life should begin her pregnancy with joy and complete her giving birth in joy." Hence the belief that Mary did not suffer in childbirth. Gregory of Nyssa contended in his treatise "De Virginitate" that Mary "did not perceive the childbirth" at all ("On Virginity," 66–67). Mary's painless childbirth is discussed as well in Kearns, *Virgin Mary*, 222.

91.   Kearns, *Virgin Mary*, 197.

92.   Sissa, "La verginità materiale," 744.

93.   John Bugge discusses the fortified castle as a metaphor of virginity in *Virginitas*, 130–34.

94.   The connections between virginity and seeing/gazing/vision—both in the positive sense here and in the negative sense that being seen is a means of unwanted sexual contact—have been explored by a number of scholars. See Bloch, "Chaucer's Maiden's Head," for a discussion of eidetic representation and virginity. In *Images for the Eye and Soul: Function and Meaning in Netherlandish Prints (1450–1650)* (Leiden, Neth.: Primavera Pers, 2006), Ilja Veldman discusses the later sixteenth-century interest, expressed in dramatic works and printmaking, in the figure of Susanna ("Lessons for Ladies," *Simiolus* 16, no. 1/2 [1986]: 113–27, 125–26). A figure of chastity from the book of Daniel, Susanna is threatened by the lecherous gaze of the elders who try to watch her bathing and later try to blackmail her into having sex. Such a representation, especially of the bathing scene, necessarily puts the viewer in the position of the lechers and blackmailers, effecting a visual pun that echoes the role of Hebrew puns in the satisfying denouement of the story itself. The figure of the chaste wife, however, more often meets with the fate of the virgin perfected by death. Before Shakespeare, Lucretia's story is told in Livy, Christine de Pizan's *The City of Ladies Book*, and Boccaccio's *De Mulieribus Claris*. Virginia was stabbed to death by her father so that she would not have to become the slave concubine of Appius Claudius. As Lucretia's story is bound up with the history of the overthrow of the monarchy in 509, Virginia's story is credited with a role in the overthrow of the decemvirate and the reestablishment of the republic in 450. Here, too, the destruction in

sacrifice of a woman serves to reestablish the bonds between men and the equilibrium of the state.

95. Discussed in Kearns, *Virgin Mary*, 197–98. The text is taken from George the Hymnist, "Kontakion for the Presentation of Mary in the Temple," in *Testi mariani del primo millenio*, ed. Georges Gharib (Rome: Città Nuova, 1990), 2:300.

96. Kearns, *Virgin Mary*, 233–34. See also Luigi S. M. Gambero, *Mary and the Fathers of the Church: The Blessed Mary in Patristic Thought* (San Francisco: Ignatius Press, 2006). Gambero recounts that Gregory tells of Zechariah's martyrdom as a consequence of this act.

97. Kearns, *Virgin Mary*, 278.

98. Kearns, *Virgin Mary*, 240–41. Mary also is frequently described as "cloistered" in later medieval traditions. See Georgiana Donavin, *Scribit Mater: Mary and the Language Arts in the Literature of Medieval England* (Washington, DC: Catholic University of America Press, 2011), 31.

99. Quoted in Graef, *Mary*, 54.

100. Jackson J. Campbell, ed. and trans., *Advent Lyrics of the Exeter Book* (Princeton, NJ: Princeton University Press, 2015), 68.

101. Discussed in Donavin, *Scribit Mater*, 202–4. See Chaucer, *The Riverside Chaucer*, ed. Larry D. Benson (Boston: Houghton Mifflin, 1987), 915n518.

102. Caputo, "Aegyptiaca from Cumae," 235–50, discusses the destruction of Isaeum statuettes, arguing that "destruction must have been brought on by Christians after the edict of Constantine (313), or probably after the Edict of Theodosius (392), because literary sources testify that the Isis cult flourished during the whole fourth century CE until the destruction of the Serapeum in Alexandria (391)" (247).

103. Waller, *Virgin Mary in English Literature*, 9–12.

104. Eamon Duffy, *The Stripping of the Altars* (New Haven, CT: Yale University Press, 1992), 171–76.

105. Waller, *Virgin Mary in English Literature*, 182, 12.

106. Transcribed in Duffy, *Stripping of the Altars*, 378. The poem has inspired Duffy's magisterial work of scholarship by the same title.

107. See S. Foster Damon, *A Blake Dictionary* (Hanover, NH: University Press of New England, 1988), 383–85.

108. My thanks to Jo Maddocks, reference librarian at the British Library, for checking the acquisition dates of the existing copies. I have not been able to consult eighteenth-century records or records of duplicate copies that might have been sold.

109. William Blake, *The Complete Poetry and Prose of William Blake*, ed. David V. Erdman (Berkeley: University of California Press, 2008), 454. Michael Davis, *William Blake: A New Kind of Man* (London: Elek, 1977), 15–22.

110. Davis, *William Blake*, 15.

111. Blake, *Complete Poetry and Prose*, 39.

112. Blake, *Complete Poetry and Prose*, 49–50.

113. Mary Wollstonecraft, *A Vindication of the Rights of Woman* (London: J. Johnson, 1792), 311.

114. Blake, *Complete Poetry and Prose*, 46.

115. Blake, *Complete Poetry and Prose*, 4–6.

116. Goethe, *Faust: Part One*, 88. Goethe does not show us this scene of the jewels surrendered to the priest; he has Mephistopheles narrate it to Faust.

117. Goethe, *Faust: Part One*, 106.

118. Goethe, *Faust: Part One*, 141.

119. Goethe, *Faust: Part Two*, 112.

120. Goethe, *Faust: Part Two*, 239.

121. Modified from Johann Wolfgang von Goethe, *Goethe's Roman Elegies*, trans. David Luke (London: Chatto and Windus, 1977), 24–25.

122. Goethe, *Goethe's Roman Elegies*, 24–25.

123. Goethe, *Goethe's Roman Elegies*, 74–75.

124. Goethe, *Goethe's Roman Elegies*, 50–51.

125. Heinrich Düntzer, *Life of Goethe*, trans. Thomas W. Lyster (London: T. Fisher Unwin, 1908), 409–10. Goethe is in fact buried in Weimar, in the Fürstengruft, the ducal burial chapel of Saxe-Weimar-Eisenach.

126. The tomb was built during the first century BCE. Metella was the daughter of Quintus Caecilius Metellus Creticus, a consul in 69 BCE and the wife of Marcus Licinius Crassus. Numerous nineteenth-century guidebooks confuse her with the notoriously promiscuous Caecilia Metella, who was the daughter of Quintus Caecilius Metellus Celer and Clodia. Known for her beauty, she married Publius Cornelius Lentulus Spinther in 53 BCE and soon afterward began an affair with Publius Cornelius Dolabella. Spinther, in a public scandal, divorced her in 45 BCE. Cicero's letters are particularly concerned with the scandal because Dolabella was his son-in-law. See Carla De Stefanis, *Via Appia, The Tomb of Cecilia Metella, and the Castrum Caetani*, ed. Rita Paris, trans. Richard Sadleir (Rome: Ministero per i Beni e le Attività Culturali Soprintendenza Archaeologica di Roma; Milan: Electa, 2000); Cicero, *Cicero's Letters: Selections*, trans. P. G. Walsh (Oxford: Oxford University Press, 2008), letter 95, 326n3. In canto 4 of *Childe Harold's Pilgrimage*, Byron expresses admiration for the tomb as well:

> There is a stern round tower of other days,
> Firm as a fortress, with its fence of stone,
> Such as an army's baffled strength delays,
> Standing with half its battlements alone,
> And with two thousand years of ivy grown,
> The garland of eternity, where wave
> The green leaves over all by time o'erthrown;—
> What was this tower of strength? Within its cave
> What treasure lay so lock'd, so hid?—A woman's grave.

He continues the theme for five more stanzas, speculating about her identity, whether she died in youth or old age, how she wore her hair, whether she had a "lovely form." He declares, "This much alone we know—Metella died, / The wealthiest Roman's wife: Behold his love or pride!" and claims that he feels "as if I had thine inmate known, / Thou tomb . . . Yet could I seat me by this ivied stone / Till I had bodied forth the heated mind / Forms from the floating wreck which Ruin leaves behind." Gordon, *Byron's Poetry and Prose*, 325–26. For an account of the portrait, see Christian Lenz, *Tischbein: Goethe in der Campagna di Roma* (Frankfurt am Main: Städelsches Kunstinstitut und Städtische Galerie, 1979).

127. Jean-Luc Nancy, *The Experience of Freedom*, trans. Bridget McDonald (Stanford, CA: Stanford University Press, 1994), 139.

Chapter Four

1. For a discussion of some of these changes in painting, see Paul Zucker, "Ruins: An Aesthetic Hybrid," *Journal of Aesthetics and Art Criticism* 20, no. 2 (Winter 1961): 119–30.

2. Petrarch, *Letters on Familiar Matters I–VIII*, 1:294.

3. In an article concerned with Hieronymus Cock's ruins prints, Christopher P. Heuer notes the Dutch golden age poet Constantijn Huygens's thoughts on such images a century later, when

a tradition of ruins representations was well established: Huygens held that ruins are "vorme-loos" (formless, amorphous) and "schilderachtig" (suitable for painting) at once. Christopher P. Heuer, "Hieronymus Cock's Aesthetic of Collapse," *Oxford Art Journal* 32, no. 3 (2009): 387.

4.   Readers of Honoré de Balzac's short story "Le Chef-d'oeuvre inconnu" ("The Unknown Masterpiece") will remember Mabuse as the revered master of the deranged genius Frenhofer.

5.   Whether he accompanied Philip to Rome or was sent later is unknown, but by 1509 Philip had returned and Gossart is registered as a resident of Middelburg. See the biographical material in *Jan Gossart's Renaissance*, An Exhibition at the Sainsbury Wing, National Gallery of Art, February 23–May 30, 2011. For a recent survey of the importance of Gossart's work for human-ist antiquarianism, see Marisa Bass, *Jan Gossart and the Invention of Netherlandish Antiquity* (Princeton, NJ: Princeton University Press, 2016).

6.   See the discussion in Maryan Ainsworth, "Introduction: Jan Gossart, the 'Apelles of Our Age,'" in *Man, Myth, and Sensual Pleasures: Jan Gossart's Renaissance; The Complete Works*, ed. Maryan Ainsworth (New Haven, CT: Yale University Press, 2010), 6.

7.   Discussed in Matthias Winner, "Vedute in Flemish Landscape Drawings of the 16th Century," in *Netherlandish Mannerism: Papers Given at a Symposium in Nationalmuseum Stockholm, September 21–22, 1984*, ed. Görel Cavalli-Björkman (Stockholm: Nationalmuseum, 1985), 91. The drawing is *View of the Colosseum in Rome*, Berlin, Kupferstichkabinett Stiftung Preuss. Kulturbesitz KdZ 12918.

8.   Vitalis's Rome poems are most fully discussed in Malcolm C. Smith, "Looking for Rome in Rome: Janus Vitalis and His Disciples," *Revue de Littérature Comparée* 51, no. 4 (1977): 510–27; and Malcolm C. Smith, "Janus Vitalis Revisited," *Revue de Littérature Comparée* 63, no. 1 (1989): 69–75. I have used his Latin transcription here. The first essay provides twelve variant versions of the epigram and includes the text from the 1552/1553 version in the *Iani Vitalis Panormitani sacrosanctae Romanae Ecclesiae Elogia* as printed in a nineteenth-century edition. See M. Smith, "Looking for Rome in Rome," 513n6—Smith lists some variants but thinks some are misprints and others are "better." It is difficult to gather what can be called a definitive text in this case, but Smith does show that the poem had a vivid impact, with twenty-eight Renaissance poets creating versions in Spanish, French, Polish, English, and Latin. In Boswell's *Life of Samuel Johnson*, Boswell records a conversation between a Mr. Cambridge and Johnson. Cambridge cites "A Spanish writer" (it is Francisco de Quevedo) who wrote "Lo que era Firme huio solamente, / Lo fugitivo permanece dura," to which Johnson snapped, "Sir, that is taken from *Janus Vitalis*; '. . . immota labescunt: et quae perpetuo sunt agitato manent.'" James Boswell, *Life of Samuel Johnson* (London: Henry Baldwin, 1791), 2:203. Nevertheless, Vitalis's own epigram, with its initiating problem of where to find Rome in Rome, owes a great deal to an earlier set of epigrams, "De Roma" and "Roma ad Hospites" by the Hungarian/Croatian humanist Janus Pannonius (Ivan Česmicki, 1434–1472). Pannonius, too, compares the built environment, which regardless of its power and permanence is subject to decay, with the ever-changing world of nature, which survives through its mutability. See Raymond Skyrme, "'Buscas en Rome a Roma': Quevedo, Vitalis, and Janus Pannonius," *Bibliothèque d'Humanisme et Renaissance* 44, no. 2 (1982): 363–67. A consequent essay by G. H. Tucker, "Le Portrait de Rome Chez Pannonius et Vitalis: Une mise au point," *Bibliothèque d'Humanisme et Renaissance* 48, no. 3 (1986): 751–56, traces Pannonius's use of the motif of Rome rising from the "cindres," or ashes, of Troy—a legacy that would appear in the "Cendres" of Du Bellay.

9.   J. V. Cunningham, *The Poems of J. V. Cunningham* (Athens, OH: Swallow Press/Ohio University Press, 1997), 118. Copyright © 1997 by J. V. Cunningham. Used by permission of Ohio University Press (www.ohioswallow.com).

10.   Philipp Fehl and Stephen Prokopoff, eds. *Raphael and the Ruins of Rome: The Poetic Dimension* (Champaign: University of Illinois, 1983), discussion of the *Speculum* at 7. The University

of Chicago Library has published a superb annotated online edition of the *Speculum*: http://
speculum.lib.uchicago.edu/ (2007).

11. Émilie d'Orgeix, "The Goldschmidt and Scholz Scrapbooks in the Metropolitan Museum of
Art: A Study of Renaissance Architectural Drawings," *Metropolitan Museum Journal* 36 (2001):
171–72. D'Orgeix suggests that Lafréry's *Speculum* was offered for individual sale as early as
1545 (192). In a more recent article, Louis Cellauro contends that there were a number of collectors' albums with this title made by different publishers and engravers in the second half of
the century and that Salamanca may have been the "real originator" of the *Speculum*. He traces
the many intersections between shop owners and often itinerant engravers in the period and
contends that Du Pérac, then working in Lafréry's shop, designed and etched the Lafréry title
page at some point between 1573 and Lafréry's death in 1577. Louis Cellauro, "'Monvmenta
Romae': An Alternative Title Page for the Duke of Sessa's Personal Copy of the *Speculum
Romanae Magnificentiae*," *Memoirs of the American Academy in Rome* 51/52 (2006/2007): 277–
81. "Palmi," "digiti," and "minuti" are the Roman measurements palm-length, finger-length,
and—one-sixtieth of a palm—a "minute." An "uncia" was the length of a thumb. The Florentine "braccia" is, as indicated, an arm's length, equivalent to two palms.

12. Cellauro, "'Monvmenta Romae,'" 280.

13. See also the reproductions of the Du Pérac prints known as the Ashby Codex in Étienne Du
Pérac, *Le Antiche Rovine di Roma nei Disegni di Étienne Du Pérac* (Milan: Amilcare Pizzi, 1990),
based on Pizzi's earlier 1960 edition. Rudolf Wittkower has contributed there an important
survey of what is known about Du Pérac, "The Du Pérac Codex: Discovering the Lost Rome,"
11–43: his prints, his reliance on images made by others, including Giovanni Antonio Dosio
and Lafréry, the reception and textual history of his work, and the relation of this codex, well
known for its discovery by Thomas Ashby and both preserved and damaged by later collectors, to the 1574 *Urbis Roma sciographia* and the 1575 *I vestigi dell'antichità di Roma*. Wittkower
concludes that the codex prints were made in two periods: "about 1565" and "about 1570."

14. Discussed in Barkan, *Unearthing the Past*, 211, passim.

15. Vitruvius, *I dieci libri dell'architettura* (Venice, 1556).

16. The Posthumus painting was discovered and acquired in Vienna in 1983 by the Prince of Liechtenstein for his collection at the Schloss Vaduz. For extensive discussions of its imagery and
the milieu of its production, see Ruth Olitsky Rubinstein, "'Tempus edax rerum': A Newly
Discovered Painting by Hermannus Posthumus," *Burlington Magazine* 127, no. 988 (July 1985):
425–33, 435–36; and Nicole Dacos, "Hermannus Posthumus pingebat 1536," in *Roma Quanta
Fuit*, 15–20.

17. My discussion of Maerten van Heemskerck here and elsewhere in this study is deeply indebted to the published work of Arthur DiFuria and as well to ongoing correspondence and
conversations with him. For van Heemskerck's drawing of the 1527 Sack of Rome, see DiFuria's
essay "The *Concettismo* of Triumph: Maerten van Heemskerck's Prints and Spanish Omnipotence in a Late Sixteenth Century Writing Cabinet," in *Prints in Translation, 1450–1575:
Image, Materiality, Space* (London: Routledge, 2016), 158–83. DiFuria discusses van Heemskerck's relation to ruins imagery as well in "The Eternal Eye: Memory, Vision and Topography
in Maerten van Heemskerck's Roman Ruin 'Vedute,'" in *Rom Zeichnen: Maerten van Heemskerck 1532–1536–37*, ed. Tatjana Bartsch and Peter Seiler (Berlin: Gebr. Mann, 2012), 157–70.
As this volume is going to press, DiFuria has published versions of these essays, and much
additional new research, in his *Maarten van Heemskerck's Rome: Antiquity, Memory, and the
Cult of Ruins* (Leiden, Neth.: Brill, 2019). His comprehensive book includes a biographical
and contextual account of van Heemskerck's drawings before and after his period in Rome
and a definitive catalog of van Heemskerck's extant drawings of Roman ruins.

18. I am indebted to Ana Cara for advice in translating this inscription. The inscriptions are of interest for many reasons, not the least of which is that they juxtapose Bourbon's historic loyalties: French, his native language, the French throne against which he committed treason, and the Spanish of the mixed Spanish and German troops that he was leading in the service of Charles V. Without arranging for provisions for his soldiers, Bourbon, and consequently the emperor, could not control his troops.

19. See Bart Rosier, "The Victories of Charles V: A Series of Prints by Maerten van Heemskerck, 1555–56," trans. Bev Jackson, *Simiolus: Netherlands Quarterly for the History of Art* 20, no. 1 (1990–91): 28.

20. Mary Tiffany Ferrer, *Music and Ceremony at the Court of Charles V* (Suffolk, UK: Boydell and Brewer, 2012), 231.

21. Such a print sequence also may be indebted to the historical "vignettes" that often were displayed across the arches of triumphal displays: there is some evidence that van Heemskerck may have helped create such a display for the emperor's triumphal procession on April 5, 1536 in Rome (Rosier, "Victories of Charles V," 35), and Cock worked as a painter of triumphal arches for Charles's ceremonial entry into Antwerp in 1549 (Heuer, "Hieronymus Cock's Aesthetic of Collapse," 395). Julia Hell discusses the tapestries depicting the triumph at Tunis that Charles commissioned from Jan Cornelisz Vermeyen—and further works of proleptic commemoration planned by his entourage of poets, historians, and mathematicians—in chapter 6 of her *Conquest of Ruins*. She draws especially on the work of Peter Burke, "Presenting and Re-presenting Charles V," in *Charles V in His Time*, ed. Hugo Soly (Antwerp: Mercatorfonds, 1999), 411–18, 426–33.

22. My summary of the 1549 entry is obliged to Mark Meadow, "Ritual and Civic Identity in Philip II's 1549 Antwerp *Blijde Incompst,*" *Nederlands Kunsthistorisch Jaarboek* 49 (1998): 36–67, and to comments in correspondence with Edward Wouk and Arthur DiFuria.

23. Rosier, "Victories of Charles V," 38. Rosier believes Granvelle also may have shown Giulio Clovio the *Victories*, for the miniaturist, his friend, also made copies of the images.

24. A rough literal translation of this title would be "Several eminent monuments of ancient ruined Rome, drawn well in living sight toward a true imitation."

25. See Heuer, "Hieronymus Cock's Aesthetic of Collapse," 401–2; he suggests that one of the Edinburgh drawings could be after the print and that there is "little evidence to suggest prints from 1551, 1561, or 1562 engraved series were based on Cock's own designs rather than those by other artists." Cock could have picked up the *Speculum Romanae* or other groups of drawings in Rome, or he could have learned about Roman ruins from Thiry, who was, as we've noted, in Antwerp in the 1550s.

26. Boudewijn Bakker and Michael Hoyle, "*Pictores, Adeste!* Hieronymus Cock Recommending His Print Series," *Simiolus: Netherlands Quarterly for the History of Art* 33, no. 1/2 (2007/2008): 60n21. Reproductions of the Baths of Diocletian prints can be viewed in *The New Hollstein, Dutch and Flemish Etchings, Engravings and Woodcuts 1450–1700, the van Doetecum Family,* ed. Ger Luijten, comp. Henk Nalis, vol. 1 (Rotterdam: Rijksprentenkabinet, 1998), 44, plates 54–80, nos. 118–61. Perhaps Granvelle was drawn to sponsoring a study of the Baths of Diocletian because of their role in Petrarch's famous letter A to Colonna. Edward Wouk has traced the role of Granvelle's patronage in Cock's career in his essay "Antoine Perrenot de Granvelle, the Aux Quatre Vents Press, and the Patronage of Prints in Early Modern Europe," *Simiolus* 38, no. 1/2 (2015/2016): 31–61. I am grateful for our correspondence in 2015 regarding the staffage figures in Cock's prints and their costumes.

27. Latin transcription appears in Bakker and Hoyle, "*Pictores, Adeste!,*" 61n31. My thanks to Samuel Stewart-Halevy for this translation.

28. Peter G. Bietenholz and Thomas B. Deutscher, *Contemporaries of Erasmus: A Biographical Register of the Renaissance and Reformation* (Toronto: University of Toronto Press, 2003), 2:123.

29. Transcribed in Bakker and Hoyle, "*Pictores, Adeste!*," 64.

30. See the contrasting images in the exhibition catalog Joris Van Grieken, Ger Luijten, and Jan Van der Stock, eds., *Hieronymus Cock: De renaissance in prent* (Brussels: Mercatorfonds; New Haven, CT: Yale University Press, 2013), 103.

31. Leon Battista Alberti, *On Painting*, trans. John Spencer (New Haven, CT: Yale University Press, 1966), 78.

32. The creative relationship between van Heemskerck and Cock is explored in Arthur DiFuria's essay "Remembering the Eternal in 1553: Maerten van Heemskerck in *Self-Portrait Before the Colosseum*," *Nederlands Kunsthistorisch Jaarboek*, no. 59 (2010): 95–99. There DiFuria also discusses the debate over whether or not Cock traveled to Rome.

33. Sixty-six printers were active in Antwerp between 1500 and 1540; they published 2,254 titles, more than half of the total book production in the Netherlands, and Antwerp played a prominent role in the last six decades of the century. Most of the works were designed for an international market, and the works were admired, too, for their excellent artisanry. In addition to Plantin, the book publishers Nutius, Steelsius, Bellerus, and van Ghelen were active. Willem Silvius and Jan/Johannes de Laet were, like the Cock family, prominent print publishers. Guido Marnef, *Antwerp in the Age of Reformation: Underground Protestantism in a Commercial Metropolis, 1550–1577*, trans. J. C. Grayson (Baltimore: Johns Hopkins University Press, 1996), 37–38.

34. For overviews of Antwerp printmaking, see Timothy Riggs and Larry Silver, eds., *Graven Images: The Rise of Professional Printmakers in Antwerp and Haarlem, 1540–1640* (Evanston, IL: Mary and Leigh Block Gallery, Northwestern University, 1993). The standard work on Aux Quatre Vents remains Timothy Riggs's 1971 dissertation at Yale University, "Hieronymus Cock (1510–1570): Printmaker and Publisher in Antwerp at the Sign of the Four Winds," photocopy (Ann Arbor, Mich.: Xerox University Microfilms, 1974, "71-31.002"). See also Van Grieken, Luijten, and Van der Stock, *Hieronymus Cock: De renaissance in prent*. Francine de Nave, *The Plantin-Moretus Museum: Printing and Publishing before 1800* (Antwerp: Museum Antwerpen, 2004), provides an overview of the history and holdings of the museum. For the engravers of the school of Fontainebleau, see Zerner, *L'école de Fontainebleau*.

35. See Zucker, *Fascination of Decay*, 21.

36. Girolamo Porro, preface to Scamozzi, *Discorsi sopra l'antichità di Roma*, n.p.

37. The Villa di Maser is also known as the Villa Barbaro. Konrad Oberhuber, "Hieronymus Cock, Battista Pittoni und Paolo Veronese in Villa Maser," in *Munuscula Discipulorum: Kunsthistorische Studien Hans Kauffmann zum 70. Geburtstag 1966*, ed. Tilmann Buddensieg and Matthias Winner (Berlin: Verlag Bruno Hessling, 1968), 207–24.

38. See the discussion of this decline in Heuer, "Hieronymus Cock's Aesthetic of Collapse," 399.

39. John Pinto, *Speaking Ruins: Piranesi, Architects, and Antiquity in 18th Century Rome* (Ann Arbor: University of Michigan Press, 2012), 26–27, suggests that Carlo Fontana peoples his drawings with ancient figures (see especially his "L'Anfiteatro Flavio"), a practice not common until the nineteenth century. He compares Fontana's work to that of Desgodetz: "Ancient architecture, with Desgodetz, is removed from its physical context and divorced from history, while in Fontana's presentation the ruins are allowed to speak in several tenses: past, present, and future," as buildings are shown in use and figures are clad in Roman costumes. Wittkower notes that whereas Du Pérac shows numerous female figures in contemporary dress, one of them is inexplicably clothed in a particular German fashion from 1525. Du Pérac, *Le Antiche Rovine*, 39.

40. Such flat hats also appear in the allegory of Africa in Jan (Johannes) Sadler's series of engravings on the four continents. The large figure of Africa herself and the small figures in the background all wear such hats. Kupferstichkabinett Box 203 2001 1. One of the earliest mentions of Maerten van Heemskerck, Hadrius Junius's *Batavia*, written between 1565 and 1570 and posthumously published in 1588, testifies that van Heemskerck was "admirably gifted in depicting, in a most attractive manner, valleys, farmhouses, rivers, straits, sailing vessels, people going to town mounted on mules or vehicles, or people walking, with wide-brimmed hats to protect them from the sun." Quoted in Ilja M. Veldman, "Maerten van Heemskerck and Hadrianus Junius: The Relationship between a Painter and a Humanist," *Simiolus* 7, no. 1 (1974): 37. Larry Silver identifies these hats as the costume of gypsies and traces them to fifteenth-century iconography; see his essay "Bruegel's Biblical Kings," in *Imago Exegetica: Visual Images as Exegetical Instruments 1400–1700*, ed. Walter S. Melion, James Clifton, and Michel Weemans (Leiden, Neth.: Brill, 2014), 821. His explanation that gypsies were often thought to be "Egyptian" may explain why the costume appears in these Africa images.

41. Vincent Ilardi, *Renaissance Vision from Spectacles to Telescopes* (Philadelphia: Memoirs of the American Philosophical Society, 2007).

42. The drawing (discussed by Heuer, "Hieronymus Cock's Aesthetic of Collapse," 390–93) is signed "H. Cock. F 1550." Scottish National Gallery, Edinburgh, inv. 1033. On page 98 of Van Grieken, Luijten, and Van der Stock, *Hieronymus Cock: De renaissance in prent*, it is juxtaposed to the engraving in a copy from the Koninklijke Bibliotheek van België, Brussels, Prentenkabinet, inv. S.I 54030.

43. Tertullian, *De idololatria*, ed. and trans. J. H. Waszink and J. C. M. van Winden (Leiden, Neth.: Brill, 1987), 73–78.

44. Stijn Bussels, *Spectacle, Rhetoric and Power: The Triumphal Entry of Prince Philip of Spain into Antwerp* (New York: Rodopi, 2012), 230. Bussels's lively study provides a good survey of all extant accounts of the features of the entry. For a discussion of the relation between baroque processions and Roman triumphs, see Richard Alewyn and Karl Sälzle, *Das große Welttheater: Die Epoche der höfischen Feste in Dokument und Deutung* (Hamburg: Rowohlt, 1959), 19–22. At times the subject of Renaissance prints, triumphs and entries nevertheless do not lend themselves readily to two-dimensional experience: ephemeral, glimpsed in passing fragments, designed to express the fullness of the state's wealth and power through displays of goods and objects, they overwhelm the viewer with a three-dimensional sensory overload of noise, light, and spectacle. As we know from the relief on the Arch of Titus, they are replete at the expense of the victims of their triumph.

45. David Freedberg, "Theory: The Question of Images," in *Art and Iconoclasm, 1525–1580: The Case of the Northern Netherlands*, ed. J. P. Filedt Kok, W. Halsema-Kubes, and Th. Kloek (The Hague: Staatsuitgeverij, 1986), 69–71. Freedberg's introduction in this catalog for the *Kunst voor de Beeldenstorm* exhibit in Amsterdam's Rijksmuseum builds on his pathbreaking earlier work, *Iconoclasm and Painting in the Netherlands 1566–1609* (Oxford: Oxford University Press, 1972).

46. Marnef, *Antwerp in the Age of Reformation*, 43–47. Bruegel moved to Brussels in 1563 and after that made few drawings for prints. See Riggs, "Hieronymus Cock," 53.

47. Cock's press, however, also flourished under the direction of his widow Volcxen Diericx, who continued his work for another thirty years—until her own death in 1600. For a history of the Family of Love in relation to Plantin, see Paul V. Blouw, "Was Plantin a Member of the Family of Love? Notes on His Dealings with Hendrik Niclaes," *Quærendo* 23, no. 1 (1993): 3–22. Blouw recounts several of the joint ventures that Plantin and Niclaes were involved in but ultimately suggests that Plantin, like Coornhert, would have been suspicious of the more grandiose claims Niclaes made for himself as a prophet and manifestation of Christ. A useful

introduction to Niclaes, the Family of Love, and their relation to later Protestant movements is Jean Dietz Moss, "'Godded with God': Hendrik Niclaes and His Family of Love," *Transactions of the American Philosophical Society* 71, no. 8 (1981): 1–89.

48.   Marnef, *Antwerp in the Age of Reformation*, 209. On the civil disorders in Antwerp and the subsequent economic decline of the city, see Jervis Wegg, *The Decline of Antwerp under Philip of Spain* (London: Methuen, 1924), 53–141; and Raymond de Roover, "The Business Organization of the Plantin Press in the Setting of Sixteenth Century Antwerp," *De Gulden Passer* 34 (1956): 110–20.

49.   Marnef, *Antwerp in the Age of Reformation*, 89.

50.   Leon Voet, *Antwerp: The Golden Age; The Rise and Glory of the Metropolis in the Sixteenth Century* (Antwerp: Mercatorfonds, 1973), 171–74.

51.   Eleanor A. Saunders, "A Commentary on Iconoclasm in Several Print Series by Maerten van Heemskerck," *Simiolus* 10, no. 2 (1978): 59–83. Saunders emphasizes that "wherever action is taken against idolatrous gods and their temples, a king with his priests or with his prophet stands in a prominent position directing the course of events, even though no such arrangement is indicated in the relevant biblical texts." She sees this element as van Heemskerck's effort to reconcile a humanist respect for the law with any iconoclasm that might be performed. His friend, the learned Reformist and humanist scholar, writer, and printmaker Dirck Volckertszoon Coornhert, helped the authorities in Haarlem keep the city calm, arguing that iconoclasm, far from bringing religious freedom and the end of the Inquisition, would evoke the government to undertake repressive measures (79–80). A particularly fine later edition by Joan (Jan) Galle of the "History of Josiah" series, originally engraved by his grandfather Philip Galle, can be found at the Plantin Moretus Museum: the destruction of the idols series begins at 133; 135 shows the destruction of Baal, with 136 and 137 showing further damage to images and 138 showing the opening of graves.

52.   Peter Arnade, *Beggars, Iconoclasts and Civic Patriots: The Political Culture of the Dutch Revolt* (Ithaca, NY: Cornell University Press, 2008), 227.

53.   Theodore Lowe DeVinne, *Christopher Plantin and the Plantin Moretus Museum in Antwerp* (New York: Grolier Book Club, 1888), 27.

54.   Arnade, *Beggars, Iconoclasts*, 265–75.

55.   Voet, *Antwerp: The Golden Age*, 241–70, surveys the cosmopolitan character of sixteenth-century Antwerp. See also Linda M. Heywood and John K. Thornton, *Central Africans, Atlantic Creoles, and the Foundation of the Americas, 1585–1660* (Cambridge: Cambridge University Press, 2007), 12–13; and Marnef, *Antwerp in the Age of Reformation*, 23–29. Marnef points out that the multiple "points of sociability" in the city, especially via the guilds and religious fraternities, were "important in the dissemination of Reformed ideas. The same applies in reverse for the penetration of the Catholic Reformation, in which, for example, the religious fraternities exercised great influence."

56.   Robert J. Wilkinson, *The Kabbalistic Scholars of the Antwerp Polyglot Bible* (Leiden, Neth.: Brill, 2007), 2–5.

57.   Wilkinson, *Kabbalistic Scholars*, 42, 67.

58.   S. A. Mansbach, "Pieter Bruegel's Towers of Babel," *Zeitschrift für Kunstgeschichte* 45, no. 1 (1982): 48.

59.   Rosenau, *Vision of the Temple*, 94. Edward Eigen discusses the early eighteenth-century reception of the Temple of Solomon in a chapter, "*The Plagiarism of the Heathens Detected*: John Wood the Elder on the Temple of Solomon," of his recent book *On Accident: Episodes in Architecture and Landscape* (Cambridge, MA: MIT Press, 2018), 124–53. There he surveys the architectural theories of John Wood the Elder of Bath, showing their relation to the historical

reception of the book of Daniel, the adaptation of classical sources by the early church fathers, debates regarding the originality and sources of *De architectura* (including their relation to the legendary, and vanished, sibillyne oracles), and the long-standing dream of an originary building/temple at the heart of Wood's conjectures.

60.   David Landau and Peter Parshall, *The Renaissance Print: 1470–1550* (New Haven, CT: Yale University Press, 1996), 221.

61.   In modern Dutch this might be rendered ALS 'T OP 'T HOOGSTE WAS / MOEST HET TOEN NIET VALLEN? I am indebted to the historian Hester Schadee for this translation.

62.   Hendrik van Cleve, *Ruinarum varii prospectus ruriumq. aliquot delineationes* (Antwerp: Philips Galle, n.d.).

63.   See Larry Silver, *Peasant Scenes and Landscapes: The Rise of Pictorial Genres in the Antwerp Art Market* (Philadelphia: University of Pennsylvania Press, 2012), 296n35.

64.   Mansbach, "Pieter Bruegel's Towers." There is no known evidence of Bruegel's own religious beliefs—he painted traditional Roman Catholic subjects such as the life of the Virgin, but they may have been selected and commissioned by his patrons. See Perez Zagorin, "Looking for Pieter Bruegel," *Journal of the History of Ideas* 64, no. 1 (2003): 76. Mansbach recounts that through his friendship with the German humanist Hans Franckert, Bruegel came to work with Cock's circle at Aux Quatre Vents and to know Christopher Plantin, who, fleeing Antwerp, stayed in Paris for eighteen months starting in 1562 because he was suspected of heresy. He returned in 1564. M. Destombes argues in his study, "A Panorama of the Sack of Rome by Pieter Bruegel the Elder," *Imago Mundi* 14 (1959): 64–73, that Bruegel painted the only extant panorama of the Sack of Rome made in the 1550s. In 1556, when Bruegel was associated with Aux Quatre Vents, Cock published a print series on the victories of Charles V (*Divi Caroli V Imp. Opt. Max. Victoriae ex multis praecipuae*) that included an image of the assault on the *Porta Torrionis* with the caption "Borbone occiso, Romana in moenia miles Caesaris ruit et miserandam diripit urbem" (Bourbon having been killed, the emperor's soldiers destroyed the ramparts of Rome and the miserable city was ransacked). Destombes suggests that "most certainly" Bruegel visited Lafréry's and Salamanca's print shops in Rome during his 1553–1554 sojourn there and that Lafréry and Aux Quatre Vents were involved in exchanging prints. He also notes that Giulio Clovio, Bruegel's collaborator, was in Rome working for Cardinal Campeggio in 1527 and was held as a prisoner during the Sack of Rome (65–68).

65.   Mansbach suggests the image of the king comes from the depictions descending from Josephus of Nimrod as tower-builder and passages in the writings of Augustine recounting Alexander the Great's ambition to build a new version of the Tower of Babel. Mansbach, "Pieter Bruegel's Towers," 44. In Josephus (book 1, chap. 4, 2–3) Nimrod's mandate to build a tower is based on ideas that human happiness should not depend on God, that the tower will be high enough to protect humans from another Flood, and that tyranny is an effective means of organizing cooperative human labor. Josephus, *Jewish Antiquities*, 1:55.

66.   Larry Silver, in "Bruegel's Biblical Kings," argues that it would be inaccurate to interpret Bruegel's paintings of kingship and war only as allegories of contemporary violence, for such a direct critique would be readily life-threatening for the artist and as well would not acknowledge the larger theological frame for Bruegel's distaste for war: Bruegel sees Christianity as a religion of peace and Christ as the "King of Kings"—a kindly and benevolent force to be absorbed through the emulation of individual followers. Silver, "Bruegel's Biblical Kings." More recently, Joseph Leo Koerner has discussed the two paintings, pointing to the Vienna painting, with its primitive huts attached to the sides of the tower and its various construction techniques, as a kind of lesson in the history of architecture. He also cites Johann-Christian Klamt's theory that the Rotterdam painting portrays, on the fourth turn of the tower's spiral,

a red baldachin proceeding amid crowds. Klamt contends that this detail indicates the retinue of the Pope and is a subtle critique of papal ceremony on the part of Bruegel. Joseph Leo Koerner, *Bosch and Bruegel: From Enemy Painting to Everyday Life* (Princeton, NJ: Princeton University Press, 2016), 298–304. He cites Johann-Christian Klamt, "Anmerkungen zu Pieter Bruegels Babel-Darstellungen," in *Pieter Bruegel und Seine Welt*, ed. Otto von Simson and Matthias Winner (Berlin: Mann, 1979), 43–50.

67.   Arno Dolders, ed., *Philips Galle: The Illustrated Bartsch* (New York: Abaris, 1987), xxvi.

68.   The frontispiece explains: DAMVS TIBI, BENIGNE LECTOR, VNO LIBELLO TANQVAMIN SPECVLO EXHIBITAS, MEMORABILIORES IVDAEAE GENTIS CLADES, VT DELICTORVM SEMPER COMITES, ITS CVM PRAESENTI, TVM POSTERAE AETATI PRO EXEMPLIS FVTVRAS (We offer you, dear reader, published in a little book as though in a mirror, the disasters of the Jewish people, which deserve to be remembered, in the present and for posterity as future examples). For a survey of scholarship regarding this series, see Marco Folin and Monica Preti, eds., *Les Villes Détruites de Maerten van Heemskerck: Images de ruines et conflits religieux dans les Pays-Bas au XVIe siècle* (Paris: INHA, 2015). Folin and Preti outline that the series has a polyvalent set of meanings: it foregrounds the inner inclination of human beings toward sin, shows the brutality of war and its consequences, narrating episodes of sacks and destructions and underscoring the suffering that ensues from sovereigns with a thirst for power. They argue that van Heemskerck and Galle are not only following the Netherlandish predilection for prints of biblical allegories but also commenting on the religious strife of their time. For discussion of the work in light of van Heemskerck's sense of himself as an artist, see two articles by Arthur J. DiFuria, "Self-Fashioning and Ruination in a Print Series by Maerten van Heemskerck," in *Culture figurative a confronto tra Fiandre e Italia dal XV al XVII secolo*, ed. Anna De Floriani and Maria Galassi (Cinisello Balsamo, It.: Silvana, 2008), 117–25; and DiFuria, "Remembering the Eternal in 1553."

69.   Martial, *Epigrams*, vol. 2 (book 8, epigram 36), trans. Walter C. Ker (London: Heineman, 1920). See the discussion in C. Smith, *Architecture in the Culture of Early Humanism*, 44, 229. Smith explains that another possible source for such comparisons is the *Greek Anthology*'s account of the walls of Babylon, the Hanging Gardens, the pyramids, and the Mausoleum of Halicarnassus, and, most magnificent of all, the Temple of Artemis at Ephesus that "mounted to the clouds" (44).

70.   Colonna, *Hypnerotomachia Poliphili*, 25: discussed in C. Smith, *Architecture in the Culture of Early Humanism*, 48–49.

71.   Dolders, *Philips Galle*, xliii, xliv.

72.   Dolders, *Philips Galle*, 354–62. The nymphs follow a series of male sea and river gods.

73.   Dolders, *Philips Galle*, 1.

Chapter Five

1.   Joachim Du Bellay, "The Ruines of Rome," trans. Edmund Spenser, in *The Shorter Poems*, by Edmund Spenser, ed. Richard A. McCabe (London: Penguin, 1999), 285.

2.   Malcolm Baker, "Representing Invention, Viewing Models," in *Models: The Third Dimension of Science*, ed. Soraya de Chadarevian and Nick Hopwood (Stanford, CA: Stanford University Press, 2004), 22.

3.   This fresco is discussed in Nagel and Wood, *Anachronic Renaissance*, 439n11. See also the guidebook by Giovanna Mariucci, *Umbria da non perdere: Guida ai 100 capolavori* (Milan: Scala, 2007), 142.

4.   See St. John Simpson, "Persepolis Graffiti: Foreign Visitors," in *Encyclopaedia Iranica*, last modified October 30, 2015, http://www.iranicaonline.org/articles/persepolis-graffiti; and

St. John Simpson, "Making Their Mark: Foreign Travellers at Persepolis," Achemenet, January 2005, http://achemenet.com/ressources/enligne/arta/pdf/2005.001-Simpson.pdf. Macaulay, *Pleasure of Ruins*, 146, cites the nineteenth-century antiquarian William Ainsworth in writing that Pietro della Valle's own signature appears on the gate at Persepolis, but no later scholars seem to confirm this assertion. Contemporary scholars give 1621 as the date of his visit to Persepolis. See Ali Mousavi, *Persepolis: Discovery and Afterlife of a World Wonder* (Boston: De Gruyter, 2012), 98–99.

5.   This is an intriguing slippage between sources of the *privilegio*. Between 1550 and 1555, Cock published a number of prints with well-documented imperial privilege from Charles V and, from 1556 to 1562, from Philip II. The 1551 *Praecipua* thus had the privilege of Charles, and the 1562 *Libello* the privilege of Philip. The Venetian state granted privileges for copying as well as for ensuring copyright, but a plethora of these *privilegi* were granted in the second half of the sixteenth century, printers bought plates from other printers, and counterfeiting was commonplace. It is therefore difficult to substantiate the integrity of Pittoni's claim. See Christopher L. C. E. Witcombe, *Copyright in the Renaissance: Prints and the Privilegio in Sixteenth-Century Venice and Rome* (Leiden, Neth.: Brill, 2004), 41–44, 7341. Witcombe's authoritative and useful book does not, unfortunately, mention Pittoni.

6.   In his introduction to Du Pérac's *Le Antiche Rovine*, Wittkower asks suggestively what the function was of the lively figures in these frames. He notes that Roman eagles lift a veil from women nursing babies in the image of the Forum, evoking Romulus and Remus; Du Pérac, like most of his peers (including, as can be seen in our fig. 25, Hieronymus Cock), would have thought the Basilica of Constantine was the Temple of Peace that Vespasian built after the Jewish war. Du Pérac frames his images of the Basilica with figures in "Jewish" or oriental costume. Wittkower, "Du Pérac Codex," 39.

7.   Gian Paolo Consoli, "Architecture and History: Vico, Lodoli, Piranesi," in *The Serpent and the Stylus: Essays on G. B. Piranesi*, ed. Mario Bevilacqua, Heather Hyde Minor, and Fabio Barry, Memoirs of the American Academy in Rome, supp. vol. 4 (Ann Arbor: University of Michigan Press, 2006), 201–2.

8.   Lola Kantor-Kazovsky, *Piranesi as Interpreter of Roman Architecture and the Origins of His Intellectual World* (Florence: Leo S. Olschki Editore, 2006), 177–78.

9.   See Zucker, *Fascination of Decay*, 99; Andrew Robison, "Giovanni Battista Piranesi," in *The Glory of Venice: Art in the Eighteenth Century*, ed. Jane Martineau and Andrew Robison (New Haven, CT: Yale University Press, 1994), 377–406. Arthur M. Hind, *Giovanni Battista Piranesi: A Critical Study* (London: Holland Press, 1922), claims that Piranesi worked in the shop of the scene painters Giuseppe and Domenico Valeriani and notes Piranesi's studies with Ferdinando Bibiena, who died in 1742 (1).

10. See Alessandra Pagliano, "Architecture and Perspective in the Illusory Spaces of Ferdinando Galli Bibiena," *Nexus Network Journal* 18, no. 3 (December 2016): 697–721, https://doi .org/10.1007/s00004-016-0295-7.

11. Matthias Winner helpfully traces the history of the Italian term *vedute* and describes the valence between first-person observation of nature and imaginary projection that "views" involved in sixteenth-century sketching and painting practices in "Vedute in Flemish Landscape Drawings." He shows the importance of the artist's standpoint and practices of copying and transferring landscape images, including the work of Jan Brueghel the Elder, Jan Gossart, Maerten van Heemskerck, and other northern artists drawing in Rome.

12. G. B. Piranesi, preface to *Le Antichità Romane* (Paris: Firmin Didot, Frères, 1835), n.p.

13. Carlo Bertelli, "Le Parlanti Rovine," in *Grafica Grafica II*, no. 2., ed. Carlo Bertelli (Rome: Calcografia Nazionale, 1976). See also Francesco Nevola, *Giovanni Battista Piranesi: I Grotteschi; Gli anni giovanili 1720–1750* (Rome: Ugo Bozzi Editore, 2010), 207.

14. John Wilton-Ely, "Design through Fantasy: Piranesi as Designer," in *Piranesi as Designer*, ed. Sarah Lawrence and John Wilton-Ely (New York: Cooper-Hewitt, National Design Museum, Smithsonian Institute, 2007), 18.

15. Maurizio Calvesi, "Nota ai 'grotteschi' o capricci di Piranesi," in *Piranesi e la cultura antiquaria: Gli antecedenti e il contesto*, ed. Anna Lo Bianco (Rome: Comune di Roma e Università degli Studi di Roma, 1983), 135–36: "di fantasioso ma anche e sopratutto di arabescato, barocco . . . e comunque per nulla inconciliabile con la presenza di significati."

16. Calvesi, "Nota ai 'grotteschi,'" 136–40. The Vico connection to Piranesi, which is based on the historical connection and correspondence Vico had with one of Piranesi's Venetian mentors, the learned Franciscan friar Carlo Lodoli, is first laid out in Maurizio Calvesi's introduction to the Italian edition of Henri Focillon's pathbreaking study of the printmaker: Maurizio Calvesi, introduction to *Giovanni-Battista Piranesi*, by Henri Focillon, ed. Maurizio Calvesi and Augusta Monferini (Bologna: Alfa, 1967), v–xlii. See also Consoli, "Architecture and History," 195–210; and Erika Naginski, "Preliminary Thoughts on Piranesi and Vico," *RES: Anthropology and Aesthetics*, no. 53/54 (Spring–Autumn 2008): 152–67.

17. Nevola, *Giovanni Battista Piranesi*, 205.

18. Giovanna Scaloni, "Carceri," in *Giambattista Piranesi, Matrici incise 1743–1753*, ed. Ginevra Mariani (Rome: Istituto Nazionale per la Grafica, Calcografia; Milan: Mazzotta, 2010), 52–53. Giovanna Scaloni is the technical and scientific coordinator of the Istituto Nazionale's vast project to publish Piranesi's *matrice* (plural of *matrix*, as introduced and described in chapter 4), held in its vaults: there are now two volumes—those incised from 1743 to 1753, as cited at the beginning of this note, and those incised in 1756–1757: *Giambattista Piranesi, Matrici incise 1756–1757*, ed. Ginevra Mariani (Rome: Istituto Nazionale per la Grafica, Calcografia; Milan: Mazzotta, 2014). For discussion of the *cisello profilatori*, see Scaloni, "La tecnica incisoria nelle tavole delle Antichità Romane," 54, in *Giambattista Piranesi, Matrici incise 1756–1757*. I extend my deepest thanks to Giovanna Scaloni and to Ginevra Mariani, the project's director, for allowing me to see a number of the copperplates and first editions, and for sharing their knowledge, during my November 2016 visit to the Calcografia.

19. It is commonly accepted that he avoided cross-hatching because it would have kept him from taking so many impressions from his plates: he claimed to take as many as four thousand.

20. Andrew Robison, "Giovanni Battista Piranesi: Prolegomena to the Princeton Collection," *Princeton University Library Chronicle* 31, no. 3 (Spring 1970): 184–85.

21. See discussion of these signatures in 225n24 of J. G. Legrand's early biography, "Notice Historique sur la Vie et les Ouvrages de J. B. Piranesi Architecte, peintre et Graveur Né a Venise en 1720 Mort a Rome en 1778," reprinted as an appendix to Gilbert Erouart and Monique Mosser, "À propos de la 'Notice historique sur la vie et les ouvrages de J.-B. Piranesi': Origine et fortune d'une biographie," in *Piranèse et les français: Colloque tenu à la Villa Médicis, 12–13 mai 1976*, ed. Georges Brunel (Rome: Edizioni dell'Elefante, 1978), 221–52. I have also consulted the edition of Legrand in Raymond Lambert, *Piranèse, Les Prisons: Présentation par Marguerite Yourcenar; Suivi de la vie de Piranèse de Jacques-Guillaume Legrand* (Paris: L'insulaire, 1999). Mario Bevilacqua discusses the strengths and shortcomings of Legrand's biography and synthesizes the available facts from it with the testimony of others, including Piranesi's first biographer, the dismissive Giovanni Ludovico Bianconi, in Mario Bevilacqua, "The Young Piranesi: The Itineraries of His Formation," in Bevilacqua, Hyde Minor, and Barry, *The Serpent and the Stylus*, 13–53.

22. Nevola, *Giovanni Battista Piranesi*, 204, suggests that Piranesi joined the ranks of the Arcadians in the autumn of 1748. John Wilton-Ely suggests in *Piranesi* (London: Arts Council of Great Britain, 1978), 21, that Piranesi inserted the inscription referring to his election to the

Arcadians in place of the Giobbe dedication, but there are versions of the plate that include both the Arcadian affiliation/Salcindio Tiseio and the dedication, such as our figure 40. See Bevilacqua, "The Young Piranesi," in Bevilacqua, Hyde Minor, and Barry, *The Serpent and the Stylus*, 13–53, esp. 14.

23. My summary of Arcadian values here is taken from Liliana Barroero and Stefano Susinno, "Arcadian Rome, Universal Capital of the Arts," in *Art in Rome in the Eighteenth Century*, ed. Edgar Peters Bowron and Joseph J. Rishel (London: Merrell; Philadelphia: Philadelphia Museum of Art, 2000), 47–76.

24. Paolo Antonio Rolli, "Solitario bosco ombroso," in *Di canzonette e di cantate libri due di Paolo Rolli*, 3 vols. (London: Presso Tommaso Edlin, 1727), bk. 1, pp. 3–4 (although the title says "due libri," in fact the collection of lyrical canzonette and longer cantate is in three parts).

25. George E. Dorris, "Goethe, Rolli, and 'Solitario Bosco Ombroso,'" *Journal of the Rutgers University Libraries* 26, no. 2 (June 1963): 33–35. See also Dorris's *Paolo Rolli and the Italian Circle in London, 1715–1744* (The Hague: Mouton, 1967), 124–26.

26. Johann Wolfgang von Goethe, *Italian Journey, 1786–1788*, trans. W. H. Auden and Elizabeth Mayer (San Francisco: North Point, 1982), 116.

27. Dorris, "Goethe, Rolli," 35.

28. For a discussion of the tensions between neoclassical and baroque aesthetics in the literary and architectural productions of the Arcadians, see Sandro Benedetti, "L'architettura dell'Arcadia, Roma 1730," in *Bernardo Vittone e la disputa fra classicismo e barocco nel settecento, Convegno promosso dall'Accademia delle Scienze di Torino* (Turin: Academia delle Scienze, 1972), 337–91.

29. Piranesi, *Prima parte*, n.p.

30. This portion of the image also makes an imaginative homology between the triangle created on the left above and across the clothesline by a ladder leaning against a wall and its consequent shadow and the figures of the two women on the right appearing on either side of, and below, the line.

31. My thanks to John Pinto for his kind advice regarding this print and for sharing his photograph of the tomb itself. As Pinto notes, Piranesi has misidentified the tomb: it actually is the tomb of the Roman general and governor of Britain Quintus Veranius. Jeanne Morgan Zarucchi discusses many of the theories of Piranesi's figures in her essay "The Literary Tradition of *Ruins of Rome* and a New Consideration of Piranesi's Staffage Figures," *Journal for Eighteenth-Century Studies* 35, no. 3 (2012): 359–80. She believes that Piranesi's four plates marked "altra veduta" are characterized especially by "a markedly negative emotional message that emphasizes decay and corruption" (367). This is an intriguing observation regarding these four *vedute*, yet Piranesi often combines, as did the printmakers of the sixteenth century, members of various classes in what we might read as a "labor and leisure" contrast. For a discussion of Piranesi's figures as influenced by the commedia dell'arte, see Roseline Bacou, "À propos des dessins de figures de Piranèse," in Brunel, *Piranèse et les français*, 33–42.

32. William Beckford, *The Travel-Diaries of William Beckford of Font-Hill* (Boston: Houghton Mifflin, 1928), 1:192.

33. Goethe, *Italian Journey*, 156–57.

34. Tanya Cooper, "Forgetting Rome and the Voice of Piranesi's 'Speaking Ruins,'" in *The Art of Forgetting*, ed. Adrian Forty and Susanne Küchler (New York: Berg, 2001), 107–25.

35. I have quoted the unattributed translation in Dorothea Nyberg's presentation of the "Original Text of Prima Parte and English Translation," in *Giovanni Battista Piranesi: Drawings and Etchings at Columbia University; An Exhibition at Low Memorial Library, March 21–April 14, 1972* (New York: Columbia University, Avery Architectural Library, 1972), 115–18.

36. This print is the largest of at least three views of the Temple of the Sibyl at Tivoli in Piranesi's total oeuvre. I have used the version at 620 × 435 mm in the Calcografia in Rome. It is registered as Taschen #934 (Focillon 766 and Wilton-Ely 196).

37. Although *Desgodetz* is the most common spelling in the art history scholarship, the name is sometimes spelled *Desgodets*, including in the Virtual International Authority file, http://viaf.org/viaf/46785030/#Desgodets,_Antoine_Babuty,_1653-1728.

38. The first caption indicates sections of the sacred area of the temple from the side of the Teverone waterfall and the second a part or fragment of the imagined Temple of Albunea. In her concerted study of the tensions between ruins and modernity in eighteenth-century Italian literature, *Ruins Past: Modernity in Italy 1744–1836* (Oxford: Voltaire Foundation, 2015), Sabrina Ferri draws a connection between early eighteenth-century discoveries in geology and stratigraphy and Piranesi's attempts at "rendering an idea of temporal strata" (90). Carolyn Springer's earlier work, *The Marble Wilderness: Ruins and Representation in Italian Romanticism, 1775–1850* (Cambridge: Cambridge University Press, 2010), is an important contribution to our understanding of how Ugo Foscolo and other poets and writers of Italian Romanticism viewed ruins as a means of inspiration for Republican values. Foscolo's long poem of 1807, *Dei Sepolcri*, written in opposition to Napoleonic edicts restricting burial grounds, holds that the veneration of the grave sites of the past—from Homer contemplating the ruins of Troy to the tombs of Michelangelo and Galileo—is vital to cultural regeneration. For Foscolo, too, ruins were models for the future and not simply sites for melancholy reflection and elegy.

39. Andrea Palladio, *Four Books on Architecture*, trans. Robert Tavernor and Richard Schofield (Cambridge, MA: MIT Press, 1997), bk. 4, images of the Temple of Vesta at Tivoli, 303–6.

40. Susan Dixon, "The Sources and Fortunes of Piranesi's Archaeological Illustrations," *Art History* 25, no. 4 (September 2002): 472–73.

41. Antoine Desgodetz, *Les édifices antiques de Rome, dessinés et mesurés très-exactement par Antoine Desgodetz architecte* (Paris: Chez Jean Baptiste Coignard, 1682), preface, second page. The most far-ranging survey of the antecedents to (and followers of) Piranesi's ruins projects is John Pinto's "The Perspective of Janus," in Pinto, *Speaking Ruins*, 11–50.

42. Giovanni Battista Piranesi to Robert Mylne, November 11, 1760, RIBA Collections, Victoria and Albert Museum, London, MyFam/4/55, with an incomplete mid-nineteenth-century translation, MyFam/4/56. I thank Vicky Wilson, curator of this archive of the Royal Institute of British Architects, for her kind assistance.

43. Frank Salmon, *Building on Ruins: The Rediscovery of Rome and English Architecture* (Aldershot, UK: Ashgate, 2000), 35–39.

44. Salmon, *Building on Ruins*, 39.

45. James Stuart and Nicholas Revett, *The Antiquities of Athens*, vol. 1 (London: John Nichols, 1762).

46. Marc-Antoine Laugier, *Essai sur l'architecture* (Paris, 1753).

47. Julien-David Le Roy, *Les ruines des plus beaux monuments de la Grèce* (Paris, 1758).

48. Johann Winckelmann, *Gedanken über die Nachahmung der griechischen Werke in der Malerey und Bildhauerkunst* (Dresden, 1755), and *Anmerkungen über die Baukunst der Alten* (Leipzig, 1762).

49. "The Roman people loathe private luxury, but they love public splendor [publicam magnificentiam diligit]." Cicero, "Pro Murena" (section 76), in *In Catilinam 1–4. Pro Murena. Pro Sulla. Pro Flacco*, Loeb edition, trans. C. Macdonald (Cambridge, MA: Harvard University Press, 1976), 169–301, 282–83. We find a similar sentiment expressed in Alberti's *De re aedificatoria*: "When you erect a wall or portico of great elegance and adorn it with door, columns, or roof, good citizens approve and express joy for their own sake, as well as for yours,

because they realize that you have used your wealth to increase greatly not only your own honor and glory, but also that of your family, your descendants, and the whole city." In Leon Battista Alberti, *On the Art of Building in Ten Books*, trans. Joseph Rykwert, Neil Leach, and Robert Tavernor (Cambridge, MA: MIT Press, 1988), 4.

50. See the discussion of this plate in Cooper, "Forgetting Rome," 116–17.

51. Giovanni Battista Piranesi, "Opinions on Architecture: A Dialogue," in *Observations on the Letter of Monsieur Mariette with Opinions on Architecture, and a Preface to a New Treatise on the Introduction and Progress of the Fine Arts in Europe in Ancient Times*, trans. Caroline Beamish and David Britt (Los Angeles: Getty Research Institute, 2002), 106.

52. Wittkower suggests that the innovations Piranesi did introduce into the interior of the church—the elevation of the apse and the communion rail, the projection of the high altar into the transept, the ornament of sphinxes resting with front paws close to a rusticated tower (borrowed from the Rezzonico arms), and new variations of half-columns and pilasters— were designed to follow aspects of Venetian architecture with its scenographic techniques and to showcase Piranesi's disregard for an architecture of mere "structural logic." He relies on Werner Körte, "Giovanni Battista Piranesi als praktischer Architekt," *Zeitschrift für Kunstgeschichte* 2 (1933): 16ff., updating that research with the details available in an account book of the restoration found at mid-twentieth century and now in the Avery Library at Columbia University in New York City. Rudolf Wittkower, "Piranesi as Architect," in *Piranesi*, ed. Robert O. Parks (Northampton, MA: Smith College Museum of Art, 1961), 108.

53. Wittkower, "Piranesi as Architect," 108.

54. John Pinto discusses Piranesi's debts to Fischer von Erlach, Francesco Bianchini, and Juvarra for the development of this archaeological sensibility in *Speaking Ruins*, 43–50.

55. As we have seen, this genre of imaginary topographies was practiced in painting by Piranesi's mentor Tiepolo—in the 1740s and 1750s, Giovanni Paolo Panini had made *capricci* of Roman monuments. His amalgams of sites of ruins stand in contrast to his more careful, near ethnographic representation of contemporary scenes of Roman life in his own *vedute*. See David Mayernik, "The *Capricci* of Giovanni Paolo Panini," in *The Architectural Capriccio: Memory, Fantasy and Invention*, ed. Lucien Steil, 33–41 (Farnham, UK: Ashgate, 2014).

56. Bowron and Rishel, *Art in Rome in the Eighteenth Century*, 578–79, plate 422.

57. See Bowron and Rishel, *Art in Rome in the Eighteenth Century*, 588, plates 438 and 439. John Pinto has suggested that Piranesi's depiction of these foundations may owe something to the massive foundations that would have been supervised by Matteo Lucchesi. John Pinto, email correspondence with author, January 14 and 15, 2018.

58. Bent Sørensen, "Some Sources for Piranesi's Early Architectural Fantasies," *Burlington Magazine* 142, no. 1163 (February 2000): 89. He mentions François Perrier's *Icones et segmenta illustrium e marmore tabularum* of 1645, a book of prints made from studies of antique sculptures, Paolo Alessandro Maffei's *Raccolta di statue antiche e moderne* of 1704, a similar collection of impressions drafted from statues, and engravings by Girolamo Frezza, Francesco Aquila, Pietro Santi Bartoli, Jan de Bisschop, Giovanni Francesco Venturini, Robert van Audenaerd, Nicolas Dorigny, and especially Jean Le Pautre.

59. Beckford, *Travel-Diaries*, 1:189.

60. Goethe, *Italian Journey*, 116.

61. In the original: "Das Pyramide des Cestius ward für diesmal mit den Augen von außen begrüßt, und die Trümmer der Antoninischen oder Caracallischen Bäder, von denen uns Piranesi so manches Effektreiche vorgefabelt, konnten auch dem malerisch gewöhnten Auge in der Gegenwart kaum einige Zufriedenheit geben." Johann Wolfgang von Goethe, *Italienische Reise* (Hamburg: Christian Wegener Verlag, 1951), 452. This passage is one of several that are

not included in the Auden and Mayer translation, *Italian Journey*. The translators admit in their introduction that they have omitted anything that would have required "a lengthy note," and they justify the liberties they take by recounting the pastiche-like practice of Goethe's own assemblage of his letters, journals, and memories between thirty and forty years after his actual visits.

62. Manfredo Tafuri, "'The Wicked Architect,' G. B. Piranesi, Heterotopia, and the Voyage," in *The Sphere and the Labyrinth: Avant-Gardes and Architecture from Piranesi to the 1970s*, trans. Pellegrino d'Acierno and Robert Connolly (Cambridge, MA: MIT Press, 1987), 25–54, at 29.

63. Tafuri, "'Wicked Architect,' G. B. Piranesi," 28–30.

64. Legrand describes Piranesi's working methods in "Suivi de la vie de Piranèse par Jacques-Guillaume Legrand" (1799), in Lambert, *Piranèse, Les Prisons*, 113–14, 145. Heather Hyde Minor has provided a lively and insightful account of the day to day atmosphere of Piranesi's "bottega" in her study of Piranesi's writings, *Piranesi's Lost Words* (State College: Pennsylvania State University Press, 2015).

65. Piranesi's litany of complaints about the lack of patrons appears as early as his preface to the *Prima parte* and presages various difficulties and quarrels that he would have with Charlemont. John Wilton-Ely discusses the Charlemont debacle in his introduction to Giovanni Battista Piranesi, *Observations on the Letter of Monsieur Mariette* (Los Angeles: Getty Research Institute, 2002), 10. A more recent account can be found in Heather Hyde Minor, "Engraved in Porphyry, Printed on Paper: Piranesi and Lord Charlemont," in Bevilacqua, Minor, and Barry, *The Serpent and the Stylus*, 123–47.

Chapter Six

1. This muse is identified in an early version of the poem as "Fancy." For the textual history, including Dyer's first version of "Grongar Hill," see Garland Greever, "The Two Versions of 'Grongar Hill,'" *Journal of English and Germanic Philology* 16, no. 2 (April 1917): 274–81. Biographical details taken from Belinda Humfrey, "John Dyer," in *Oxford Dictionary of National Biography* (Oxford: Oxford University Press, [2004]), https://doi.org/10.1093/ref:odnb/8350.

2. All citations from Dyer's work are from John Dyer, *Poems* (London: J. Dodsley, 1770).

3. Quoted in John Fleming, *Robert Adam and His Circle in Edinburgh and Rome* (London: John Murray, 1962), 166. Fleming is quoting from Adam's letters in October 1755.

4. The inscription DIS MANIB—ROBERTI ADAM SCOT—ARCHITECTI—PRAESTANTISS—I.B.P.—FAC COERAVIT can be unpacked as follows: Dis Manibus (dedicated to the Manes/the dead, a common Roman inscription type used on tombstones)—Robert Adam Scot—Architect—Most Excellent—G. B. Piranesi—Fac[iundum] Coeravit (Undertook to have this built, a phrase likely borrowed from an inscription on one of the arches of the *pons Fabricius* connecting the city to the island in the Tiber). On the dedication page of the Campus Martius volume, Piranesi writes, in an only partially visible Latin inscription on a column fragment, that Adam is a celebrated British architect. These inscriptions seem both in-jokes and a means of implying that the ancients could proleptically memorialize their eighteenth-century admirers. Piranesi's relationship to Robert and James Adam is surveyed in John Wilton-Ely, "'Amazing and Ingenious Fancies': Piranesi and the Adam Brothers," in Bevilacqua, Hyde Minor, and Barry, *The Serpent and the Stylus*, 214–17. For biographical material, Wilton-Ely also relies on the dedicatee of his essay, John Fleming, and Fleming's *Robert Adam and His Circle*.

5. Citations from Robert Adam's letters and replies in this chapter come from the collection of Adam family correspondence in the Guild Hall Library, London: The Brothers Adam 1754–1807, "Business Documents" MSS 3070. The letters here are written to Messrs. Innes and Clerk, their financial agents in London.

6. A digital analysis of the histories of architects on the grand tour is available in Giovanna Cesarini et al., "British Travelers in Eighteenth-Century Italy: The Grand Tour and the Profession of Architecture," *American Historical Review* 122, no. 2 (April 2017): 425–50.

7. Harry F. Mallgrave, *Modern Architectural Theory: A Historical Survey, 1673–1968* (Cambridge: Cambridge University Press, 2005), 26.

8. Quoted in Roderick Graham, *Arbiter of Elegance: The Biography of Robert Adam* (Edinburgh: Birlinn, 2009), 219.

9. See the discussion in John Wilton-Ely's introduction to Piranesi, *Observations on the Letter of Monsieur Mariette*, 14–24.

10. Lesley Lawrence, "Stuart and Revett: Their Literary and Architectural Careers," *Journal of the Warburg Institute* 2, no. 2 (October 1938): 128–46, Chambers quotation at 137. Chambers's *Treatise* first appeared in 1759 and was reissued in several editions incorporating various materials from these early editions under slightly revised titles.

11. Giovanni Battista Piranesi, "Opinions on Architecture: A Dialogue," in Piranesi, *Observations*, 102–14, at 107–8.

12. Quoted in Lawrence, "Stuart and Revett," 134, 137.

13. Quoted in Salmon, *Building on Ruins*, 43.

14. Recounted in Lawrence, "Stuart and Revett," 130. Lawrence takes the latter anecdote from "An Account of the Extraordinary Escape of James Stewart Esq., commonly called Athenian Stewart, from being put to death by some Turks, in whose company he happened to be travelling. Communicated by Dr. Thomas Percy, Bishop of Dromore, as related to his Lordship by Stewart himself," *European Magazine*, November 1804, 369–70.

15. Wood, "To the Reader," in *Ruins of Palmyra*, b.

16. Robert Wood, *The Ruins of Balbec, otherwise Heliopolis in Coelosyria* (London, 1757), 4.

17. Wood, *Ruins of Palmyra*, a, 1.

18. Wood, *Ruins of Palmyra*, 2.

19. Wood, *Ruins of Balbec*, 1.

20. Robert Adam, *Ruins of the Palace of the Emperor Diocletian at Spalatro in Dalmatia* (London, 1764), 4.

21. Wood, *Ruins of Palmyra*, 33–34.

22. Wood, "To the Reader," in *Ruins of Palmyra*.

23. See vols. 55–57, Robert Adam drawings, Soane Museum, which contain Adam's work from the Roman period. We should note the use of the passive voice here. Robert Adam had a dubious habit of obscuring the contributions of others, and particularly the work of Clérisseau. He often uses only the first person for achievements that were collaborative, and even today it is up to connoisseurs to determine which of the drawings in Robert Adam's collections and publications are by Clérisseau—the consensus is most and no doubt the best of them. Adam's major work, his folio of the Palace of Diocletian at Spalatro (today's Split), has only the engraver's name on each plate, with no attribution for the draftsman. At the same time, Clérisseau's character has been perhaps immoderately celebrated in the historical record because J. J. Legrand, the biographer of Piranesi, was Clérisseau's son-in-law. See the account of these issues in Thomas J. McCormick, *Charles-Louis Clérisseau and the Genesis of Neo-Classicism* (Cambridge, MA: MIT Press, 1990), 23–98. A printed sample of the Adam Brothers drawings

from the period can be found in the catalog edited by A. A. Tait, *The Adam Brothers in Rome: Drawings from the Grand Tour* (London: Scala / Soane Museum, 2008).

24. This summary of drawing techniques relies on Salmon, *Building on Ruins*, 45, and my brief observations of the Adam albums at the Soane Museum in January 2013. I am grateful for the kind assistance of Stephen Astley during that visit.

25. Nagel and Wood, *Anachronic Renaissance*, 93.

26. Stuart and Revett, *Antiquities of Athens*, vol. 3, chap. 5, plate 1.

27. Stuart and Revett, *Antiquities of Athens*, vol. 3, 37.

28. Wilton-Ely, "Amazing and Ingenious Fancies," 225; Clérisseau's improving erasures are also discussed in Salmon, *Building on Ruins*, 43.

29. See John A. Pinto, "Diocletian's Palace and the Adam Style," in *Robert Adam and Diocletian's Palace in Split*, ed. Joško Belamarić and Ana Šverko (Zagreb: Institute of Art History, 2017), 357–69, in which Pinto, at 366, describes how Adam attempted to make "improvements" by changing dimensions of peristyle capitals and eliminating details. Nevertheless, Adam's folio itself now preserves otherwise vanished aspects of the city's Western Gate. See, in the same volume, Krasanka Majer Jurišić, "Adam's Print of the Western Gate of Diocletian's Palace: A Resource for the Study of the Communal Buildings of Split in the Eighteenth Century," 309–23.

30. See John Wilton-Ely's account of James's failed 1761 Parliament project in "Amazing and Ingenious Fancies," 232. James had not reached a level of mastery in drawing adequate to his ambition, and he relied on his associates from Rome—Clérisseau, Antonio Zucchi, and others—to make the presentation drawings.

31. Drawings of the orders—the Scottish order by James himself, the British order in a presentation drawing by Zucchi—can be seen in Tait, *Adam Brothers in Rome*, 135, 138.

32. Piranesi, "Opinions on Architecture," 110–11.

33. William Hamilton to [Giovanni Battista] Piranesi, October 3, 1767, record ID 105361, accession no. MA 321.49, Pierpont Morgan Library, New York. Citation here is from Wilton-Ely, "Amazing and Ingenious Fancies," 233n54, where Wilton-Ely also discusses this period of exchange between Piranesi and the Adam brothers (232–34). The folio was published in 1769, yet the letter is dated two years before—Piranesi must have sent unbound sheets.

34. Robert seems to have convinced Clérisseau to tutor him in drawing and accompany him on his sketching excursions from this moment forward. Later Clérisseau would accompany James on his own grand tour. Robert believed that Clérisseau had held back some of his own drawings for his own profit. See McCormick, *Charles-Louis Clérisseau*, 71–74. Within a few years the Adam family seems to have been financing Clérisseau's assistance. The Guildhall records of the Adam family business include a letter from Edinburgh on December 14, 1757: "There is a French gentleman whose name is Charles Lewis Clerrisseau [*sic*] who has been along with our R.A. [Robert Adam] ever since he went abroad. We have agreed with him to transact some affairs for us in Italy, for which trouble he may have an occasion to value on us frequently for some time . . . monthly."

35. It is intriguing to find a character reference to Father Jacquier in Goethe's *Italian Journey*, in an entry from January 1787: "Some days ago I visited a Franciscan called Father Jacquier who lives on the Trinità dei Monti. He is a Frenchman by birth and well-known for his books on mathematics. He is very old, but very nice and sympathetic. He has known many eminent men in his time and even spent some months with Voltaire, who grew very fond of him" (155).

36. McCormick, *Charles-Louis Clérisseau*, 103–12. The room is rarely available to visitors and even more rarely is photography allowed, which makes the Boscaro study all the more useful. Cristian Boscaro, "Rilievo metrico e cromatico della Stanza delle Rovine nel Convento della Trinità dei Monti a Roma," in *Prospettive architettoniche conservazione digitale, divulgazione e*

studio, vol. 2, ed. Graziano Mario Valenti (Rome: Sapienza Università Editrice, 2016), 361–74. I am deeply grateful to Andrea Jemolo Archivio for granting me permission to use their striking photograph of the room in and on this volume.

37. *Adam Brothers in Rome*, 64. On the same page, the catalog includes a discussion of Robert's harebrained scheme for rebuilding Lisbon after the earthquake of 1755, noting that his grandiose ideas "had the advantage of Clerisseau's [*sic*] assistance and council." Adam made a small ink plan and provided a bird's-eye perspective, annotated in French, and that was the extent of his intervention.

38. McCormick, in *Charles-Louis Clérisseau*, 64, indicates that Francesco Bartolozzi was hired to insert figures into Clérisseau's drawings of Diocletian's palace. If so, one wonders whether this disabled person may have been intended to appear in the Temple of Aesculapius, where he would have been seeking healing.

39. Denis Diderot, *Diderot on Art*, vol. 2, *The Salon of 1767*, ed. and trans. by John Goodman (New Haven, CT: Yale University Press, 1995), 217.

40. Goethe, *Italian Journey*, 120–21.

41. See David Karmon, "A Sixteenth-Century Meteor in the Roman Forum," in Karmon, *Ruin of the Eternal City*, 77–116.

42. Leon Battista Alberti, *Leon Battista Alberti's Delineation of the City of Rome*, ed. Mario Carpo and Francesco Furlan, trans. Peter Hicks (Tempe: Arizona Center for Medieval and Renaissance Studies, 2007). The "delineation" is not a map or diagram but an ingenious device: a circle (horizon) and within it, a revolving spoke (radius). Alberti chose 175 sites either within Rome or along its walls; each site is identified by an angle to be read on the circle and a distance from the center to be read on the spoke. Coordinating the locations on the circle and spoke produces a point that then can be both located and joined to other sites, hence giving some sense as well of the path of the walls and the Tiber. Anyone who wants to use the device can determine the scale of his or her delineation by adjusting the size of the circle.

43. The Adam works can be seen in McCormick, *Charles-Louis Clérisseau*, 48–49; the Clérisseau works on p. 143 and 149 respectively. Clérisseau's "Architectural Fantasy" is at the Hermitage; his other works listed here are at the Soane Museum.

44. John D. Bandiera, "Form and Meaning in Hubert Robert's Ruin Caprices: Four Paintings of Fictive Ruins for the Château de Méréville," *Art Institute of Chicago Museum Studies* 15, no. 1 (1989): 20–37, 82–85. In a richly detailed and considered recent book, Nina Dubin explores the relations between Robert's paintings on ruin and disaster and the climate of financial chaos in late eighteenth-century France. She links Robert's concern with not only Roman but also contemporary and imaginary ruins to the problems speculation poses to "futures" of all kinds. Nina Dubin, *Futures and Ruins: Eighteenth-Century Paris and the Art of Hubert Robert* (Los Angeles: Getty Research Institute, 2010).

45. Constantin-François de Chassebœuf was named a count by Napoleon and invented the name "Volney" for himself as an amalgamation of "Voltaire" and "Ferney."

46. Volney, *The Ruins; or, A Survey of the Revolutions of Empires*, trans. James Marshall, with an intro. by Jonathan Wordsworth (1811; repr., West Yorkshire, UK: Orley, 2000), 2. Although this volume translates Volney's title as "a survey of the revolutions of empires" the French title more accurately reflects the contents of the book as "meditations on the revolutions of empires."

47. Volney, *Ruins*, 7–8. Volney's vision of a belated visitor looking at ruins on the banks of the Thames was manifested in Gustave Doré's well-known 1872 engraving of a visitor from New Zealand contemplating the ruins of Saint Paul's Cathedral. We remember, too, that Volney's text was, in translation, a book from which Mary Shelley's monster Frankenstein learns English and obtains a sense of human history.

48. Volney, *Ruins*, 186.

49. See A. Gobert, "Franklin et Volney," *French Review* 9, no. 5 (April 1936): 391–403.

50. Diderot, *Diderot on Art*, 2:217.

51. In the same period Robert produced another, smaller, painting of the Louvre in ruins which was for a time at Tsarskoy Seloe, the tsar's summer palace outside Saint Petersburg, and now is held by the Louvre. In this version, the building is depicted in an even more advanced state of decay: a few amorphous figures of seated women in what seems to be contemporary dress and a distant vague figure of a watchman are all that are left of the figures that had staffed the 1796 pendant image. Significantly, the work also is much smaller. Dubin, *Futures and Ruins*, 175, argues that this sketch-like version of the Louvre in ruins is from 1798–1799, while the Louvre's online database says "about 1796." John Bandiera, in "Form and Meaning," 36, gives 1786 as the date of this painting without explanation. Dubin's argument that Robert's view is late—and consequently shows further "decay" of the elements in this imaginary scene—is convincing and raises suggestive questions about the degree of "finish" or polish in the depiction of ruined matter. At the same time, the vague figures and use of smoke, the generic fragments scattered about the foreground, link this painting, too, to the influences on Robert during his sojourn in Rome: Giovanni Paolo Panini and Piranesi above all.

52. Quoted in Brian Lukacher, *Joseph Gandy: An Architectural Visionary in Georgian England* (London: Thames and Hudson, 2006), 30–31. Lukacher quotes from Gandy's letters in a manuscript volume called "The Gandy Green Book" that has now disappeared. Typed transcripts of the book can be found in the libraries of the Soane Museum and in the Drawings Collection of the Royal Institute of British Architects. All discussion of Gandy here is drawn from Lukacher's study.

53. Antoine-Chrysostome Quatremère De Quincy, "Première Lettre," in *Lettres à Miranda sur le déplacement des monuments de l'art de l'Italie* (Paris: Éditions Macula, 1989), 87.

54. His only realized works were his offices for the now-destroyed Phoenix Fire and Pelican Life Insurance Offices in London, Doric House in Bath, and the remodeling of Swerford Park house in Oxfordshire. Ever loyal to his firsthand experiences of classical architecture, he nevertheless found himself caught up in a Gothic revival upon his return to England.

55. See the discussion in Lukacher, *Joseph Gandy*, 162–64.

56. Cited in Lukacher, *Joseph Gandy*, 165.

57. See Salmon, *Building on Ruins*, 54.

58. Gordon, *Byron's Poetry and Prose*, 82–84.

59. Gordon, *Byron's Poetry and Prose*, 82–84.

60. Dyer, *Poems*, 36–37.

61. Henry Home, Lord Kames, *Elements of Criticism* (London: A. Millar; Edinburgh: A. Kincaid and Bell, 1762), 3:313. For the Home–Adam friendship, see Fleming, *Robert Adam and His Circle*, 307–12.

62. Goethe, *Italian Journey*, 434–35.

63. That is, a house in the form of a ruin. Paolo Clini and Riccardo Gulli, *Il San Giovanni di Girolamo Genga: Codici e strumenti per la conservazione* (Florence: Alinea, 2008), 26.

64. Geoffrey Beard, *The Work of John Vanbrugh* (New York: Universe/Rizzoli, 1986), 37–50.

65. Batty Langley, *New Principles of Gardening; or, The Laying Out and Planting Parterres, Groves, Wildernesses, Labyrinths, Avenues, Parks, &c., After a More Grand and Rural Manner* (London: A. Bettesworth and J. Batley; J. Pemberton et al., 1728), xv.

66. These works are surveyed in the Soane Museum catalog *Visions of Ruin: Architectural Fantasies and Designs for Garden Follies* (London: Soane Museum, 1999). See also the discussion of ruins in English gardens in John Dixon Hunt, "Picturesque Mirrors and the Ruins of the Past," in *Gardens and the Picturesque* (Cambridge, MA: MIT Press, 1992), 171–92.

67. See Diana Ketcham, *Le Désert de Retz: A Late Eighteenth-Century French Folly Garden, the Artful Landscape of Monsieur de Monville* (Cambridge, MA: MIT Press, 1997), 2–3. Information in the discussion here also comes from my notes of a formal tour of the site in spring 2014. Ketcham helpfully explores the many precedents for the forms Monville chose (18) and surveys theories of the park's meaning, particularly a theory that it represents the progress of a Masonic ritual, and authorship—that not Monville, but rather Hubert Robert or Étienne-Louis Boullée or another contemporary architect or painter or garden designer was behind the plans for the "fabriques" and their placement.

68. John Pinto points out that, figuring a modular height of eight diameters, the column actualized would have reached a height of four hundred feet (email correspondence with the author, January 14, 2018). Intended as a truncated form, it is perhaps even more gigantic by not being realized.

69. Ketcham, *Le Désert de Retz*, 16.

70. Ketcham, *Le Désert de Retz*, 1–2.

Chapter Seven

1. Alberti, *On Painting*. He adds, "I certainly censure such men." He also warns of the dangers of the overwrought: "But it is best to avoid the vitiating effect of those who wish to eliminate every weakness and make everything too polished. In their hands the work becomes old and squeezed dry before it is finished" (97).

2. For a survey of aesthetic attitudes toward the *non finito*, from Pliny to the present, see the essays in Kelly Baum, Andrea Bayer, and Sheena Wagstaff, eds., *Unfinished: Thoughts Made Visible* (New York: Metropolitan Museum of Art, 2016). The early uses of the particular term are discussed on p. 14, but the concept arises throughout, and Carmen C. Bambach provides a useful essay on Michelangelo and Leonardo, 30–41; Andrea Bayer on Renaissance approaches to the unfinished in general, 18–29. My own essay on the unfinished in literature, 140–47, has been adapted for this chapter.

3. Kant, *Critique*, 101–4.

4. For example, Percy asked both Thomas Warton and Lord Hailes to finish the ballad "The Child of Elle." See Percy–Warton Correspondence, 1761–1765, no. 42560, folio 121, and Percy–Hailes Correspondence, 1762–1783, no. 32337, folio 25, both in British Library, London. He also asked Warton to finish "The Squire's Tale of Chaucer"; see Percy–Warton Correspondence, 1761–1775, no. 42560, folio 97, British Library. I discuss many of the ways that ballads were "distressed" or intentionally antiquated "antiques" in the period in Susan Stewart, "Notes on Distressed Genres," in *Crimes of Writing: Problems in the Containment of Representation* (Durham, NC: Duke University Press, 1994), 66–101.

5. Homer, *Homer: The Iliad*, 2nd ed., ed. Michael Silk (Cambridge: Cambridge University Press, 2004), 6. Martin West, *Studies in the Text and Transmission of the Iliad* (Munich: K. G. Saur, 2001), 8, mentions that the poem was copied "thousands of times" by ancient and medieval hands. For "Barbara Allen," see Arthur Kyle David Jr., ed., *Traditional Ballads of Virginia, Collected under the Auspices of the Virginia Folk-Lore Society* (Cambridge, MA: Harvard University Press, 1929), 629.

6. F. J. Miller, "Evidences of Incompleteness in the *Aeneid* of Virgil," *Classical Journal* 4, no. 8 (June 1909): 341–55. See also James J. O'Hara, "The Unfinished *Aeneid*?," in *A Companion to Vergil's "Aeneid" and Its Tradition*, ed. Joseph Farrell and Michael C. J. Putnam (Chichester, UK: Wiley-Blackwell, 2014), 96–106.

7. R. M. Cummings, ed., *Edmund Spenser: The Critical Heritage* (London: Routledge, 1996), 120.

8. Derek Pearsall, ed., *Chaucer: The Canterbury Tales* (London: Routledge, 1985), 8.

9.   For a recent translation of Michelangelo's sonnets, see Michelangelo Buonarroti, *Complete Poems of Michelangelo*, trans. John Frederick Nims (Chicago: University of Chicago Press, 2000).

10. Shakespeare, "Sonnet 55," in *Complete Sonnets and Poems*, 439.

11. Gilpin, "On Picturesque Beauty," 21–22.

12. Jane K. Brown, "Faust," in *The Cambridge Companion to Goethe*, ed. Lesley Sharpe (Cambridge: Cambridge University Press, 2002), 89.

13. We might note that such theories were precursors to what would become, in the nineteenth century, an era of speculative systems. Charles Darwin, G. F. Hegel, and Karl Marx constructed theories that offered open, ever-evolving and unfinished visions of human physical, spiritual, and material development. A fourth great theorist, Sigmund Freud, posed in contrast a restricted economy of psychological drives, where the repression of one element would lead to the efflorescence of a corresponding element. Even so, the actual process of psychoanalysis suggested a never-ending hermeneusis of both conscious and unconscious experiences.

14. William Gilpin, "On Picturesque Travel," in *Three Essays*.

15. In *Fracture and Fragmentation in British Romanticism* (Cambridge: Cambridge University Press, 2010), Alexander Regier ably summarizes recent debates regarding the literary fragment, contrasting critics who consider the fragment to be a genre, often linked to themes of ruin, and those who join him in centering their concerns upon fragmentation as a process of composition or making (24–25). Marjorie Levinson's influential 1986 book, *The Romantic Fragment Poem*, offers a typology of fragment works based in how more or less severed the work was from its context of production and the degree to which the work was dependent on a knowledge of other works, including works by the fragment's author. Marjorie Levinson, *The Romantic Fragment Poem* (Chapel Hill: University of North Carolina Press, 1986), 49–50. Although Levinson holds that the British fragment poem was distinct from traditions of German aesthetics, her definition of a "true fragment" as a work that requires the reader to supply the entire context of the work actually is quite close to Friedrich Schlegel's famous aphorism: "A fragment, like a miniature work of art, has to be entirely isolated from the world and complete in itself like a porcupine." Friedrich Schlegel, *Athenaeumsfragment* 206, in *Philosophical Fragments*, trans. Peter Firchow (Minneapolis: University of Minnesota Press, 1991), xii. Regier's work, with its interest in fracture and fragmentation as Romantic modes extending to the literary criticism of the late twentieth century, is substantially influenced by Philippe Lacoue-Labarthe and Jean-Luc Nancy's study of the collapse of self-presence and self-unity in Jena school aesthetics and post-Kantianism in general: Philippe Lacoue-Labarthe and Jean-Luc Nancy, *The Literary Absolute*, trans. Philip Barnard and Cheryl Lester (Albany: State University of New York Press, 1988). Two particularly useful books linking architectural and literary ruin and fragmentation are Elizabeth Harries's study of eighteenth-century British culture, *The Unfinished Manner: Essays on the Fragment in the Later Eighteenth Century* (Charlottesville: University of Virginia Press, 1994), and Robert Harbison's recent far-ranging study of aesthetic practices of fragmentation from ancient mosaics to cubism and experimental modernism, *Ruins and Fragments*.

16. See Thora Brylowe, "Of Gothic Architects and Grecian Rods: William Blake, Antiquarianism and the History of Art," *Romanticism* 18, no. 1 (2012): 93. My account here of Blake's early schooling and preference for popular over classical antiquarian traditions is taken from this study (89–95). See also Morris Eaves, *The Counter-Arts Conspiracy: Art and Industry in the Age of Blake* (Ithaca, NY: Cornell University Press, 1992); and an earlier essay by Eaves, "Blake and the Artistic Machine: An Essay in Decorum and Technology," *PMLA* 92 (1977): 903–

27, which explains Blake's equal repugnance toward mechanistic techniques of drawing and printing as they developed in the period.

17. Here, during a period when British war preparations against France were in full force, Blake introduces as well the figure of Shiloh as representative of French peace and liberty. Chapter 1, "War Unchained," of David Erdman's *Blake: Prophet against Empire* (Princeton, NJ: Princeton University Press, 1977), 3–19, and the discussion of Shiloh on pp. 309–13 remain the best guides to these issues. Blake's preceding poem *The Four Zoas* describes in Night 1 the breakdown of peace negotiations between Britain and France and Shiloh and Jerusalem in ruins.

18. Blake, *Complete Poetry and Prose*, chap. 3, plate 60: line 48, p. 211.

19. Blake, "Jerusalem," in *Complete Poetry and Prose*, plates 60–61, pp. 209–12.

20. Blake, *Complete Poetry and Prose*, 705.

21. Harold Bloom, "Commentary," in Blake, *Complete Poetry and Prose*, 931. The word *spectre* has a particular meaning in Blake's cosmology, signifying the mental image as opposed to the created manifestation of the Emanation.

22. Blake, "Jerusalem," in *Complete Poetry and Prose*, "Jerusalem," plate 98, p. 258.

23. Blake, "Jerusalem," in *Complete Poetry and Prose*, plate 27, p. 171.

24. Blake, "Jerusalem," in *Complete Poetry and Prose*, plate 43, p. 191.

25. W. J. T. Mitchell, *Blake's Composite Art: A Study of the Illuminated Poetry* (Princeton, NJ: Princeton University Press, 1978), 215. More recently Saree Makdisi has made a compelling case that the "open" quality of the relation between text and image in Blake's work, and between the plates themselves, speaks to Blake's desire to "rouze" us from our habits of production and reception. He writes, "For Blake developed a mode of production that necessarily produced heterogeneous products at precisely the historical moment when manufacturers— not just those in the art world—were seizing on the potential offered by another mode of production that would ultimately reorient not only the ways in which people work but the entire cultural and political organization of societies all over the world in order to spew out a stream of identical [as Blake called them] 'Good for Nothing Commodit[ies].'" Saree Makdisi, "The Political Aesthetic of Blake's Images," in *The Cambridge Companion to William Blake*, ed. Morris Eaves (Cambridge: Cambridge University Press, 2003), 130–31. See as well the discussion of Blake's *Jerusalem* in light of an English ruins poem tradition concerned with the fate of the nation and nationalism in Janowitz, *England's Ruins*, 145–76. Janowitz distinguishes between what she finds to be an "active" sublime state of ruin, such as we find in Blake, and a landscape ruin characterized by "inertia," found in the picturesque, adding, "This [distinction] runs parallel to the distinction between the apparent naturalness and therefore permanence of the picturesque ruin and the transience of Blake's urban ruins. The nation in *Jerusalem* is in a state of continual fallings-apart and recoveries. Demolishing and creating are the twin labors of Los: 'In fears / He built it, in rage & in fury. It is the Spiritual Fourfold / London, continually building & continually decaying desolate'" (153).

26. Geoffrey Hartman, "Wordsworth, Inscriptions, and Romantic Nature Poetry," in *Beyond Formalism: Literary Essays 1958–1970* (New Haven, CT: Yale University Press, 1970), 206–30.

27. I have relied on the relevant volumes of the Cornell Wordsworth: William Wordsworth, *"The Ruined Cottage" and "The Pedlar,"* ed. James A Butler (Ithaca, NY: Cornell University Press, 1979); William Wordsworth, *The Salisbury Plain Poems of William Wordsworth*, ed. Stephen Gill (Ithaca, NY: Cornell University Press, 1975); and, for "Michael" and "Tintern Abbey," William Wordsworth, *Lyrical Ballads and Other Poems, 1797–1800*, ed. James Butler and Karen Green (Ithaca, NY: Cornell University Press, 1992).

28. William Wordsworth, *Early Poems and Fragments, 1785–1797*, ed. Carol Landon and Jared Curtis (Ithaca, NY: Cornell University Press, 1997), 426.

29. William Wordsworth, "Incipient Madness," fragment from *"The Ruined Cottage" and "The Pedlar,"* 468. For a pioneering psychoanalytic reading of the fragment, see Mary Jacobus, "The Ordinary Sky: Wordsworth, Blanchot, and the Writing of Disaster," in the web-based journal *Romantic Circles* (2008): https://www.rc.umd.edu/praxis/psychoanalysis/jacobus /jacobus.html.

30. Goethe, *Conversations with Eckermann* (Cambridge, MA: Da Capo Press, 1998), 46–47.

31. John Denham, *Cooper's Hill* (London, 1643), 5.

32. Thomas Warton [the Younger], *Poems: A New Edition* (London: T. Becket, 1777), 31–35.

33. William Wordsworth, *The Borderers*, ed. Robert Osborn (Ithaca, NY: Cornell University Press, 1982), 83.

34. Mary Moorman, *William Wordsworth: The Early Years* (1957; repr., Oxford: Oxford University Press, 1968), 402–3.

35. David Bromwich, "The French Revolution and 'Tintern Abbey,'" in *Disowned by Memory: Wordsworth's Poetry of the 1790s* (Chicago: University of Chicago Press, 2000), 69–91; Nicholas Roe, "The Politics of the Wye Valley: Re-placing 'Tintern Abbey,'" in *The Politics of Nature: Wordsworth and Some Contemporaries* (London: Palgrave Macmillan, 1992), 117–36. Other scholars have underscored the poem's expression of William Wordsworth's dislike of cities, his conversion from an early pantheistic nature worship to philosophy, and the complexities of his relationship with Dorothy. See, for example, Stephen Gill, "The Philosophic Poet," in *The Cambridge Companion to Wordsworth*, ed. Stephen Gill (Cambridge: Cambridge University Press, 2003), 142–59; and David Simpson, *Wordsworth's Historical Imagination* (New York: Routledge, 1987), 109–13.

36. William Gilpin, *Observations on the River Wye*, 2nd ed. (London: Blamire, 1789), 50–52.

37. See Marjorie Levinson, "Insight and Oversight: Reading 'Tintern Abbey,'" in *Wordsworth's Great Period Poems* (Cambridge: Cambridge University Press, 1986), 14–57. Levinson's argument is not simply that Wordsworth has an obligation to represent what is difficult or unpleasant to a picturesque sensibility in the actual scene; she contends that much of the power of his great meditative poems comes from the suppression of reality in this fashion. For considered critiques of this approach, see Bromwich, "French Revolution," 75; and David Ferry, review of *Wordsworth's Great Period Poems*, by Marjorie Levinson, *Studies in Romanticism* 30, no. 1 (Spring 1991): 113–20.

38. William Gilpin, *An Essay on Prints* (London: J. Robson, 1768).

39. See the discussion of Wordsworth's "rebellion against engravings" in his later work in Peter Simonsen, *Wordsworth and Word-Preserving Arts: Typographic Inscription, Ekphrasis and Posterity in the Later Work* (Basingstoke, UK: Palgrave Macmillan, 2007), esp. 21–25.

40. William Wordsworth, "Tintern Abbey," in *Lyrical Ballads*, 116–17.

41. "On Nature's Invitation Do I Come" can be read as a single poem in *The Poetical Works of William Wordsworth*, ed. William Knight (London: MacMillan, 1896), 2:118–19. The star images appear on page 119, lines 40 and 43. For the incorporation of these lines into "The Recluse," see William Wordsworth, *Home at Grasmere*, ed. Beth Darlington (Ithaca, NY: Cornell University Press, 1977), 43–47, where the poem is at lines 71–97 and 100–125.

42. Gilpin, *Essay on Prints*, 17–18.

43. James Thomson, *Winter, a Poem* (London, 1730), 23, emphasis added.

44. Warton, *Poems*, 35.

45. William Wordsworth, *"The Ruined Cottage" and "The Pedlar,"* 42.

46. William Wordsworth, *"The Ruined Cottage" and "The Pedlar,"* 42–44.

47. Simon Jarvis, "Wordsworth and Idolatry," *Studies in Romanticism* 38, no. 1 (Spring 1999): 3–27, suggests that Margaret's husband Robert's whittling and toy making and the pedlar's pow-

ers of suffusing his world with meanings he shares only with God are yoked to Wordsworth's engagement with theological doctrines of iconoclasm and critiques of idolatry—doctrines and critiques which Jarvis effectively shows continue to have an impact on contemporary Wordsworth studies as materialist critics aim to demystify the "Romantic ideology."

48. Robert Southey, "English Eclogues," in *Joan of Arc, Ballads, Lyrics, and Minor Poems* (London, 1857), 242–43.

49. James Averill, *Wordsworth and the Poetry of Human Suffering* (Ithaca, NY: Cornell University Press, 1980). Quentin Bailey, *Wordsworth's Vagrants: Police, Prisons, and Poetry in the 1790s* (Farnham, UK: Ashgate, 2011). Averill discusses the tragic trajectory of many of Wordsworth's poems, and his thoughts on "Hart-leap Well" emphasize that Wordsworth's ruined structures (here "The Pleasure-house is dust:—behind, before" until Nature returns with her beauty and bloom) acquire importance because of the stories attached to them (221). Bailey's rigorously historical study gives us insight into the law's role in the ruination of persons.

50. W. Wordsworth, *"The Ruined Cottage" and "The Pedlar,"* 72.

51. W. Wordsworth, *Salisbury Plain Poems*, 145.

52. The B version of the poem has simply "of Nature with our restless thoughts?," in Wordsworth, *"The Ruined Cottage" and "The Pedlar,"* 57.

53. W. Wordsworth, *"The Ruined Cottage" and "The Pedlar,"* 58.

54. W. Wordsworth, *"The Ruined Cottage" and "The Pedlar,"* 75.

55. W. Wordsworth, *Lyrical Ballads*, 253.

56. W. Wordsworth, *Lyrical Ballads*, 257.

57. W. Wordsworth, *Lyrical Ballads*, 259.

58. W. Wordsworth, *Lyrical Ballads*, 256–57.

59. Giotto had shown two scenes from this story: the first depicts Joachim among the shepherds when his sacrifice has been denied, the second Joachim's withdrawal to the sheepfold and his dream. See Jules Lubbock, *Storytelling in Christian Art from Giotto to Donatello* (New Haven, CT: Yale University Press, 2006), 50.

60. Geoffrey Hartman, *Wordsworth's Poetry, 1787–1814* (New Haven, CT: Yale University Press, 1964), xvii.

61. To summarize Johnston's findings: The first drafts of *The Recluse* are simultaneous to the completion of the two-part *Prelude* of 1799; part 1, book 1 of *The Recluse*, "Home at Grasmere" is drafted in 1800–1801, with the thirteen-book *Prelude* completed in 1805 and "Home at Grasmere" resumed in 1806. In 1808 Wordsworth returns to *The Recluse* with "The Tuft of Primroses," and in 1809 he begins "The Excursion" with the story of the Solitary, working on it until 1812 and then, for the next two years, he completes the five books devoted to the Pastor, books 5–9. Kenneth Johnston, "Wordsworth and 'The Recluse,'" in Gill, *Cambridge Companion to Wordsworth*, 70–89.

62. Dorothy Wordsworth, *Journals* (London: Macmillan, 1904), 1:57.

63. W. Wordsworth, *Lyrical Ballads*, 268.

Chapter Eight

1. Percy Shelley, "Ozymandias," in *The Complete Poetry of Percy Bysshe Shelley*, vol. 3, ed. Donald Reiman, Neil Fraistat, and Nora Crook (Baltimore: Johns Hopkins University Press, 2012), 326–27. I have transcribed here the 1811 published version; the fair copy MS has several slight variations.

2. Throughout this discussion of "The Waste Land," I have relied upon Lawrence Rainey's authoritative *The Annotated Waste Land with Eliot's Contemporary Prose*, 2nd ed. (New Haven,

CT: Yale University Press, 2005). Rainey works with the final (but first produced) version of the poem with notes, published by Boni and Liveright in December 1922. Earlier drafts (in a not completely reliable account of their chronological order—see *Annotated Waste Land*, 17–18) and Pound's emendations are published in T. S. Eliot, *The Waste Land: A Facsimile and Transcript of the Original Drafts Including the Annotations of Ezra Pound*, ed. Valerie Eliot (London: Faber and Faber; New York: Harcourt, Brace, 1971).

3.   Eliot, *Annotated Waste Land*, 70.

4.   Eliot, *Annotated Waste Land*, 71.

5.   Jessie L. Weston, *From Ritual to Romance* (Cambridge: Cambridge University Press, 1920).

6.   Eliot, *Annotated Waste Land*, 30, 38.

7.   Eliot, *Annotated Waste Land*, 58.

8.   Eliot, *Annotated Waste Land*, 57, 58, 60, 64, 67.

9.   Eliot, *Annotated Waste Land*, 206n16.

10. The poem as well alludes to the legend of Amyclae (or Amyklai). This town, described by Pausanias, was associated with the myth of Apollo and Hyacinth and perished from its own mandate of silence: after several false alarms, the people vowed not to report the approach of enemies and so were successfully surprised by their attacking neighbors, the Spartans. Pausanias, *Guide to Greece*, 2:63–69. Pausanias goes into detail about the images carved there on the throne of Apollo, and the Apollo/Hyacinth allusions, but does not mention the legend regarding the town's silence. The legend is recorded, however, in the late fourth- or early fifth-century Virgil commentary of Marus Servius Honoratus, who records the proverb TACITIS REGNAVIT AMYCLIS (silence ruled Amyclae). Virgil, *Aeneid*, ed. T. E. Page (London: Macmillan, 1900), 336n564.

11. Eliot, *Annotated Waste Land*, 69, 70, 74.

12. Horace, *Odes*, 255.

13. Shakespeare, "Sonnet 55," 439.

14. Claire Colomb, *Staging the New Berlin: Place Marketing and the Politics of Urban Reinvention Post-1989* (New York: Routledge, 2013), 210.

15. For an astute summary of the Nazi relation to ruins, and Speer's "theory," see Julia Hell, "Imperial Ruin Gazers, or Why Did Scipio Weep?," in Hell and Schönle, *Ruins of Modernity*, 184–88. Hell discusses the long legacy of imperial fascination with ruins, from the Roman preoccupation with the story of Troy and the erasure of Carthage to the "neo-Roman" frames of the Hapsburg conquests and twentieth-century fascism in her new study, *Conquest of Ruins*. In addition to the survey of the triumphs of Charles V after his victory at Tunis cited earlier, Hell's work brings forward the role of imitation in empire building and colonial practices, not only in Europe but also in the South Pacific and Latin America. She follows the imperial ruins theme into strands of twentieth-century political thought, including the work of Hannah Arendt, Carl Schmitt, and Martin Heidegger. For a useful summary of Arendt's insights into natality as a remedy for ruin, and for the tradition of ruins discourse running from doctrines of original sin to Kierkegaardian despair to Heidegger on *ruinanz* and Walter Benjamin's notion of progress as a catastrophe, see Susannah Young-ah Gottlieb, *Regions of Sorrow: Anxiety and Messianism in Hannah Arendt and W. H. Auden* (Stanford, CA: Stanford University Press, 2003), 136–37.

16. Lucia Allais's just-published *Designs of Destruction: The Making of Monuments in the Twentieth Century* (Chicago: University of Chicago Press, 2018) underscores the complexity of this homology. In this deeply researched study of twentieth-century monument policies, from the League of Nations to UNESCO's World Heritage sites, she traces the many paradoxical (and often accidental) ways that monuments survived the devastation of world wars, becoming

alike sites of significance, crude profit, and aesthetic experimentation. Allais reveals how a web of practices—bureaucracy, paperwork, diplomacy, tourism, techniques of "conservation" via damage and alteration, and, more recently, the sentimental "packaging" provided by new media—determined, and continues to determine, the fate of structures and designations of their "monumental" status. She specifically discusses the place of ruination in UNESCO policies of the 1960s into the mid-1970s, noting that ruin is not merely an "imperial effect" of the abandonment of colonized peoples. Instead, she demonstrates, "even as ruins, architectural monuments in the post-colony functioned as instruments of culturalization" (216).

Works Cited

Abraham, Herbert. *Asphalts and Allied Substances*. Princeton, NJ: D. Van Nostrand, 1960.

Adam, Robert. *Ruins of the Palace of the Emperor Diocletian at Spalatro in Dalmatia*. London, 1764.

Adler, Cyrus, and Isidore Singer, eds. *Jewish Encyclopedia*. 12 vols. New York: Funk and Wagnalls, 1906.

Agamben, Giorgio. *Nymphs*. Translated by Amanda Minervini. London: Seagull Books, 2013. Translation of *Ninfe*. Turin: Bollati Boringhieri Editore, 2007. Page references are to the 2013 edition.

Ainsworth, Maryan W. "Introduction: Jan Gossart, the 'Apelles of Our Age.'" In *Man, Myth, and Sensual Pleasures: Jan Gossart's Renaissance; The Complete Works*, edited by Maryan Ainsworth, 3–7. New Haven, CT: Yale University Press, 2010.

Alberti, Leon Battista. *Leon Battista Alberti's Delineation of the City of Rome (Descriptio vrbis Roma)*. Edited by Mario Carpo and Francesco Furlan. Translated by Peter Hicks. Tempe: Arizona Center for Medieval and Renaissance Studies, 2007.

———. *On Painting*. Translated by John R. Spencer. New Haven, CT: Yale University Press, 1966.

———. *On the Art of Building in Ten Books*. Translated by Joseph Rykwert, Neil Leach, and Robert Tavernor. Cambridge, MA: MIT Press, 1988.

Alchermes, Joseph. "*Spolia* in Roman Cities of the Late Empire: Legislative Rationales and Architectural Reuse." *Dumbarton Oaks Papers* 48 (1994): 167–78.

Alcock, Susan, John F. Cherry, and Jaś Elsner, eds. *Pausanias: Travel and Memory in Roman Greece*. Oxford: Oxford University Press, 2001.

Alewyn, Richard, and Karl Sälzle. *Das große Welttheater: Die Epoche der höfischen Feste in Dokument und Deutung*. Hamburg: Rowohlt, 1959.

Alexander, Michael, ed. and trans. *The Earliest English Poems*. 3rd ed. London: Penguin, 1991.

Allais, Lucia. *Designs of Destruction: The Making of Monuments in the Twentieth Century*. Chicago: University of Chicago Press, 2018.

Anderson, James C. Jr. *Roman Architecture in Provence*. Cambridge: Cambridge University Press, 2012.

André-Salvini, Béatrice. "Das Erbe von Babylon." In *Babylon: Mythos und Wahrheit*, 2 vols., edited by Joachim Marzahn and Günther Schauerte, 29–37. Berlin: Staatliche Museen; Munich: Hirmer Verlag, 2008. Exhibition catalog.

Angèli da Barga, Pietro. *De privatorum, publicorumque aedificiorum urbis Romae eversoribus epistola*. Florence: Sermartellius, 1589. Bayerische StaatsBibliotek. http://reader.digitale -sammlungen.de/resolve/display/bsb11211092.html.

Aristotle, *Complete Works of Aristotle*. Edited by Jonathan Barnes. Princeton, NJ: Princeton University Press, 2014.

Arnade, Peter. *Beggars, Iconoclasts and Civic Patriots: The Political Culture of the Dutch Revolt*. Ithaca, NY: Cornell University Press, 2008.

Arndt, Ernst Moritz. "Der Rabenstein," *Märchen und Jugenderinnerungen*. 2 vols. Berlin: G. Reimer, 1843.

Ascoli, Albert, and Unn Falkeid, eds. *The Cambridge Companion to Petrarch*. Cambridge: Cambridge University Press, 2015.

Augustine of Hippo. *City of God*. Translated by Henry Bettenson. London: Penguin, 1972.
———. *Confessions*. Translated by R. S. Pine-Coffin. London: Penguin, 1961.
———. *On Christian Doctrine*. Translated by D. W. Robertson Jr. Indianapolis: Bobbs-Merrill, 1958.

Averill, James H. *Wordsworth and the Poetry of Human Suffering*. Ithaca, NY: Cornell University Press, 1980.

Ayers, Andrew. *The Architecture of Paris: An Architectural Guide*. Stuttgart: Edition Axel Menges, 2003.

Bacou, Roseline. "À propos des dessins de figures de Piranèse." In Brunel, *Piranèse et les français*, 33–42.

Bailey, Quentin. *Wordsworth's Vagrants: Police, Prisons, and Poetry in the 1790s*. Farnham, UK: Ashgate, 2011.

Baker, Malcolm. "Representing Invention, Viewing Models." In *Models: The Third Dimension of Science*, edited by Soraya de Chadarevian and Nick Hopwood, 19–42. Stanford, CA: Stanford University Press, 2004.

Bakker, Boudewijn, and Michael Hoyle. "*Pictores, Adeste!* Hieronymus Cock Recommending His Print Series." *Simiolus: Netherlands Quarterly for the History of Art* 33, no. 1/2 (2007/2008): 53–66.

Bamford, Karen, and Naomi J. Miller, eds. *Maternity and Romance Narratives in Early Modern England*. Oxford: Routledge, 2016.

Bandiera, John D. "Form and Meaning in Hubert Robert's Ruin Caprices: Four Paintings of Fictive Ruins for the Château de Méréville." *Art Institute of Chicago Museum Studies* 15, no. 1 (1989): 20–37 and 82–85.

Barkan, Leonard. "Rome." In *The Classical Tradition*, edited by Anthony Grafton, Glenn W. Most, and Salvatore Settis, 839–50. Cambridge, MA: Belknap Press of Harvard University Press, 2013.
———. *Unearthing the Past: Archaeology and Aesthetics in the Making of Renaissance Culture*. New Haven, CT: Yale University Press, 1999.

Barroero, Liliana, and Stefano Susinno. "Arcadian Rome, Universal Capital of the Arts." In Bowron and Rishel, *Art in Rome in the Eighteenth Century*, 47–76.

Barthes, Roland. *The Neutral*. Translated by Rosalind Kraus and Denis Hollier. New York: Columbia University Press, 2007.

Barton, George. "Shinar." In Adler and Singer, *Jewish Encyclopedia*, 11:290–91.

Bass, Marisa. *Jan Gossart and the Invention of Netherlandish Antiquity*. Princeton, NJ: Princeton University Press, 2016.

Baudelaire, Charles. *Oeuvres complètes*. Edited by Y.-G. Le Dantec. Paris: Éditions Gallimard, 1961.

Baum, Kelly, Andrea Bayer, and Sheena Wagstaff, eds. *Unfinished: Thoughts Made Visible*. New York: Metropolitan Museum of Art, 2016. Exhibition catalog.

Beard, Geoffrey. *The Work of John Vanbrugh*. New York: Universe/Rizzoli, 1986.

Beard, Mary. "Re-reading (Vestal) Virginity." In *Women in Antiquity: New Assessments*, edited by Richard Hawley and Barbara Levick, 166–77. New York: Routledge, 1995.

———. "The Sexual Status of Vestal Virgins." *Journal of Roman Studies* 70 (1980): 12–27.

Beard, Mary, John North, and Simon Price, eds. *Religions of Rome: A Sourcebook*. Vol. 2. Cambridge: Cambridge University Press, 1998.

Beckford, William. *The Travel-Diaries of William Beckford of Font-Hill*. Edited by Guy Chapman. 2 vols. Cambridge: Cambridge University Press; Boston: Houghton Mifflin, 1928.

Bede. *The Ecclesiastical History of the English People; The Greater Chronicle; Bede's Letter to Egbert*. Edited by Judith McClure and Roger Collins. Oxford: Oxford University Press, 1999.

Belamarić, Joško, and Ana Šverko, eds. *Robert Adam and Diocletian's Palace in Split*. Zagreb: Institute of Art History, 2017.

Benedetti, Sandro. "L'architettura dell'Arcadia, Roma 1730." In *Bernardo Vittone e la disputa fra classicismo e barocco nel settecento*, vol. 1, 337–91. Turin: Accademia delle Scienze di Torino, 1970.

Beowulf. Edited and translated by R. M. Liuzza. Peterborough, ON: Broadview Press, 2012.

Bernardin de Saint-Pierre. *Études de la nature par Jacques-Henri-Bernardin de Saint Pierre, avec des notes par M. Aimé-Martin*. Vol. 2, *Étude douzième*. Paris: Chez Lefevre, 1836.

———. *Studies of Nature. By James-Henry-Bernardin de Saint-Pierre*. Translated by Henry Hunter. 5 vols. London, 1796.

Bertelli, Carlo. "Le Parlanti Rovine." In *Grafica Grafica II*, no. 2., edited by Carlo Bertelli. Rome: Calcografia Nazionale, 1976.

Bevilacqua, Mario. "The Young Piranesi: The Itineraries of His Formation." In Bevilacqua, Hyde Minor, and Barry, *The Serpent and the Stylus*, 13–53.

Bevilacqua, Mario, Heather Hyde Minor, and Fabio Barry, eds. *The Serpent and the Stylus: Essays on G. B. Piranesi*. Memoirs of the American Academy in Rome, supp. vol. 4. Ann Arbor: University of Michigan Press, 2006.

Bietenholz, Peter G., and Thomas B. Deutscher. *Contemporaries of Erasmus: A Biographical Register of the Renaissance and Reformation*. 3 vols. Toronto: University of Toronto Press, 2003.

Blake, William. *The Complete Poetry and Prose of William Blake*. Edited by David V. Erdman. New York: Anchor, 1982.

Bloch, R. Howard. "Chaucer's Maiden's Head: 'The Physician's Tale' and the Poetics of Virginity." *Representations*, no. 28 (1989): 113–34.

Bloom, Harold. "Commentary." In Blake, *Complete Poetry and Prose*, 894–972.

Blouw, Paul V. "Was Plantin a Member of the Family of Love? Notes on His Dealings with Hendrik Niclaes." *Quærendo* 23, no. 1 (1993): 3–22.

Blunt, Anthony. "The Hypnerotomachia Poliphili in 17th Century France." *Journal of the Warburg Institute* 1, no. 2 (October 1937): 117–37.

Boscaro, Cristian. "Rilievo metrico e cromatico della Stanza delle Rovine nel Convento della Trinità dei Monti a Roma." In *Prospettive architettoniche conservazione digitale, divulgazione e studio*, vol. 2, edited by Graziano Mario Valenti, 361–74. Rome: Sapienza Università Editrice, 2016.

Boswell, James. *Life of Samuel Johnson*. 2 vols. London: Henry Baldwin, 1791.

Bowron, Edgar Peters, and Joseph J. Rishel, eds. *Art in Rome in the Eighteenth Century*. London: Merrell; Philadelphia: Philadelphia Museum of Art, 2000. Exhibition catalog.

Bracciolini, Poggio. *De varietate fortunae*. Critical edition with introduction and commentary by Outi Merisalo. Helsinki: Suomalainen Tiedeakatemia, 1993.

Brenk, Beat. "Spolia from Constantine to Charlemagne: Aesthetics versus Ideology."

In "Studies on Art and Archaeology in Honor of Ernst Kitzinger." Special issue, *Dumbarton Oaks Papers* 41 (1987): 103–9.

Brilliant, Richard, and Dale Kinney, eds. *Reuse Value: Spolia and Appropriation in Art and Architecture from Constantine to Sherrie Levine.* Farnham, UK: Ashgate, 2011.

Bromwich, David. "The French Revolution and 'Tintern Abbey.'" In *Disowned by Memory: Wordsworth's Poetry of the 1790s.* Chicago: University of Chicago Press, 2000.

Brown, Jane K. "Faust." In *The Cambridge Companion to Goethe*, edited by Lesley Sharpe, 84–100. Cambridge: Cambridge University Press, 2002.

Brunel, Georges, ed. *Piranèse et les français: Colloque tenu à la Villa Médicis, 12–13 mai 1976.* Rome: Edizioni dell'Elefante, 1978.

Brylowe, Thora. "Of Gothic Architects and Grecian Rods: William Blake, Antiquarianism and the History of Art," *Romanticism* 18, no. 1 (2012): 89–104.

Buddensieg, Tilmann. "Gregory the Great, the Destroyer of Pagan Idols: The History of a Medieval Legend Concerning the Decline of Ancient Art and Literature." *Journal of the Warburg and Courtauld Institutes* 28 (1965): 44–65.

Bueno, Christina. *The Pursuit of Ruins: Archaeology, History, and the Making of Modern Mexico.* Albuquerque: University of New Mexico Press, 2017.

Bugge, John. *Virginitas: An Essay in the History of a Medieval Ideal.* The Hague: Martinus Nijhoff, 1975.

Buonarroti, Michelangelo. *Complete Poems of Michelangelo.* Translated by John Frederick Nims. Chicago: University of Chicago Press, 2000.

Burckhardt, Jacob. *Civilization of the Renaissance in Italy.* Translated by S. Middlemore. London: Penguin, 1990.

Burke, Peter. "Presenting and Re-presenting Charles V." In *Charles V in His Time*, edited by Hugo Soly, 411–18, 426–33. Antwerp: Mercatorfonds, 1999.

Burnet, Thomas. *The Theory of the earth: containing an account of the original of the earth, and of all the general changes which it hath already undergone, or is to undergo, till the consummation of all things.* London: R. Norton, for Walter Kettilby, 1691.

Bussels, Stijn. *Spectacle, Rhetoric and Power: The Triumphal Entry of Prince Philip of Spain into Antwerp.* New York: Rodopi, 2012.

Calasso, Robert. *The Marriage of Cadmus and Harmony.* Translated by Tim Parks. New York: Knopf, 1993.

Callimachus. *The Poems of Callimachus.* Translated by Frank Nisetich. Oxford: Oxford University Press, 2001.

Calvesi, Maurizio. Introduction to *Giovanni-Battista Piranesi*, by Henri Focillon, v–xlii. Edited by Maurizio Calvesi and Augusta Monferini. Bologna: Alfa, 1967.

———. "Nota ai 'grotteschi' o capricci di Piranesi." In *Piranesi e la cultura antiquaria: Gli antecedenti e il contesto*, edited by Anna Lo Bianco, 135–40. Rome: Comune di Roma e Università degli Studi di Roma, 1983.

Camden, William. *Britain, or A chorographicall description of the most flourishing kingdomes, England, Scotland, and Ireland, and the islands adjoyning, out of the depth of antiquitie beautified with mappes of the severall shires of England: written first in Latine by William Camden Clarenceux K. of A. Trans. newly into English by Philémon Holland Doctour in Physick: finally, revised, amended, and enlarged with sundry additions by the said author.* London: Printed by F. K[ingston,] R. Y[oung,] and I. L[egatt] for George Latham, 1637.

Cameron, Alan. *The Last Pagans of Rome.* Oxford: Oxford University Press, 2011.

Campbell, Jackson J., ed. and trans. *Advent Lyrics of the Exeter Book.* Princeton, NJ: Princeton University Press, 2015.

Caputo, Paolo. "Aegyptiaca from Cumae: New Evidence for Isis Cult in Campania; Site and Materials." In Casadio and Johnston, *Mystic Cults*, 235–50.

Carpo, Mario. *Architecture in the Age of Printing: Orality, Writing, Typography, and Printed Images in the History of Architectural Theory*. Translated by Sarah Benson. Cambridge, MA: MIT Press, 2001.

Casadio, Giovanni, and Patricia A. Johnston, eds. *Mystic Cults in Magna Graecia*. Austin: University of Texas Press, 2009.

Cellauro, Louis. "'Monvmenta Romae': An Alternative Title Page for the Duke of Sessa's Personal Copy of the *Speculum Romanae Magnificentiae*." *Memoirs of the American Academy in Rome* 51/52 (2006/2007): 277–95.

Cesarini, Giovanna, Giorgio Caviglia, Nicole Coleman, Thea De Armond, Sarah Murray, and Molly Taylor-Polesky. "British Travelers in Eighteenth-Century Italy: The Grand Tour and the Profession of Architecture." *American Historical Review* 122, no. 2 (April 2017): 425–50.

Chaucer, Geoffrey. *The Riverside Chaucer*. Edited by Larry D. Benson. Boston: Houghton Mifflin, 1987.

Christian, Kathleen Wren. *Empire without End: Antiquities Collections in Renaissance Rome, c. 1350–1527*. New Haven, CT: Yale University Press, 2010.

Cicero. *Cicero's Letters: Selections*. Translated by P. G. Walsh. Oxford: Oxford University Press, 2008.

———. "Pro Murena" (section 76). In *In Catilinam 1–4. Pro Murena. Pro Sulla. Pro Flacco*, translated by C. Macdonald, 169–301. Loeb edition. Cambridge, MA: Harvard University Press, 1976.

Claridge, Amanda, Judith Toms, and Tony Cubberley, eds. *Rome: An Oxford Archaeological Guide*. Oxford: Oxford University Press, 1998.

Clini, Paolo, and Riccardo Gulli. *Il San Giovanni di Girolamo Genga: Codici e strumenti per la conservazione*. Florence: Alinea, 2008.

Colomb, Claire. *Staging the New Berlin: Place Marketing and the Politics of Urban Reinvention Post-1989*. New York: Routledge, 2013.

Colonna, Francesco. *Hypnerotomachia Poliphili*. Translated by Joscelyn Godwin. London: Thames and Hudson, 1999.

Connelly, Joan Breton. *Portrait of a Priestess: Women and Ritual in Ancient Greece*. Princeton, NJ: Princeton University Press, 2007.

Consoli, Gian Paolo. "Architecture and History: Vico, Lodoli, Piranesi." In Bevilacqua, Hyde Minor, and Barry, *The Serpent and the Stylus*, 195–212.

Coogan, Michael D. *The Old Testament: A Historical and Literary Introduction to the Hebrew Scriptures*. Oxford: Oxford University Press, 2014.

Cooper, Tanya. "Forgetting Rome and the Voice of Piranesi's 'Speaking Ruins.'" In *The Art of Forgetting*, edited by Adrian Forty and Susanne Küchler, 107–25. New York: Berg, 2001.

Cozens, Alexander. *A New Method of Assisting the Invention in Drawing Original Compositions of Landscape*. London: J. Dixwell, 1785.

Cummings, R. M., ed. *Edmund Spenser: The Critical Heritage*. London: Routledge, 1996.

Cunningham, J. V. *The Poems of J. V. Cunningham*. Athens, OH: Swallow Press/Ohio University Press, 1997.

Curran, Brian A., Anthony Grafton, Pamela O. Long, and Benjamin Weiss. *Obelisk: A History*. Cambridge, MA: Burndy Library/MIT Press, 2009.

Dacos, Nicole. *La découverte de la Domus Aurea et la formation des grotesques à la Renaissance*. Studies of the Warburg Institute, vol. 31. Leiden, Neth.: Brill, 1969.

————. *Roma Quanta Fuit: Tre pittori fiamminghi nella Domus Aurea*. Translated by Maria Baiocchi. Rome: Donzelli Editore, 1995.

Dalley, Stephanie. *The Mystery of the Hanging Gardens of Babylon*. Oxford: Oxford University Press, 2015.

Damon, S. Foster. *A Blake Dictionary*. Hanover, NH: University Press of New England, 1988.

Dante Alighieri. *The Divine Comedy of Dante Alighieri: Inferno*. A verse translation by Allen Mandelbaum. New York: Bantam, 1982.

David, Arthur Kyle Jr., ed. *Traditional Ballads of Virginia, Collected under the Auspices of the Virginia Folk-Lore Society*. Cambridge, MA: Harvard University Press, 1929.

Davies, Gordon. *The Earth in Decay: A History of British Geomorphology, 1578–1878*. London: Macdonald, 1969.

Davis, Michael. *William Blake: A New Kind of Man*. Berkeley: University of California Press, 1977.

Denham, John. *Cooper's Hill*. London, 1643.

Derrida, Jacques. "Des Tours de Babel." In *Difference in Translation*, edited and translated by Joseph F. Graham, 191–225. Ithaca, NY: Cornell University Press, 1985.

Desgodetz, Antoine. *Les édifices antiques de Rome, dessinés et mesurés très-exactement par Antoine Desgodetz architecte*. Paris: Chez Jean Baptiste Coignard, 1682.

Desrochers, Brigitte. "Ruins Revisited: Modernist Conceptions of Heritage." *Journal of Architecture* 5 (Spring 2000): 35–45.

De Stefanis, Carla. *Via Appia, The Tomb of Cecilia Metella, and the Castrum Caetani*. Edited by Rita Paris. Translated by Richard Sadleir. Rome: Ministero per i Beni e le Attività Culturali Soprintendenza Archaeologica di Roma; Milan: Electa, 2000.

Destombes, M. "A Panorama of the Sack of Rome by Pieter Bruegel the Elder." *Imago Mundi* 14 (1959): 64–73.

DeVinne, Theodore Lowe. *Christopher Plantin and the Plantin Moretus Museum in Antwerp*. New York: Grolier Book Club, 1888.

Diderot, Denis. *Diderot on Art*. Vol. 2, *The Salon of 1767*, edited and translated by John Goodman. New Haven, CT: Yale University Press, 1995.

————. *Salons*. Edited by Jean Seznec and Jean Adhémar. 3 vols. Oxford: Oxford University Press, 1975–1983.

DiFuria, Arthur. "The *Concettismo* of Triumph: Maerten van Heemskerck's Prints and Spanish Omnipotence in a Late Sixteenth Century Writing Cabinet." In *Prints in Translation, 1450–1575: Image, Materiality, Space*, 158–83. London: Routledge, 2016.

————. "The Eternal Eye: Memory, Vision and Topography in Maerten van Heemskerck's Roman Ruin 'Vedute.'" In *Rom Zeichnen: Maerten van Heemskerck 1532–1536–37*, edited by Tatjana Bartsch and Peter Seiler, 157–70. Berlin: Gebr. Mann, 2012.

————. *Maarten van Heemskerck's Rome: Antiquity, Memory, and the Cult of Ruins*. Leiden, Neth.: Brill, 2019.

————. "Remembering the Eternal in 1553: Maerten van Heemskerck in *Self-Portrait Before the Colosseum*," *Nederlands Kunsthistorisch Jaarboek*, no. 59 (2010): 91–108.

————. "Self-Fashioning and Ruination in a Print Series by Maerten van Heemskerck." In *Culture figurative a confronto tra Fiandre e Italia dal XV al XVII secolo*, edited by Anna De Floriani and Maria Galassi, 117–25. Cinisello Balsamo, It.: Silvana, 2008.

Dillon, Brian. *Ruins*. Boston: MIT Press; London: Documents of Contemporary Art, 2011.

Diodorus Siculus. *The Library of History*. Vol. 2, *Books 2.35–4.58*. Translated by C. H. Oldfather. Loeb Classical Library. Cambridge, MA: Harvard University Press, 1935.

Dionysus of Halicarnassus. *Roman Antiquities*. Translated by Earnest Cary. Loeb ed. Cambridge: Harvard University Press, 1937.

Dixon, Susan. "The Sources and Fortunes of Piranesi's Archaeological Illustrations," *Art History* 25, no. 4 (September 2002): 469–87.

Dolders, Arno, ed. *Philips Galle: The Illustrated Bartsch*. Netherlandish Artists, vol. 56. Norfolk, CT: Abaris, 1987.

Donavin, Georgiana. *Scribit Mater: Mary and the Language Arts in the Literature of Medieval England*. Washington, DC: Catholic University of America Press, 2011.

Donne, John. *The Variorum Edition of the Poetry of John Donne*. Vol. 6, *The Anniversaries and the Epicedes and Obsequies*, edited by Gary A. Stringer, Ted-Larry Pebworth, John T. Shawcross, Ernest W. Sullivan II, and Paul A. Parrish. Bloomington: Indiana University Press, 1995.

d'Orgeix, Émilie. "The Goldschmidt and Scholz Scrapbooks in the Metropolitan Museum of Art: A Study of Renaissance Architectural Drawings." *Metropolitan Museum Journal* 36 (2001): 171–72.

Dorris, George E. "Goethe, Rolli, and 'Solitario Bosco Ombroso.'" *Journal of the Rutgers University Libraries* 26, no. 2 (June 1963): 33–35.

———. *Paolo Rolli and the Italian Circle in London, 1715–1744*. The Hague: Mouton, 1967.

Drayton, Michael. *The Works of Michael Drayton*. Edited by J. William Hebel. 5 vols. Oxford: Basil Blackwell and Mott, 1961.

Du Bellay, Joachim. *Les regrets; suivi de Les antiquités de Rome, Le Songe / Du Bellay*. Edited and annotated by François Roudaut. Paris: Librairie générale française, 2002.

———. "The Ruines of Rome." Translated by Edmund Spenser. In Spenser, *Shorter Poems*, 272–88.

Dubin, Nina. *Futures and Ruins: Eighteenth-Century Paris and the Art of Hubert Robert*. Los Angeles: Getty Research Institute, 2010.

Duffy, Eamon. *The Stripping of the Altars*. New Haven, CT: Yale University Press, 1992.

Düntzer, Heinrich. *Life of Goethe*. Translated by Thomas W. Lyster. London: T. Fisher Unwin, 1908.

Du Pérac, Étienne. *Le Antiche Rovine di Roma nei Disegni di Étienne Du Pérac*. Milan: Amilcare Pizzi, 1990.

Dürer, Albrecht. *Literary Remains of Albrecht Dürer*. Edited by William Martin Conway. Cambridge, 1889.

Dyer, John. *Poems*. London: J. Dodsley, 1770.

Eaves, Morris. "Blake and the Artistic Machine: An Essay in Decorum and Technology," *PMLA* 92 (1977): 903–27.

———. *The Counter-Arts Conspiracy: Art and Industry in the Age of Blake*. Ithaca, NY: Cornell University Press, 1992.

Edwards, Catherine. *Writing Rome: Textual Approaches to the City*. Cambridge: Cambridge University Press, 1996.

Effros, Bonnie. "Monuments and Memory: Repossessing Ancient Remains in Early Medieval Gaul." In *Topographies of Power in the Early Middle Ages*, edited by Mayke de Jong and Frans Theuws, 93–118. Leiden, Neth.: Brill, 2001.

Eigen, Edward. *On Accident: Episodes in Architecture and Landscape*. Cambridge, MA: MIT Press, 2018.

Eisner, Robert. *Travelers to an Antique Land: The History and Literature of Travel in Greece*. Ann Arbor: University of Michigan Press, 1991.

Eliot, T. S. *The Annotated Waste Land with Eliot's Contemporary Prose*. Edited by Lawrence Rainey. 2nd ed. New Haven, CT: Yale University Press, 2005.

———. *The Waste Land: A Facsimile and Transcript of the Original Drafts Including the Annotations of Ezra Pound*. Edited by Valerie Eliot. London: Faber and Faber; New York: Harcourt, Brace, 1971.

Elsner, Jaś. *Imperial Rome and Christian Triumph*. Oxford: Oxford University Press, 1998.

Erdman, David. *Blake: Prophet against Empire*. Princeton, NJ: Princeton University Press, 1977.

Fant, J. Clayton. "Rome's Marble Yards." *Journal of Roman Archaeology* 14 (2001): 167–98.

Fehl, Philipp, and Stephen Prokopoff, eds. *Raphael and the Ruins of Rome: The Poetic Dimension*. Champaign: University of Illinois, Krannert Art Museum, 1983. Exhibition catalog.

Fermor, Patrick Leigh. *Mani: Travels in the Southern Peloponnese*. 1958. Reprint, New York: New York Review of Books, 2006.

Ferrer, Mary Tiffany. *Music and Ceremony at the Court of Charles V*. Suffolk, UK: Boydell and Brewer, 2012.

Ferri, Sabrina. *Ruins Past: Modernity in Italy 1744–1836*. Oxford: Voltaire Foundation, 2015.

Ferry, David. Review of *Wordsworth's Great Period Poems*, by Marjorie Levinson. *Studies in Romanticism* 30, no. 1 (Spring 1991): 113–20.

Fleming, John. *Robert Adam and His Circle in Edinburgh and Rome*. London: John Murray, 1962.

Fleming, Robin. *Britain after Rome: The Fall and Rise, 400–1070*. London: Penguin, 2011.

Flower, Harriet. *The Art of Forgetting: Disgrace and Oblivion in Roman Political Culture*. Chapel Hill: University of North Carolina Press, 2006.

Folin, Marco, and Monica Preti, eds. *Les Villes Détruites de Maerten van Heemskerck: Images de ruines et conflits religieux dans les Pays-Bas au XVIe siècle*. Paris: INHA, 2015.

Fowler, Don. "The Ruin of Time: Monuments and Survival at Rome." In *Roman Constructions: Readings in Postmodern Latin*, 193–217. Oxford: Oxford University Press, 2000.

Françon, Marcel. "Francesco Colonna's Poliphili Hypnerotomachia and Pantagruel." *Italica* 31, no. 3 (September 1954): 136–37.

———. "Francesco Colonna's 'Poliphili Hypnerotomachia' and Rabelais." *Modern Language Review* 50, no. 1 (January 1955): 52–55.

Franke, Detlef. *Das Heiligtum des Heqaib auf Elephantine*. Heidelberg: Heidelberger Orientverlag, 1994.

Frazer, J. G. *Pausanias's Description of Greece*. 1898. Reprint, Cambridge: Cambridge University Press, 2012.

Freedberg, David. *Iconoclasm and Painting in the Netherlands 1566–1609*. Oxford: Oxford University Press, 1972.

———. "Theory: The Question of Images." In *Art and Iconoclasm, 1525–1580: The Case of the Northern Netherlands*, edited by J. P. Filedt Kok, W. Halsema-Kubes, and W. Th. Kloek, 69–71. Amsterdam: Rijksmuseum; The Hague: Staatsuitgeverij, 1986. Exhibition catalog.

Freud, Sigmund. *Civilization and Its Discontents*. Edited and translated by James Strachey. New York: W. W. Norton, 1961.

Fuchs, Samuel. "Hammurabi." In Adler and Singer, *Jewish Encyclopedia*, 6:198–200.

Gambero, Luigi. *Mary and the Fathers of the Church: The Blessed Mary in Patristic Thought*. San Francisco: Ignatius Press, 2006.

George the Hymnist. "Kontakion for the Presentation of Mary in the Temple." In *Testi mariani del primo millenio*, edited by Georges Gharib, 4 vols. Rome: Città Nuova, 1990.

Gibbon, Edward. *The Autobiographies of Edward Gibbon*. Edited by John Murray. London: John Murray, 1896.

Gill, Stephen. *The Cambridge Companion to Wordsworth*. Cambridge: Cambridge University Press, 2003.

———. "The Philosophic Poet." In Gill, *Cambridge Companion to Wordsworth*, 142–59.

Gilpin, William. *An Essay on Prints*. London: J. Robson, 1768.

———. *Observations on Several Parts of the Countries of Cambridge, Norfolk, Suffolk, and Essex. Also on Several Parts of North Wales; relative chiefly to Picturesque Beauty, in Two Tours, the former made in the year 1769. The latter in the year 1773*. London: 1809.

———. *Observations on the River Wye, and Several Parts of South Wales, &c. relative chiefly to Picturesque Beauty, made in the summer of the year 1770*. 2nd ed. London: Blamire, 1789.

———. *Three Essays: On Picturesque Beauty; On Picturesque Travel; and On Sketching Landscape; to Which Is Added a Poem, on Landscape Painting*. London: R. Blamire, 1792.

Ginsberg, Robert. *Aesthetics of Ruins*. Amsterdam: Rodopi, 2004.

Glendinning, Miles. "The Conservation Movement: A Cult of the Modern Age." *Transactions of the Royal Historical Society*, 6th ser., 13 (2003): 359–76.

Gobert, A. "Franklin et Volney." *French Review* 9, no. 5 (April 1936): 391–403.

Godwin, Joscelyn. *The Real Rule of Four*. New York: Disinformation Books, 2004.

Goethe, Johann Wolfgang von. *Conversations with Eckermann*. Cambridge, MA: Da Capo Press, 1998.

———. *Faust: Part One*. Edited and translated by David Luke. Oxford: Oxford University Press, 2008.

———. *Faust: Part Two*. Edited and translated by David Luke. Oxford: Oxford University Press, 2008.

———. *Goethe's Roman Elegies*. Translated by David Luke. London: Chatto and Windus, 1977.

———. *Italian Journey, 1786–1788*. Translated by W. H. Auden and Elizabeth Mayer. San Francisco, North Point, 1982.

———. *Italienische Reise*. Hamburg: Christian Wegner Verlag, 1951.

Gohau, Gabriel. *Histoire de la géologie*. Translated by Albert V. Carozzi and Marguerite Carozzi. New Brunswick, NJ: Rutgers University Press, 1990.

Gombrich, Ernst. *Art and Illusion*. Princeton, NJ: Princeton University Press, 1961.

———. "The Evidence of Images." In *Interpretation: Theory and Practice*, edited by Charles Southward Singleton, 35–104. Baltimore: Johns Hopkins University Press, 1969.

Gordon, George [Lord Byron]. *Byron's Poetry and Prose*. Edited by Alice Levine. New York: Norton, 2010.

Graef, Hilda. *Mary: A History of Doctrine and Devotion*. London: Sheed and Ward, 1965.

Grafton, Anthony, ed. *Rome Reborn: The Vatican Library and Renaissance Culture*. New Haven, CT: Yale University Press; Washington, DC: Library of Congress; Vatican City: Biblioteca Apostolica Vaticana, 1993. Exhibition catalog.

Graham, Roderick. *Arbiter of Elegance: The Biography of Robert Adam*. Edinburgh: Birlinn, 2009.

Greever, Garland. "The Two Versions of 'Grongar Hill.'" *Journal of English and Germanic Philology* 16, no. 2 (April 1917): 274–81.

Gregory of Nyssa. "On Virginity." In *Saint Gregory of Nyssa: Ascetical Works*, edited and translated by Virginia Woods Callahan, 3–76. Fathers of the Church Patristic Series, vol. 58. Washington, DC: Catholic University of America Press, 1967.

Griggs, Tamara. "Promoting the Past: The Hypnerotomachia Poliphili as Antiquarian Enterprise." *Word and Image: A Journal of Verbal/Visual Enquiry* 14, no. 1/2 (January–June 1998): 17–39.

Hansen, Maria Fabricius. *The Eloquence of Appropriation: Prolegomena to an Understanding of Spolia in Early Christian Rome*. Rome: L'Erma di Bretschneider, 2003.

Harbison, Robert. *Ruins and Fragments*. London: Reaktion Books, 2015.

Harries, Elizabeth. *The Unfinished Manner: Essays on the Fragment in the Later Eighteenth Century*. Charlottesville: University of Virginia Press, 1994.

Harrison, Robert. *Rome, la pluie, a quoi bon la littérature?* Translated by Florence Naugrette. Paris: Flammarion, 1994.

Hartman, Geoffrey. "Wordsworth, Inscriptions, and Romantic Nature Poetry." In *Beyond Formalism: Literary Essays 1958–1970*, 206–30. New Haven, CT: Yale University Press, 1970.

———. *Wordsworth's Poetry, 1787–1814*. New Haven, CT: Yale University Press, 1964.

Haskell, Francis. *History and Its Images*. New Haven, CT: Yale University Press, 1993.

Hell, Julia. *The Conquest of Ruins: The Third Reich and the Fall of Rome*. Chicago: University of Chicago Press, 2018.

———. "Imperial Ruin Gazers, or Why Did Scipio Weep?" In Hell and Schönle, *Ruins of Modernity*, 184–88.

Hell, Julia, and Andreas Schönle, eds. *Ruins of Modernity*. Durham, NC: Duke University Press, 2010.

Henle, Mary, ed. *Vision and Artifact*. New York: Springer, 1976.

Herodotus. *The History*. Translated by David Grene. Chicago: University of Chicago Press, 1987.

Heuer, Christopher P. "Hieronymus Cock's Aesthetic of Collapse." *Oxford Art Journal* 32, no. 3 (October 2009): 387–408.

Heywood, Linda M., and John K. Thornton. *Central Africans, Atlantic Creoles, and the Foundation of the Americas, 1585–1660*. Cambridge: Cambridge University Press, 2007.

Hind, Arthur M. *Giovanni Battista Piranesi: A Critical Study*. London: Holland Press, 1922.

Hobbes, Thomas. *The Moral and Political Works of Thomas Hobbes of Malmesbury*. London: n.p., 1750.

Holmes, Urban T. "Mediaeval Gem Stones." *Speculum* 9, no. 2 (April 1934): 195–204.

Home, Henry, Lord Kames. *Elements of Criticism*. 3 vols. London: A. Millar; Edinburgh: A. Kincaid and Bell, 1762.

Homer. *Iliad*. Translated by Robert Fagles. New York: Penguin, 1990.

———. *Homer: The Iliad*. Edited by Michael Silk. 2nd ed. Landmarks of World Literature. Cambridge: Cambridge University Press, 2004.

Horace. *The Odes of Horace*. Translated by David Ferry. New York: Farrar, Straus and Giroux, 1997.

Hui, Andrew. *The Poetics of Ruins in Renaissance Literature*. New York: Fordham University Press, 2017.

Humfrey, Belinda. "John Dyer." In *Oxford Dictionary of National Biography*. Oxford: Oxford University Press, 2004; online ed., https://doi.org/10.1093/ref:odnb/8350.

Hunt, John Dixon. "Picturesque Mirrors and the Ruins of the Past." In *Gardens and the Picturesque*, 171–92. Cambridge, MA: MIT Press, 1992.

Hypnerotomachia Poliphili. Edited and with commentary by Lucia A. Ciapponi and Giovanni Pozzi. 2 vols. Padua, It.: Editrice Antenore, 1980.

Ilardi, Vincent. *Renaissance Vision from Spectacles to Telescopes*. Philadelphia: Memoirs of the American Philosophical Society, 2007.

Jacobus, Mary. "The Ordinary Sky: Wordsworth, Blanchot, and the Writing of Disaster." *Romantic Circles*, 2008. https://www.rc.umd.edu/praxis/psychoanalysis/jacobus/jacobus.html.

Jahn, Otto. *Über Darstellungen des Handwerks und Handelsverkehrs Auf Antiken Wandgemälden*. Leipzig: Hirzel, 1868.

Jakob, Michael. "On Mountains: Scalable and Unscalable." Translated by Timothy Attanucci. In *Landform Building: Architecture's New Terrain*, edited by Stan Allen and Marc McQuade, 136–64. Zurich: Lars Müller, 2011.

James, Henry. *Italian Hours*. 1909. Reprint, New York: Ecco Press, 1987.

Jameson, Anna. *Legends of the Madonna as Represented in the Fine Arts*. London: Longman, 1857.

Janowitz, Anne. *England's Ruins: Poetic Purpose and the National Landscape*. Cambridge: Basil Blackwell, 1990.

Jarvis, Simon. "Wordsworth and Idolatry." *Studies in Romanticism* 38, no. 1 (Spring 1999): 3–27.

Johnston, Kenneth. "Wordsworth and 'The Recluse.'" In Gill, *Cambridge Companion to Wordsworth*, 70–89.

Jonas, Hans. "Jewish and Christian Elements in Philosophy: Their Share in the Emergence of the Modern Mind." In *Philosophical Essays: From Ancient Creed to Technological Man*, 21–44. Englewood Cliffs, NJ: Prentice Hall, 1974.

Josephus, Flavius. *The genuine and complete works of Flavius Josephus, the celebrated warlike, learned and authentic Jewish historian*. Translated by William Whiston. Dublin: Thomas Morton Bates, 1796.

———. *Jewish Antiquities*. Vol. 1. Translated by H. St. J. Thackeray. Loeb Classical Library, vol. 242. Cambridge, MA: Harvard University Press, 1930.

Jurišić, Krasanka Majer. "Adam's Print of the Western Gate of Diocletian's Palace: A Resource for the Study of the Communal Buildings of Split in the Eighteenth Century." In Belamarić and Šverko, *Robert Adam and Diocletian's Palace in Split*, 309–23.

Kahn, Louis. "Kahn" [interview with Louis Kahn]. *Perspecta* 7 (1961): 9–28.

Kant, Immanuel. *Critique of the Power of Judgment*. Edited by Paul Guyer. Translated by Paul Guyer and Eric Matthews. Cambridge: Cambridge University Press, 2001.

Kantor-Kazovsky, Lola. *Piranesi as Interpreter of Roman Architecture and the Origins of His Intellectual World*. Florence: Leo S. Olschki Editore, 2006.

Karmon, David. *The Ruin of the Eternal City: Antiquity and Preservation in Renaissance Rome*. Oxford: Oxford University Press, 2011.

Kearns, Cleo McNelly. *The Virgin Mary, Monotheism and Sacrifice*. Cambridge: Cambridge University Press, 2008.

Ketcham, Diana. *Le Désert de Retz: A Late Eighteenth-Century French Folly Garden, the Artful Landscape of Monsieur de Monville*. Cambridge, MA: MIT Press, 1997.

Kim, Anna M. "Creative Iconoclasms in Renaissance Italy." In *Striking Images: Iconoclasms Past and Present*, edited by Stacy Boldrick, Leslie Brubaker, and Richard Clay, 65–80. Burlington, VT: Ashgate, 2013.

Kinney, Dale. "Spolia." In *St. Peter's in the Vatican*, edited by William Tronzo, 16–47. Cambridge: Cambridge University Press, 2005.

———. "Spolia: Damnatio and Renovatio Memoriae." *Memoirs of the American Academy in Rome* 42 (1997): 117–48.

Kittel, Gerhard, Gerhard Friedrich, and Geoffrey W. Bromiley, eds. *Theological Dictionary of the New Testament*. Grand Rapids, MI: Eerdmans, 1985.

Kleinbub, Christian. "Bramante's Ruined Temple and the Dialectics of the Image." *Renaissance Quarterly* 63, no. 2 (Summer 2010): 412–58.

Kristeva, Julia. "Stabat Mater." Translated by Leon S. Roudiez. In *The Kristeva Reader*, edited by Toril Moi, 160–86. New York: Columbia University Press, 1986.

Lacoue-Labarthe, Philippe, and Jean-Luc Nancy. *The Literary Absolute*. Translated by Philip Barnard and Cheryl Lester. Albany: State University of New York Press, 1988.

Lactantius. *Divine Institutes*. Edited by Anthony Bowen and Peter Gamsey. Liverpool: Liverpool University Press, 2004.

Lambert, Raymond. *Piranèse, Les Prisons: Présentation par Marguerite Yourcenar; Suivi de la vie de Piranèse de Jacques-Guillaume Legrand*. Paris: L'insulaire, 1999.

Lamp, Kathleen S. *A City of Marble: The Rhetoric of Augustan Rome*. Columbia: University of South Carolina Press, 2013.

Lanciani, Rodolfo. *Ancient and Modern Rome*. New York: Cooper Square Publishers, 1963.

———. *The Destruction of Ancient Rome: A Sketch of the History of the Monuments*. New York: Macmillan, 1899.

———. *The Ruins and Excavations of Ancient Rome*. 1897. Reprint, New York: Benjamin Blom, 1967.

Landau, David, and Peter Parshall. *The Renaissance Print: 1470–1550*. New Haven, CT: Yale University Press, 1996.

Langley, Batty. *New Principles of Gardening; or, The Laying Out and Planting Parterres, Groves, Wildernesses, Labyrinths, Avenues, Parks, &c., After a More Grand and Rural Manner*. London: A. Bettesworth and J. Batley; J. Pemberton et al., 1728.

Lansford, Tyler. *The Latin Inscriptions of Rome: A Walking Guide*. Baltimore: Johns Hopkins University Press, 2009.

Larson, Jennifer. *Greek Nymphs: Myth, Cult, Lore*. Oxford: Oxford University Press, 2001.

Laugier, Marc-Antoine. *Essai sur l'architecture*. Paris: Chez Duchesne, 1753.

Lavin, Marilyn Aronberg. "Piero's Meditation on the Nativity." In *The Cambridge Companion to Piero della Francesca*, edited by Jeryldene M. Wood, 66–75. Cambridge: Cambridge University Press, 2002.

Lawrence, Lesley. "Stuart and Revett: Their Literary and Architectural Careers." *Journal of the Warburg Institute* 2, no. 2 (October 1938): 128–46.

Lee-Jeffries, Hester. *England's Helicon: Fountains in Early Modern Literature and Culture*. Oxford: Oxford University Press, 2007.

Lefaivre, Liane. *Leon Battista Alberti's Hypnerotomachia Poliphili: Re-cognizing the Architectural Body in the Early Italian Renaissance*. Cambridge, MA: MIT Press, 1997.

Legrand, J.-G. "Notice Historique sur la Vie et les Ouvrages de J. B. Piranesi Architecte, peintre et Graveur Né a Venise en 1720 Mort a Rome en 1778." Reprinted as an appendix to Gilbert Erouart and Monique Mosser, "À propos de la 'Notice historique sur la vie et les ouvrages de J.-B. Piranesi': Origine et fortune d'une biographie," in Brunel, *Piranèse et les français*, 221–52.

———. "Suivi de la vie de Piranèse par Jacques-Guillaume Legrand" (1799). In Lambert, *Piranèse, Les Prisons*, 91–152.

Lenz, Christian. *Tischbein: Goethe in der Campagna di Roma*. Frankfurt am Main: Städelsches Kunstinstitut und Städtische Galerie, 1979.

Leonardo da Vinci. *A Treatise of Painting, Translated from the Original Italian, And adorn'd with a great Number of Cuts*. London: Senex and Taylor, 1721.

Le Roy, Julien-David. *Les ruines des plus beaux monuments de la Grèce*. Paris, 1758.

Levinson, Marjorie. "Insight and Oversight: Reading 'Tintern Abbey.'" In *Wordsworth's Great Period Poems*, 14–57. Cambridge: Cambridge University Press, 1986.

———. *The Romantic Fragment Poem*. Chapel Hill: University of North Carolina Press, 1986.

Liuzza, R. M. "The Tower of Babel: The Wanderer and the Ruins of History." *Studies in the Literary Imagination* 36, no. 1 (Spring 2003): 1–35.

Livy. *The Rise of Rome: Books I–V*. Translated by T. J. Luce. Oxford: Oxford University Press, 1998.

Lubbock, Jules. *Storytelling in Christian Art from Giotto to Donatello*. New Haven, CT: Yale University Press, 2006.

Lucan. *The Civil War*. Translated by J. D. Duff. Loeb Classical Library. Cambridge, MA: Harvard University Press, 1928.

Lucretius. *De Rerum Natura*. Translated by W. H. D. Rouse. Loeb Classical Library. Cambridge, MA: Harvard University Press, 1989.

Luijten, Ger, ed. *The New Hollstein, Dutch and Flemish Etchings, Engravings and Woodcuts 1450–1700, the van Doetecum Family*. Compiled by Henk Nalis. Part 1 of 4. Rotterdam: Rijksprentenkabinet, 1998.

Lukacher, Brian. *Joseph Gandy: An Architectural Visionary in Georgian England*. London: Thames and Hudson, 2006.

Macaulay, Rose. *Pleasure of Ruins*. New York: Barnes and Noble, 1953.

MacLachlan, Bonnie. "Women and Nymphs at the Grotta Caruso." In Casadio and Johnston, *Mystic Cults*, 204–16.

MacMullen, Ramsay. "The Epigraphic Habit in the Roman Empire." *American Journal of Philology* 103, no. 3 (Autumn 1982): 233–46.

Makdisi, Saree. "The Political Aesthetic of Blake's Images." In *The Cambridge Companion to William Blake*, edited by Morris Eaves, 110–32. Cambridge: Cambridge University Press, 2003.

Mallgrave, Harry F. *Modern Architectural Theory: A Historical Survey, 1673–1968*. Cambridge: Cambridge University Press, 2005.

Mansbach, S. A. "Pieter Bruegel's Towers of Babel." *Zeitschrift für Kunstgeschichte* 45, no. 1 (1982): 43–56.

Mariucci, Giovanna. *Umbria da non perdere: Guida ai 100 capolavori*. Milan: Scala, 2007.

Marnef, Guido. *Antwerp in the Age of Reformation: Underground Protestantism in a Commercial Metropolis, 1550–1577*. Translated by J. C. Grayson. Baltimore: Johns Hopkins University Press, 1996.

Martial. *Epigrams*. Translated by Walter C. Ker. 2 vols. London: Heineman, 1920.

Marvell, Andrew. *The Poems and Letters of Andrew Marvell*. Edited by H. M. Margoliouth. Revised by Pierre Legouis with the collaboration of E. E. Duncan-Jones. Oxford: Clarendon Press, 1971.

The Marvels of Rome: Mirabilia Urbis Romae. Edited and translated by Francis Morgan Nichols. 2nd ed., with new introduction, gazetteer, and bibliography by Eileen Gardiner. New York: Italica Press, 1986. First published 1889 by Ellis and Elvey (London).

Maso di Banco: La Capella di San Silvestro. Edited by Cristina Acidini Luchinat and Enrica Neri Lusanna. Milan: Electa, 1998.

Mayernik, David. "The *Capricci* of Giovanni Paolo Panini." In *The Architectural Capriccio: Memory, Fantasy and Invention*, edited by Lucien Steil, 33–41. Farnham, UK: Ashgate, 2014.

Mazzocco, Angelo. "Petrarca, Poggio, and Biondo: Humanism's Foremost Interpreters of Roman Ruins." In *Francis Petrarch, Six Centuries Later: A Symposium*, edited by Aldo Scaglione, 353–63. Chapel Hill, NC: Department of Romance Languages; Chicago: Newberry Library, 1975.

McCabe, Richard A. "The Masks of Duessa: Spenser, Mary Queen of Scots, and James VI." *English Literary Renaissance* 17, no. 2 (1987): 224–42.

McCormick, Thomas J. *Charles-Louis Clérisseau and the Genesis of Neo-Classicism*. Cambridge, MA: MIT Press, 1990.

McGowan, Margaret. *The Vision of Rome in Late Renaissance France*. New Haven, CT: Yale University Press, 2000.

Meadow, Mark. "Ritual and Civic Identity in Philip II's 1549 Antwerp *Blijde Incompst.*" *Nederlands Kunsthistorisch Jaarboek* 49 (1998): 36–67.

Meiss, Millard. *Andrea Mantegna as Illuminator: An Episode in Renaissance Art, Humanism and Diplomacy.* New York: Columbia University Press, 1957.

Metelli, Fabio. "The Perception of Transparency." *Scientific American* 230, no. 4 (April 1974): 90–98.

———. "What Does 'More Transparent' Mean? A Paradox." In Henle, *Vision and Artifact,* 19–24.

Miller, F. J. "Evidences of Incompleteness in the *Aeneid* of Virgil." *Classical Journal* 4, no. 8 (June 1909): 341–55.

Milton, John. *Paradise Lost.* Edited by Scott Elledge. New York: W. W. Norton, 1975.

Minor, Heather Hyde. "Engraved in Porphyry, Printed on Paper: Piranesi and Lord Charlemont." In Bevilacqua, Hyde Minor, and Barry, *The Serpent and the Stylus,* 123–47.

———. *Piranesi's Lost Words.* State College: Pennsylvania State University Press, 2015.

Mitchell, W. J. T. *Blake's Composite Art: A Study of the Illuminated Poetry.* Princeton, NJ: Princeton University Press, 1978.

Moorman, Mary. *William Wordsworth: The Early Years.* 1957. Reprint, Oxford: Oxford University Press, 1968.

Morison, Stanley. "Early Humanistic Script and the First Roman Type." *Library* 4-24, no. 1/2 (September 1, 1943): 1–29.

Mortier, Roland. *La poétique des ruines en France.* Geneva: Librairie Droz, 1974.

Moss, Jean Dietz. "'Godded with God': Hendrik Niclaes and His Family of Love." *Transactions of the American Philosophical Society* 71, no. 8 (1981): 1–89.

Mousavi, Ali. *Persepolis: Discovery and Afterlife of a World Wonder.* Boston: De Gruyter, 2012.

Nagel, Alexander, and Christopher Wood. *Anachronic Renaissance.* New York: Zone Books, 2010.

Naginski, Erika. "Preliminary Thoughts on Piranesi and Vico." *RES: Anthropology and Aesthetics,* no. 53/54 (Spring–Autumn 2008): 152–67.

Nancy, Jean-Luc. *The Experience of Freedom.* Translated by Bridget McDonald. Stanford, CA: Stanford University Press, 1994. First published as *L'expérience de la liberté* (Paris: Editions Galilée, 1988). Page references are to the Stanford edition.

Nash, Ernest. "Hidden Visual Patterns in Roman Architecture and Ruins." In Henle, *Vision and Artifact,* 95–103.

Nave, Francine de. *The Plantin-Moretus Museum: Printing and Publishing before 1800.* Antwerp: Museum Antwerpen, 2004.

Nees, Lawrence. "Theodulf's Mythical Silver Hercules Vase, Poetica Vanitas and the Augustinian Critique of the Roman Heritage." *Dumbarton Oaks Papers* 41 (1987): 443–51.

Nevola, Francesco. *Giovanni Battista Piranesi: I Grotteschi; Gli anni giovanili 1720–1750.* Rome: Ugo Bozzi Editore, 2010.

Nicolson, Marjorie Hope. *Mountain Gloom and Mountain Glory: The Development of the Aesthetics of the Infinite.* Ithaca, NY: Cornell University Press, 1959.

Nyberg, Dorothea. "Original Text of Prima Parte and English Translation." In *Giovanni Battista Piranesi: Drawings and Etchings at Columbia University; An Exhibition at Low Memorial Library, March 21–April 14, 1972,* 115–18. New York: Columbia University, Avery Architectural Library, 1972.

Oberhuber, Konrad. "Hieronymus Cock, Battista Pittoni und Paolo Veronese in Villa Maser." In *Munuscula Discipulorum: Kunsthistorische Studien Hans Kauffmann zum 70. Geburtstag 1966,* edited by Tilmann Buddensieg and Matthias Winner, 207–24. Berlin: Verlag Bruno Hessling, 1968.

O'Hara, James J. "The Unfinished *Aeneid*?" In *A Companion to Vergil's "Aeneid" and Its Tradition*, edited by Joseph Farrell and Michael C. J. Putnam, 96–106. Blackwell Companions to the Ancient World, Literature and Culture. Chichester, UK: Wiley-Blackwell, 2014.

Orr, James, ed. *New Testament Apocryphal Writings*. London: J. M. Dent, 1903.

Ovid. *Ovid: Fasti*. Translated by Anne Wiseman and Peter Wiseman. Oxford: Oxford University Press, 2011.

———. *Ovid: Metamorphoses*. Translated by A. D. Melville. Oxford: Oxford University Press, 1986.

Pagliano, Alessandra. "Architecture and Perspective in the Illusory Spaces of Ferdinando Galli Bibiena." *Nexus Network Journal* 18, no. 3 (December 2016): 697–721. https://doi.org/10.1007/s00004-016-0295-7.

Palladio, Andrea. *Four Books on Architecture*. Translated by Robert Tavernor and Richard Schofield. Cambridge, MA: MIT Press, 1997.

Panofsky, Erwin. *Early Netherlandish Painting*. Cambridge, MA: Harvard University Press, 1953.

Paracelsus. "A Book on Nymphs, Sylphs, Pygmies, Salamanders, and Other Spirits." In *Four Treatises of Theophrastus von Hohenheim called Paracelsus*, translated by Henry E. Sigerist, 223–53. Baltimore: Johns Hopkins University Press, 1941.

Parker, Holt N. "Why Were the Vestals Virgins? Or the Chastity of Women and the Safety of the Roman State." *American Journal of Philology* 125, no. 4 (Winter 2004): 563–601.

Parkinson, Richard B., ed. *Reading Ancient Egyptian Poetry: Among Other Histories*. Oxford: Blackwell, 2009.

———, trans. *The Tale of Sinuhe and Other Ancient Egyptian Poems 1940–1640 B.C.* Oxford: Oxford University Press, 1999.

Pausanias. *Guide to Greece*. Translated by Peter Levi. London: Penguin, 1971.

Pearsall, Derek, ed. *Chaucer: The Canterbury Tales*. London: Routledge, 1985.

Pérez-Gomez, Alberto. "The Hypnerotomachia Poliphili by Francesco Colonna: The Erotic Nature of Architectural Meaning." In *Paper Palaces: The Rise of the Renaissance Architectural Treatise*, edited by Vaughan Hart and Peter Hicks, 86–104. New Haven, CT: Yale University Press, 1998.

Petrarch, Francesco. *L'Africa: Edizione critica per cura di Nicola Festa*. Florence: G. C. Sansoni, 1926.

———. *Letters on Familiar Matters I–VIII*. Translated by Aldo S. Bernardo. 3 vols. New York: Italica Press, 2005.

———. *Petrarch's Lyric Poems: The "Rime sparse" and Other Lyrics*. Edited and translated by Robert M. Durling. Cambridge, MA: Harvard University Press, 1976.

Petronius. *The Satyricon of Petronius*. Translated by William Arrowsmith. Ann Arbor: University of Michigan Press, 1959.

Petrucci, Armando. *Public Lettering: Script, Power, and Culture*. Translated by Linda Lappin, Chicago: University of Chicago Press, 1993.

Petter, Donna Lee. *The Book of Ezekiel and Mesopotamian City Laments*. Orbis Biblicus et Orientalis, vol. 246. Fribourg, Switz.: Academic Press, 2011.

Piggott, Stuart. *Ruins in a Landscape: Essays in Antiquarianism*. Edinburgh: Edinburgh University Press, 1976.

Pinto, John. "Diocletian's Palace and the Adam Style." In Belamarić and Šverko, *Robert Adam and Diocletian's Palace in Split*, 357–69.

———. *Speaking Ruins: Piranesi, Architects, and Antiquity in 18th Century Rome*. Ann Arbor: University of Michigan Press, 2012.

Piranesi, Giovanni Battista. *Giambattista Piranesi, Matrici incise 1743–1753*. Edited by Ginevra Mariani. Rome: Istituto Nazionale per la Grafica, Calcografia; Milan: Mazzotta, 2010.

———. *Giambattista Piranesi, Matrici incise 1756–1757*. Edited by Ginevra Mariani. Rome: Istituto Nazionale per la Grafica, Calcografia; Milan: Mazzotta, 2014.

———. *Le Antichità Romane*. 4 vols. Paris: Firmin Didot, Frères, 1835.

———. *Observations on the Letter of Monsieur Mariette with Opinions on Architecture, and a Preface to a New Treatise on the Introduction and Progress of the Fine Arts in Europe in Ancient Times*. Translated by Caroline Beamish and David Britt. Los Angeles: Getty Research Institute, 2002.

———. *Prima parte di architetture, e prospettive*. Rome: Stamperia de' Fratelli Pagliarini, 1743.

Plattes, Gabriel. *A Discovery of Subterraneall Treasure, viz. Of all manner of Mines and Mineralls, from the Gold to the Coale*. London: by I. Okes for Jasper Emery, 1639. Reprinted in facsimile for the Institute of Mining and Metallurgy. Ilkey, UK: Scolar Press, 1980.

Plutarch. *Lives*. Vol. 1, *Thesus and Romulus; Lycurgus and Numa; Solon and Publicola*. Translated by Bernadotte Perrin. Loeb Classical Library, vol. 46. Cambridge, MA: Harvard University Press, 1914.

———. "Romulus," 11. In *Lives*, vol. 1, 118–21.4.

Porter, J. I. "Sublime Monuments and Sublime Ruins in Ancient Aesthetics." *European Review of History: Revue européenne d'histoire* 18, no. 5/6 (2011): 685–96.

Procopius. *History of the Wars*. Translated by H. B. Dewing. 7 vols. Loeb Classical Library. Cambridge, MA: Harvard University Press, 1916.

Propertius. *Elegies*. Edited and translated by G. P. Goold. Cambridge, MA: Harvard University Press, 1990.

Purchas, Samuel. *Hakluytus Posthumus, Or Purchas His Pilgrimes*. Vol. 10. 1905. Reprint, Cambridge: Cambridge University Press, 2015.

Quatremère De Quincy, Antoine-Chrysostome. *Lettres à Miranda sur le déplacement des monuments de l'art de l'Italie*. Paris: Éditions Macula, 1989.

Ray, John. *Three physico-theological discourses . . . wherein are largely discussed the production and use of mountains, the original of fountains, of formed stones, and sea-fishes bones and shells found in the earth, the effects of particular floods and inundations of the sea, the eruptions of vulcano's, the nature and causes of earthquakes: with an historical account of those two late remarkable ones in Jamaica and England*. London: William Innys, 1713. First published 1693 by Sam. Smith (London).

Reeves, William, ed. and trans. *The apologies of Justin Martyr, Tertullian, and Minutius Felix, in defence of the Christian religion, with the Commonitory of Vincentius Lirinensis concerning the primitive rule of faith, translated from their originals with notes, for the advantage chiefly of English readers, and a preliminary discourse upon each author, together with a prefatory dissertation about the right use of the Fathers*. 2 vols. London: A. and J. Churchill, 1709.

Regier, Alexander. *Fracture and Fragmentation in British Romanticism*. Cambridge: Cambridge University Press, 2010.

Riegl, Alois. "The Modern Cult of Monuments: Its Character and Its Origin." Translated by Kurt W. Forster and Diane Ghirardo. *Oppositions* 25 (1982): 21–51.

Riggs, Timothy. "Hieronymus Cock (1510–1570): Printmaker and Publisher in Antwerp at the Sign of the Four Winds." PhD diss., Yale University, 1972. Microfilm. Photocopy. Ann Arbor, Mich.: Xerox University Microfilms, 1974. "71-31.002."

Riggs, Timothy, and Larry Silver, eds. *Graven Images: The Rise of Professional Printmakers in Antwerp and Haarlem, 1540–1640*. Evanston, IL: Mary and Leigh Block Gallery, Northwestern University, 1993.

Robison, Andrew. "Giovanni Battista Piranesi." In *The Glory of Venice: Art in the Eighteenth Century*, edited by Jane Martineau and Andrew Robison, 377–406. New Haven, CT: Yale University Press, 1994.

———. "Giovanni Battista Piranesi: Prolegomena to the Princeton Collection." *Princeton University Library Chronicle* 31, no. 3 (Spring 1970): 165–206.

Roe, Nicholas. "The Politics of the Wye Valley: Re-placing 'Tintern Abbey.'" In *The Politics of Nature: Wordsworth and Some Contemporaries*, 117–36. London: Palgrave Macmillan, 1992.

Rohleder, Johannes. "The Cultural History of Limestone." In *Calcium Carbonate from the Cretaceous Period into the 21st Century*, edited by Wolfgang Tegethoft, 55–135. Basel: Springer, 2001.

Rolli, Paolo Antonio. *Di canzonette e di cantate libri due di Paolo Rolli*. 3 vols. London: Presso Tommaso Edlin, 1727.

Roover, Raymond de. "The Business Organization of the Plantin Press in the Setting of Sixteenth Century Antwerp." *De Gulden Passer* 34 (1956): 104–20.

Roscher, W. H, ed. *Ausführliches Lexikon der griechischen und römischen Mythologie*. 6 vols. Leipzig: B. G. Teubner, 1884–1937.

Rosenau, Helen. *Vision of the Temple: The Image of the Temple of Jerusalem in Judaism and Christianity*. London: Oresko, 1979.

Rosier, Bart. "The Victories of Charles V: A Series of Prints by Maerten van Heemskerck, 1555–56." Translated by Bev Jackson. *Simiolus: Netherlands Quarterly for the History of Art* 20, no. 1 (1990/1991): 24–38.

Rowland, Ingrid D. *The Culture of the High Renaissance: Ancients and Moderns in Sixteenth-Century Rome*. Cambridge: Cambridge University Press, 1998.

———. "Raphael, Angelo Colocci, and the Genesis of the Architectural Orders." *Art Bulletin* 76 (1994): 81–104.

Rubinstein, Ruth Olitsky. "'Tempus edax rerum': A Newly Discovered Painting by Hermannus Posthumus." *Burlington Magazine* 127, no. 988 (July 1985): 425–33, 435–36.

Ruskin, John. *The Works of John Ruskin*. Vol. 8, *The Seven Lamps of Architecture*, edited by E. T. Cook and Alexander Wedderburn. London: George Allen, 1903.

Salmon, Frank. *Building on Ruins: The Rediscovery of Rome and English Architecture*. Aldershot, UK: Ashgate, 2000.

Sanzio da Urbino, Raphael. *Raffaello gli scritti*. Edited by Ettore Camesasca. Milan: Biblioteca universale Rizzoli, 1994.

———. *Raffaello nei documenti*. Edited by Vincenzo Golzio. Vatican City: Pontificia insigne accademia di belle arti e lettere dei virtuosi al Pantheon, 1936.

———. *Tutti gli scritti*. Edited by E. Camesasca. Milan: Rizzoli, 1956.

Saunders, Eleanor A. "A Commentary on Iconoclasm in Several Print Series by Maerten van Heemskerck." *Simiolus* 10, no. 2 (1978): 59–83.

Scaloni, Giovanna. "Carceri." In *Giambattista Piranesi, Matrici incise 1743–1753*, edited by Ginevra Mariani, 52–69. Rome: Istituto Nazionale per la Grafica, Calcografia; Milan: Mazzotta, 2010.

———. "La tecnica incisoria nelle tavole delle Antichità Romane." In *Giambattista Piranesi, Matrici incise 1756–1757*, edited by Ginevra Mariani, 49–66. Rome: Istituto Nazionale per la Grafica, Calcografia; Milan: Mazzotta, 2014.

Scamozzi, Vincenzo. *Discorsi sopra l'antichità di Roma*. Venice: Appresso Francesco Ziletti, 1582.

Scapecchi, Piero. "*L'Hypnerotomachia Poliphili* e il suo autore." *Accademie e biblioteche d'Italia* 51 (1983): 286–98.

Schama, Simon. *Landscape and Memory*. New York: Knopf, 1995.

Schlegel, Friedrich. *Philosophical Fragments*. Translated by Peter Firchow. Minneapolis: University of Minnesota Press, 1991.

Schmid, Hansjörg. *Der Tempelturm Etemenankí in Babylon*. Mainz, Ger.: P. von Zabern, 1995.

Scodel, Ruth. "The Achaean Wall and the Myth of Destruction," *Harvard Studies in Classical Philology* 86 (1982): 33–50.

Semler, L. E. "Robert Dallington's *Hypnerotomachia* and the Protestant Antiquity of Elizabethan England." *Studies in Philology* 103, no. 2 (Spring 2006): 208–41.

Seneca. *Epistles 93–124*. Translated by Richard M. Gummere. Loeb Classical Library. Cambridge, MA: Harvard University Press, 1925.

Shakespeare, William. *Complete Sonnets and Poems*. Edited by Colin Burrows. New York: Oxford University Press, 2002.

Shelley, Percy. "The Coliseum: A Fragment." In *The Complete Works of Percy Bysshe Shelley*, 10 vols., edited by Roger Ingpen and Walter Edwin Peck, 6:299–306. London: Ernest Benn, 1926–1960.

———. *Letters of Percy Shelley*. Vol. 2, *Shelley in Italy*, edited by Frederick Jones. Oxford: Oxford University Press, 1964.

———. "Ozymandias." In *The Complete Poetry of Percy Bysshe Shelley*, vol. 3, edited by Donald H. Reiman, Neil Fraistat, and Nora Crook, 326–27. Baltimore: Johns Hopkins University Press, 2012.

Shepard, Paul. *Man in the Landscape: A Historic View of the Esthetics of Nature*. 1967. Reprint, College Station: Texas A&M University Press, 1991.

Silver, Larry. "Bruegel's Biblical Kings." In *Imago Exegetica: Visual Images as Exegetical Instruments 1400–1700*, edited by Walter Mellon, James Clifton, and Michel Weemans, 791–831. Leiden, Neth.: Brill, 2014.

———. "Nature and Nature's God: Landscape and Cosmos of Albrecht Altdorfer," *Art Bulletin* 81, no. 2 (June 1999): 194–211.

———. *Peasant Scenes and Landscapes: The Rise of Pictorial Genres in the Antwerp Art Market*. Philadelphia: University of Pennsylvania Press, 2012.

Simmel, Georg. "Die Ruine." In *Philosophische Kultur: Gesammelte Essais*, 137–54. Leipzig: W. Klinkhardt, 1911.

Simonsen, Peter. *Wordsworth and Word-Preserving Arts: Typographic Inscription, Ekphrasis and Posterity in the Later Work*. Basingstoke, UK: Palgrave Macmillan, 2007.

Simpson, David. *Wordsworth's Historical Imagination*. New York: Routledge, 1987.

Simpson, St. John. "Making Their Mark: Foreign Travellers at Persepolis." *Achemenet*, January 2005. http://www.achemenet.com/ressources/enligne/arta/pdf/2005.001-Simpson.pdf.

———. "Persepolis Graffiti: Foreign Visitors." In *Encyclopaedia Iranica*. Article published and last modified October 30, 2015. http://www.iranicaonline.org/articles/persepolis-graffiti.

Simpson, William Kelly, ed. *The Literature of Ancient Egypt: An Anthology of Stories, Instructions, Stelae, Autobiographies and Poetry*. Translated by Robert K. Ritner, Vincent A. Tobin, and Edward Wente. 3rd ed. New Haven, CT: Yale University Press, 2003.

Sissa, Giulia. "La verginità materiale: Evanescenza di un oggetto." *Quaderni Storici*, n.s., 25, no. 75.3 (December 1990): 739–56.

Skyrme, Raymond. "'Buscas en Rome a Roma': Quevedo, Vitalis, and Janus Pannonius." *Bibliothèque d'Humanisme et Renaissance* 44, no. 2 (1982): 363–67.

Smith, Christine. *Architecture in the Culture of Early Humanism*. New York: Oxford University Press, 1992.

Smith, Malcolm C. "Janus Vitalis Revisited." *Revue de Littérature Comparée* 63, no. 1 (1989): 69–75.

———. "Looking for Rome in Rome: Janus Vitalis and His Disciples." *Revue de Littérature Comparée* 51, no. 4 (1977): 510–27.

Smith, William. *A Smaller Dictionary of Greek and Roman Antiquities*. London: J. Murray, 1868.

Sørensen, Bent. "Some Sources for Piranesi's Early Architectural Fantasies." *Burlington Magazine* 142, no. 1163 (February 2000): 82–89.

Southey, Robert. *Joan of Arc, Ballads, Lyrics, and Minor Poems*. London, 1857.

Spenser, Edmund. *The Faerie Queene*. Edited by Thomas Roche, with the assistance of C. Patrick O'Donnell. London: Penguin, 1978.

———. *The Poetical Works of Edmund Spenser*. Edited by J. C. Smith and E. De Selincourt. London: Oxford University Press, 1912.

———. *The Shorter Poems*. Edited by Richard A. McCabe. London: Penguin, 1999.

Springer, Carolyn. *The Marble Wilderness: Ruins and Representation in Italian Romanticism, 1775–1850*. Cambridge: Cambridge University Press, 1987.

Staples, Ariadne. *From Good Goddess to Vestal Virgin*. London: Routledge, 1998.

Staub, Susan C. "While She Was Sleeping: Spenser's 'Goodly Storie' of Chrysogone." In Bamford and Miller, *Maternity and Romance Narratives*, 13–32.

St. Clair, William. *Lord Elgin and the Marbles: The Controversial History of the Parthenon Sculptures*. 3rd ed. Oxford: Oxford University Press, 1998.

Stephens and Catherwood Revisited: Maya Ruins and the Passage of Time. Washington, DC: Dumbarton Oaks Research Library and Collection, 2015. Exhibition catalog.

Stewart, Susan. *Crimes of Writing: Problems in the Containment of Representation*. Durham, NC: Duke University Press, 1994.

Stewering, Roswitha. "Architectural Representations in the 'Hypnerotomachia Poliphili' (Aldus Manutius, 1499)." *Journal of the Society of Architectural Historians* 59, no. 1 (March 2000): 6–25.

———. *Architektur and Natur in der "Hypnerotomachia Poliphili" (Manutius, 1499) und die Zuschreibung des Werkes an Niccolò Lelio Cosmico*. Hamburg: LIT, 1996.

———. "Who Wrote the 'Hypnerotomachia Poliphili'? Arguments for a New Author." In *La réception européenne du Songe de Poliphile: Littérature, jardin et architecture* (Actes du Colloque de Mulhouse-Einsiedeln), edited by M. Mosser, W. Oechslin, and G. Polizzi. Einsiedeln, Switz.: Stiftung Bibliothek Werner Oechslin, 1999. Proceedings of a congress held in Einsiedeln, July 4, 1999.

Stinger, Charles L. *The Renaissance in Rome*. Bloomington: Indiana University Press, 1998.

Stoneman, Richard. *Palmyra and Its Empire: Zenobia's Revolt against Rome*. Ann Arbor: University of Michigan Press, 1992.

Strabo. *Geography*. Translated by H. C. Hamilton and William Falconer. London: Bohn, 1854.

Strachan, Michael. *Thomas Coryat*. Oxford: Oxford University Press, 1962.

Strohman, Anne-Marie. "Deferred Motherhood in Spenser's *The Faerie Queene*." In Bamford and Miller, *Maternity and Romance Narratives*, 33–48.

Struck, Peter T. "Allegory and Ascent in Neo-Platonism." In *The Cambridge Companion to Allegory*, edited by Rita Copeland and Peter T. Struck, 57–70. Cambridge: Cambridge University Press, 2010.

Stuart, James, and Nicholas Revett. *The Antiquities of Athens*. London: John Nichols, 1794.

Suetonius. *Suetonius: Julius, Augustus, Tiberius, Gaius, Caligula*. Vol. 1. Translated by J. C. Rolfe. Loeb Classical Library. Cambridge, MA: Harvard University Press, 1914.

Swisher, Michael. "Beyond the Hoar Stone." *Neophilologus* 86 (2002): 133–36.

Synesius of Cyrene. *The Letters of Synesius of Cyrene*. Translated and with introduction and notes by Augustine FitzGerald. Oxford: Oxford University Press, 1926.

Tafuri, Manfredo. "'The Wicked Architect,' G. B. Piranesi, Heterotopia, and the Voyage." In *The Sphere and the Labyrinth: Avant-Gardes and Architecture from Piranesi to the 1970s*, translated by Pellegrino d'Acierno and Robert Connolly, 25–54. Cambridge, MA: MIT Press, 1987.

Tait, A. A. *The Adam Brothers in Rome: Drawings from the Grand Tour*. London: Scala / Soane Museum, 2008. Exhibition catalog.

Tanizaki, Jun'ichirō. *In Praise of Shadows*. Translated by Thomas Harper and Edward Seidensticker. New York: Vintage Books, 2006.

Tertullian. *De idololatria*. Edited and translated by J. H. Waszink and J. C. M. van Winden. Leiden, Neth.: Brill, 1987.

Thomson, James. *Winter, a Poem*. London, 1730.

Trippe, Rosemary. "The 'Hypnerotomachia Poliphili,' Image, Text and Vernacular Poetics." *Renaissance Quarterly* 55, no. 4 (Winter 2002): 1222–58.

Tucci, Pier Luigi. *The Temple of Peace in Rome*. Cambridge: Cambridge University Press, 2017.

Tucker, G. H. "Le Portrait de Rome Chez Pannonius et Vitalis: Une mise au point." *Bibliothèque d'Humanisme et Renaissance* 48, no. 3 (1986): 751–56.

Uberti, Fazio degli. *Il Dittamondo di Fazio degli Uberti*. Edited by Vincenzo Monti. Milan: Giovanni Silvestri, 1826.

van Cleve, Hendrik. *Ruinarum varii prospectus ruriumq. aliquot delineationes*. Antwerp: Philips Galle, n.d.

van der Noot, Jan. *A theatre wherein be represented as wel the miseries & calamities that follow the voluptuous worldlings, as also the greate ioyes and plesures which the faithfull do enioy. An argument both profitable and delectable, to all that sincerely loue the word of God. Devised by S. John van-der Noodt*. London: Henry Bynneman, 1569.

Van Grieken, Joris, Ger Luijten, and Jan Van der Stock, eds. *Hieronymus Cock: De renaissance in prent*. Brussels: Mercatorfonds; New Haven: Yale University Press, 2013. Exhibition catalog.

Van Heck, Adrianus. *Breviarium Urbis Romae Antiquae*. Leiden, Neth.: Brill, 2002.

Varner, Eric. *Mutilation and Transformation: Damnatio Memoriae and Roman Imperial Portraiture*. Monumenta Graeca et Romana, vol. 10. Leiden, Neth.: Brill, 2004.

Vasari, Giorgio. *Le vite de' più eccellenti pittori, scultori, e architettori nelle redazioni del 1550–1568*. Edited by Rosanna Bettarini. 6 vols. Florence: Sansoni, 1966–69.

Veldman, Ilja. *Images for the Eye and Soul: Function and Meaning in Netherlandish Prints (1450–1650)*. Leiden, Neth.: Primavera Pers, 2006.

———. "Lessons for Ladies: A Selection of Sixteenth and Seventeenth-Century Dutch Prints." *Simiolus* 16, no. 1/2 (1986): 113–27.

———. "Maerten van Heemskerck and Hadrianus Junius: The Relationship between a Painter and a Humanist." *Simiolus* 7, no. 1 (1974): 35–54.

Venturi, Adolfo. *Storia dell'Arte italiana*. 11 vols. Milan: Hoepli, 1926.

Vidler, Anthony. "X Marks the Spot: The Obelisk in Space." In *The Scenes of the Street and Other Essays*, 221–32. New York: Monacelli Press, 2011.

Viollet-le-Duc, Eugène. *Dictionnaire raisonné de l'architecture française du XIe au XVIe siècle.* 9 vols. Paris: Édition Bance-Morel, 1854–68.

Virgil. *Aeneid.* Edited by T. E. Page. London: Macmillan, 1900.

———. *The Aeneid of Virgil: A Verse Translation.* Translated by Rolfe Humphries. New York: Charles Scribner, 1951.

Visions of Ruin: Architectural Fantasies and Designs for Garden Follies. London: Soane Museum, 1999. Exhibition catalog.

Vitruvius. *I dieci libri dell'architettura.* Venice: Francesco Marcolini, 1556.

Voet, Léon. *Antwerp: The Golden Age; The Rise and Glory of the Metropolis in the Sixteenth Century.* Antwerp: Mercatorfonds, 1973.

Volney [Constantin-François de Chassebœuf]. *The Ruins; or, A Survey of the Revolutions of Empires.* Translated by James Marshall, with an introduction by Jonathan Wordsworth. 1811. Reprint, West Yorkshire, UK: Orley, 2000.

Voragine, Jacobus de. *The Golden Legend: Readings on the Saints.* Translated by William Granger Ryan, with an introduction by Eamon Duffy. Princeton, NJ: Princeton University Press, 2012.

Waller, Gary. *The Virgin Mary in Late Medieval and Early Modern English Literature and Popular Culture.* Cambridge: Cambridge University Press, 2011.

Warner, Marina. *Alone of All Her Sex: The Myth and Cult of the Virgin Mary.* 1976. Reprint, Oxford: Oxford University Press, 2013.

Warton, Thomas [the Younger]. *Poems: A New Edition.* London: T. Becket, 1777.

Wegg, Jervis. *The Decline of Antwerp under Philip of Spain.* London: Methuen, 1924.

Wells, Robin Headlam. *Spenser's "Faerie Queene" and the Cult of Elizabeth.* London: Croom Helm, 1983.

West, Martin. *Studies in the Text and Transmission of the Iliad.* Munich: K. G. Saur, 2001.

Weston, Jessie L. *From Ritual to Romance.* Cambridge: Cambridge University Press, 1920.

White, Arthur. *Plague and Pleasure: The Renaissance World of Pius II.* Washington, DC: Catholic University of America Press, 2014.

White, Roger. "Scrap or Substitute: Roman Material in Anglo-Saxon Graves." In *Anglo-Saxon Cemeteries: A Reappraisal,* edited by Edmund Southworth, 125–52. Stroud, UK: A. Sutton, 1991. Proceedings of a conference held at Liverpool Museum, 1986.

Wildfang, Robin Lorsch. *Rome's Vestal Virgins: A Study of Rome's Vestal Priestesses in the Late Republic and Early Empire.* London: Routledge, 2006.

Wilkins, David G. *Maso di Banco: A Florentine Artist of the Early Trecento.* New York: Garland, 1985.

Wilkins, E. H. *Life of Petrarch.* Chicago: University of Chicago Press, 1961.

Wilkins, John. *The Discovery of a World in the Moone; or, A Discovrse Tending to Prove That 'Tis Probable There May Be Another Habitable World in That Planet.* London: E. G. for Michael Sparl and Edward Forrest, 1638.

Wilkinson, Robert J. *The Kabbalistic Scholars of the Antwerp Polyglot Bible.* Leiden, Neth.: Brill, 2007.

Wilton-Ely, John. "'Amazing and Ingenious Fancies': Piranesi and the Adam Brothers." In Bevilacqua, Hyde Minor, and Barry, *The Serpent and the Stylus,* 213–37.

———. "Design through Fantasy: Piranesi as Designer." In *Piranesi as Designer,* edited by Sarah Lawrence and John Wilton-Ely, 11–91. New York: Cooper-Hewitt, National Design Museum, Smithsonian Institute, 2007.

———. Introduction to Piranesi, *Observations on the Letter of Monsieur Mariette,* 14–24.

———. *Piranesi*. London: Arts Council of Great Britain, 1978.

Winckelmann, Johann. *Anmerkungen über die Baukunst der Alten*. Leipzig: J. G. Dyck, 1762.

———. *Gedanken über die Nachahmung der griechischen Werke in der Malerey und Bildhauerkunst*. 2nd ed. Dresden and Leipzig: Walther, 1756.

Winner, Matthias. "Vedute in Flemish Landscape Drawings of the 16th Century." In *Netherlandish Mannerism: Papers Given at a Symposium in Nationalmuseum Stockholm, September 21–22, 1984*, edited by Görel Cavalli-Björkman, 85–96. Nationalmuseum Skriftserie, vol. 4. Stockholm: Nationalmuseum, 1985.

Witcombe, Christopher L. C. E. *Copyright in the Renaissance: Prints and the Privilegio in Sixteenth-Century Venice and Rome*. Leiden, Neth.: Brill, 2004.

Wittkower, Rudolf. "The Du Pérac Codex: Discovering the Lost Rome." In Du Pérac, *Le Antiche Rovine di Roma*, 11–43.

———. "Piranesi as Architect." In *Piranesi*, edited by Robert O. Parks, 99–109. Northampton, MA: Smith College Museum of Art, 1961. Exhibition catalog.

Wollstonecraft, Mary. *A Vindication of the Rights of Woman: With Strictures on Political and Moral Subjects*. London, 1792.

Wood, Robert. *The Ruins of Balbec, otherwise Heliopolis in Coelosyria*. London, 1757.

———. *The Ruins of Palmyra, otherwise Tedmor, in the Desart*. London, 1753.

Woodward, Christopher. *In Ruins*. New York: Pantheon, 2001.

Woolf, Greg, ed. *The Cambridge Illustrated History of the Roman World*. Cambridge: Cambridge University Press, 2003.

———. "Monumental Writing and the Expansion of Roman Society in the Early Empire." *Journal of Roman Studies* 86 (1996): 22–39.

Wordsworth, Dorothy. *Journals*. 2 vols. London: Macmillan, 1904.

Wordsworth, William. *The Borderers*. Edited by Robert Osborn. Ithaca, NY: Cornell University Press, 1982.

———. *Early Poems and Fragments, 1785–1797*. Edited by Carol Landon and Jared Curtis. Ithaca, NY: Cornell University Press, 1997.

———. *Home at Grasmere: Part First, Book First, of "The Recluse."* Edited by Beth Darlington. Ithaca, NY: Cornell University Press, 1977.

———. *Lyrical Ballads and Other Poems, 1797–1800*. Edited by James Butler and Karen Green. Ithaca, NY: Cornell University Press, 1992.

———. *The Poetical Works of William Wordsworth*. Edited by William Knight. 11 vols. London: MacMillan, 1896.

———. *"The Ruined Cottage" and "The Pedlar."* Edited by James A Butler. Ithaca, NY: Cornell University Press, 1979.

———. *The Salisury Plain Poems of William Wordsworth*. Edited by Stephen Gill. Ithaca, NY: Cornell University Press, 1975.

Wouk, Edward H. "Antoine Perrenot de Granvelle, the *Aux Quatre Vents* Press, and the Patronage of Prints in Early Modern Europe." *Simiolus* 38, no. 1/2 (2015/2016): 31–61. Paper presented in conjunction with the exhibition *Hieronymus Cock: De renaissance in prent*, Brussels, June 6, 2013.

Wragge-Morley, Alexander. "A Strange and Surprising Debate: Mountains, Original Sin and 'Science' in Seventeenth-Century England." *Endeavour* 33, no. 2 (June 2009): 76–80.

Wu Hung. *A Story of Ruins: Presence and Absence in Chinese Art and Visual Culture*. Princeton, NJ: Princeton University Press, 2012.

Young-ah Gottlieb, Susannah. *Regions of Sorrow: Anxiety and Messianism in Hannah Arendt and W. H. Auden*. Stanford, CA: Stanford University Press, 2003.

Yourcenar, Marguerite. *Memoirs of Hadrian*. Translated by Grace Frick in collaboration with the author. New York: Farrar, Straus and Giroux, 1963. First published 1951 by Librairie Plon (Paris).

Zagorin, Perez. "Looking for Pieter Bruegel." *Journal of the History of Ideas* 4, no. 1 (2003): 73–96.

Zarucchi, Jeanne Morgan. "The Literary Tradition of *Ruins of Rome* and a New Consideration of Piranesi's Staffage Figures." *Journal for Eighteenth-Century Studies* 35, no. 3 (2012): 359–80.

Zerner, Henri. *L'école de Fontainebleau: Gravures*. Paris: Arts et Métiers Graphiques, 1969.

Zucker, Paul. *Fascination of Decay: Ruins; Relics—Symbol—Ornament*. Ridgewood, NJ: Gregg Press, 1968.

———. "Ruins: An Aesthetic Hybrid." *Journal of Aesthetics and Art Criticism* 20, no. 2 (Winter 1961): 119–30.

Photography Credits

All photographs without other source attribution are by the author.

PLATE 1, FIGS. 65, 76: Scala / Art Resource, New York.

PLATES 2, 8, FIG. 32: Erich Lessing / Art Resource, New York.

PLATE 3: bpk Bildagentur / Gemäldegalerie / Jörg P. Anders / Art Resource, New York.

PLATE 4: HIP / Art Resource, New York.

PLATE 5: © Liechtenstein, The Princely Collections, Vaduz-Vienna / Scala, Florence / Art Resource, New York, 2019.

PLATE 6, FIGS. 17, 18: © National Gallery, London / Art Resource, New York.

PLATE 7: Kavaler / Art Resource, New York.

PLATE 9: Andrea Jemolo, Fotografia e Archivio d'Architettura e Arte, Rome.

PLATE 10, FIG. 66: Soane Museum, London.

FIGS. 1, 14, 58, 78, 79: Wikimedia Commons.

FIGS. 3, 36, 38, 39, 51, 61, 62: Marquand Library of Art and Archaeology, Princeton University.

FIGS. 4, 20, 44, 49, 50, 52, 57, 63: Metropolitan Museum of Art, New York.

FIG. 11: bpk Bildagentur / Antikensammlung / Johannes Laurentius / Art Resource, New York.

FIGS. 16, 22, 24, 31, 34, 35, 47, 48, 73: © The Trustees of the British Museum. All rights reserved.

FIG. 19: Princeton University Art Museum.

FIGS. 21, 40, 41, 42, 43, 45, 46, 64, 71: Department of Rare Books and Special Collections, Princeton University Library.

FIG. 23: Istituto centrale per la grafica; reproduced by kind permission of the Ministero dei Beni e delle Attività Culturali e del Turismo, Rome.

FIGS. 25, 26, 27: National Gallery of Art, Washington, DC.

FIG. 28: National Galleries of Scotland.

FIG. 29: Museo Nacional del Prado / Art Resource, New York.

FIG. 33: Museum Plantin-Moretus (collection Printroom), Antwerp—UNESCO, World Heritage.

FIG. 68: The Morgan Library and Museum, New York.

FIG. 69: © Victoria and Albert Museum, London.

FIG. 70: National Museum of New Zealand, Te Papa, Tongarewa.

FIG. 72: The Arthur Ross Collection, Yale University Art Gallery.

FIG. 74: © The Trustees of the British Museum / Art Resource, New York.

FIG. 75: © 1984 by Yale University Press.

FIG. 77: Courtesy of Amelia and Joe Worsley.

Index

Mitchell, W. J. T., 236

models, 157; architectural, 193; for figures,
175; ruins as, 193, 204, 233, 270, 316, 316n38

Monophysites, 108

monotheism, 24

Montano, Benito Arias, 144–45, 151

monuments: age value, acquiring of, 17;
Arch of Constantine, 61–62, 212; Arch of
Hadrian (Athens), 223; Arch of Marius
(Orange), 6; Arch of Septimius Severus,
284n27; Arch of Titus, 58, 60, 219; Baths
of Caracalla, 193, 198, 200, 212; Baths
of Diocletian, 68–69, 131, 137–38, 198,
307n26; Capitol, 4, 20, 35, 61, 68–69, 71,
106, 132, 177, 191, 198, 232, 277n5; Castel
Sant'Angelo (Mausoleum of Hadrian),
126, 128, 159, 192, 289n34; *castra* of
Diocletian (Palmyra), 202; Colosseum,
7–8, 13, 34, 63, 66–67, 123, 126, 130, 132,
137–39, 146–47, 150, 159, 177, 181, 198,
212, 216, 219, 248, 278n12; column of
Marcus Aurelius, 159; as controversial,
269; Flaminian obelisk, 58–59, 159, 259;
Forum, 62, 67, 75, 106, 126, 129, 132,
159, 182, 212, 219, 288n20, 313n6; Forum
Boarium, 72, 126; Forum of Nerva, 72,
152–53; Hercules Temple, 72, 201; Lateran
obelisk, 291n54; and memory, 53; Meta
Romuli, 72; Palace of Diocletian (Split),
200–201, 204–11, 319n23, 320n29, 321n38;
Palace of Domitian, 148–49; Palatine, 2,
35, 80, 85, 148–49, 176, 197–98, 248, 295n93,
295n9; Pantheon, 198, 212, 216, 219; *pons
Fabricius*, 318n4; Pyramid of Cestius,
8–9, 116, 126, 193, 198, 224; and ruins, 54;
Saint Peter's, 62, 64, 66–68, 72, 74–75,
126–27, 129, 150, 177, 254; Septizodium,
72–73, 126, 159, 161, 212, 269; Solarium
obelisk (Obelisk of Psammetichus and
Horologium), 288n23; Tempietto, 126–27;
Temple of Bel (Palmyra), 61, 203; Temple
of Castor and Pollux, 182, 219; Temple
of Concord, 198; Temple of Hadrian
(Hadrianeum), 182; Temple of Janus,
126; Temple of Jove (Jupiter), 20, 61, 198;
Temple of Jupiter d'Agrigente (Sicily), 7;
Temple of Jupiter Stator, 176; Temple of
Minerva, 71; Temple of Peace (Basilica
of Constantine), 76, 132–33, 198, 294n92,
313n6; Temple of Rome and Augustus,
62; Temple of Romulus and Remus, 61,
198; Temple of the Sibyl, 178; Temple of
Venus and Roma, 206; Temple of Vesta
(Roman Forum), 67; Temple of Vesta
(Tivoli), 28–29, 178, 182–83, 223–24,
316n36, 316n39; Torre delle Milizie
(Nero's Tower), 198; Trajan's column,
198; Triumphal Arch of Marcus Aurelius,
72; Vatican obelisk, 64–65; Vatican *pigna*
(pine cone), 64–65; as word, 53; World
War II, destruction in, 281n44

Monville, François Nicolas Henri Racine
de, 223–25

Mor, Anthonis, 127

Morel, Jean-Marie, 223

Moretus, Jan, 134

Morris, William, 18

Mortier, Roland, 287n2

mountains, 30; Creation story, 27; dramatic
transformation, places of, 26; exalting
of, 283n19; in *Faust*, 31; fear of, 26,
283n14; flaws of, 25; and materiality, 28,
31; megalithic forms, 27–28; mountain
ruins, 25, 27–28, 32, 66, 114, 186, 198, 262;
"thingness" of, 25

Mulmutius, Dunwallo, 103–4

Mylne, Robert, 182, 199–200

Nabopolassar, 48

Nancy, Jean-Luc, 324n15; *The Experience of
Freedom*, 117

Napoleon Bonaparte, 66, 216

National Gallery (London), 76

National Gallery of Scotland, 137

Nativity (Pinturicchio), 158

Nativity scenes, 76–80

Natural History (Pliny the Elder), 229

nature: alienation from, 23; Arcadians,
attitudes toward, 174; building in consonance with, 184; built environment,
source of damage to, 5–7, 16–17, 19, 26,
32, 37, 45, 269, 278n9; destruction of, xiii,
27, 270–71; and erosion, 33; and geology,
283n19, 316n38; laws of, 214; nature
imagery, 67, 86; ruins, as version of Fall,
27; ruins, compared to natural forms, 4,
32, 204, 233; state of, 214; and vegetation,
6–8; in Wordsworth, 245, 250–51. *See also*
earthquakes; fire; floods; mountains;
water